D1548477

SCIENCE AND THE INTERNET
Communicating Knowledge
in a Digital Age

Edited by

Alan G. Gross
University of Minnesota

and

Jonathan Buehl
The Ohio State University

Afterword by Charles Bazerman

Baywood's Technical Communications Series
Series Editor: Charles H. Sides

Baywood Publishing Company, Inc.
AMITYVILLE, NEW YORK

Baywood Publishing Company, Inc.

26 Austin Avenue
P.O. Box 337
Amityville, NY 11701
(800) 638-7819

E-mail: baywood@baywood.com
Web site: baywood.com

Library of Congress Catalog Number:
ISBN: 978-0-89503-897-5 (cloth : alk. paper)
ISBN: 978-0-89503-898-2 (paper)
ISBN: 978-0-89503-899-9 (e-pub)
ISBN: 978-0-89503-900-2 (e-pdf)
http://dx.doi.org/10.2190/SCI

Library of Congress Cataloging-in-Publication Data

Names: Gross, Alan G. | Buehl, Jonathan.
Title: Science and the Internet : communicating knowledge in a digital age / edited by Alan G. Gross, and Jonathan Buehl ; afterword by Charles Bazerman.
Description: Amityville, New York : Baywood Publishing Company, [2015] | Series: Baywood's technical communications series
Identifiers: LCCN 2015036696| ISBN 9780895038975 (clothbound : alk. paper) | ISBN 9780895038982 (paperbound : alk. paper) | ISBN 9780895039002 (epdf) | ISBN 9780895038999 (epub)
Subjects: LCSH: Science--Computer network resources. | Communication in Science. | Internet research.
Classification: LCC Q224.5 .S36 2015 | DDC 501/.4--dc23
LC record available at http://lccn.loc.gov/2015036696

Table of Contents

http://dx.doi.org/10.2190/SCIC1

CHAPTER 1

Revolution or Evolution?
Casing the Impact of Digital Media
on the Rhetoric of Science

Jonathan Buehl

ABSTRACT

This introductory chapter for *Science and the Internet: Communicating Knowledge in a Digital Age* describes a recent controversy in biochemistry to frame the intellectual commitments of the entire collection. After NASA researchers published findings that a rare bacterium can use arsenic instead of phosphorous in its biomolecules, a critical scientist used her blog to voice concerns about the research. Comments on her blog posts from experts and lay readers hint at the range of ways that the Internet is changing scientific discovery, the circulation of scientific knowledge, and access to scientific conversations.

REVOLUTION OR EVOLUTION?

In December 2010, a team of NASA researchers led by astrobiologist Felisa Wolfe-Simon made a remarkable announcement: Bacteria living in California's Mono Lake can replace the phosphorous in their biomolecules with arsenic (Wolfe-Simon, Blum, Kulp, Gordon, Hoeft, Pett-Ridge et al., 2010). A first-of-its-kind discovery, the extraordinary biochemistry of species GFAJ-1 offered "proof" that life could exist in environments without phosphorous; that is, in environments whose chemistries differ vastly from ours. In other words, different kinds of life might exist on planets with scant resemblance to Earth.

1

The team's findings appeared in the journal *Science*, and NASA widely publicized the research. Footage of an elaborate press conference was broadcast on major television news channels, and video of the entire event was uploaded to YouTube. Although circulating video on the Internet is no longer novel, other aspects of the Mono Lake project's digital life are emblematic of Internet-enabled rhetorical processes that are changing scientific practice.

On December 4, just two days after the initial announcement and online prepublication of the article, Rosie Redfield, a microbiologist at the University of British Columbia, posted a 2,100-word critique of the Mono Lake research on her blog RRResearch. After identifying apparent flaws in the researchers' methods, analyses, and reasoning, Redfield questioned the motives of *Science* and the NASA team:

> I don't know whether the authors are just bad scientists or whether they're unscrupulously pushing NASA's "There's life in outer space!" agenda. I hesitate to blame the reviewers, as their objections are likely to have been overruled by *Science*'s editors in their eagerness to score such a high-impact publication. (2010)

Like many blogs, RRResearch allows readers to post comments about its stories. The comments on Redfield's "Arsenic-associated bacteria (NASA's claims)" post included general affirmations (e.g., "Way to go, Rosie."), additional critiques of Wolfe-Simon's paper, refinements of Redfield's arguments, and links to other blogs. Other readers posted poems about biochemistry, criticisms of Wolfe-Simon's demeanor during the press conference, identifications of Redfield's typos, and corrections (but not outright refutations) of Redfield's calculations. Most of these comments were posted by other scientists, but nonexpert laypeople also entered the conversation. For example, self-identified nonexpert Zinegata (2010) wondered about some of Redfield's commentary:

> I'd just like to make a clarification—why did Dr. Redfield suggest to use standard *E. coli* in the end of the article? Is this to have some kind of control group to verify the methodology? Wouldn't standard *E. coli* simply die when they are put in an arsenic solution? I'm a bit of a layman, so please forgive my ignorance.

Other comments included reflections on scientific behavior and the principles of peer review—the traditional mechanism for establishing and policing scientific knowledge. For example, Sanford May (2010) was particularly upset by the medium Redfield chose to present her critique:

> This whole thing is grossly inappropriate. You should have sent this to the journal of record FIRST, where it can be properly reviewed. You're not some advanced hobbyist layman with a good idea but no standing. You'd almost certainly be given a full hearing in the appropriate forum.

The comment goes on to suggest that in blogging her criticism Redfield damaged her professional ethos:

> Since this constitutes a formal challenge without review, I urge you to take it down until it has been properly reviewed. And I'd keep accusations like the above quoted out of any formal challenge. You come across like you have an ax to grind, and while that may make you a star on the Internet, it'll cost you respect in the professional community. Probably already has.

Other commentators did not agree that a peer-reviewed response is the only appropriate tool for critiquing published scientific claims. For example, a respondent identified as PetHW (2010) replied that peer-reviewed forums should not be the only rhetorical spaces available to scientists:

> I do not think that every single opinion and comment we, as scientists, have or make should be peer-reviewed. If they decided to publish this paper too soon, then they must face the consequences of their decision and questionable science. The paper is out there for anybody to comment.

Others suggested that blogs offer a form of peer review that is even more productive than the traditional process. One commentator described the speed and efficacy of the blog medium:

> What I perceived is that a load of valuable ideas, suggestions and knowledge finds its way to this blog and within 2 days this complex piece of work is thoroughly analyzed, erroneous information is corrected within an hour by specialized people (+ review), new insight is born and supplied with feedback and it leads to a scientific "report" which is immediately reviewed on contents and language.
>
> And I think: Wouldn't it be perfect if this process would become the standard for scientific research? The knowledge for everything is somewhere and every somewhere is connected to the Internet. I'm afraid that the old fashioned way with the magazines, at least for the millions of "half way publications," is not suitable anymore. (Erik, 2010)

Other comments concurred that blogs might be superior peer-reviewed venues for advancing scientific knowledge. For instance, Joy Kennedy (2010) compared the epistemological affordances of blogs to those or traditional journals:

> I do have to say, however, that I wish my field had a forum such as this for vetting and responding to published research. If we are looking for a viable alternative to the current system of peer-reviewed publications, which often screens IN bad science and screens OUT good science with null findings, I think we've found it. In just a few days, we have achieved a thorough critique by an expert in the field, which has in turn been reviewed and further

critiqued by other experts in the same and related fields. The result is a thorough and accurate assessment of the original work.

The public scrutiny of the Wolfe-Simon paper was not overlooked. When the print version of the paper finally appeared in *Science* in June of 2011, the journal also printed 8 of the 25 "Technical Comments" it had received about the article, "the most *Science* has published for any one paper" (Pennisi, 2011, p. 1137). It also printed a "News & Analysis" piece by Elizabeth Pennisi entitled "Concerns About Arsenic-Laden Bacterium Aired" (2011). Although the story is not an outright defense of the Wolfe-Simon paper, it does paint the research in positive light while subtly questioning the role of scientific blogs. Its opening sentence makes a seemingly conservative statement about privileged channels of scientific critique: "The debate that erupted 5 months ago . . . is finally being aired in the scientific literature rather than on blogs" (Pennisi, 2011, p. 1137). Pennisi (2011) notes that the vetted technical comments in *Science* "formally raise many of the criticisms that were quickly hurled" through blogs (p. 1137). In short, the appropriateness of the sanctioned peer-reviewed forum is juxtaposed with the reckless speed of the Internet.

Redfield continued to activate the rhetorical affordances of the Internet as she blogged about experiments she planned and ran on samples of GFAJ-1 received from the Wolfe-Simon team. Most of these posts are summaries, but some offer open questions about how to investigate the bacterium. For instance, a July 2011 post, which was framed as an open email from Redfield to three collaborators, invited comments on her experimental process:

> I'm confident that I can find a suitable growth condition for the $\pm$P/$\pm$As growth experiments. But this probably won't be exactly the same condition reported by Wolfe-Simon et al., so we need to decide whether it's appropriate to use my growth condition to test their observation. (Redfield, 2011)

She followed a detailed description of her plans to determine appropriate growth conditions with a query: "Do you think that this would be seen as a valid test of the reported result?" In response, an anonymous comment offered some rhetorical advice:

> I think it is essential to test exactly the same medium used by Wolfe-Simon, including tungsten, to show that there is no growth (assuming that will be the case). After that, testing her claims about arsenic under slightly different conditions would be good enough for the scientific community. (Anonymous, 2011)

The author's advice is grounded by his or her knowledge of the rhetorical norms of the discourse community; that is, he or she knows what will be "good enough" for the sake of argument. In this case, the blog becomes a space for considering the connections between scientific methods and argumentation.

The asynchronous and occasionally tempestuous conversations about GFAJ-1that played out in the pages of *Science* and on the Web pages of the blogosphere raise interesting questions about science and rhetoric. Is the Internet changing the scope, meaning, and timing of scientific peer review? Is the Internet reconfiguring the rhetorical boundaries of scientific practice? Is the Internet fundamentally changing the nature of scientific collaboration? Of scientific argumentation? These are but a few of the questions addressed by the chapters in this collection on science and the Internet.

Assessing the effects of the Internet on the rhetoric of science—and indeed all forms of epistemic rhetoric—requires critical perspective. It is easy to be seduced by the Internet's seemingly profound—perhaps revolutionary— implications. As the case of GFAJ-1 suggests, the Internet has accelerated the pace of scientific communication to peers and to other publics. It promises wider and more fruitful collaborative networks, enabling full documentation of experiments and the universal and immediate scrutiny of results. Elsewhere, the multimodal affordances of the Internet have even enabled alternative formats of scientific publishing, such as videographic journals (e.g., *The Journal of Visualized Experiments*) and live-streamed experiments (see Sidler's contribution to this volume). Some scholars (including the editors of this collection) would argue that collectively these changes are altering science's social structure and its epistemology, leading to greater democracy within the scientific community and to the increased credibility of experimental results. But is the term "revolutionary" an appropriate descriptor for these changes? How large an "impact" has the Internet really had on science and its rhetorics?

In reviewing Science and Technology Studies scholarship on new media and knowledge creation, the Virtual Knowledge Studio (VKS) notes that most work addressing the "informationization of academic work" falls into one of three categories: "impact talk, deconstruction of impact talk, and detailed empirical description" (2008, p. 321). The phrase "impact talk" describes commentary that reflects technological determinism: the Internet is the main character in a master narrative of revolutionary change. According to VKS, impact talk about the Internet can be compelling because the narrative seems to hold up in many contexts: "First-time users, as well as more advanced users, of a particular Internet-based tool can ground their experiences in a coherent story about the 'impact of the Internet'" (p. 320). But the determinism underwriting impact talk can pose philosophical and methodological problems. As Eduardo Aibar (2010) has explained, "Particular technologies are usually taken as something given or coming out of the blue: they are just there and social scientists are expected to explain what their effects on society will be" (p. 178). Such determinism fails to account for the social forces that shape technology as a much as technology shapes them.

Deconstructions of impact talk challenge or at least qualify the Internet's effects on the social systems that produce knowledge. For example, John MacKenzie Owen's *The Scientific Article in the Age of Digitization* (2007) concludes that claims of an impending digital revolution in science are hyperbolic and misguided strains of technological determinism. Such claims, he shows, began in the 1970s, and yet the traditional scientific journal article has endured the advent and proliferation of various incarnations of e-journals. Predictions of revolution, he argues, say more about the philosophical and political positions of the prophets that the realities of scientific communication. Moreover, such claims label evolutionary socially grounded processes as revolutionary technologically driven events (p. 221).

Owen supports his claims with a thorough empirical study of electronic journals from 1987 to 2004, which quantifies the uptake and application of new technological affordances. After coding 86 scientific journals against 15 criteria and analyzing his results, Owen determined that electronic publishing has not revolutionized science:

> There is no evidence that digitization has transformed the practice of scientific authorship at the level of the journal article. This study has found that authors show little interest in adopting new ways of documenting and presenting research results by means of the research article, or in deviating too far from the traditional culture of scientific communication. (2007, pp. 224–225)

We find Owen's framework productive, but his study ends at 2004, just before the advent of many significant developments in digitized scientific publishing, such as those leveraging Web 2.0 technologies. These more recent technological developments warrant reexamining Owen's conclusions. Moreover, as many of the cases collected here show, social media and multimedia technologies are changing rhetorical practices both in journals and in other contexts. Owen's exclusive focus on journal articles is too narrow to examine fully the diverse sites where rhetors use digitally mediated discourse to create and circulate scientific knowledge. To be fair, Owen's work is a dedicated study of the scientific journal and the articles therein and not a study of scientific rhetoric more broadly conceived. As many chapters in this collection show, the Internet's influence on the invention, production, and circulation of knowledge claims is significant in arrays of genres and contexts. These arrays include scientific journal articles, but not exclusively.

Most of the chapters of *Science and the Internet* fall into the last of the categories of "Internet and academic research" scholarship posed by the VKS— detailed empirical description. Collectively, they argue that rhetorical theory can illuminate science and the Internet without resorting to hyperbolic "impact talk" or dismissive deconstruction. Rhetoric offers tools for analyzing specific social actions enabled and mediated by Internet technologies in order to generalize about the Internet's rhetorical role in communicating modern science. Labeling the magnitude and nature of the Internet's effect on science is less important (for us) than understanding—at a functional level—how the Internet is used in creating and distributing scientific knowledge. We leave it for our readers to decide if these new technological affordances and rhetorical practices are evolutionary or revolutionary.

The chapters in *Science and the Internet* approach a common question: How is the Internet changing how science is communicated? Although these textual, contextual, and empirical analyses isolate the local effects of information technologies on specific rhetorical activities, they can be grouped into two broad categories: communicating to (and among) scientists and communicating to (and among) nonexperts.

The chapters in the first section are arranged according to the lifecycle of scientific arguments. The first of these chapters considers how technologies influence the creation of scientific knowledge; that is, how the Internet can affect rhetorical invention in science. Blogs offer one mechanism for refining scientific and rhetorical procedures transparently and collectively, as Redfield's open invitation for comments about her methodology suggests. However, blogs are just one mechanism for collaborative invention. Chad Wickman's chapter demonstrates how "open science" movements are changing the discursive and material practices of scientists. Wickman's study of open access notebooks— laboratory notebooks posted online—shows how digital mediation has transformed what were once private paper archives into dynamic, collaborative rhetorical spaces with global audiences.

The other chapters on communication between scientists consider how networked technologies are changing the representation, circulation, and reception of knowledge within and between scientific communities: How might the Internet affect the arrangement, style, and delivery of scientific arguments? How has the Internet changed the ways in which peers react to their colleagues' arguments? Blogs like Redfield's allow researchers to self-publish informal scientific arguments, but formal scientific forums are also adapting to the rhetorical affordances of the Internet, and new digital tools have expanded how data is represented and used. Joseph Harmon's quantitative study of electronic articles published in 2010 and 2011 offers an updated survey of the proliferating affordances offered by the Internet. His findings demonstrate how much has changed and not changed since Owen conducted his study.

The case of GFAJ-1 is but one example of how Internet-enabled genres and processes are changing the where, how, and who of peer review. Alan Gross shows how Retraction Watch and other blogs use the narrative mode and ironic stance of investigative journalism to comment on problematic published research; he also shows the limits of these tactics of critique. Christian Casper examines how informal postpublication comments have become institutionalized through online commenting features integrated into the electronic interfaces of two journals. Michelle Sidler shows how scientists have taken the process of peer review to the next level by liveblogging replication experiments that refute published claims. Together, these chapters demonstrate how the Internet enables new, richer, and more democratic mechanisms for the communal policing of scientific knowledge.

The contributions to the second half of *Science and the Internet* describe how nonexperts receive and react to scientific knowledge communicated through digital channels. Chapters in this section include case studies of lay interaction with professional scientists (e.g., a blog gave layperson Zinegata a forum to ask questions about Redfield's critique), but they also offer accounts of digital technologies transforming how science is accommodated for broader publics.

Jeanne Fahnestock provides a case study of the Web presence of a controversial claim about adult human neurogenesis; that is, the brain can grow new neurons in areas dedicated to higher reasoning. By tracking how the arguments of different researchers were represented on blogs, listservs, and news sites as well as in YouTube videos and other genres, Fahnestock charts the unique affordances and problems of popularizing science via the Web.

Sara Wardlaw's chapter examines a different Web-enabled genre for popularizing science: the podcast. Confirming earlier work on print science journalism, Wardlaw verifies her analysis of wonder appeals in a Radiolab podcast on parasites through close readings of online comments from users. Thus, she demonstrates one of the key methodological advantages of studying rhetoric on the Web—mineable sources of reception evidence.

Three chapters investigate the role of the Internet in risk communication. Kostelnick and Kostelnick examine relationships between specific digital affordances—data visualization tools used in earth science—and specific rhetorical and ethical problems, such as expressing certainty and probability when describing the risks of natural disasters to the public. Two chapters address Internet-enabled risk communication and the Fukushima Daiichi nuclear disaster. James Wynn examines how digital technologies have transformed the representation of risk offered by radiation maps. His comparison of printed radiation maps from previous disasters with recent digital maps of the Fukushima event demonstrates how verbal and visual rhetorical choices are affected by technological affordances, contextual factors, and available scientific details. Ashley R. Kelley and Carolyn Miller approach the Fukushima disaster through "parascientific" genres, such as posts on Facebook, Twitter, Wikipedia, and other social media sites. They show how these Internet channels offered nonexperts in Japan the means to communicate information about the event; that information was then commented upon by speculating experts, thereby "eroding" the boundaries between expert and nonexpert communities.

The section on accommodating science via the Internet concludes with a chapter on online science writing and informal science learning. In this study of the Science Museum of Minnesota's Science Buzz blog, Stacey Pigg, William Hart-Davidson, Jeff Grabill, and Kirsten Ellenbogen use rhetorical discourse analysis to document how blog posts demonstrate learning about science. Their close reading of a popular blog thread identifies factors that encourage public engagement with scientific topics, which has implications for how science-learning institutions position themselves on the Web.

In a concluding reflection chapter, Charles Bazerman offers a candid assessment of the rhetoric of science in the Internet era in the light of the contributions to this volume. Bazerman situates the conclusions of these cases in relation to the longer history of scientific communication, and he identifies additional opportunities for studying the Internet's influence on the scientific article and other genres.

REFERENCES

Aibar, E. (2010). A critical analysis of information society conceptualizations from an STS point of view. *tripleC: Cognition, Communication, Cooperation, 8*(2), 177–182.

Anonymous. (2011, July 20). Email to my GFAJ-1 collaborators [Blog comment]. *RRResearch*. Retrieved from http://rrresearch.fieldofscience.com

Erik. (2010, December 8). Arsenic-associated bacteria (NASA's claims) [Blog comment]. *RRResearch*. Retrieved from http://rrresearch.fieldofscience.com

Kennedy, J. (2010, December 9). Arsenic-associated bacteria (NASA's claims) [Blog comment]. *RRResearch*. Retrieved from http://rrresearch.fieldofscience.com

May, S. (2010, December 7). Arsenic-associated bacteria (NASA's claims) [Blog comment]. *RRResearch*. Retrieved from http://rrresearch.fieldofscience.com

Owen, J. M. (2007). *The scientific article in the age of digitization.* Dordrecht, The Netherlands: Springer.

Pennisi, E. (2011). Concerns about arsenic-laden bacterium aired. *Science, 332*(3), 1136–1137.

PetHW. (2010, December 7). Arsenic-associated bacteria (NASA's claims) [Blog comment]. *RRResearch*. Retrieved from http://rrresearch.fieldofscience.com

Redfield, R. (2010, December 4). Arsenic-associated bacteria (NASA's claims) [Blog post]. *RRResearch*. Retrieved from http://rrresearch.fieldofscience.com

Redfield, R. (2011, July 20). Email to my GFAJ-1 collaborators [Blog post]. *RRResearch*. Retrieved from http://rrresearch.fieldofscience.com

Virtual Knowledge Studio (VKS). (2008). Messy shapes of knowledge—STS explore informationization, new media, and academic work. In E. Hackett, O. Amsterdamska, M. Lynch, & J. Wajcman (Eds.), *The handbook of science and technology studies* (3rd ed., pp. 319–352). Cambridge, MA: MIT Press.

Wolfe-Simon, F., Blum, J. S., Kulp, T. R., Gordon, G. W., Hoeft, S. E., Pett-Ridge, J., et al. (2010). A bacterium that can grow by using arsenic instead of phosphorus. *Science, 332*(6034), 1163–1166.

Zinegata. (2010, December 9). Arsenic-associated bacteria (NASA's claims) [Blog comment]. *RRResearch*. Retrieved from http://rrresearch.fieldofscience.com

http://dx.doi.org/10.2190/SCIC2

CHAPTER 2

Learning to "Share your Science": The Open Notebook as Textual Object and Dynamic Rhetorical Space

Chad Wickman

ABSTRACT

Laboratory notebooks have historically provided scientists with an important resource for documenting, warranting, and communicating the outcomes of their day-to-day research. Over the past decade, however, the genre has undergone some interesting changes: once a situated, print-bound activity, the practice of note making has begun to develop into a highly distributed, multimedia undertaking—a development that is beginning to reconfigure the traditional relationship between the laboratory, scientific community, and broader public sphere. The growing movement toward "open notebook science" (see Bradley, 2006; Bradley, Owens, & Williams, 2008) specifically raises questions about the ways in which notebooks function as a proprietary safeguard for individual scientists and as a dynamic rhetorical space within which groups of scientists and other stakeholders can present, discuss, revise, and circulate information. Through analysis of OpenWetWare, a Web-based scientific community, this chapter examines how scientists use familiar genres to balance the relationship between stability and change as they make the transition from traditional rhetorical practices that focus on individual ownership to emerging rhetorical practices that focus on the open sharing of information through digital infrastructures. I will argue specifically that open notebooks reinforce a type of "shared praxis" (Nielsen, 2011) that is necessary for open access to take hold in the scientific community and that may be contributing to a broader shift in the rhetorical and epistemological dimensions of scientific research culture.

INTRODUCTION

The Art of Scientific Writing, a style guide for practitioners in the natural sciences, emphasizes the importance of written communication for sharing information,

11

publishing findings, and generally contributing to one's field of inquiry. Among the genres the authors discuss—from reports to dissertations to journal articles—they pay early and detailed attention to the laboratory notebook, describing it as the "'germ cell' of the scientific literature" (Ebel, Bliefert, & Russey, 2004, p. 16). I mention this quote not simply to point out what might be evident to many scholars of rhetoric: namely, that writing is an essential component of scientific communication and knowledge production. More interesting to me is how the authors explicitly characterize the laboratory notebook as progenitor to a larger and more complex body of scientific discourse. This is no trivial statement. It is a telling one, however, in that it speaks to the constructive role that texts play not just in the dissemination of published findings but also in the seemingly mundane, day-to-day work of scientists at the laboratory bench.

Laboratory notebooks have historically provided scientists with a textual resource for documenting their inquiry and thereby establishing proprietary ownership over their inventions and discoveries. The fact that the genre warrants its own section in a well-known guide to scientific writing only affirms its ongoing relevance to students of science and working professionals alike. Yet similar to other genres of scientific communication, the laboratory notebook has undergone some interesting changes over the past decade. Once a situated, print-bound activity, the practice of note making has begun to develop into a highly distributed, multimedia undertaking—a development that is beginning to reconfigure the traditional relationship between the laboratory, scientific community, and broader public sphere. The growing movement toward "open notebook science" (see Bradley, 2006; Bradley, Owens, & Williams 2008) specifically raises questions about the ways in which notebooks function as a proprietary safeguard for individual scientists and as a dynamic rhetorical space within which groups of scientists and other stakeholders can present, discuss, revise, and circulate information.

Open access is a recognized yet still-evolving phenomenon in the scientific community. Sometimes referred to as Open Science, or Science 2.0, it involves making one's research, from raw data to journal publications, freely available to anyone who might benefit from it (see Willinsky, 2006).[1] In a 2006 blog post, chemist Jean-Claude Bradley coined the term "open notebook science" to

---

[1] Scientists sometimes do this of their own accord, and they are sometimes required to do so. For instance, the NIH implemented a policy in 2008, under the Consolidated Appropriations Act, that requires "all investigators funded by the NIH [to]submit or have submitted for them to the National Library of Medicine's PubMed Central an electronic version of their final, peer reviewed manuscripts upon acceptance for publication, to be made publicly available no later than 12 months after the official date of publication" (nih.gov). While the long-term impact of such policies has yet to be determined, a growing number of scientists have actively begun to support open access practices. The 2012 boycott of Elsevier by mathematicians and other researchers is just one recent example. See Brienza (2012) for a general overview of the "Academic Spring" movement.

describe a method of sharing information analogous to the open-source-software movement. It is "a way of doing science," he suggests, "in which . . . you make all your research freely available to the public and in real time. . . . The underlying philosophy is that there should be no insider information" (Poynder, 2010). Under this description, the image of the individual scientist making notes in the laboratory takes on a new look: it now includes a vast network of scientists, technical experts, and other interested parties who openly share information using Web-based technologies. There is a democratic—and perhaps even non-agonistic—impulse at work in the open access movement that emphasizes the value of freeing knowledge for humanitarian purposes. Open notebook infra-structures help to accommodate this need by providing a nontraditional rhetorical space within which to communicate and deliberate about the sometimes-mundane details of laboratory practice (see Borgman, 2007).

The very metaphor "open notebook science" calls to mind the physical rela-tionship between scientists and the writing they perform in the dynamic flow of their day-to-day research. In many ways, to "open" one's notebook is to reveal intimate details related to the process of inquiry and, more personally, to one's unique thought processes. Advocates of open notebook science see the practical benefits of sharing their data and technical expertise freely with others; and, for scientists like Jean-Claude Bradley, they also find value in promoting a philosophy that privileges collective problem solving over individual ownership. Opportunities for rhetorical study abound on both accounts. Within the scope of this chapter, I specifically take steps to define the open notebook as a textual object and examine open note making as a dynamic rhetorical activity. These steps include describing new and emerging features of the notebook genre, exploring how the practice of note making mediates research- and teaching-related activities in an online scientific community, and theorizing how open notebooks are contributing to the development of open access as a viable paradigm for scientific communication in the 21st century. By addressing these foci, I hope to illustrate the tensions involved in open notebook science and the potential benefits that accrue from collaborating in a densely networked Web 2.0 environment.

The focus of this chapter is an online scientific community, OpenWetWare, that specializes in the study and application of synthetic biology. I designed a case study of the site to explore how it functions as an open notebook and to investigate how it promotes communal standards for note making through the use of semiformalized templates and a flexible, wiki-based infrastructure. My analysis suggests that open notebooks borrow from conventional features of the genre—for example, they provide a textual space within which to document routine laboratory work—but shift the locus of writing activity away from the individual scientist and toward a broader community of practitioners. Note making thus preserves its traditional function as a semiprivate meditational means (dialogue with oneself or one's collaborators) but takes on a new role as an object of public deliberation (dialogue with audiences outside the immediate laboratory context). Sites like OpenWetWare in particular reveal how scientists use a familiar genre to balance the relationship between stability and change as they make the transition from traditional rhetorical practices that focus on proprietary ownership to emerging rhetorical practices that focus on the open sharing of information through digital infrastructures. I will argue, specifically, that open notebooks reinforce a type of "shared praxis" (Nielsen, 2011), which is necessary for open access to take hold in the scientific community and which may be contributing to a broader shift in the rhetorical and epistemological dimensions of scientific research culture.

THE SCIENTIFIC NOTEBOOK AS GENRE
AND TEXTUAL OBJECT

Scholars have investigated the constructive power of genre across a diverse range of institutional and disciplinary contexts. Nowhere is this more apparent than in the sciences. Bazerman's (1988) study of scientific writing in the early modern period, for instance, demonstrates how the experimental report emerged in response to specific rhetorical problems and thereby assisted in the formation of a coherent research culture (see Atkinson, 1999; Gross, Harmon, & Reidy, 2002). "By examining the emergence of a genre," Bazerman suggests, "we can identify the kinds of problems the genre was attempting to solve and how it went about solving them" (p. 63). Berkenkotter and Huckin's (1995) related study traces the 20th-century evolution of the experimental article and the ways in which textual practices shape the construction of scientific knowledge. According to them, genres are "sites of contention between stability and change. They are inherently dynamic, constantly (if gradually) changing over time in response to the sociocognitive needs of individual users" (p. 6; see Orlikowski & Yates, 1994; Schryer, 1994). More recently, scholars have begun to examine how the ongoing integration of digital media into the world of scientific publishing has begun to impact the genre's form and function (see Owen, 2007).

The experimental article has been a generative object of analysis for examining the role of writing and rhetoric in science. Yet other research genres, like notebooks, have not gone unnoticed. Indeed, researchers have used these texts to explore the microhistorical and tacit dimensions of experimental inquiry (see Gooding, 1990a, 1990b; Holmes, 1984, 1990, 2004; Holmes, Renn, & Rheinberger, 2003); the social and rhetorical dimensions of scientific invention and discovery (see Bazerman, 1999; Campbell, 1990; Crick, 2005; Gross, 2006); and the semiotic dimensions of writing and representation in the context of laboratory practice (see Kozma, Chin, Russell, & Marx, 2000; Wickman, 2010). Collectively, these scholars illustrate how notebooks contributed to important episodes in the history of science and technology, and they confirm that notebooks continue to provide scientists with a constructive resource for carrying out their day-to-day inquiry. What they have not fully investigated, however, is how digitization and recent developments in open access communication have begun to impact the genre and therefore the ways in which it mediates the relationship between scientists, their objects of study, and the audiences with whom they share their work. I believe that approaching notebooks from this perspective specifically offers a basis both for identifying how emerging features of the genre respond to new rhetorical problems and exigencies and for theorizing how the genre helps to reinforce specific types of social and rhetorical action both in the laboratory and in broader public forums.

Notebook Transformations and the Evolution of a Genre

The move toward electronic notebooks and open access recordkeeping is gaining momentum within the scientific community. Even so, not all agree that it is a welcome development. Waldrop (2008) claims that the "wide-open approach to science still faces intense skepticism" (para. 15) from scientists over what emerging textual practices signify for issues of privacy—for example, protecting the anonymity of research participants—and intellectual property—for example, establishing proprietary ownership over inventions and discoveries. Elliot (2011) suggests that electronic laboratory notebooks have "helped hundreds of organizations to organize records and retain research knowledge" but do not necessarily "eliminate the need for proper records management" (para. 18). And Giles (2012) raises questions about what it means for notebooks to "go paperless" at all. Implicit in these arguments is the assumption that note making is a more or less codified textual practice that, depending on medium, can either positively or negatively impact scientific research activity. Even a cursory investigation of notebooks, however, reveals them to be increasingly diverse in their form and function, whether referring to print, electronic, digital, or open access versions of the genre.

Scientists have traditionally used print notebooks to achieve multiple objectives. A short list would include the following: recording technical procedures and outcomes in the laboratory, interpreting one's research findings over time, facilitating collaboration through shared textual space, and staking claims to intellectual property. Electronic notebooks function similarly to their print counterparts but offer a different set of affordances. Most prominently perhaps, they facilitate recordkeeping through specially designed software programs that can be used to record, archive, index, search, and share vast amounts of information (see Butler, 2005). According to Myers (2003), electronic notebooks offer "clear advantages to the researcher" and "provide a strong driver away from paper records" (p. 1; see Rubacha, Rattan, & Hosselet, 2011). Myers argues, however, that to be successfully integrated into scientific practice, they must afford the same advantages as print notebooks, for instance, in terms of providing scientists with an *in situ* technology for sharing information between practitioners who are focused on common problems (see Klokmose & Zander, 2010; Myers, Fox-Dobbs, Laird, Le, Reich,& Curtz, 1996; Tabard, Mackay, & Eastmond, 2008; Talbott, Peterson, Schwidder, & Myers, 2005; Turner & Turner, 1997). Adopting an electronic medium in itself does not radically alter the exigency for keeping a notebook—for example, it still addresses the problem of recording information for personal and proprietary use—but it does influence how notebooks organize research activity and therefore how they contribute to processes of scientific knowledge production.

The electronic notebook is a precursor to more recent developments in notebook technology. Over the past decade in particular, scientists have increasingly begun to use—and often repurpose—digital media to suit their own, specialized needs in the laboratory. I differentiate between electronic and digital notebooks on two accounts. The first tend to be designed with software that relate to discipline-specific laboratory practices and institutional needs. So, for example, a group of scientists or technicians may share common devices and/or programs that can be used to optimize workflow and share information with one another. The second do not necessarily require specialized software designed for technical or scientific disciplines. Indeed, scientists often use common word processing programs like Microsoft Word or Web infrastructures like blogs to record and share their work with each other. It is worth mentioning that to keep a digital notebook often involves posting information online and making it available to audiences that extend beyond institutional collaborations. Under this description, one's notebook may be accessed by anyone with an Internet connection, but the information is not completely "open" in the sense that it is still nonmodifiable—for example, if it takes the form of a secured PDF file—and thus does not fundamentally alter the traditional relationship between producer/rhetor and user/audience.

Open notebooks combine the affordances of print, electronic, and digital media. Like print media, scientists use them to facilitate inquiry and document laboratory practices; like electronic media, scientists use them to record, archive, index, search, and circulate information in an efficient way; and like digital media, scientists use them to post information online and thereby make their research available to anyone who might benefit from it. Open notebooks also contribute at least two novel features to the genre: notebook entries tend to be designed exclusively for public consumption and use, and notebooks can be modified by different users and not just the original writer or writers.[2] The model

---

[2] The definition of "open" or "open notebook" is not fully settled. Jean-Claude Bradley (2006) has argued, for instance, that *open notebook* refers to making one's research notes immediately available online. I choose to modify this definition to include information that can be readily accessed *and modified* by different audiences. The latter definition, which I use throughout the remainder of this chapter, attempts to account for the collaborative nature of note making and thus the collective nature of knowledge production that takes place in some online spaces.

for sender-receiver is not wholly different from a print scenario where the writer anticipates how the reader will engage with the text and where the reader brings his or her own interpretive lens and background knowledge to the situation. Yet there is a key difference, and that is, the reader in this case is also a potential collaborator and producer of the text in an explicit way. As I define it here, the open notebook is not an *immutable mobile* in Latour's (1990; see Latour, 1987; Latour & Woolgar, 1986) sense of the term, but rather a type of *fluid object* (see de Laet & Mol, 2000) that serves a generally recognizable purpose but can be adapted to context-specific needs. Given these characteristics, it is somewhat unclear whether open notebooks actually constitute an extension of the genre or, more radically, a complete break from it. What we do know is that the rhetorical situation for note making is changing as it begins to accommodate new media, wider audiences, and novel exigencies related to open access.

A commonplace within the North American genre studies scholarship is that genres are not static vehicles for delivering information. Rather, in Miller's (1984) well-known phrasing, they are "typified rhetorical actions based in recurrent situations" (p. 159). The situation for keeping an open notebook is not completely typified in the way Miller describes; indeed, open notebook science itself is an emerging phenomenon and therefore presents a challenge for anyone who attempts to theorize it as a "type" of rhetorical activity. My inclination, however, is to characterize recent developments in the genre as a productive tension between stability and change that is still unfolding; that is, open notebooks are recognizable enough to invite a particular response yet flexible enough to accommodate, and reinforce, emergent forms of social and rhetorical action. Geisler (2001) suggests that "a key characteristic of texts used for internal control . . . is their public character, which makes compliance or failure to comply an observable fact" (p. 4). Texts that "jump the wall," she argues, move from private meditational means to public motive and, in doing so, become a "culturally-valued" outcome of activity (p. 9). With traditional notebooks, this would involve an active attempt to share one's work outside the laboratory context. But with open notebooks, writing is *always* a public activity. It is therefore always constrained by one's ability either to adhere to or depart from communal standards for note making. My aim in the remainder of this chapter is to show how these claims take shape in the context of an online scientific community.

EMERGENT CONTEXTS FOR WRITING IN SCIENCE

My interest in laboratory notebooks grew out of a previous study that explored processes of writing and representation in a chemical physics laboratory. Through that inquiry, I found these texts being used in a variety of ways: for example, *technically* (scientists use them to record and archive procedural information); *epistemically* (scientists use them to generate meaning and interpret phenomena in the flow of laboratory inquiry); and *rhetorically* (scientists use them to stabilize meaning over time and develop propriety ownership over the outcomes of their research). From these perspectives, notebooks offer a valuable resource for theorizing scientific writing from the perspective of *in situ* laboratory activity. Specifically, we can situate them in relation to specific tasks; we can study them in relation to workplace ensembles and collaborative activities; we can examine them in relation to other textual practices; and we can theorize them as a type of meaning- and knowledge-constructive rhetorical technology. A similar method applies to these study of open notebook science, only it requires that we adapt our print-based thinking about scientific texts to accommodate emerging forms of writing activity that take place in online spaces.

I initially approached the website OpenWetWare (OWW) as a dynamic network and eventually as an identifiable community that is bound together by a range of textual practices. The site itself served as a general object of study to bound off my analysis; but, I also focused on discrete written interactions as a means to explore how scientists and other stakeholders negotiate object-referents through the practice of note making and open notebook production. I gained access to OWW by composing a letter to the organization that manages the site and by becoming an official member of the community.[3] The following methods contributed to my data-collection efforts: observations and field notes, visual mapping of the site, analysis of intertextual relationships and written interactions, and semistructured interviews with members of the community. I also looked to other open notebook practices outside of OWW as a point of comparison. (The *UsefulChem Project* [n.d.] is a well-known example that builds on similar principles related to open access but defines and manifests them in different ways.) Over time, I narrowed my focus to two objects of analysis: the site itself and the way it functions as an open notebook; and notebook templates within the site and the way they structure rhetorical dynamics between members of the community. I describe these processes in greater detail in the following sections.

OpenWetWare: Learning to "Share Your Science"

OpenWetWare was launched in May 2005 by a group of graduate students at the Massachusetts Institute of Technology (MIT) who wanted to coordinate their work through a shared Web space (see Waldrop, 2008). Over time, the project developed into a much larger collective of practitioners and students

---

[3] I made my presence known in different ways: for example, by obtaining IRB approval for this research; by writing to executive members of the organization; by contacting individual members directly; and by developing my own Web space on the site. OWW itself is a diverse space with a diverse membership base. My presence was therefore not as noticeable as it would typically be in a physical research environment.

who use the site as a resource for obtaining and sharing information related to the field of biology and the discipline of biological synthesis. OWW's stated mission is to

> support open sharing of research, education, publication, and discussion in biological sciences and engineering. We promote and support collaborations among researchers, students, and others who are working towards these goals. We believe that open sharing of research improves the quality and pace of scientific and engineering research. (OWW, n.d.)

The early vision for the community was based on a "Science 2.0" philosophy that encouraged members to exchange information in the most efficient manner possible and therefore make "good use of 21st century technology for sharing and publishing . . . with societal goals of openness regarding the development and constructive application of technology" (OWW, n.d.). The OWW community originally consisted of only a handful of graduate students and related laboratories, but over the past 7 years, it has continued to proliferate. At the time of this writing, in 2012, the site has received over 80 million page views and includes over 11,000 members from countries that span the globe. I see these numbers as evidence of a growing interest both in synthetic biology—a common area of interest for members of the OWW community—and open notebook science—a related interest that many in the community share.

Synthetic biology is an emerging discipline that has grown in interest over the past decade. According to Benner and Sismour (2005), synthetic biologists "extract from living systems interchangeable parts that might be tested, validated as construction units, and reassembled to create devices that might (or might not) have analogues in living systems" (p. 533; see Andrianantoandro, Basu, Karig, & Weiss, 2006; Knight, 2005). The possibilities for application are vast. Endy (2005), an early advocate for OWW and co-founder of the Biobricks Foundation, argues that open, reliable, and standardized information are key components for helping synthetic biology fulfill human needs. In an article published in the scientific journal *Nature*, he suggests, specifically, that

> the biological engineering community would benefit from the development of technologies and the promulgation of standards that support the definition, description and characterization of the basic biological parts, as well as standard conditions that support the use of parts in combination and overall system operation. (p. 450)

The very existence of a community like OWW responds to this need both directly and indirectly. On the one hand, the site provides the biology community with a usable infrastructure within which to share procedural information related to biological engineering. On the other hand, it standardizes the process of note making, transforming it from an individual meditational means to a collective and public rhetorical activity and thus promotes the growth of synthetic biology as a coherent body of research. (It is worth noting that Endy's students helped to launch OWW based on an earlier model they developed called "Endipedia.") The Biobricks Foundation, a public-benefit organization devoted to the study and production of standardized biological parts, or Biobricks, now manages the site.

Open notebook science is compelling in part because it seeks to create access to information that might not be made available through other forms of scientific communication. This is one recognizable feature of the genre; that is, scientists have traditionally used notebooks to document successes *and* failures whereas only the former have traditionally made their way into published journal articles (see Medawar, 1964). Early developers of OWW recognized the potential value of sharing laboratory notes with other researchers in the synthetic biology community. We can see this explicitly stated in a grant proposal OWW submitted to the National Science Foundation (NSF) in 2006:

> The process of biological research generates and makes use of a wide variety of information, most of which is either inaccessible or unrecorded. For example, research papers and conference proceedings typically only summarize completed projects and results, while biological databases store and share heavily refined experimental data. Most of the remaining knowledge, and the process through which that knowledge is produced, is not recorded in any structured form or made available. . . . As a result, much biological research knowledge is consigned to individual and collective lore. (2006, p. 1)

According to the proposal, OWW provides an important space not only for sharing the minutiae of research—what we might refer to as the "germ cells" of the scientific literature—but also for laying bare the very process of knowledge production. The recording of failure is a particularly relevant example: just because an experiment did not work out as hypothesized does not render it worthless to scientists (and students of science) working on similar projects. Interestingly, the grant proposal makes an implicit argument about the ways in which genres constrain scientific communication and thus influence the larger scientific enterprise. In this case, the open notebook offers affordances to researchers that other genres, or even other media within the same genre, may not offer.

OWW as Open Notebook

OWW is designed using wiki software and is therefore "open" in the sense that any member can freely modify the structure or, on a more fine-grained level, revise individual notebook entries. Members represent countries from around the world and join the site for any number of reasons. Some are synthetic biologists interested in promoting their research; some are practitioners coordinating the work that takes place in their laboratories; and some are students who are fulfilling course requirements. OWW thus provides a space for practicing scientists to communicate about their research but also serves as a pedagogical resource for those who are learning to be scientists (or simply, who might want to learn more about synthetic biology). There is some overt regulation of communicative activity in this setting—for example, users must go through a process of joining the site if they want to create a new page or modify existing information—but overall, the community governs itself through collective norms that are reinforced through different note making practices. In this section, I focus on the features of OWW that enable it to function as an open notebook.

OWW's homepage is designed to organize important pages on the site and sometimes link them to other related information on the Web. These include the following: protocols, materials, labs & groups, courses, blogs, and a lab notebook software program. *Protocols* and *materials* are dynamic wiki spaces where technical information gets shared with and modified by members of the community. *Labs & groups* identify different organizations affiliated with OWW and provide links to individual pages both within and outside the site. *Courses* provide information related to science classes offered at different universities in the United States and around the world. *Blogs* provide a setting within which members can communicate about general issues related to biology and biological engineering. And the *software program* provides a template for creating an individual notebook that one can use to record information and share it with others. Together, these pages orient users to OWW as an open notebook and more generally as a networked community of practitioners.

The site-as-open-notebook responds to a familiar exigence in the sense that it provides users with a space within which to record their day-to-day laboratory work. In this way, it functions similarly to other notebook media. Yet OWW promotes a more collective approach to note making and more broadly to the construction of procedural knowledge. *Protocols* and *materials* in particular facilitate this practice. Protocol entries tend to focus on the communication of techniques for carrying out procedures in the laboratory; and material entries tend to focus on the communication of techniques for producing physical artifacts. They each rely on the completion of technical tasks, but the former tend to be techniques for acting while the latter tend to be artifacts that mediate activity or can be acted upon. Protocol and material entries look like pages in a print notebook in the sense that they communicate technical information through multiple semiotic resources; one significant difference however is that the information is immediately and publicly accessible and can be openly modified by members of the OWW community.

Protocols and materials cover a range of subject areas related to the study and application of synthetic biology. Some entries get modified regularly while others rarely get modified at all. These wiki pages function in similar ways, but I focus on protocols here because they tend to get revised more often, and by a greater number of members, than other entries on the site. The current template for uploading protocols developed over time (2006–present) and through ongoing interactions between individual members. The structure itself is relatively linear and includes the following headings: *overview, materials, procedure, notes, references,* and *contact.* Users simply adopt these categories to generate their individual entries or conversely, input alternative categories or subsections as they see fit. (They can do this by accessing the page's source code.) The template thus provides constraints for note making activity but is flexible enough to accommodate localized needs. The entry titled Agarose Gel Electrophoresis offers one illustrative example of the OWW protocol. It includes the following headings adapted from the template structure: *general procedures, casting gels, buffers, loading dyes, notes, see also,* and *external links.* Generally, it looks like a normal, albeit cleaned-up, page out of a print-based laboratory notebook.

The "History" link at the top of the page allows users to trace how the Agarose Gel Electrophoresis (AGE) protocol evolved between April 25, 2005 (the date of the original entry) and April 29, 2010 (a recent modification). Altogether, 12 users contributed to it over a 5-year span, and over 50 changes were made between the first and last entry. These changes suggest that procedural knowledge communicated on OWW is the result of a dynamic interaction between users rather than an instrumental reporting of technical data. For instance, the aim of the original entry was to "prepare gels for gel electrophoresis" (April 25, 2005). Approximately 6 months later, however, a different user off-loaded the existing information to another page using a hyperlink and changed the protocol to "Agarose gel electrophoresis." The protocol thus evolved from a narrow focus on material production—that is, how to prepare a gel— to a broader focus on laboratory techniques that use material products—that is, how to perform the gel electrophoresis technique. Once the original objective was modified, it offered a basis for other participants to add new text (e.g., step-by-step directions), visuals (e.g., an image of the agarose gel under UV light), and data displays (e.g., a table that displays rules of thumb for the procedure). The final result is a usable protocol and a page that has stabilized through ongoing collaboration between community members.

The networked structure of OWW allows practitioners to supplement individual entries through an intertextual weaving of hyperlinks that guide users to internal and external sources. Protocol pages typically include two types. The first connect to other pages on the site and often relate to the procedure itself. So, for instance, the AGE page includes links to materials that are necessary to carry out the protocol (e.g., preparing agarose gel) and to similar entries generated by other individuals or groups within the site (e.g., affiliated labs that have developed their own AGE procedures). The second connect to external websites that provide alternative techniques for carrying out the protocol in question. AGE includes several hyperlinks to pages outside OWW, and each one gets rated on a "3-star" system so that readers have some sense of whether it is viable information to consult. One benefit of connecting to other resources on the Web is that the AGE page can provide users—some of whom may be novices just learning to perform laboratory tasks—with information delivered in a range of formats. These include the typical written instructions, visual images, and data displays; but they also include media like virtual simulations. Users can thus learn about AGE from several perspectives: whether by consulting the entry on OWW and the revisions that were made to the protocol over time, by researching the embedded hyperlinks to see how they might supplement their understanding through other information found on the site and on the Web, or by experimenting with tools for enacting material techniques in virtual spaces.

The fact that the AGE page underwent several transformations over a 5-year span suggests that even the most basic (or seemingly basic) procedural knowledge is a product of communal interaction. Sometimes this takes place over days and weeks; and sometimes it takes place over months and years. The "Talk" function embedded within the wiki facilitates this process by providing a mechanism within which members can communicate with one another about the changes they feel would improve individual entries. Consider an example taken from the AGE page:

> Hi Mike, nice additions to Agarose gel electrophoresis consensus protocol. Would be great to have that as an image. I saw something similar once in the Roche LabFAQ but the image is copyrighted. See you around on OWW—Jakob 06:31, 29 June 2009 (EDT).

The writing displayed in the "talk" between scientists confirms that members communicate with each other directly and not only through their contributions to different protocols. And sometimes they discuss the most viable methods both for completing technical work in the laboratory *and* for sharing it on OWW. The object of this activity is not always something that can be discussed as, say, one might discuss a new species of insect; indeed, synthetic biologists actively design and engineer biological parts and systems that do not necessarily exist in nature. The object-referent for these scientists, whether engineered materials or protocols, might therefore be considered an active negotiation of meaning through procedural discourse rather than a straightforward representation of technical knowledge that they simply share with one another. In principle, the negotiation itself could go on for an unlimited period of time, but I have found that protocols and materials do stabilize as procedures get worked out through ongoing community interactions.

OWW and the Standardization of Note Making Activity

A strategic issue for early users of OWW was whether protocols should be dynamically generated or whether they should be based on templates that the community proposes, creates, and approves (e.g., via steering committee). On the one hand, the open nature of the site is valuable for creating new knowledge through collective interactions and collaborative problem solving. On the other hand, the open nature of the site can be messy, and perhaps obstructive, if everyone has a unique method for uploading and sharing information. The notebook software program embedded within the site responds to both needs; that is, it provides a template for uploading information that exists as part of the wiki structure and can be modified by other members of the OWW community; and the templates can be modified to accommodate (semi-) personal use by individuals and subgroups within the site. Members who use the program thus move from note making that takes place within a general structure to one that takes place in a more circumscribed space, which, I have found, tends to get used for individualized needs. The creation of a standardized yet flexible notebook program contributes to the efficiency of research and communicative activity and reflects an intentional effort to stabilize the ways in which users access and modify information on the site.

The exigency for using the notebook program varies depending on the user and audience. Individual scientists may use it to record their personal findings and share them with the OWW community; teachers may use it to orient students to laboratory techniques and writing practices; and students may use it simply because they want to pass their courses or learn how to contribute to OWW through their writing.[4] I have found that the pedagogical function in particular illustrates the power of note making to reinforce disciplinary norms related both to research and communication. The NSF grant proposal referenced earlier in the chapter is telling in this regard: "By exposing students to OWW via their courses," the authors suggest, "we will train a new cadre of researchers to systematically and digitally document and share not only experimental results but also the detailed context for those results" (2006, p. 3). I take two points of interest from this statement. First, the authors see how notebooks function as a pedagogical resource in the undergraduate classroom, and second, they appear well aware of the connection between writing and disciplinary enculturation. Over time, the logic goes, students will become practicing scientists who have learned to "share their science"—including the "detailed context" for experimental results—and open access will be less an argument to be made than it will be a common practice in the scientific community.

Multiple groups associated with OWW use the notebook program to organize their laboratory activities. One instructive example comes from American University's Biomaterials Design Lab (BDL), where the professor and principal investigator, Dr. Matt Hartings, requires undergraduate students to document

---

[4] As evidence of the latter, OWW has used the notebook program for students taking part in the International Genetically Engineered Machine (iGEM) competition.

their laboratory work using the notebook program. The process of note making for these members is similar to other writing that takes place on the site—for example, inputting and modifying information—but is oriented toward a different set of outcomes. In this case, Dr. Hartings (expert scientist) uses the site and the notebook program as a medium for teaching undergraduates (novice scientists) how to carry out field-specific procedures in the laboratory, and document and interpret the outcomes of the procedures they perform. Students record their work in notebooks, all of which are linked to the BDL homepage on OWW, and Hartings assesses their entries by embedding his own comments on individual pages. Students in turn respond to his comments and in doing so, learn how to rhetorically present their findings in the style of an expert practitioner.

The template for the notebook program includes just two categories for inputting information. The first is *Description/Abstract*, and the second is *Notes*. It also includes two additional features that differentiate it from other templates used within the site: a calendar that highlights the date of each entry, and a search engine that can be used to locate information related to notebook entries in particular. Hartings tailored his course template to include the following: *Objective*, *Description*, *Data*, and *Notes*. While a simple modification, it is not a trivial one. Indeed, the professor in this case takes advantage of the template's flexibility and uses it to bridge the materiality of laboratory inquiry with a textual practice that connects students with a networked collective of practitioners in the field. Hartings's model for constructing a notebook page accomplishes at least two objectives: it orients students to the technical tasks involved in carrying out laboratory protocols and it orients them to rhetorical tasks involved in documenting their work in an open notebook that potentially can be accessed and modified by members of the OWW community. Both are necessary for students to become facile with technical procedures they need to perform at the laboratory bench and with the rhetorical techniques that will enable them to become contributing members of a scientific discipline.

Students create their own notebooks through OWW, and Hartings uses entries as a space within which to guide them in completing and documenting their work. Similar to materials and protocols, it is possible to trace these interactions through the "Revision History" feature located on individual notebook pages. A September 2011 entry in Hartings's notebook, for instance, required students to carry out a technical procedure related to nanoparticle synthesis and document their outcomes in their OWW notebooks. Once the task was completed, he then commented on the entries individually. These comments included questions like, "What do you make of your data?" and "What do you think it means?" Hartings also directed students toward scholarly literature that they read as a class, asking, "Is this consistent with what Bakishi et al [*sic*] see in their paper for nanoparticle synthesis?" Students responded to these questions by correcting their calculations, adding visual displays and including more textual explanation to the entry. The rhetorical situation here combines the material and technical dimensions of laboratory practice with the rhetorical dimensions of recording data, interpreting and displaying it, and situating one's work within the broader field of study. And it all takes place within a pedagogical framework where the professor is teaching students not only how to perform but also how to share their science.

The dynamic between Hartings and his students is one that we might find in any number of classroom settings. It goes something like this: professor assigns task; student completes task; professor assesses task; student respond to assessment (and so on). The relationship here, however, is different in the sense that this interaction takes place on OWW and is therefore a public activity. Indeed, different members of the group can consult each other's work, and other members of the OWW community can contribute their own insights if they so choose. Similar to other forms of note making on the site, these notebook entries "jump the wall" (see Geisler, 2001) when they move from private meditational means to public motive. Only in this situation, the relationship is somewhat more complex because it involves a decidedly educational component; that is, notebook entries that once mediated between professor and student now take on a much wider audience. It is not only an expert practitioner posting his or her research to the Web; it is a more systematic attempt to enculturate an upcoming generation into particular ways of approaching laboratory tasks—completing technical procedures—and writing about the outcomes of those tasks—interpreting, structuring, and displaying information in the form of notebook entries that provide detailed contexts for experimental results. It may be that professor Hartings is simply attempting to help his students "get it right." Yet a more nuanced view might suggest that he is showing them how to process information in the style of an expert scientist and, just as important, how to build knowledge through collaborative interactions in general and through the practice of open notebook science in particular.

CONCLUSIONS AND DIRECTIONS

Open notebook science is just one of many new practices emerging within the complex ecology of 21st-century scientific communication, but I believe it usefully illustrates how scientists are attempting to balance the relationship between stability and change through a familiar textual practice. The laboratory notebook genre has traditionally been "fuzzy" (see Medway, 2002) in the sense that individual texts tend to share a common exigence but also tend to be somewhat idiosyncratic to the individual scientist or group. With electronic notebooks, however, the process of uploading information becomes increasingly standardized through predesigned templates. Note making in turn begins to resemble a relatively streamlined process of data entry. Open notebook sites like OWW converge these two phenomena in the sense that they provide a dynamic yet structured space within which scientists can share information with others on the Web. The flexibility of the wiki ensures that note making is not a wholly standardized or rote activity, and the public and modifiable nature of notebook entries ensures that individual writers must at least remain accountable to community norms (lest they find themselves at odds with the community). Through this process, notebook entries become less fuzzy, more recognizable in their form and function, and potentially more powerful in their ability to reinforce particular habits of writing and rhetorical action.

Online communities like OWW offer many possibilities for collaborative inquiry and collective problem solving. Yet on a broader scale, the power of open notebook science is potentially inhibited if there is no clear standard for communicating about problems and the techniques used for solving them. And here is where open notebooks have some role to play in transforming scientific research culture. Nielsen (2011) argues that

> if we're to amplify collective intelligence . . . participants must share a body of knowledge and techniques. It's that body of knowledge and techniques that they use to collaborate. When this shared body exists, we'll call it a *shared praxis*, after the word *praxis*, meaning the practical application of knowledge." (p. 75, Nielsen's emphasis)

Notebooks are not the only way to create a shared body of knowledge in the sciences. Admittedly, a variety of textual genres exist for this very purpose. Even so, the practice of open note making does represent a move to make all research available—and not just the finished work that makes its way into journal articles or other formal publication outlets. Some open notebooks function as an archive of details gleaned from research undertaken by scientists, like Jean-Claude Bradley, who are willing to make their work public in real time. Under this description, sharing knowledge becomes an act of making information available and accessible. An open notebook infrastructure like OWW, however, represents a somewhat different prospect for the idea of open notebook science as an emergent model of scientific communication—precisely *because* it reinforces shared praxis both through communal standards of note making and through the reporting of practical techniques that lie at the heart of much scientific inquiry. It does this in at least two ways: first, by providing a flexible infrastructure within which members can share, revise, and otherwise communicate about their research over time; and second, by providing dynamic templates that promote rhetorical action based on principles of open access and collective problem solving. These features contribute to the typification of open note making as a textual practice and, for OWW in particular, the stabilization of procedural knowledge related to synthetic biology.

I began this chapter by discussing how the *art of scientific writing* characterized the laboratory notebook as a "germ cell of the scientific literature." The authors of that style guide were referring primarily to a print-based genre; for them, the laboratory notebook is just the beginning of a long process through which knowledge takes shape and gets communicated beyond the laboratory walls. I believe that the germ cell metaphor still applies today but invites an alternative reading given our current technological landscape. Note making is no longer only a starting point for the communication of science; indeed, it is also a *telos*, which over time may begin to effect subtle changes in the scientific research culture. When scientists "open their notebooks" to the world, they are sharing information, but they are also promoting a new way of thinking about knowledge production. Studies of laboratory life have described science as a competitive enterprise where scientists produce immutable and mobile inscriptions, amass allies, and construct barriers between themselves and others. I would argue that this agonistic model comes into question when they begin to integrate principles of open access into their research and communication. With open notebook science in particular, scientists are not only attempting to win arguments, they are also learning to "share their science" and thus facilitate a collective approach to knowledge production—one that benefits from increasingly fluid boundaries between the classroom, laboratory, scientific community, and broader public sphere.

What I hope to have shown in this chapter is that open notebook science is a promising development within the open access movement. Yet like other developments in open access, it is not without its complications. At the very least, it will take a genuine effort on the part of individual scientists to communicate information that may potentially undercut their claims to intellectual property. We can see this happening on a very public stage (e.g., the "Academic Spring" movement), and we can see this happening in everyday practice (e.g., scientists who use sites like OWW to share their science and promote their research). There is a question here of self-interest—getting credit for one's intellectual work—and communal interest—contributing to a body of knowledge for the sake of improving the human condition. Open notebooks have an increasingly vital role to play in this process. And as writing researchers and rhetoricians, we have an increasingly central role to play in showing how and the extent to which emerging textual practices contribute to the production and dissemination of scientific knowledge. When we do this, we are not critiquing the epistemology of science through rhetorical study, but rather we are showing how rhetoric itself contributes to conversations about the relationship between science and society in a digital age.

REFERENCES

Andrianantoandro, E., Basu, S., Karig, D. K., & Weiss, R. (2006). Synthetic biology: New engineering rules for an emerging discipline. *Molecular Systems Biology.* Retrieved from http://www.nature.com

Atkinson, D. (1999). *Scientific discourse in sociohistorical context: The philosophical transactions of the Royal Society of London, 1675–1975.* Mahwah, NJ: Erlbaum.

Bazerman, C. (1988). *Shaping written knowledge: The genre and activity of the experimental article in science.* Madison, WI: University of Wisconsin Press.

Bazerman, C. (1999). *The languages of Edison's light.* Cambridge, MA: MIT Press.

Benner, S. A., & Sismour, M. A. (2005). Synthetic biology. *Nature Reviews Genetics, 6,* 533–543.

Berkenkotter, C., & Huckin, T. (1995). *Genre knowledge in disciplinary communication: Cognition/culture/power.* New York, NY: Routledge.

Borgman, C. (2007). *Scholarship in the digital age: Information, infrastructure, and the Internet.* Cambridge, MA: MIT Press.

Bradley, J. C. (2006, September 26). *Open notebook science.* Retrieved from http://drexel-coas-elearning.blogspot.com/2006/09/open-notebook-science.html

Bradley, J. C., Owens, K., & Williams, A. (2008). Chemistry crowdsourcing and open notebook science. *Nature Precedings.* doi: 10.1038/npre.2008.1505.1

Brienza, C. (2012). Opening the wrong gate?: The academic spring and scholarly publishing in the humanities and social sciences. *Publishing Research Quarterly, 28,* 159–171.

Butler, D. (2005). Electronic notebooks: A new leaf. *Nature, 436,* 20–21.

Campbell, J. A. (1990). Scientific discovery and rhetorical invention: The path to Darwin's origin. In H. W. Simons (Ed.), *The rhetorical turn: Invention and persuasion in the conduct of inquiry* (pp. 58–90). Chicago, IL: University of Chicago Press.

Crick, N. (2005). "A capital and a novel argument": Charles Darwin's notebooks and the productivity of rhetorical consciousness. *Quarterly Journal of Speech, 91,* 337–364.

de Laet, M., & Mol, A. (2000). The Zimbabwe bush pump: Mechanics of a fluid technology. *Social Studies of Science, 30,* 225–263.

Ebel, H. F., Bliefert, C., & Russey, W. E. (Eds.). (2004). *The art of scientific writing: From student reports to professional publications in chemistry and related fields.* Germany: Wiley-VCH.

Elliot, M. H. (2011). *New debates over intellectual property protection and ELN.* Retrieved from http://www.scientificcomputing.com

Endy, D. (2005). Foundations for engineering biology. *Nature, 438,* 449–453.

Geisler, C. (2001). Textual objects: Accounting for the role of texts in the everyday life of complex organizations. *Written Communication, 18,* 296–325.

Giles, J. (2012). *Going paperless: The digital lab.* Retrieved from http://www.nature.com

Gooding, D. (1990a). Mapping experiment as a learning process: How the first electromagnetic motor was invented. *Science, Technology, & Human Values, 15,* 165–201.

Gooding, D. (1990b). *Experiment and the making of meaning: Human agency in scientific observation and experiment.* Dordrecht, The Netherlands: Kluwer.

Gross, A. G. (2006). *Starring the text: The place of rhetoric in science studies.* Carbondale, IL: Southern Illinois University Press.

Gross, A. G., Harmon, J. E., & Reidy, M. S. (2002). *Communicating science: The scientific article from the 17th century to the present.* New York, NY: Oxford University Press.

Holmes, F. L. (1984). Lavoisier and Krebs: The individual scientists in the near and deeper past. *Isis, 75,* 131–142.

Holmes, F. L. (1990). Laboratory notebooks: Can the daily record illuminate the broader picture? *Proceedings of the American Philosophical Society, 134*, 349–366.

Holmes, F. L. (2004). *Investigating pathways: Patterns and stages in the careers of experimental scientists.* New Haven, CT: Yale University Press.

Holmes, F. L., Renn, J., & Rheinberger, H.-J. (2003). *Reworking the bench: Research notebooks in the history of science.* Dordrecht, The Netherlands: Kluwer.

Klokmose, C. N., & Zander, P. (2010). Rethinking laboratory notebooks. In M. Lewkowicz, P. Hassanaly, M. Rohde, & V. Wulf (Eds.), *Proceedings of COOP 2010: Proceedings of the 9th international conference on Designing Cooperative Systems* (pp. 119–139). New York, NY: Springer.

Knight, T. F. (2005). Engineering novel life. *Molecular Systems Biology.* Retrieved from http://www.nature.com

Kozma, R., Chin, E., Russell, J., & Marx, N. (2000). The roles of representations and tools in the chemistry laboratory and their implications for chemistry learning. *The Journal of the Learning Sciences, 9*, 105–143.

Latour, B. (1987). *Science in action: How to follow scientists and engineers through society.* Cambridge, MA: Harvard University Press.

Latour, B. (1990). Drawing things together. In M. Lynch & S. Woolgar (Eds.), *Representation in scientific practice* (pp. 19–69). Cambridge, MA: MIT Press.

Latour, B., & Woolgar, S. (1986). *Laboratory life: The construction of scientific facts.* Princeton, NJ: Princeton University Press.

Medway, P. (2002). Fuzzy genres and community identities: The case of architecture students' sketchbooks. In R. Coe, L. Lingard, & T. Teslenko (Eds.), *The rhetoric and ideology of genre: Strategies for stability and change* (pp. 123–153). Cresskill, NJ: Hampton.

Medawar, P. (1964, August 1). Is the scientific paper fraudulent? *Saturday Review,* pp. 42–43.

Miller, C. (1984). Genre as social action. *Quarterly Journal of Speech, 70*, 151–167.

Myers, J. D. (2003). Collaborative electronic notebooks as electronic records: Design issues for the secure electronic laboratory notebook (ELN). In *Proceedings of the fourth international symposium on collaborative technologies and systems, 35*, 13–22.

Myers, J. D., Fox-Dobbs, C., Laird, J., Le, D., Reich, D., & Curtz, T. (1996). Electronic laboratory notebooks for collaborative research. In *Proceedings of the 5th workshop on enabling technologies: Infrastructure for collaborative enterprises* (pp. 19–21). Washington, DC: IEEE Computer Society.

Nielsen, M. (2011). *Reinventing discovery: The new era of networked science.* Princeton, NJ: Princeton University Press.

OpenWetWare (OWW). (n.d.). *About.* Retrieved August 1, 2012, from http://openwetware.org/images/7/72/OWWv17.pdf

OpenWetWare (OWW). (2006). *NSF Grant Application.* Retrieved August 1, 2012, from http://openwetware.org/images/7/72/OWWv17.pdf

Orlikowski, W. J., & Yates, J. (1994). Genre repertoire: The structuring of communicative practices in organizations. *Administrative Science Quarterly, 39*, 541–574.

Owen, J. M. (2007). *The scientific article in the age of digitization.* Dordrecht, The Netherlands: Springer.

Poynder, R. (2010). *Interview with Jean-Claude Bradley: The impact of open notebook science*. Retrieved from http://www.infotoday.com/it/sep10/Poynder.shtml

Rubacha, M., Rattan, A. K., & Hosselet, S. C. (2011). A review of electronic laboratory notebooks available in the market today. *Journal of Laboratory Automation, 16*, 90–98.

Schryer, C. F. (1994). The lab vs. the clinic: Sites of competing genres. In A. Freedman & P. Medway (Eds.), *Genre and the new rhetoric* (pp. 105–124). London, UK: Taylor & Francis.

Tabard, A., Mackay, W., & Eastmond, E. (2008). From individual to collaborative: The evolution of prism, a hybrid laboratory notebook. In *Proceedings of the 2008 ACM conference on computer supported cooperative work* (pp. 569–578). New York, NY: ACM.

Talbott, T., Peterson, M., Schwidder, J., & Myers, J. D. (2005). Adapting the electronic laboratory notebook for the semantic era. In W. McQuay & W. W. Smari (Eds.), *Proceedings of the 2005 international conference on collaborative technologies and systems* (pp. 136–143). Washington, DC: IEEE Computer Society.

Turner, P., & Turner, S. (1997). Supporting cooperative work using shared notebooks. In J. Hughes (Ed.), *Proceedings of the fifth European conference on computer supported cooperative work* (pp. 281–295). Dordrecht, The Netherlands: Kluwer.

UsefulChem Project. (n.d.). *Wikispaces*. Retrieved August 1, 2013, from http://usefulchem.wikispaces.com/

Waldrop, M. M. (2008). Science 2.0. *Scientific American, 298*, 68–73.

Wickman, C. (2010). Writing material in chemical physics research: The laboratory notebook as locus of technical and textual integration. *Written Communication, 27*, 259–292.

Willinsky, J. (2006). *The access principle: The case for open access to research and scholarship*. Cambridge, MA: MIT Press.

http://dx.doi.org/10.2190/SCIC3

CHAPTER 3

The Scientific Journal: Making It New?

Joseph E. Harmon

ABSTRACT

In the early 1990s, as the first digital scientific journals were coming online, Stevan Harnad made the prescient observation that "Electronic journals should not and will not be mere clones of paper journals, ghosts in another medium." But the earliest Web-based scientific articles looked much like clones of their print versions, except for the addition of hyperlinks to the different article sections and references. Is that still the case two decades later? To assess what, if anything, has changed compared with the typical print-only scientific article of the 20th century, the author asked a common set of questions of a random selection of 150 scientific research articles for the period 2010–2011. These articles were chosen from the 10 most highly cited science journals, as well as 5 journals available to readers without any payment or institutional subscription ("open access"). This analysis captured evolutionary changes that have occurred in the byline, abstract, master finding system, visual presentation, and argumentative structure of the digital scientific article, as well as the contents pages for the scientific journal. The case is made that now is a time of extraordinary fecundity with regard to communicative variations from 20th-century practices, directly and indirectly propelled by the personal computer and Internet.

> The future is already here. It's just not evenly distributed yet.
> —William Gibson

In a provocative 1992 essay for the *New York Times*, novelist Robert Coover predicted the death of books of fiction and their transfiguration in a nonlinear hypertext form:

> Much of the novel's alleged power is embedded in the line, that compulsory author-directed movement from the beginning of a sentence to its period, from the top of the page to the bottom, from the first page to the last. . . . But true freedom from the tyranny of the line is perceived as only really possible now at last with the advent of hypertext, written and read on the computer.

As one of the many novelists and poets heavily influenced by Ezra Pound's (1935) injunction to "make it new," Coover confidently extrapolated that hypertext would push literary experimentation in a new direction. From the perspective of 2 decades later, however, it is now clear that Coover's vision of the end for creative writing as we have known it since the invention of the printing press has yet to materialize. The typical novel or book of poems or collection of essays we read on Kindle, iPad, laptop, or other electronic device—at least those written by prominent writers like David Foster Wallace, or Zadie Smith, or Joyce Carol Oates, or even Robert Coover—is not all that appreciably different from their modernistic predecessors in printed book form. We still, more or less, read "from the top of the page to the bottom, from the first page to the last." There are no embedded visuals, videos, or audio files. There is no color. We do not interact with these literary texts other than to advance or bookmark the page. The "tyranny" of the line and page continues to reign.

This chapter will be arguing that much of the above is *not* the case for the typical present-day issue of any of the leading scientific journals. That thesis may sound counterintuitive since, in contrast to modern literary artists, scientists are not purposely trying to either make their communications "new" stylistically or "intentionally disorient readers for artistic effect" (Bernstein, 1999), in fact, quite the contrary. Nonetheless, the case will be made here that the scientific literature is in the midst of a turbulent transitional period, where the print era is still very much in evidence, yet driven in part by technological changes, the dawn of the "post-Gutenberg era" has spawned an incredible explosion of variations on the 20th-century norms. This transition is symbolized by the typical Web version of a scientific article, where the digital contents page offers links to a PDF file for printing and reading on paper and an HTML version for reading on the Web—icons for the old and new sitting side by side on the computer screen.

In part, this chapter is meant as a follow-up to *Communicating Science: The Scientific Article from the 17th Century to the Present* by Gross, Harmon, and Reidy (2002). In a series of chapters covering each of the last 4 centuries, we analyzed a large corpus of whole articles and short passages from French, English, and German scientific journals. Our analysis focused on the changes over the past 4 centuries in the writing style, organization, and argumentative structure of the selected articles. Our corpus began in 1665, the year the first scientific journals were founded in Paris and London, and ended in the mid-1990s, the time during which we gathered our sample of articles for analysis.

In the mid-1990s, the webification of the scientific literature was still in a very early stage. We did note that about half the 35 journals in our 20th-century sample were on the Web (p. 186), but did not then have a large enough sample to make any observations about the effect, if any, on individual articles.

In a later quantitative study of the scientific literature, *The Scientific Article in the Age of Digitization*, Owen (2005) analyzed 86 peer reviewed scientific journals that had initiated publication on the Web between 1987 and 2001 (along with 100 peer reviewed digital journals in the humanities, law, social science, and other disciplines). Surprisingly, his principal conclusion was that,

> contrary to pretentious claims and expectations about the impact of digitization on scientific communication [p. 5]. . . , the journal article as a communicative form for reporting on research and disseminating scientific knowledge does not seem to have been transformed by . . . [the Internet]: it remains a digital copy of the printed form. (p. 11)

Owen views the current situation as preserving and extending "existing functions and values rather than as an innovation that radically transforms a communicative practice that has evolved over the centuries" (p. 55). In other words, gradual evolutionary, not revolutionary change, has occurred in the communicative aspects of the research article in the typical digital journal to date. Owen's sample included such journals as the *Brazilian Electronic Journal of Economics*, *Internet Journal of Chemistry*, and *Journal of Cotton Science*, but not the most highly cited scientific journals producing printed and electronic issues like *Nature*, *Physical Review*, *Journal of the American Chemical Society*, or even the highly successful open access journals founded by the Public Library of Science (PLoS). My contention is that the latter set constitutes the best journals to scrutinize if one wants to discover what innovations, if any, have surfaced in the digital scientific journal and the research articles therein. Such journals have the wide readership and prestige necessary to introduce Web-based innovations that scientists will gladly embrace in exchange for publication of their manuscripts. Also important, the journal publishers as well as the authors themselves have the necessary financial resources, technical knowhow, and manpower to implement such changes, even if only on a trial basis.

To tackle the basic question "What's changed, if anything?" between the printed articles of the 20th century and the digital articles of the 21st century, I closely examined a random selection of scientific research articles published in 2010 and 2011. These articles were chosen from the 10 most highly cited science journals for the period 1999–2009 (Thomson Reuters, 2009). These 10 journals not only represent the elite journals of science, but also a long history of article publication in print (see Table 3.1, left column). The oldest (*NEJM*) has been in existence for over 200 years; the youngest (*PRB*), over 40 years, though it is an offshoot of *Physical Review*, founded in 1893. All but one (*APL*)

Table 3.1 Science Journals Analyzed and Year Founded

Most-cited science journals	First year	Open-access science journals	First year
New England Journal of Medicine (NEJM)	1812	PLoS Biolog	2003
		PLoS Medicine	2004
Astrophysical Journal (AJ)	1849		
		PLoS One	2006
Nature	1869		
		Journal of Modern Physics (JMP)	2010
Journal of American Chemical Society (JACS)	1879		
		International Journal of Geosciences (IJG)	2010
Science	1880		
Journal of Biological Chemistry (JBC)	1905		
Proceedings of the National Academy of Sciences (PNAS)	1915		
Physical Review Letters (PRL)	1958		
Applied Physics Letters (APL)	1962		
Physical Review B (PRB)	1970		

still issue a print version of each issue, although according to its website, *JBC* only continues to publish printed issues "for now." All offer HTML and PDF versions of individual articles, except the two *Physical Review* journals (PDF only). All 10 journals require payment or subscription for access to all articles in their latest issues. Also included in my sample are five journals available to all readers without any payment or institutional subscription—three from PLoS and two recent startup open access journals (also listed in Table 3.1, right column). I analyzed 10 randomly selected articles from each of the 15 journals in Table 3.1 (150 total). I also gathered information about the homepage and first page to a 2011 issue of each of the journals.

In this chapter, I argue that there are substantive differences between the typical printed scientific article in the 20th century and the linked, multimedia article accessible through websites in the 21st century. These differences do not concern literary style per se, but strategies that "counter the line's power" by means of visualization, intertextuality, interactivity, and compartmentalization of information into discrete sections for readers with different special interests. Also changing is the meaning of authorship, an indirect consequence of the Internet era. These differences are best understood not in the common metaphors for dramatic change, such as "revolution" or "paradigm shift," but in terms of evolutionary variations and origins that can be traced to long before the Internet era. And it is probably too soon to tell which variations evident on the Web today will prove enduring. Yet even at this early stage, the digital scientific article in the leading scientific journals listed in Table 3.1 looks substantially different from the print-only article of the previous century. Exhibit A: compare Figure 3.1 and Figure 3.2.

AUTHORSHIP

One of the marked differences between Figures 3.1 and 3.2 concerns the list of authors and their institutional affiliations. The Goodman and Rich (1962) article has two authors, both from the same U.S. research organization. The Aron, Klein, Pham, Kramer, Wurst, and Klein article (2010) has six authors, from three German research organizations. This difference reflects one of the variations in the 21st-century scientific article: its composition is a highly social activity, often involving participants from different countries and organizations, presumably exchanging texts, data, and images via the Internet.

Through the 19th century, scientific articles seldom had more than one author. And for their sample of 20th-century articles, Gross et al. (2002) calculated an average of a little over two authors per article, with a maximum of five. On the basis of these data, they concluded that the practice of 20th-century science was "largely the product of an individual or very small group trying to solve a limited problem within a larger research field" (p. 175). Such a statement would appear to be greatly in need of updating. Recent quantitative studies have reported that single authors generated "the papers of singular distinction in science and engineering and social science in the 1950s, but the mantle of extra-ordinarily cited work has passed to teams by 2000" (Wuchty, Jones, & Uzzi, 2007, p. 1038), and that after 1975 these collaborations increasingly involved multiple universities (Jones, Wuchty, & Uzzi, 2008).

The results from analyzing the bylines in my 21st-century sample of highly cited journals support these recent conclusions. The average number of authors per article was 12, higher by a factor of nearly 6 compared with the 20th-century sample of Gross et al. (2002). There were only two single-author articles, while two had author lists running into the hundreds. The average number of institutions listed in the bylines was also impressively high, 5.7, and almost half (47%) of the sample involved an international collaboration. Not too surprisingly, the most represented countries in the bylines were the same ones that have been major players in scientific research over the past several centuries: United States (named in 45% of the bylines), Germany (17%), United Kingdom (17%), and

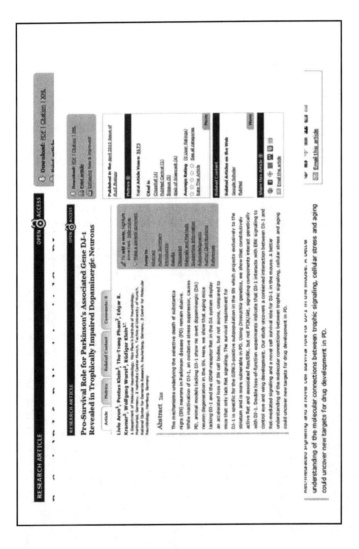

Figure 3.1. Screen shot of a digital article from *PLoS Biology* (Aron et al., 2010). Tabs open to article itself, metrics regarding community reception, related articles on the Web, and reader comments. Shaded box adjacent to abstract is for navigating article contents, adding a note to a selected passage, and making a general comment. Shaded box at upper right has links for PDF and XML versions, reprint ordering, and citation information. "Metrics" shows total article views and citations received to date. Links to social media at lower right.

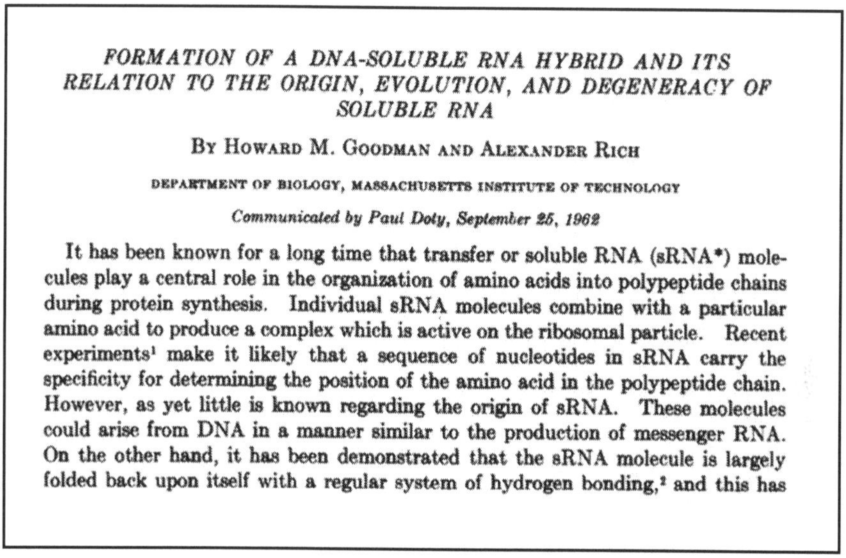

FORMATION OF A DNA-SOLUBLE RNA HYBRID AND ITS RELATION TO THE ORIGIN, EVOLUTION, AND DEGENERACY OF SOLUBLE RNA

BY HOWARD M. GOODMAN AND ALEXANDER RICH

DEPARTMENT OF BIOLOGY, MASSACHUSETTS INSTITUTE OF TECHNOLOGY

Communicated by Paul Doty, September 25, 1962

It has been known for a long time that transfer or soluble RNA (sRNA*) molecules play a central role in the organization of amino acids into polypeptide chains during protein synthesis. Individual sRNA molecules combine with a particular amino acid to produce a complex which is active on the ribosomal particle. Recent experiments[1] make it likely that a sequence of nucleotides in sRNA carry the specificity for determining the position of the amino acid in the polypeptide chain. However, as yet little is known regarding the origin of sRNA. These molecules could arise from DNA in a manner similar to the production of messenger RNA. On the other hand, it has been demonstrated that the sRNA molecule is largely folded back upon itself with a regular system of hydrogen bonding,[2] and this has

---

Figure 3.2. The first printed page of a 1962 PNAS article.
Reprinted with permission from Goodman, H. M., & Rich, A. (1962).
Formation of a DNA-soluble RNA hybrid and its relation to
the origin, evolution, and degeneracy of soluble RNA.
Proceeding of the National Academy of Sciences, 48, 2101-2109.

France (11%). One journal (*APL*) also has an interesting variation on the byline, including world maps with the geographic locations of the authors' home institutions. This feature further reinforces the truly international nature of much 21st-century scientific practice.

The authorship data for the open access literature sample (Table 3.1, right column) were slightly lower but no less impressive: average number of authors, 7.8, and participating institutions, 3.2. About 30% involved an international effort. These lower numbers are largely due to the two journals in the sample with negligible citation impact factors (*JMP* and *IJG*), both of which had many articles with one or two authors representing a single institution (24%). Interestingly, these two journals appear to be a host site for posting articles by scientists from Russia, China, and countries without a long continuous tradition of scientific publishing (Egypt, Iran, Brazil, Turkey, Iraq, etc.). They thus give a voice to scientists working in underrepresented countries within the pages of English-language scientific journals. This finding is consistent with another recent quantitative study reporting that open access journals are widening "the global circle of those who can participate in science and benefit from it" (Evans & Reimer, 2009).

For the sample as a whole, the article bylines clearly reflect the fact that scientific practice today is largely a collaborative effort involving multiple authors from different research institutions, often performing highly specialized tasks in different countries. Obviously the lengthy lists in the bylines are not directly a product of digital publication. But it is hard to imagine the existence of such large collaborative teams without the ease of communicating verbal messages, images, articles, and data through the Internet.

ABSTRACT

Especially over the last century, scientific communication has grown increasingly complex and specialized (Gross et al., 2002, pp. 161–162; Hayes, 1992). In partial compensation for the challenged reader, the heading "Abstract" was invented in the early 20th century (Gross et al., 2002, p. 176). Its purpose is to summarize what was done, how it was done, and what was discovered (Harmon & Gross, 2007, pp. 3–18). Few articles of any length are now without one. Not surprisingly, then, all the scientific articles in my sample except three have such abstracts (the exceptions are a literature review and two articles only a page in length). Armed with such information, the reader can make an informed decision on whether to read further; moreover, whatever the complexities of the main text, he or she will be provided upfront with the main message in relatively straightforward language to more easily "follow the argument" and grasp the main points.

Clearly, Web publication has caused the journals in my sample to think seriously about how to better communicate complex information to a more diverse learned audience. Observe that the Goodman and Rich (1962) article has no heading abstract (see Figure 3.2), as was unusual but not uncommon in the mid-20th century, while the Aron et al. (2010) article has not only a heading abstract, but also an "author summary" (link in box next to heading abstract of Figure 3.1) of about the same length whose stated purpose on the PLoS website is "to make findings accessible to an audience of both scientists and nonscientists. . . . Ideally aimed to a level of understanding of an undergraduate student." All research articles in the three PLoS journals include such author summaries, as do *PNAS* and *JBC* (see Figure 3.3). Moreover, nearly all the journals (*Nature, Science, PNAS, PRL, PRB, NEJM, PLoS Biology,* and *PLoS Medicine*) offer links to synopsis or news type stories written by editors or other scientists for at least some of the articles in a given issue. While such author and editor summaries can also be added to print articles, the Web facilitates their widespread adoption because of the lack of restrictions over space.

Other journals in the sample have adopted different approaches to combat article complexity. Two (*JACS* and *APL*) are taking advantage of the ease of displaying images and text on the Web to literally catch the readers' eyes. For

ATP Synthase Complex of *Plasmodium falciparum*

DIMERIC ASSEMBLY IN MITOCHONDRIAL MEMBRANES AND RESISTANCE TO GENETIC DISRUPTION*

Praveen Balabaskaran Nina, Joanne M. Morrisey, Suresh M. Ganesan, Hangjun Ke, April M. Pershing, Michael W. Mather and Akhil B. Vaidya[1]

⊞ Author Affiliations

⌐[1] To whom correspondence should be addressed: Drexel University College of Medicine, 2900 Queen Ln., Philadelphia, PA 19129. Tel.: 215-991-8557; Fax: 215-848-2271; E-mail: avaidya@drexelmed.edu.

Capsule

Background: The role of ATP synthase in blood stages of malaria parasites has been unclear.

Results: Canonical subunits were targeted to the mitochondrion, could not be deleted by gene disruption, and were present in large complexes.

Conclusion: *Plasmodium* ATP synthase is likely essential and forms a dimeric complex.

Significance Composition, properties, structure, and drugability of the complex should be fully investigated.

Abstract

The rotary nanomotor ATP synthase is a central player in the bioenergetics of most organisms. Yet the role of ATP synthase in malaria parasites has remained unclear, as blood stages of *Plasmodium falciparum* appear to derive ATP largely through glycolysis. Also, genes for essential subunits of the F_O sector of the complex could not be detected in the parasite genomes. Here, we have used molecular genetic and immunological tools to investigate the localization, complex formation, and functional significance of predicted ATP synthase subunits in *P. falciparum*. We generated transgenic *P. falciparum* lines expressing seven epitope-tagged canonical ATP synthase subunits, revealing localization of all but one of the subunits to the mitochondrion. Blue native gel electrophoresis of *P. falciparum* mitochondrial membranes suggested the molecular mass of the

Figure 3.3. An example of an article incorporating an abstract of an abstract followed by a traditional heading abstract (Nina et al., 2011). Reproduced with permission. Copyright © 2011 The American Society for Biochemistry and Molecular Biology.

instance, the contents page to the physics journal *APL* shows the usual lists of titles and authors, but also a one- or two-sentence abstract of the abstract and the key image. In the example of Figure 3.4, the title announces the major claim in a noun phase, the abstract of the abstract elaborates on that claim in two complete sentences, and the graph visually represents the claim. Following the link in the lower right corner then sends interested readers to the actual heading abstract and byline. Finally, *NEJM* articles all have abstracts divided into four discrete components: a paragraph on the background, one on the methods, another for results, and yet another for conclusions—all linked to corresponding sections in the main text. In all these elite journals, freed from the space restrictions in the printed issues, there appears to be a genuine effort to add content to ensure that all readers, whatever their expertise, can follow the main points.

INTER- AND INTRATEXTUALITY

In general, the aim of the scientific research article is to solve a problem whose importance, originality, and need are established by means of other texts. This task involves, of course, scholarly citation. Gross et al.'s analysis (2002) found that the number, format, and placement of citations in the scientific literature have evolved continuously over time. In their 17th century sample, only about a third had any citations whatsoever, normally incorporated into or adjacent to running text with minimal bibliographic information or consistency (p. 43). In the 18th- and 19th-century samples, more than half had citations incorporated into the text or placed at the bottom of the page as footnotes (pp. 85, 131). The citation format varied widely from journal to journal, and even article to article in a given

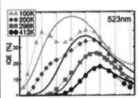

Temperature-dependence of the internal efficiency droop in GaN-based diodes

J. Hader, J. V. Moloney, and S. W. Koch

The temperature dependence of the measured internal efficiencies of green and blue emitting InGaN-based diodes is analyzed. With increasing temperature, a strongly decreasing strength of the loss mechanism responsible for droop is found which is in contrast to the usually assumed behavior of Auger losses.

Appl. Phys. Lett. 99, 181127 (2011)

Figure 3.4. An example of an abstract from the APL contents page.
Reprinted with permission from Hader, J., Moloney, J. V., & Koch, S. W. (2011).
Temperature-dependence of the internal efficiency in GaN-based diodes.
Applied Physics Letters 99, 181127. Copyright 2011, AIP Publishing, LLC.

journal. Also during this time, the average number of citations within a section of text and the number of citation elements (author name, article title, page number, etc.) slowly grew. In the 20th century, while the citation density in the text body increased fourfold and the citation format standardized, the placement of the citations shifted from the bottom of the page to a list at the end (pp. 169, 180).

The Goodman and Rich (1962) article is typical of the 20th century. The 25 citations are gathered in full at the end, numbered, and uniformly presented. In each case, Goodman and Rich provide the author names, journal name, volume, first page, and year of publication. The key information for finding the article—journal name, volume, and first page—are differentiated by typeface: italics for journal name, bold for volume, plain font for page number. To interfere minimally with reading, the citations are interwoven into the text only by their superscripted number. These references are dispersed throughout the text body, not confined to the beginning or end, making the entire article, in a sense, "intertextual." This intertextuality serves two purposes: it rewards scientists for having provided the article's authors with information about their research that was employed in a productive way, and it provides the readers with additional reading material about the research problem, methods details, supporting information about the main claims being made, and so forth.

The intertextuality of the scientific text continues to evolve in the 21st century, spurred on by the Internet. As exemplified by the Aron et al. (2010) article, the reference numbers in the text body and the reference list at the end remain. What's different is that in all the HTML-based articles in my sample, the reference numbers are linked to the actual citation, and the actual citation is linked to the corresponding article or its abstract. Readers thus can follow a reading path of hyperlink in running text, to bibliographic details in the reference list, to actual cited article, or at least its abstract; then to another set of superscripted numbers, citation details, and cited article; and so forth. Such deviations from the main pathway can lead to the reader making connections with the original article wholly unimagined by the author. Yet whatever alternative reading paths readers may follow, there always remains the central argument as originally formulated by the author.

The intertextuality of the digital article has spread beyond the web of citations within it. The digital scientific article often includes links to one or more of the following: published works in the same journal by the authors (53% of 15 journals sampled had them), articles on the same topic by other authors not cited in the reference list (73%), articles related to keywords chosen by the authors (33%), information about manufacturers of equipment and materials used in experiments or databases to relevant subject matter such as the Protein Data Bank (7%), articles that cite the subject article after publication (93%), written comments by readers and the authors' responses (53%), and even blogs on the subject matter (20%). This dense intertextuality is the one feature of the digital scientific article that profoundly distinguishes it from its printed brethren.

The *intra*textuality of the scientific article is also important. As pointed out by Gross et al. (2002), one of the more remarkable characteristics of the 20th-century scientific article is its elaborate finding system of section headings, graphic legends, numbered citations, and numbered equations, which evolved gradually over time. This master finding system also allows readers to navigate more easily among the diverse components of the article; they can thus extract the desired bits of theory, methods, results, and conclusions without necessarily having to read the text from front to back. The finding system acts like a map, allowing readers to easily direct their attention on select components within the argument being made. In the digital scientific article like that of Aron et al. (2010), this finding system has been augmented by a linked contents segment at the top (see Figure 3.1), links from section heading to actual section, links from figure or table called out in running text to actual figure or table, links from citation number in text to bibliographic information in the reference list to actual reference, and so forth. The element of greatest interest to any given reader within an article is thus a click away. And those readers more comfortable with the traditional print version can download and print a PDF version (upper right in Figure 3.1).

VISUALIZATION

Flip through the pages or scroll down the screen of a research article in any of the journals from Table 3.1. It will be abundantly evident that scientists communicate routinely not only through words but also through tables and images. In *Communicating Science*, Gross et al. (2002) observed that one of the main factors contributing to communicative change over time is "the increasing prominence of visual representations, and their integration into argument" (p. 231). In their 20th-century sample, Gross et al. found the percentage of numbered figures and tables steadily increasing over that century (p. 172). Overall, they also found the average percentage of space visuals occupied in a 20th-century article to be a hefty 26% (18% figures, 8% tables). The most prominent type of visual was the data graph: an average of 57% of articles had at least one (72% after 1950). About 50% of articles had at least one table.

The visuals in the aforementioned article by Goodman and Rich (1962) are fairly typical of 20th-century practices. The article has one table of data and eight graphs of data trends displayed in five figures. The table and figures occupy about 20% of the article's length. They all have numbers and captions and are integrated into the text close to first mention. Figure 3.5 reproduces one of the graphs.

The data gathered in the present study suggest that—in large part due to the abundance of new computer-based instruments for converting data into images, usually in color, and the relative ease of incorporating such images into a digital

Saturation experiments: The experiments described in Figure 1a and b showed that more sRNA could be annealed to the DNA if a larger amount was added to the annealing mixture. This immediately suggests the possibility of attempting to saturate the sRNA sites on the DNA by increasing the amount of sRNA in the annealing mixture. The results of experiments of this type are shown in Figure 3.

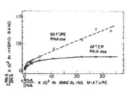

A constant amount of DNA (45 γ) was annealed with varying amounts of sRNA over a 300-fold range in concentration. The dashed curve shows that the amount of attached sRNA in the hybrid band goes up steadily while the solid curve shows that the ribonuclease-resistant part saturates. A plateau appears as a mass ratio of sRNA to DNA of 0.025 per cent. Thus, only a very small portion of the DNA is able to accept an sRNA molecule in hybrid formation. Furthermore, these results show that the preparation does not contain ribosomal RNA, since DNA-ribosomal RNA hybrids contain six times more RNA.[6] If cold ribosomal RNA is added to the annealing mixture, it does not compete with the bonding of sRNA, thereby suggesting that the ribosomal RNA sites are different from the sRNA sites.

FIG. 3.—The amount of *E. coli* P[32] sRNA found in the *E. coli* DNA band is plotted as a function of increasing amounts of P[32] sRNA in the annealing mixture. All preparations were annealed with 45 γ DNA and varying amounts of P[32] sRNA (0.005 to 1.50 γ P[32] sRNA, specific activity = 5.6 × 10[6] cpm/γ). The O.D.$_{260}$ and cpm before and after ribonuclease digestion were measured through the band region as described in *Methods*.

The genome in *E. coli* contains a DNA molecular weight equivalent of 4 × 10[9].[12] Knowing this, and using the molecular weight of *E. coli* sRNA (25,500), we may calculate from the plateau in Figure 3 that there are approximately 40 sRNA sites in the *E. coli* genome. If we assume that there is one site per sRNA molecule, this number provides a direct estimate of the degeneracy of the amino acid code.

Figure 3.5. A graph integrated into text by Goodman and Rich (1962). Reprinted with permission from Goodman, H. M., & Rich, A. (1962). Formation of a DNA-soluble RNA hybrid and its relation to the origin, evolution, and degeneracy of soluble RNA. *Proceeding of the National Academy of Sciences, 48,* 2101-2109.

article—the visual has become much more prominent and far more colorful. The visuals in the Aron et al. (2010) article contrast markedly from those in Goodman and Rich (1962). This article has 125 images displayed in eight figures (i.e., about 16 images per figure) and occupying about 38% of the article's length. These visual assemblages consist of various arrangements of bar graphs (30), photographs at the microscopic scale (92), and Western blots of genetic components (3). Of the 125 images, 63% are color. What's more, the article has Supporting Information not available in the print version, which consists of 50 additional images displayed in four figures.

In terms of visual density, the Aron et al. (2010) article is a somewhat extreme example. In our 21st-century sample, the average percentage of space that visuals occupy in the main text is 28% (23% figures, 5% tables). While the overall average is not dramatically higher compared with the 20th century, it would appear that the space allotted to figures has grown at the expense of tables. The averages for numbers of images and tables per article are also illuminating: tables, only 1.4, and images, a robust 14, about half of which are in color. (These data are for the main text only, not any supplementary information.) Moreover, these visuals are more data driven than in previous centuries: nearly 90% had at least one graph representing data trends, but usually many more than one.

The greatest change in visual presentation in the 21st century concerns use of color. The first appearance of color figures in printed scientific documents dates back to the 15th century, when astronomical figures in some books were hand colored (see Metropolitan Museum of Art, 2006). And the journal *Botanical Magazine* has routinely printed color botanical images since its first issue in 1787. Yet for the 20th-century sample of Gross et al. (2002), the number of color figures was so small as to be not worth counting. With about half the images in our 21st-century sample being in color, there can be little doubt that the ease of generating a digital image and displaying it on the Web has ignited a riot of color in the digital scientific article.

The presentation of figures has also changed dramatically. In the 17th and 18th centuries, the physical integration of figure with text tended to be haphazard in large part as a result of limitations in printing practices. Figures might appear gathered together at the end of each article or at the end of the individual journal. They might appear in the margins. They might appear on separate pages from the text within an article or integrated into the page close to their mention in the text. They might or might not have descriptive captions. They might or might not be numbered. The tighter integration of text with the accompanying images, along with titles and numbers, did not occur until well into the 19th century, when innovations in imaging technology made this economically practical.

The presentation of 21st-century figures on the Web differs markedly from earlier centuries. All the journals in my sample, except for the four that do not offer HTML articles (*PRL*, *PRB*, *JMP*, and *IJG*), display the images in a thumb-nail size immediately after its first mention in a paragraph. For each figure, readers have the option of either ignoring it altogether, clicking on a link to view it in a much more easily scrutinized size, copying the figure for use in another electronic document, or viewing and copying the figure as a PowerPoint slide (Figure 3.6). The last option is available presumably for use of figures as a teaching tool. While rare in earlier centuries, multicomponent figures such as Figure 3.6 are rampant in my 21st-century sample. Meaning emerges as a consequence of not only the interaction between image and text, as exemplified in Figure 3.5, but also that among the diverse images within the figure. Like color, creating such visual assemblages has always been possible, but it is hard to imagine their widespread adoption before the invention of the personal computer for their creation and Web for their dissemination.

Video and interactive images are brand new forms of visualization in the scientific article that further contribute to visual prominence. However, on the

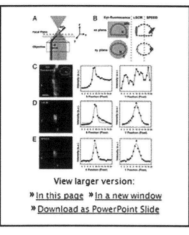

Fig. 1. SPEED microscopy. (*A*) Optics. The simplified optical diagram illustrates the different excitation beam paths of the SPEED (blue), the LSCM (cyan), and the wide–field epifluorescence (light blue) microscopy. The laser beam in the SPEED microscopy was focused into a diffraction-limited spot in the focal plane (dotted line) from the edge of the objective. An angle of 45° was formed between the iPSFs of the SPEED microscopy and the LSCM when the incident laser beam was shifted 237 µm (*d*) off the center of the objective (Fig. S2). (*B*) Illumination volumes in the three microscopes. The diagram demonstrates the NPCs inside (green) and outside (gray) the illumination volume in the *xy* and *xz* planes. *N*, nucleus; *C*, cytoplasm. (*C*) Multiple GFP–NPCs were excited using wide–field epifluorescence microscopy. The adopted area is enclosed by the blue box in the image of the entire fluorescent nuclear envelope (*Inset*). (Scale bar, 1 µm.) (*D*) GFP–NPCs were illuminated by the LSCM. The fluorescent spot was fit by a Gaussian function in both *x* and *y* directions. (*E*) Only a single GFP–NPC was excited in the illumination volume of the SPEED microscopy.

View larger version:
» In this page » In a new window
» Download as PowerPoint Slide

Figure 3.6. An example of a multicomponent figure with caption. Reprinted with permission from Ma, J., & Yang, W. (2010). Three-dimensional distribution in the nuclear pore core complex obtained from single-molecule snapshots. *Proceedings of National Academy of Sciences, 107*, 7305-7310.

basis of my sample, they cannot yet be said to be routine: only six articles in my sample have them (4%). The future prospects would appear to be bright, however, as they re-create processes or represent changes in data or objects over time in several ways not possible with static images. First, interested readers can see what the scientist saw in the laboratory or field, giving an entirely new dimension to "virtual witnessing": examples drawn from our sample include videos showing the behavior of mice in a laboratory setting (Yizhar, Fenno, Prigge, Schneider, Davidson, O'Shea, et al., 2011), the movement of a biological substance from the cytoplasm to the nucleus within a cell (Ma & Yang, 2010), and a villager walking through coals before revelers in a Spanish town as part of an annual ritual (Konvalinka, Xygalatas, Bulbulia, Schjodt, Jegindo, Wallot et al., 2011). Second, readers can view objects from different perspectives, for example, by rotating a microscopic section of a mouse spleen (Bodin, Ellmerich, Kahan, Tennent, Lowsuh, Gilbertson, et al., 2010) or a vertebrae limb bud (Boehm et al., 2010). Finally, readers can view data as they change over time: in our sample, that includes a set of graphs demonstrating the stabilization over time of the quantum state in a microsystem by means of a continuous feedback loop (Sayrin, Dotsenko, Zhou, Peaudecerf, Rybarczyk, Gleyzes et al., 2011). All the above moving pictures appear in a section called Supplemental Information (of which, more later), which is separated from the main body and not included in the PDF version. It seems safe to predict that these sorts of moving pictures will soon migrate into the main body and increase in frequency.

One final note on visualization and its increased prominence. Several of the sample journals also display all the figures within an article in a separate segment on the screen at the article top or side. For example, *Nature* displays all figures in a horizontal band after the abstract and before the introduction. With this arrangement, the reader can both read the abstract and scroll through all figures in an article and more easily make a judgment as to its worth before jumping into a sea of specialized terms and data.

ARGUMENTATIVE STRUCTURE

According to Gross et al. (2002, pp. 229–231), the typical early scientific article was either a straightforward description of the natural world or a narrative centered on a string of loosely connected experiments or observations, often arranged chronologically. Over time, however, the article evolved a modular structure (abstract, introduction, methods, etc.) suited to authorship by a small group of researchers and designed to present each article's argument in a roughly similar way and level of detail. A question worth asking is, has, will, or can the hypertext nature of Web publication change the basic structure of that argument?

David Kolb (1994, 1996, 2008) asked that same question about scholarship in the humanities, particularly his discipline of philosophy. In the end, he seems to have reluctantly concluded that in general, "A philosophical argument (or a mathematical proof) cannot be presented as a cloud of disjointed statements," and that attempts to escape the bounds of linear argument have largely failed or only transformed a single linear argument into a set of linked linear arguments. Yet he remained hopeful that hypertext might one day lead to a new form of discourse "composed of fragmentary paths . . . with neither atomistic disintegration nor final unity." In a similar vein, Landow (2006) asserted that "one of the fundamental characteristics of hypertext is that it is composed of linked texts that have no primary axis of organization" (p. 56). If such is the case, then the digital scientific article is not hypertext and probably never will be. True, readers can and do browse through a digital scientific article following an orderly but nonlinear path, yet the same can be claimed of printed scientific texts (Charney, 1993). And in both cases, scientist-readers know that the text, when read from beginning to end, has as its "primary axis of organization" an argument of Aristotlean rigor: basically, a research problem is introduced and contextualized, a method for its solution is described, the results from having applied the method are presented and discussed, conclusions are drawn, intellectual and material assistance is acknowledged, and literature sources are listed. Indeed, in most articles, whether in print or on the Web, the boundaries of these components are signaled by section headings or different font size. Those headings in the Goodman and Rich (1962) article are Introduction, Methods and Materials, Results, Discussion, Summary, Acknowledgments, and References. The Aron et al. (2010) article has similar headings: Abstract, Acknowledgments, Author Summary, Introduction, Results, Discussion, Supporting Information, Author Contributions, and References.

If anything, the structure of the digital scientific article is even more regimented than ever before: all data-driven articles in my sample conformed to this argumentative structure or a slight variation on it. The digital articles in eight journals (*JBC, PNAS, JACS, NEJM, AJ,* and three PLOS journals) include a box with sectional headings and navigational links (consult Figure 3.1, right side). In these journals, the basic structure differs little if at all from article to article. The other three journals providing HTML files (*Science, Nature,* and *APL*) mostly publish very short articles with no need for any headings, though they do still more or less conform to the standard structure.

With regard to their 20th-century sample, Gross et al. (2002, p. 185) mentioned two major variations in structure, appearing in the *Journal of the Chemical Society* and *Journal of the American Chemical Society* in the early part of that century. These articles were typically divided into two distinct parts. The first half distilled the essence of the discovery and its intellectual context and was aimed at an audience of chemists in general. The second provided the experimental method and results in enough detail to satisfy experts in the subject matter. This sensible variation did not take hold in the scientific literature at-large during the 20th century. But now a similar variation is routine in two of the journals in Table 3.1, *Nature* and *Science.* Within the space of several thousand words, the article itself, available in the printed issue or as PDF from the Web, conforms to the typical article structure but does so with minimal experimental details, results, tables of data, and visuals. It is aimed at scientist-readers interested only in the main points and underlying argument. But there is also a link to Supplemental Information, available only through the Web, conveying the experimental methods, results, and such, for experts with a strong interest in the subject matter (90% of articles in the two journals have supporting information).

Nearly 83% of the articles in seven other journals (*JBC, PNAS, JACS, NEJM,* and the three PLOS journals) also include Supplemental Information, but the articles themselves are more of standard length (5,000–10,000 words) and structure.

The Supplemental Information provides authors with a space for additional technical details (mostly methods and results) that would have had to have been dropped because of space considerations in the past, as well as any videos, interactive images, or audio files. The length runs from a few pages to 151. Because of Supplemental Information, these journals can thus accommodate much longer arguments in a way that does not burden readers uninterested in the full details.

READER COMMENTS AND STATISTICS

A little more than half the journals in Table 3.1 (*JBC*, *PNAS*, *Nature*, *Science*, *NEJM*, and three PLoS journals) allow readers to comment on articles after publication, where links to those comments along with any author responses are incorporated into the digital article. The Aron et al. (2010) article has a comments tab at the top (Figure 3.1), but no comments yet entered. That is fairly typical. Of the 80 articles randomly selected from such journals, only 11 (14%) had technical comments attached (1 to 3 each), 7 of which appeared in the three PLoS journals. Even though widely available, online commentary remains anemic.

In contrast to the most-cited journals, the open access journals also provide statistics on what articles readers have viewed (see right side of Figure 3.1). These data should give scientist-authors some encouragement that their articles are read, or at least skimmed, by more than a few. The PLoS journals report number of views for each article, the average in my sample being a robust 4,418 (the Aron et al. [2010] article had 7,536 views as of July 2012). And even though the two other journals (*JMP* and *IJG*) are only recently founded and have negligible citation impact factors, their average reported number of downloads per article (one step beyond simply viewing) also appear impressive, 422. In a sense, readers implicitly vote on an article's potential interest by simply viewing or downloading it. In the PLoS journals, readers can actually rate articles on a scale of 1 to 5, but they seldom do so.

Such statistics give scientist-authors a sense of the reception of their writing and scientist-readers a sense of what articles have received major attention in a given issue or journal. When a healthy number of views or downloads is displayed with the article itself, it serves a rhetorical purpose as well: adding authority to the contents being reported beyond the reputation of the authors or their institutional affiliations or the citation impact factor of the journal itself.

JOURNAL CONTENTS PAGES

A tangential component to the earlier-mentioned finding system for the scientific article is the journal contents page—a listing of authors, article titles, and corresponding page numbers for a single journal issue. This useful index has been around since the very first scientific journals in the 17th century. The most-cited journals in my sample have essentially two contents pages: one for the journal itself, another for each issue. Anyone examining these pages on the Web (e.g., Figure 3.7) will come away with little doubt that a major transformation in journal contents has occurred: they are now portals to new knowledge, edification, and even entertainment and social engagement.

Perhaps the most dramatic difference between print and digital scientific journals is that the latter also function as virtual libraries. The contents pages for all 10 journals offer portals to browsable electronic archives that cover all previously published articles back to the first issue. And visitors to a journal's homepage can view not only research articles before the print issue but also most viewed, most cited, most downloaded, and most emailed, as well as recently published articles judged by the editors to deserve special attention, articles on a narrow topic, and articles covered by the news media.

As another strategy for capturing reader attention, four of the most-cited journals (*Science, Nature, NEJM,* and *JACS*) offer "multimedia centers" composed of scientific images displayed for the reader's aesthetic pleasure or edification or both; podcasts highlighting the contents of individual issues or other newsworthy matters; instructional webinars and visuals; slideshows on a variety of scientific topics; and short videos produced by the journal or authors of articles. For the most part, the purpose of these multimedia centers is not to convey arguments for original knowledge claims—the primary function of the research article itself—but to present stories about science meant to reach those without specialized knowledge of the subject matter and present science and scientists to a wider readership in a more personal light. *JACS*, for example, has a link called "Video Abstracts," which leads to an archive of short videos (typically about 5 minutes), which are produced by the authors of published articles; *Science, Nature, NEJM,* and *JBC* have podcasts summarizing issue contents; *PNAS* has podcasts on various topics as well as interviews with scientists about their research; and for teaching purposes, *NEJM* posts videos of microscopic physical abnormalities in patients.

The digital journal has also embraced the world of social media. In the print era, the main means for scientist-authors to contribute to a journal besides research articles was letters to the editor. Mostly, these letters commented upon published research articles or sociopolitical issues that concerned the journal's readership. They were normally published some weeks or months after submittal and seldom drew a published response. Social media accessed through the journal homepage are now transforming this once fairly sedate section of the scientific journal (Figure 3.8). As a result, readers for some of the journals can immediately post a tweet, blog, or Facebook comment about a published article or issue and, if it is controversial, spark a lively or even contentious debate. With the introduction of social media, journals are entering the freewheeling public sphere of gossiping, complaining, exchanging information on professional experiences,

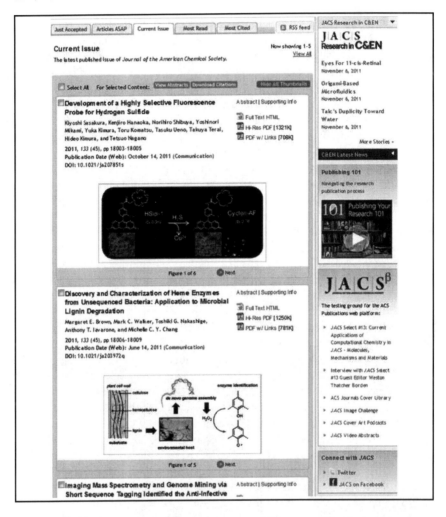

Figure 3.7. A sample issue home page from JACS. November 2011. Retrieved from http://pubs.acs.org/toc/jacsat/133/45/. Image reprinted with permission from Sasakura et al. (2011). Development of a highly selective fluorescence probe for hydrogen sulfide. *Journal of the American Chemical Society*, *133*(45), 18003-18005. Copyright © 2011 American Chemical Society.

deliberating, and even ranting on occasion. At present, 4 of the 10 elite journals in my sample have links to such social media. Not coincidentally, these are the same four journals with robust multimedia centers: *Science, Nature, NEJM,* and *JACS.*

CONCLUSION

In *Communicating Science,* Gross et al. (2002) attempted to explain communicative change over time by means of a communicative selection theory. They contended that over time, the scientific journal has evolved into a complex network designed to meet the needs of varying and constantly emerging scientific communities. In evolutionary terms,

> in the case of the scientific article, the genotype is a set of predispositions: to create arguments . . . to transform these arguments into sentences and paragraphs, and finally, to order these sentences and paragraphs according to well-organized organizational constraints. These predispositions are behavioral tendencies generally shaped by learning. . . . When the situation calls for it, scientists activate these predispositions to create a scientific article. (p. 218)

This evolution, of course, does not mean that the 21st-century embodiment is "better" than those of the 17th or 18th centuries. Evolutionary theories are incompatible with any notion of progress that implies successive betterment. The only notion of "better" that any evolutionary theory can tolerate is that of "better adapted" to prevailing conditions.

The history of the scientific journal supports the hypothesis that its current communicative and argumentative practices evolved, and continue to evolve, as a consequence of variation and selective survival. And yet, as Owen (2005) concluded in an earlier study, whether HTML or PDF, whether the science or humanities, there is a strong impression of attempting to simulate the relative permanence of printed publication. The founder of the physics preprint archive (arXiv), Paul Ginsparg (2011), has expressed a similar view:

> The transition to article formats and features better suited to modern technology than to print on paper has also been surprisingly slow. Page markup formats, such as PDF, have only grudgingly given way to XML-based ones that support features such as manipulable graphics, dynamic views, linked annotations and semantic markup. Part of this caution is a result of the understandable need to maintain a stable archive of research literature, as provided by paper over centuries. (p. 147)

My contention here, however, is that numerous permutations on the 20th-century norm are sprouting up in many digital articles published by the elite

Figure 3.8. Screen shot of the *PLoS Biology* home page showing social media. Retrieved from http://blogs.plos.org.

scientific journals, along with their associated homepages. These variations include multimedia centers, complete archives of back issues, social media, links to most-cited and most-viewed articles, image albums, abstracts of abstracts, summaries aimed at general audience, supplemental information omitted from print articles, reader statistics, reader commentary, and so forth. Top-drawer scientific journals are doing whatever they can to "make it new." Worth noting here is that the agents behind these innovations are largely software engineers, Web designers, and the editorial staff of journals, along with article authors. Recently, Elsevier Publishing developed what it called "The Article of the Future" (articleofthefuture.com), which is really an amalgamation of many existing features among the elite journals and is therefore more accurately called "The State-of-the-Art Digital Article." What of the current permutations will eventually be transmitted to the *typical* digital article or journal homepage of the future cannot be asserted with any authority. One can rest assured, however, that evolution will continue as it always has, but now catalyzed by the new communicative variations afforded by digital publication.

CODA: HUMANITIES JOURNALS ON THE WEB

As part of the instructions to contributors of this volume, the contributing authors were asked, "Does your investigation of one or another aspect of scientific communication have any implications for communication in the humanities?" Comparing the online variations of the elite scientific journals with those in the humanities suggests that there is no comparison: the digital research articles (whether formatted as HTML or PDF) in the elite humanities journals are typically simulations of the printed version, and the contents of the journal homepages carries only marginally more information than what can be found in the printed issues from the 20th century. In 2005, Peter Suber noted that "open access isn't undesirable or unattainable in the humanities. But it is less urgent and harder to subsidize than in the sciences." The same might also be said about implementation of Web-based features. This statement applies to prestigious journals like *PMLA* (*Journal of the Modern Language Association*), *Isis* (*Journal of the Society of History of Science*), *Journal of Philosophy*, *Configurations*, *Music Perception*, *College Composition and Communication*, and the like. It even holds for recently founded online journals. For example, within the past decade, the Open Humanities Press (OHP) established 11 open access journals in "response to the crisis in scholarly publishing in the humanities"; tellingly, of these 11, the articles in all but one are in the form of PDF or HTML files with straight text and few if any links or images. An exception is *Vectors: Journal of Culture and Technology in a Dynamic Vernacular*, which "brings together visionary scholars with cutting-edge designers and technologists to propose a rethinking of the dynamic relation of form to content in academic research"(OHP, n.d). Of course, an innovative website does not necessarily translate to innovative scholarship. Moreover, for humanities journals, in which the articles are primarily composed of words with few if any visuals and are written in the form of the traditional linear essay, the print model appears to serve their online needs perfectly well for the most part.

In contrast to humanities journals, the elite and PLoS scientific journals have been in the vangaurd of adopting the Web for many reasons: the typical readers and writers are comfortable with being first users of new technology, these journals have sizable financial resources to draw upon to test and implement new Internet features, these journals can get away with steep author charges for open access to all, and their writers establish their reputations almost exclusively by publishing journal articles, not scholarly monographs. (For a comparison of the business models in scientific and humanities journals, see Waltham, 2010; Harley, Acord, Earl-Novell, Lawrence, & Judson King, 2010.) Moreover, several factors made the scientific article especially well suited for early adaptation to the Web: its historic emphasis on visual as well as verbal communication; its standard modular, hypertext-like structure; its heavy reliance on research protocols and data too profuse for the typical article length; and the rapid creation of an enormous electronic archive of past journal articles plus extensive citation information about them (in Science Citation Index).

While innovative examples of online articles and journals in the humanities remain outside the mainstream, they do exist. See, for example, the use of multimedia in Favro and Johanson's model article (2010) in the *Journal of the Society of Architectural Historians*.

REFERENCES

Aron, L., Klein, P., Pham, T.-T., Kramer, E. R., Wurst, W., & Klein, R. (2010). Pro-survival role for Parkinson's associated gene DJ-1 revealed in trophically impaired dopaminergic neurons. *PLoS Biology, 8*(4), e1000349.

Bernstein, M. (1999). Structural patterns and hypertext rhetoric. *ACM Computing Surveys.* Retrieved from http://dl.acm.org/citation.cfm?id=345966&CFID=75143083&CFTOKEN=10827851

Bodin, K., Ellmerich, S., Kahan, M. C., Tennent, G. A., Loesch, A., Gilbertson, J. A., et al. (2010). Antibodies to human serum amyloid P component eliminate visceral amyloid deposits. *Nature, 468*, 93–97.

Boehm, B., Westerberg, H., Lesnicar-Pucko, G., Raja, S., Rautschk, M., Cotterell, J., et al. (2010). The role of spatially controlled cell proliferation in limb bud morphogenesis. *PLoS Biology, 8*(7), e1000420.

Charney, D. (1993). A study in rhetorical reading: How evolutionists read "The Spandrels of San Marco." In J. Selzer (Ed.), *Understanding scientific prose* (pp. 203–231). Madison, WI: University of Wisconsin Press.

Coover, R. (1992, June 21). The end of books. *New York Times Book Review.* Retrieved from http://www.nytimes.com/books/98/09/27/specials/coover-end.html

Evans, J. A., & Reimer, J. (2009). Open access and global participation in science. *Science, 323,* 1025.

Favro, D., & Johanson, C. (2010). Death in motion: Funeral processions in the Roman Forum. *Journal of the Society of Architectural Historians, 69,* 12–37.

Ginsparg, P. (2011). ArXiv at 20. *Nature, 476,* 145–147.

Goodman, H. M., & Rich, A. (1962). Formation of a DNA-soluble RNA hybrid and its relation to the origin, evolution, and degeneracy of soluble RNA. *Proceedings of the National Academy of Sciences, 48,* 2101–2109.

Gross, A. G., Harmon, J. E., & Reidy, M. (2002). *Communicating science: The scientific article from the 17th century to the present.* Oxford, UK: Oxford University Press.

Hader, J., Moloney, J. V., & Koch, S. W. (2011). Temperature-dependence of the internal efficiency in GaN-based diodes. *Applied Physics Letters, 99,* 181127.

Harley, D., Acord, S. K., Earl-Novell, S., Lawrence, S., & Judson King, C. (2010). *Assessing the future landscape of scholarly communication: An exploration of faculty values and needs in seven disciplines.* Berkeley, CA: Center for Studies in Higher Education, University of California.

Harmon, J. E., & Gross, A. G. (2007). *The craft of scientific communication.* Chicago, IL: University of Chicago Press.

Hayes, D. P. (1992). The growing inaccessibility of science. *Nature, 356,* 739–740.

Jones, B. F., Wuchty, S., & Uzzi, B. (2008). Multi-university research teams: Shifting impact, geography, and stratification in science. *Science, 322,* 1259–1262.

Kolb, D. (1994). Socrates in the labyrinth. In G. P. Landow (Ed.), *Hyper/text/theory* (pp. 323–342). Baltimore, MD: Johns Hopkins University Press.

Kolb, D. (1996). Discourse across links. In C. Ess (Ed.), *Philosophical perspectives on computer-mediated communication* (pp. 15–26). Albany, NY: State University of New York Press.

Kolb, D. (2008). The revenge of the page. In P. Brusilovksy & H. C. Davis (Eds.), *Proceedings of 19th ACM conference on hypertext and hypermedia.* New York, NY: Association of Computing Machinery.

Konvalinka, I., Xygalatas, D., Bulbulia, J., Schjødt, U., Jegindø, E.-M., Wallot, S., et al. (2011). Synchronized arousal between performers and related spectators in a fire-walking ritual. *Proceedings of National Academy of Sciences, 108,* 8514–8519.

Landlow, G. P. (2006). *Hypertext 3.0: Critical theory and new media in an era of globalization.* Baltimore, MD: Johns Hopkins University Press.

Ma, J., & Yang, W. (2010). Three-dimensional distribution in the nuclear pore core complex obtained from single-molecule snapshots. *Proceedings of National Academy of Sciences, 107,* 7305–7310.

Metropolitan Museum of Art. (2006). Johannes de Sacrobosco, Regiomontanus, Georg von Peuerbach. *Sphaera mundi.* In *Heilbrunn timeline of art history.* Retrieved from http://www.metmuseum.org/toah/works-of-art/17.45

Nina, P. B., Morrisey, J. M., Ganesan, S. M., Ke, H., Pershing, A. M., Mather, M. W., et al. (2011). ATP synthase complex of Plasmodium falciparum: Dimeric assembly in mitochondrial membranes and resistance to genetic disruption. *Journal of Biological Chemistry, 286,* 41312–41322.

Open Humanities Press (OHP). (n.d.). "Vectors." *Open Humanities Press*. Retrieved June 11, 2012, from http://www.openhumanitiespress.org/vectors.html

Owen, J. S. M. (2005). *The scientific article in the age of digitization*. Amsterdam, The Netherlands: Springer.

Pound, E. (1935). *Make it new: Essays by Ezra Pound*. New Haven, CT: Yale University Press.

Sasakura, K., Hanaoka, K., Shibuya, N., Mikami, Y., Kimura, Y., Komatsu, T., et al. (2011). Development of a highly selective fluorescence probe for hydrogen sulfide. *Journal of the American Chemical Society, 133*(45), 18003–18005.

Sayrin, C., Dotsenko, I., Zhou, X., Peaudecerf, B., Rybarczyk, T., Gleyzes, S., et al. (2011). Real-time quantum feedback prepares and stabilizes photon number states. *Nature, 477,* 73–77.

Suber, P. (2005). Promoting open access in the humanities. *Syllecta Classica, 16,* 231–246.

Thomson Reuters. (2009). Top ten most-cited journals, 1999–2009. *Science Watch*. Retrieved from http://sciencewatch.com/dr/sci/09/aug2-09_2

Waltham, M. (2010). The future of scholarly journal publishing among social science and humanities associations. *Journal of Scholarly Publishing, 41,* 257–324.

Wuchty, S., Jones, B. F., & Uzzi, B. (2007). The increasing dominance of teams in production of knowledge. *Science, 316,* 1036–1039.

Yizhar, O., Fenno, L. E., Prigge, M., Schneider, F., Davidson, T. J., O'Shea, D. J., et al. (2011). Neocortical excitation/inhibition balance in information processing and social dysfunction. *Nature, 477,* 171–178.

http://dx.doi.org/10.2190/SCIC4

CHAPTER 4

Evaluation After Publication: Setting the Record Straight in the Sciences

Alan G. Gross

ABSTRACT

The blogs *Retraction Watch* and *Abnormal Science* have reinvented investigative journalism in the interest of keeping science accurately on course, detecting error, ferreting out fraud and plagiarism, and publicizing their presence. *Retraction Watch* promotes transparency by disseminating to all interested parties the retraction of articles that are erroneous, fraudulent, or plagiarized; *Abnormal Science* actually detects instances in which either fraud or plagiarism seems likely. Both sites rely on informants, largely anonymous, to accomplish their aims. This reliance forces them to resolve the ethical dilemma that anonymity brings in its wake: must sources reveal their identity if they are to be trusted? Those maintaining sites that deal directly with fraud and plagiarism, sites like *Abnormal Science* must also take the law of libel carefully into consideration. Although the evidence of alleged fraud or plagiarism may be presented, neither fraud nor plagiarism may be alleged.

> Tell truth and shame the devil.
> —Hotspur, *Henry IV*

Are personal blogs merely personal diaries online, rehearsals of trivialities of interest only to their creators, intimate friends, and nosy neighbors? Yes and no. In some cases, personal blogs have been reconfigured so as to preserve the immediacy inherent in the genre and the moral purpose inherited from famous ancestors, like *Boswell's London Journal* and *The Diary of Anne Frank,* works that shape scattered incidents into meaningful lives. In Ivan Oransky and Adam Marcus's *Retraction Watch*, and Joerg Zwirner's *Abnormal Science,* everyday professional life is encountered, reflected on, and infused with moral purpose. Marcus, Oransky, and Zwirner see themselves as successful only to the extent that scientific journals openly retract erroneous, plagiarized, or fraudulent articles and at the same time tell the scientific public exactly why they are doing so. They are conservatives, motivated by the pressing need to keep science true to an established principle: self-correction. In my view, *Retraction Watch* and *Abnormal Science* succeed in the task they undertake: setting the scientific record straight by turning their personal blogs into a form of investigative journalism, reborn on the Web. They do so by activating a set of institutional imperatives, shared by the scientists and science journals they criticize, norms first articulated by the sociologist of science, Robert Merton (1968): the expectation that published research is original, that it is generated by agreed-upon methods, that it has survived the skeptical scrutiny of the authors' peers, that it is free of the influence of special interests unrelated to science, and that it will be shared freely with one's fellows. Because of this shared legacy, the error, plagiarism, and fraud that Marcus, Oransky, and Zwirner expose and publicize cannot be easily dismissed; nor can their insistence on open acknowledgement be readily gainsaid.

SETTING THE RECORD STRAIGHT
IN THE SCIENCES

After reading Chaucer's *Canterbury Tales*—after the sweeping Prologue, the dramatic Pardoner's Tale, the raucous Miller's Tale, the sermon that is the Parson's Tale—readers come upon what may well be the world's first Retraction Notice:

> Now I pray to all who hear or read this little treatise, that if there is anything in it that they like, they thank our Lord Jesus Christ for it, from whom proceeds all wisdom and goodness. And if there is anything that displeases them, I pray also that they ascribe it to the fault of my ignorance and not to my will, which would readily have spoken better if I had the knowledge. For our book says, "All that is written is written for our doctrine," and that is my intention. Therefore I beseech you, for the mercy of God, that you pray for me that Christ have mercy on me and forgive my sins, especially my translations and compositions of worldly vanities, which I revoke in my retractions. (1933, p. 314)

In acknowledging error, some editors of science journals lack the poet's candor. One minced no words, responding to Marcus and Oransky's (2011a) request for reasons with the following terse comment: "It's none of your damn business." This reluctance to admit error with candor and dispatch can have serious consequences. When Tsou, Talia, Pinney, Kendzicky, Piera-Velazquez, Jimenez et al. (2012) published an article on the effect of oxidative stress, they found useful a much-cited article in the *Journal of Biological Chemistry* by two Japanese researchers, Naohito Aoki and Tsukasa Matsuda (2000), published 12 years before. Their discussion contains a paragraph in which a conclusion of this earlier article is incorporated into their argument by means of endnote 42, a reference to PTP1B, an enzyme. We can safely ignore the details of their argument, paying attention only to the fact that one of Aoki and Matsuda's conclusions has become part of it, as revealed by our italics:

> We examined the expression and function of PTP1B, which has been reported to be a negative regulator of receptor tyrosine kinases such as PDGFR (30, 31). The association between PTP1B and PDGFR is further supported by a study using PTP1B-knockout mice (38). In addition to the PDGFR pathway, PTP1B appears to be a negative regulator in both insulin and leptin signaling pathways (39, 40). *Epidermal growth factor receptor (41) and tyrosine-phosphorylated proteins such as STAT-5 (42) have also been shown to be targets of PTP1B.* Although the expression of PTP1B was similar in normal dermal fibroblasts and SSc dermal fibroblasts (Figure 4B), the activity of PTP1B was significantly lower in SSc fibroblasts, suggesting that only a portion of the expressed PTP1B is active in SSc fibroblasts. (Tsou et al., 2012)

Were reference 42 eliminated, the article's case would not fail, though it would be weakened. As it turns out, it must be weakened, for in March of the previous year, the Japanese paper had been retracted: "This article has been withdrawn by the authors" was all that was said. This omission provoked only consternation on the part of the two editors of *Retraction Watch*:

> Whoa there! TMI! [too much information] Don't share so much!
> Alas, that's all [the editor] wrote. In fact, neither the abstract nor the article itself is marked as retracted, so it's worse than useless. (Marcus & Oransky, 2011g)

It would be a serious mistake to say that Marcus and Oransky are just reporting; they are deeply engaged in the politics of change, a politics with important epistemic consequences. True, they are merely publicizing error, not detecting it. Nevertheless, they are not merely participants, but leaders in the process of scientific self-correction.

What is *Retraction Watch*? Begun by two medical journalists, it is a blog with a difference. It was hosting about 100,000 page views a month shortly after its launch and by mid-2014 claimed 33,490 followers, a testimony to its importance as an influence in setting the record of science straight. In an entry called "What people are saying about *Retraction Watch*" (Marcus & Oransky, 2011g), the site posts prominent endorsements of its mission. In a Twitter feed, John Rennie, former editor-in-chief of *Scientific American*, says that the blog is "one of the most important recent developments in science journalism." In Columbia Journalism Review, Craig Silverman calls *Retraction Watch* "a new blog that should be required reading for anyone interested in scientific journalism or the issue of accuracy." Ben Goldacre of the *Guardian* concludes, "Ivan Oransky and Adam Marcus are two geeks who set up a website called *Retraction Watch* because it was clear that retractions are often handled badly." An editorial in the Ottawa Citizen asserts:

> Fortunately, there are some people in the world of science who think more attention should be paid to retractions. Two of them have started a popular blog, *Retraction Watch*, which has shed light on about 200 retractions since its inception a year ago. The authors, both medical journalists, hope to "open a window onto the world of scientific publishing, and, by implication, science itself." If scientific publishers cared more about transparency than damage control, that window would be easier to pry open, and science would be better for it. (Making Science Transparent, 2011)

What is *Abnormal Science*? It is a German blog written by Zwirmer (2011a), a former university science professor. Unlike *Retraction Watch*, *Abnormal Science* is devoted, first to revealing, then to publicizing error, plagiarism, and fraud. Like *Retraction Watch*, it is a blog deeply implicated in the politics of change, the process of setting the record of science straight:

> With this blog I hope to contribute to a critique of the absence of transparency and of the secretive machinations of German universities when it comes to scientific misconduct. The public review of cases in the news illustrates serious flaws in the process of revealing misconduct. The behavior of the German Ombudsman is a notorious example.

WHAT SCIENCE BLOGS REVEAL

What is revealed in these science blogs need not be the consequence of scientific misconduct. On January 7, 2011, *Retraction Watch* reported that an article had been retracted because researchers mistakenly used the wrong mice, the result of a misreading of a confusing catalogue entry (Marcus & Oransky, 2011b). On January 19, an article that appeared in the *Journal of the National Cancer Institute* was quickly withdrawn by its authors: a conceptual error had been made. Of the latter case, *Retraction Watch* commented, "No misconduct involved—just good old-fashioned self-correcting science. So we applaud Baker, Simon, their co-authors, and the JNCI [*Journal of the National Cancer Institute*]" (Marcus & Oransky, 2011c).

Nevertheless, retractions very often involve plagiarism and fraud. For plagiarism, the rule is this: the ideas that scientists present to their publics should be entirely original, except where a citation is provided; their prose should also be wholly theirs, except where quotation marks are present. When Reginald Smith published virtually the same paper in two journals, he clearly violated this principle. A paper published in the *European Respiratory Journal* was retracted by editorial fiat for the same reason:

> Although the two papers were not exactly identical, there were overlaps between the two papers, and more importantly, the authors have failed to mention the existence of a closely related paper, using the same cohort of patients, and being submitted to another journal. We do not say whether this was intentional or simply due to a misunderstanding of our journal's policy, but the fact that the authors have failed to report (either to us or to the chief editor of Respiratory Medicine) of this almost concomitant submission of two very closely related papers was real and undisputable. (Marcus & Oransky, 2010)

However defined, plagiarism is an offense against, and only against, the social community that is science; it does not affect the community's knowledge base. It has no epistemic consequences. It is its effect on scientific knowledge that makes fraud the graver offense. The case of Silvia Bulfone-Paus, a case we reconstruct from *Retraction Watch* and *Abnormal Science*, reveals the importance of the Internet and its blogs in ferreting out fraud, pursuing the truth relentlessly despite considerable institutional opposition. Marcus and Oransky and Zwirner provide us with a window into institutional resistance to detecting and correcting fraud and in punishing offenders.

What is symptomatic of an article in need of retraction on account of fraud? Grant Steen (2011) investigated the characteristics of such articles, determining that in general they were published in journals with a relatively high impact factor, reflecting the ambition of their first authors; that they frequently had a relatively large number of co-authors, a tactic that obscures responsibility; that they were very often one of a series, a repetition indicating a pattern of deception; and finally, that the delay between publication and retraction was typically long, resulting in large part from the authors' reluctance to admit fault. The Bulfone-Paus case exhibits all of the characteristics Steen detects (Frost, 2010; Marcus & Oransky, 2011d, 2011e, 2011f). Some 12 of her papers were retracted after an extended period of delay, clearly marked by resistance on her part. On average, these papers had nearly eight authors. Their impact factor averaged 5.813, over double the average for journals in immunology, Bulfone-Paus' field.

The first hint of difficulty with Bulfone-Paus' work surfaces in November 2009, when Karin Wiebauer, a PhD working in her laboratory at the German Research Center Borstel, alerts her to the possibility that some papers published by her research team may contain manipulated images. Far from acting at once, Bulfone-Paus waits until February 29, 2010, to inform her superiors of the possibility. Only in May is an internal investigation initiated. Apparently as a result of this investigation (its report is never released), in July 2010 an external investigation begins, headed by Werner Seeger of the University of Giessen.

In the meantime, the Internet has not been silent on this matter. In his private blog, Martin Frost, a pseudonym for a person unknown to any of the parties in the investigation, openly accuses Bulfone-Paus of fraud. The first reaction of the scientific community is severely critical of interference that it regards as gratuitous and unwarranted. In September, a *Nature* editorial (A destabilizing force, 2010) accuses Frost of carrying out a "trial-by-Internet" and threatening "the impartiality of misconduct inquiries." In October, Frost receives a letter from a Hamburg law firm, presumably initiated by Bulfone-Paus, asking him to remove his allegedly libelous comments. He does not comply. In November–December 2010, the report of the external committee is made public. It concludes that two post-doctoral students, co-authors Elena Bulanova and Vadim Budagian, are responsible for image manipulation; however, there is no falsification of data "in the sense that anything was made up." There is no doubt, however, that "fundamental responsibility" for any scientific misconduct has to rest on the senior author, also Director of Immunology and Cell Biology. Despite this finding, there is no reason for wholesale retraction because there was no indication, the report asserts, that the "core findings" of these papers were in any way undermined by the fraudulent images. In November, pending the public release of this report, Bulfone-Paus is asked to resign as Director. She does not comply.

In December, an email from Karin Wiebauer appears on Martin Frost's blog (2010). This appearance represents the turning of the tide against Bulfone-Paus. In less than perfect and often bold-faced English, Wiebauer details the difficulties she had in getting a hearing for her warnings and later, her accusations of fraud, accusations that point directly at Bulfone-Paus.

> Incidentally, in the long year, that followed my email to Silvia on 4th November 2009, I took great pains to stay on the "legal" route for whistleblowers, trying to keep this case within the limits of the scientific community and, most notably, acting always under my full name.

> Did it lead me anywhere? It didn't. Instead, I had to endure the mindboggling lies and/or excuses of all parties involved in this case of scientific misconduct, starting with **Prof. Bulfone-Paus** and including the poor co-worker condemned to reproduce non-existing data, the **Editors-in-Chief of Journal of Immunology and Molecular and Cellular Biology**, the **speakers of ombudsman**—and other committees, and—last not least— the **"Deutsche Forschungsgemeinschaft"** (DFG) [German Research Society]: This organization provided most of the money that enabled Prof.

Bulfone-Paus to publish a series of science fiction articles for the past 10 years (SFB 506/C5, SFB 415/A10). It also approved the establishment of SFB 877 (the successor of SFB 415) that contains a proposal by Prof. Bulfone-Paus, which was based in part on publications that were purportedly under investigation.

These accusations are accompanied by a visual series that make the degree of image manipulation abundantly clear. My Figure 4.1 is one of Wiebauer's mash-ups. It is hard to believe in Bulfone-Paus' innocence when we see her Figure 5D transformed by Photoshop into Figure 3B.

Now the story approaches its climax. On March 16, Research Center Borstel receives an open letter, signed by 24 researchers from the United States, England, Sweden, Germany, Italy, and Israel, a stout defense of Bulfone-Paus as a researcher above reproach. It is clear testimony to the high regard for her achievements within the relevant scientific community. On April 6, the Board of Directors of the Research Center Borstel responds, defending its case against Bulfone-Paus. They point to "Silvia Bulfone-Paus's prolonged failure to be completely up-front about the nature and extent of the fraud occurring in her lab." They add that "Silvia Bufone-Paus received repeated warnings (in writing) from her former co-worker Dr. Karin Wiebauer as early as January 2004." Finally, they dismiss those who would trivialize the consequences of her misconduct:

> It has been stated that, since many of the incriminated manipulations "only" concern Western Blots showing loading controls, the main results reported in the papers appeared not to be affected by the manipulations. The data supporting this contention, however, have not yet been examined by independent referees from the respective Journals.

Finally, they state unequivocally that "the principal investigator bears full responsibility for any faulted data in publications." As a consequence of their brief, Bulfone-Paus has been demoted: She will no longer be Director.

What is the motivation for Bulfone-Paus' misconduct? Why did this competent and talented researcher commit fraud? According to Robert Merton (1968), there are five shared norms essential to the proper conduct of science—originality, communalism, universalism, disinterestedness, and organized skepticism. These do not describe the way all scientists behave; they describe the way all scientists ought to behave. Science editors whose retraction notices lack candor violate the norm of communalism; plagiarists violate the norm of originality; fraudsters, like Bulfone-Paus, violate the norms of disinterestedness, universalism, and organized skepticism. Why?

They do so because there is a problem with these norms. Behaving well may be a necessary condition for a successful scientific career; it is never sufficient. Adherence determines only membership in good standing; it does not determine relative status, the size of one's share in the rewards one's fellows can offer. This

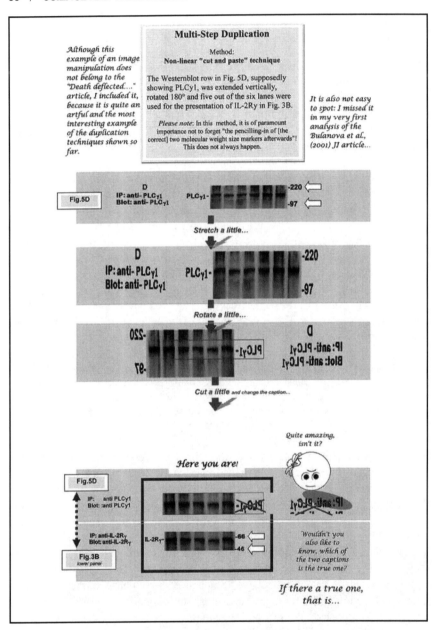

Figure 4.1. Wiebauer's mash-up illustrating fraud in an article by Bulfone-Paus et al. (1999). Adapted from pages 3 and 4 of "Bulfone-Paus et al. 1999 Part 3," a PDF attachment of Wiebauer (2010). Retrieved from http://martinfrost.ws/htmlfiles/dec2010/blame-elena-vadim.html.

size is a consequence of the significance of scientists' work to their peers, its impact on their particular community and on science as a whole. While it is possible to increase one's status without deviating from any community norms, it is also possible to achieve the same result more swiftly simply by violating them. In a healthy community, there is consensus that the benefits from adherence will exceed those of violation—that crime does not pay. But if this consensus does not obtain routinely—if adherence is perceived by some as a path to failure in the competition for status—a state of anomie may well arise. For some at least, the norms cease to be compelling. As more and more norm violations succeed, as they lead to an increase in status for more and more members of the community, anomie deepens and spreads; as it does, deviant behavior spreads. If the infection becomes general, the community becomes pathological: deviant behavior becomes the norm. Scientists can no longer be trusted to do trustworthy science (Merton, 1968).

The temptation to which Bulfone-Paus succumbed is not hers alone; it is widespread in the biomedical community of which she is a member, a community that suffers from increasing anomie, a state of affairs in which the norms of originality, communality, universalism, disinterestedness, and organized skepticism are in constant peril. Too often in biomedical articles, recommendations and conclusions are not supported by data; too often their significance is exaggerated (Boutron, Dutton, Ravaud, & Altman, 2010; Gøtszche, 2006; Hewitt, Mitchell, & Torgerson, 2008; Martinson, Anderson, & de Vries, 2005). Too often, conclusions are biased by financial ties to sponsoring pharmaceutical companies (Bennett, Lai, Henke, Bartnato, Armitage, & Sartor, 2010; Norris, Herxheimer, Lexchin, & Mansfield, 2005, pp. 48–55; Yank, Rennie, & Bero, 2007). Too often, there is a lack of transparency: protocols are not presented and vital methodological information is missing (Hopewell, Dutton, Yu, Chan, & Altman, 2010; Martinson et al., 2005). Too often, industry-supported studies in medical journals are more likely to report positive findings, regardless of the evidence, and to support new and off-label treatments over standard ones (Jefferson, Pietrantoni, Debalini, Rivetti, & Demicheli, 2009; Jørgensen, Hilden, & Gøtzsche, 2006; Yank et al., 2007). Despite the heavy involvement of industry in funding research, a survey established that only 26% of North American medical journals required disclosure of any conflict of interest that might arise from drug company subsidies (Norris et al., 2005).

As a consequence of these trends, we might infer that the number of candidates for retraction exceeds by far the number of articles actually retracted: Bulfone-Paus and her fellows, exposed by *Retraction Watch*, are the tip of the iceberg. This is indeed the case. On the basis of one count, between 1995 and 2004, there were 328 retractions out of 5,041,587 articles listed in PubMed (Redman, 2008). This is an absurdly small number (33 per year or 0.0065%), given the articles likely in need of retraction. A survey of over 3,000 researchers funded by the National Institutes of Health reported that one third of the respondents admitted to "a range of questionable practices that are striking in their breadth and prevalence" (Martinson, 2005). Owning up to falsifying results was rare (0.3%), though still significantly higher than the number of papers actually retracted. If 0.3% of 5,041,587 papers are fraudulent, then 15,125 are; that is 1,513 a year.

There are other problems. The study provides evidence of undue influence. A substantial number of respondents acknowledged changing important aspects of a study owing to pressure from the funding source (15.5%). Also alarming was the fact that 27.5% of respondents self-reported sloppy recordkeeping, a practice that makes extremely difficult the assessment of human error, experimental replicability, or fraud. In addition, the results of this survey may be an underestimation because, in all probability, misbehaving scientists were less likely to respond and those responding were more likely to underreport their deviance. The problems such unprofessional practices create would not be solved, however, even if all fraudulent, biased, or otherwise tainted articles were eventually retracted. Retraction does nothing to purge the literature of the many citations to retracted articles, citations that permanently infect the literature (Howard, 2011). Indeed, retracted articles are cited, even after retraction, partly because retractions are often hidden behind a pay-wall. Witness the Aoki-Matsuda problem.

WHY SCIENCE BLOGS ARE PERSUASIVE

The websites of Marcus and Oransky and Zwirner are engaged in a heroic quest, designed to rescue, not just bioscience, but all science from the throes of error and self-deception. To do so, they turn the recent past into a story with a moral, a Pilgrim's Progress of scientists caught in the snares of institutional constraints, tempted by sin into deviance. But can such moral journeys rest, as those of Marcus and Oransky and Zwirner largely rest, on the accusations of anonymous whistle-blowers? Should not accusations of plagiarism and fraud be pursued only through proper institutional channels, behind closed doors, rather than aired in public? And if pursued beyond proper channels, should whistle-blowers be permitted to remain anonymous?

Those in favor of proper channels alone ignore the evidence that such channels fail to work properly more often than not, a fact that *Retraction Watch* and *Abnormal Science* regularly document and as the Bulfone-Paus case amply demonstrates. Speaking of the German Ombudsman in charge of investigating fraud, Zwirner (2011d) vents his understandable frustration at the approach through proper channels:

> Fig. 3C is obviously and unequivocally manipulated. The correct control stain (double color stain) could prove it beyond doubt. . . . Instead you accept the wrong control stain (single color). An analogy to your approach would

be that a court accepted a kitchen knife as weapon in a homicide case although the victim had a gunshot wound in the forehead and the suspect offender was in possession of the gun in question.

Those against anonymity seem unaware that the public forum afforded by a blog is well suited for exposing the evidence for plagiarism and fraud. What counts in the cases reported in *Retraction Watch* and *Abnormal Science* is, after all, not the motive of the whistleblower but the evidence produced in defense of claims. Moreover, those against anonymity seem also unaware that whistle-blowing legislation has repeatedly failed to protect whistleblowers from retalia-tion (Dworkin, 2007). Those against anonymity also ignore the fact that blogs allow anyone to respond almost immediately to an accusation, including those most knowledgeable about what really happened: the accused. Finally, those in favor of anonymity ignore the existence of libel law as a protection for the accused.

Stories with a moral like those in *Retraction Watch* and *Abnormal Science* are the routine products of investigative journalism (Ettema & Glasser, 1998). In such journalism, "narrative is an instrument of both cognitive and moral understanding. More than that, narrative is the instrument by which these two intellectual impulses are united" (Ettema & Glasser, 1998, p. 128). It is a union abetted by irony, a tool designed to persuade readers to share the authors' indignation at the violation of Merton's norms and to spur the demand for a return to their adherence (Ettema & Glasser, 1998, p. 87). In telling Bulfone-Paus' story, for example, *Retraction Watch* combines cognitive and moral understanding in a single narrative, one honed throughout by structural and verbal irony. Structural irony contrasts her respected position with her reprehensible conduct, apparently trying to quash a whistleblower in her lab and threatening to sue another. This ironic stance is seconded by its verbal counterpart (Marcus & Oransky, 2011e):

> Some of the notices have gone into great detail about what was wrong with the original papers, and journals have even allowed the team to declare that some of the results had been replicated. One simply said there had been misconduct.

Then there's this [retraction notice]:

> This article has been withdrawn by the authors.

That certainly clears things right up.

This verbal irony is also seconded by readers who comment on the case, one of whom is none other than Joerg Zwirner:

> EMBO Journal editor Bernd Pulverer has done science a disservice. Without good cause he provided platform to people (shall we still call them scien-tists?) who gambled away their credibility. Key experiments reproduced and

> confirmed? No proof? No evidence? Come on! Bulfone-Paus is not worthy
> of our trust anymore. (Zwirner, 2011a)

In other *Retraction Watch* cases, where the violation seems particularly outrageous, irony's siblings, sarcasm and ridicule, play a significant role. For example, in one post, Marcus (2011b) writes, "A team of Australian medical writers who analyzed four decades worth of retractions has reached the conclusion—we trust you're sitting—that people in their profession are more honest than, well, the rest of us." This freedom to belittle does not extend to the Web equivalent of face-to-face interaction, an indication that Marcus and Oransky's moral compass is in order. Responding to a comment, Marcus's tone is as always sober, indicating by a modulation that ridicule extends only to the article, not to its authors:

> Our skepticism stems largely from the significant limitation of the study—
> the inability to analyze papers in which the work of medical writers has
> not been disclosed—and the implicit claim that medical writers add a
> veneer of ethical purity. In our view, transparency and the willingness
> to disclose (authorship, pharma involvement, etc.) probably are the best
> insurance against misconduct. (Marcus, 2011a)

Marcus and Oransky and Zwirner also extend the permissible scope of investigative reporting by their willingness to editorialize, to make their moral mission explicit. It is this willingness that is behind a *Retraction Watch* entry that attempts to give journals retraction grades. The most impressive of the 12 retraction notices analyzed acknowledge misconduct and do not permit the authors to make unsubstantiated claims concerning the remaining worth of their retracted papers. Less worthy notices mention that there are irregularities but do not tell us what they are. Even less worthy notices say nothing whatever about the cause of the retraction. The four worst notices specify exactly what was wrong, but then allow "the authors to claim—without the journal editors having reviewed any findings, one of them told us—that the data and conclusions had been confirmed." For example, "The authors declare that key experiments presented in the majority of these figures were recently reproduced and that the results confirmed the experimental data and the conclusions drawn from them" (Marcus & Oransky, 2011f). Zwirner (2011c) goes even further out on a moral limb in his attack on a melanoma study that, he alleges, continues to recruit patients in defiance of medical plausibility:

> The official website of the Department of Dermatology, the first and fore-
> most purpose of which is to inform patients, their physicians as well as
> scientists and students delivers false, misleading informations [*sic*] on a
> large scale dendritic cell-based tumor vaccination trial. The website is an
> important tool for the recruitment of melanoma patients in future trials with

dendritic cell-based immune therapy. From the perspective of patients and their physicians it is totally inacceptable [*sic*] that the true fate of this multicenter study and the inefficacy of the dendritic cell therapy as found in that trial is not revealed.

Reader commentary extends investigative reporting's scope even further. In *Retraction Watch*, dozens comment, some only once, some seldom, some frequently. Some prefer pseudonyms; some reveal their identity either directly or indirectly. The case of ktwop, alias of Krishna Pillai, a research engineer with a doctorate, reveals what a frequent commentator can contribute to reinforce the goals of investigative journalism by employing its methods: straight reporting informed by structural irony, criticism edged with sarcasm, editorializing. Commenting on the precarious state of academic integrity in Chinese science, ktwop employs structural irony when replying to one of Marcus and Oransky's posts:

> After a quick trial, a local court in Beijing convicted urologist Xiao Chuang-Guo on 10 October of assaulting two well-known advocates of academic integrity in China. One victim of the attacks was Fang Shimin, freelance writer and self-appointed watchdog of research misconduct. Fang had questioned Xiao's academic achievements, but this was not what prompted the attack, Xiao claimed. Xiao told the court that he had a decade-long personal conflict with Fang, mainly because Fang had insulted Xiao's wife and teacher. (ktwop, 2010)

A comment on an English case of scientific fraud is edged with sarcasm:

> Perhaps friend Jatinder can follow the example of "zu Googleberg." [A reference to a German Defense Minister, Karl Theodor zu Guttenberg, dismissed over a plagiarism scandal.] As the plagiarist he has retracted his own PhD and Angela Merkel has let him continue in his job. But he has a personal fortune of € 300 million to fall back on! (ktwop, 2011b)

Of a journal editor who was not forthcoming about the reasons for retraction, ktwop editorializes:

> It is increasingly obvious that it is not just the ethics of researchers which can be involved in retractions. The ethics of the journal editors and the journals themselves (including their peer-review process) are obviously very relevant. He may be a wonderful surgeon and husband for all I know but as an editor-in-chief he is no role-model and he does not impress. (ktwop, 2011a)

For Marcus and Oransky, for Zwirner, and for their reader-commentators, narrative tinged with irony is the tool with which to judge and to transform the moral order so that it conforms more closely to the acknowledged norms of science.

There are limits to this approach. *Retraction Watch* never probes beneath the surface to the source behind misconduct, to science as a social institution, to an enterprise that has silently incorporated into itself incentives at odds with its norms. To its credit, *Abnormal Science* does raise this issue, though Zwirner (2011b) lacks the tools to address it adequately:

> There has been a neglect of the sociological aspects of scientific misbehavior to this day. One might argue that misconduct in science is as much a sociological phenomenon as a scientific or legal issue. Such reasoning has already been voiced in regard to doping in sports. . . . However, to keep sports as well as science clean, it might prove to be insufficient to focus exclusively on the scientist who personally fabricated, falsified or plagiarized, or the athlete who used performance enhancers. Such a personalization of misconduct might distract from other, equally important causes of failures of compliance with accepted standards in science and sports.

Still, it would be unfair to judge *Retraction Watch* and *Abnormal Science* against a standard they were not designed to meet. Their achievement is nothing less than remarkable: two journalists and one former scientist have succeeded in reinventing investigative journalism on the Web, creatively exploiting its possibilities in pursuit of a better world of science, one more in conformity with its own high standards.

CONCLUSION

Without the Internet, enterprises like *Retraction Watch* and *Abnormal Science* are inconceivable. Neither newspapers nor television nor radio could focus so relentlessly on a single topic of no interest to a general audience but of considerable importance to every citizen. No other medium could maintain an instantly available archive of cases, a history of scientific misconduct and retraction as it unfolds. No other medium could make reader comments an integral part of its developing stories. No other medium could provide Twitter feeds that keep the blog up-to-date, literally minute by minute. No other medium could provide such ready access to other relevant Internet sources, including other blogs or related articles. The story of *Retraction Watch* and *Abnormal Science* is the tale of nodes in a network of expanding knowledge and epistemic, social, and moral critique. Both blogs seriously influence how we know. By correcting error, *Abnormal Science* does so directly by publicizing error and opening a window to the efforts of others in doing so; *Retraction Watch* does so indirectly. Bulfone-Paus' exposure is a prime example of private endeavors working in the public interest, an enterprise made possible and made public by the Internet. We have a case, probably not the last case, of a prominent researcher seriously misbehaving. It is a case that shows us that science is far from self-correcting and that it can no longer insulate its lapses from wider public opinion operating in virtual space. As a result of the efforts of these bloggers, we—all of us—have a firmer sense of the state of knowledge at the research front in particular fields of scientific endeavor.

REFERENCES

A destabilizing force. (2010). [Editorial] *Nature, 467,* 7312.

Aoki, N., & Matsuda, T. (2000). A cytosolic protein-tyrosine phosphatase PTP1B specifically dephosphorylates and deactivates prolactin-activated STAT5a and STAT5b. *Journal of Biological Chemistry, 275,* 39718–39726.

Bennett, C. L., Lai, S. Y., Henke, M., Bartnato, S. E., Armitage, J. O., & Sartor, O. (2010). Association between pharmaceutical support and basic science research on erythropoiesis-stimulating agents. *Archives of Internal Medicine, 170*(16), 1490–1498.

Boutron, I., Dutton, S., Ravaud, P., & Altman D. G. (2010). Reporting and interpretation of randomized controlled trials with statistically nonsignificant results for primary outcomes. *JAMA, 303*(20), 2058–2064.

Bulfone-Paus, S., Bulanova, E., Pohl, T., & Budagian, V. (1999). Death deflected: IL-15 inhibits TNF-N1-mediated apoptosis in fibroblasts by TRAF2 recruitment to the IL-15RN1 chain. *FASEB Journal, 13,* 1575–1585. [retracted]

Chaucer, G. (1933). *The poetical works.* (F. N. Robinson, Ed.). Boston, MA: Houghton Mifflin.

Dworkin, T. M. (2007). Sox and whistleblowing. *Michigan Law Review, 105,* 1757–1780.

Ettema, J. S., & Glasser, T. S. (1998). *Custodians of conscience: Investigative journalism and public virtue.* New York, NY: Columbia University Press.

Frost. M. (2010). *Frost's meditations.* Retrieved from http://www.martinfrost.ws/htmlfiles/dec2010/blame-elena-vadim.html

Gøtzsche, P. C. (2006). Believability of relative risks and odds ratios in abstracts: Cross sectional study. *BMJ, 333,* 231–234.

Hewitt, C., Mitchell, N., & Torgerson, D. (2008). Heed the data when results are not significant. *BMJ, 336,* 23–25.

Hopewell, S., Dutton, S., Yu, L., Chan, A., & Altman, D. G. (2010). The quality of reports of randomized trials in 2000 and 2006: Comparative study of articles indexed in PubMed. *BMJ,* 340, c723. doi: 10.1136/bmj.c723

Howard, J. (2011). Despite warnings, biomedical scholars cite hundreds of retracted papers. *Chronicle of Higher Education, 57*(32), 2–3.

Jefferson, T., Pietrantoni, C. D., Debalini, M. G., Rivetti, A., & Demicheli, V. (2009). Relation of study quality, concordance, take home message, funding, and impact in studies of influenza vaccine: Systematic review. *BMJ, 338.* doi: 10.1136/bmj.b354

Jørgensen, A. W., Hilden, J., & Gøtzsche, P. C. (2006). Cochrane reviews compared with industry supported meta-analyses and other meta-analyses of the same drugs: Systematic review. *BMJ, 333.* doi: 10.1136/bmj.38973.444699.OB

ktwop. (2010, October 7). Do plagiarism, fraud, and retractions make it more difficult to trust research from China? [Blog comment]. *Retraction Watch.* Retrieved December 17, 2011, from http://retractionwatch.wordpress.com/2010/10/07/do-plagiarism-fraud-and-retractions-make-it-more-difficult-trust/#more-496 ktwop. (2011a, January 5). Why was that paper retracted? Editor to *Retraction Watch*: "It's none of your business" [Blog comment]. *Retraction Watch*. Retrieved from http://retractionwatch.wordpress.com/2011/01/05/why-was-that-paper-retracted-editor-to-retraction-watch-its-none/#more-1261

ktwop. (2011b, February 21). Ahluwalia did not tell UCL he had been dismissed from Cambridge [Blog comment]. *Retraction Watch*. Retrieved from http://retraction watch.wordpress.com/2011/02/21/ahluwalia-did-not-tell-ucl-he-had-been-dismissed-from-cambridge/#more-1817

Making science transparent. (2011, August 12). [Editorial] *The Ottawa Citizen*. Retrieved from http://search.proquest.com/

Marcus, A. (2011a, February 3). Three more Bulfone-Paus rejection notices, in *Journal of Immunology* [Blog comment]. *Retraction Watch*. Retrieved from http://retraction watch.wordpress.com/2011/02/03/three-more-bulfone-paus-retraction-notices-out-in-journal-of-imm/#more-1656

Marcus, A. (2011b, April 15). Want to avoid a retraction? Hire a medical writer, say medical writers. *Retraction Watch*. Retrieved from http://retractionwatch.com/2011/04/15/want-to-avoid-a-retraction-hire-a-medical-writer-say-medical-wri/

Marcus, A., & Oransky, I. (2010, December 28). Nearly identical twins: *European Respiratory Journal* retracts another asthma in pregnancy paper similar to another by the same group. *Retraction Watch* [Blog post]. Retrieved from http://retraction watch.wordpress.com/2010/12/28/nearly-identical-twins-european-respiratory-journal-retracts-ast/#more-1199

Marcus, A., & Oransky, I. (2011a, January 5). Why was that paper retracted? Editor to *Retraction Watch*: "It's none of your business" [Blog post]. *Retraction Watch*. Retrieved from http://retractionwatch.wordpress.com/2011/01/05/why-was-that-paper-retracted-editor-to-retraction-watch-its-none/#more-1261

Marcus, A., & Oransky, I. (2011b, January 7). Authors of *Journal of Immunology* paper retract it after realizing they have ordered the wrong mice [Blog post]. *Retraction Watch*. Retrieved from http://retractionwatch.wordpress.com/2011/01/07/authors-of-journal-of-immunology-paper-retract-it-after-realizin/#more-1274

Marcus, A., & Oransky, I. (2011c, January 19). A lightning-fast *JNCI* retraction shows how science should work [Blog post]. *Retraction Watch*. Retrieved from http://retractionwatch.wordpress.com/2011/01/19/a-lightning-fast-jnci-retraction-shows-how-science-should-work/#more-1416

Marcus, A., & Oransky, I. (2011d, February 3). Three more Bulfone-Paus rejection notices, in *Journal of Immunology* [Blog post]. *Retraction Watch*. Retrieved from http://retractionwatch.wordpress.com/2011/02/03/three-more-bulfone-paus-retraction-notices-out-in-journal-of-imm/#more-1656

Marcus, A., & Oransky, I. (2011e, February 15). Bulfone-Paus retraction notice appears in the *Journal of Biological Chemistry* [Blog post]. *Retraction Watch*. Retrieved from http://retractionwatch.wordpress.com/2011/02/15/bulfone-paus-retraction-notice-appears-in-the-journal-of-biologi/#more-1747

Marcus, A., & Oransky, I. (2011f, March 14). As last of 12 Bulfone-Paus retractions appears, a (disappointing) report card on journal transparency [Blog post]. *Retraction Watch*. Retrieved from http://retractionwatch.wordpress.com/2011/03/14/as-last-of-12-promised-bulfone-paus-retractions-appears-a-disapp/#more-2048

Marcus, A., & Oransky, I. (2011g, March 21). Freedom from Information Act? Another *JBC* retraction untarnished by the facts [Blog post]. *Retraction Watch*. Retrieved from http://retractionwatch.wordpress.com/?s=matsuda

Martinson, B. C., Anderson, M. S., & de Vries, R. (2005). Scientists behaving badly. *Nature*, *435*(7043), 737–738.

Merton. R. K. (1968). *Social theory and social structure*. New York, NY: Free Press.

Norris, P., Herxheimer, A., Lexchin, J., & Mansfield, P. (2005). Drug promotion: What we know, what we have yet to learn: Reviews of materials in the WHO/HAI database on drug promotion. *World Health Organization*, WHO/EDM/PAR/2004.3.

Redman, B. K. (2008). Empirical developments in retraction. *Journal of Medical Ethics*, *34*, 807–809.

Steen, G. (2011). Retractions in the scientific literature: Do authors deliberately commit research fraud? *Journal of Medical Ethics*, *37*, 113–117.

Tsou, P., Talia, N. N., Pinney, A. J., Kendzicky, A., Piera-Velazquez, S., Jimenez, S. A., et al. (2012). Effect of oxidative stress on protein tyrosine phosphatase 1B in scleroderma dermal fibroblasts. *Arthritis and Rheumatism*, *64*(6), 1978–1989.

Wiebauer, K. (2010, December 3). Fraud perfected—Accusations deflected? [or] How to duplicate and plagiarize one's own data [or] Data manipulation: A guided tour through an expanding universe. [PDF files]. Attachments to correspondence reproduced on *Frost's Meditations* [Blog entry]. Retrieved December 4, 2010 from http://martinfrost.ws/htmlfiles/dec2010/blame-elena-vadim.html

Yank, V., Rennie, D., & Bero, L. A. (2007). Financial ties and concordance between results and conclusions in meta-analyses: Retrospective cohort study. *BMJ*. doi: 10.1136/bmj.39376.447211.BE

Zwirner, J. (2011a, February 3). Three more Bulfone-Paus rejection notices, in *Journal of Immunology* [Blog comment]. *Retraction Watch*. Retrieved from http://retraction watch.wordpress.com/2011/02/03/three-more-bulfone-paus-retraction-notices-out-in-journal-of-imm/#more-1656

Zwirner, J. (2011b, September 15). SMS alert at Erlangen: The sociological aspects of scientific misconduct [Blog post]. *Abnormal Science*. Retrieved from http://abnormalscienceblog.wordpress.com/2011/09/15/sociological-aspects-of-scientific-misconduct/#more-748

Zwirner, J. (2011c, September 19). SMS alert at Erlangen: The mystery of a cancer study [Blog post]. *Abnormal Science*. Retrieved from http://abnormalscienceblog.word press.com/2011/09/19/sms-alert-in-erlangen-the-mystery-of-a-cancer-study/#more-761

Zwirner, J. (2011d, September 27). German Ombudsman et al.: Systematic suppression of evidence. *Abnormal Science*. Retrieved from http://abnormalscienceblog.word press.com/2011/09/27/german-ombudsman-et-al-systematic-suppression-of-evidence/#more-790

http://dx.doi.org/10.2190/SCIC5

CHAPTER 5

The Online Research Article and the Ecological Basis of New Digital Genres

Christian F. Casper

ABSTRACT

Among the most significant outcomes of the emergence and evolution of digital communication technology are the ways in which it enables formerly disparate genres to exist within the same milieu. In other words, genres that rarely interacted in print media find themselves suddenly thrown together in the new digital world, and the ecological implications are often fascinating. This chapter explores this development by examining the particular case of online scientific journals and the interactions between existing and new genres in these publications, and it proposes a conception of genre in digital space based explicitly on its role within an "ecosystem" of texts.

Scholars of communication and rhetoric have been interested in scientific genres for some time. In fact, much of the seminal work in genre since the 1980s has dealt with scientific texts (e.g., Bazerman, 1988, 1994; Berkenkotter & Huckin, 1995; Miller, 1984, 1994; Schryer, 1993, 1994; Swales, 1990, 2004), and these studies have helped us understand the inherently social nature of genres (Miller, 1984), their key role in community formation and cohesion (Miller, 1994), and the ways that genres evolve and interact in assemblages (Bazerman, 1994; Devitt, 1991; Orlikowski & Yates, 1994; Spinuzzi, 2002, 2004; Spinuzzi & Zachry, 2000; Swales, 2004; Yates & Orlikowski, 2002).

One of the most important developments in genre studies has been the recognition that no genre is an island. Genres act together to play particular roles in the communication of a community, much as particular species fill particular niches in a biological ecosystem. Several models of genre assemblages[1] have been proposed over the years, including genre sets (Devitt, 1991), genre systems (Bazerman, 1994; Yates & Orlikowski, 2002), genre repertoires (Orlikowski & Yates, 1994), and genre ecologies (Spinuzzi, 2002; Spinuzzi & Zachry, 2000), in addition to Swales's (2004) several "constellations" of genres. These models are not mutually exclusive, but they do foreground different aspects of the uses of genres that can be more or less useful depending on the artifacts at hand and the questions asked.[2]

Owen (2007) describes the research article as having undergone a process that he calls "encapsulation," whereby the basic form of the genre remains constant even as its medium of delivery changes. Contending that scientific journals have passed the point at which they were likely to be significantly changed by digital media (pp. 213–214), he explains that the research article has simply migrated online, like moving a potted plant (p. 218). However, I argue here that a complete consideration of a genre should not treat it as if in a vacuum but should also take into account the "ecosystem" of genres in which it operates. Changes that occur in the generic environment in which a text sits can have important implications for the practice of its discourse community. The discourse being carried out in new electronic annotation and discussion genres may very well change the discursive environment in which the research article sits, so even if the research article is not changing formally, its role as a text in the generic milieu of science may very well be evolving with its environment. My study of new genres that interact with the research article addresses how the research article evolves as a genre even if it may not noticeably change in form. In short, I argue here that developments in electronic media and their deployment in online communication of scientific research suggest a conception of genre evolution that focuses more on a genre's role in its textual ecosystem than on any changes in its "anatomical" form.

METHODOLOGY

To begin to address these questions, I undertook a critical and empirical study of four tools for feedback on published research in science: comments and notes in an innovative online journal called *PLOS ONE*, published by the

---

[1] In a very useful article on some of these models Spinuzzi (2004) uses the term *assemblages* without its Deleuzian implications, and here so do I.

[2] Crawford, Hurd, & Weller (1996), Garvey & Griffith (1972), and Hahn (2001) have proposed models of the scientific communication process, which, although not framed as descriptions of genre assemblages per se, are useful for understanding how scholars have conceptualized the interplay of various kinds of texts related to scientific research.

nonprofit publisher Public Library of Science (PLOS), and "e-letters" and traditional letters to the editor (which are published both in print and online) in the highly regarded, well-established journal *Science*. *PLOS ONE* and *Science* are both interdisciplinary journals publishing research from a wide variety of fields. Established in 1880 with financial support from Thomas Edison, *Science* has become one of the most prestigious scientific journals in the world, rivaling its British counterpart *Nature*. *PLOS ONE* has been published only since December 2006 but has become widely known largely due to its open access, subscription-free publication policy and experimentation with novel forms of online communication. Unlike the other journals published by PLOS, such as *PLOS Biology* and *PLOS Genetics*, *PLOS ONE* employs a unique standard of prepublication peer review in which submissions are evaluated only on the soundness of the methodology and interpretation of the data and not on the work's perceived importance or significance. Among this family of journals, *PLOS ONE* is where new online communication features are typically tried out first, so it provided the richest source of data for this study.

(During the publication process of this book, *PLOS ONE* eliminated the notes function and converted all existing notes to comments. I inquired about this to PLOS's product manager, and he explained that the program was shuttered because the notes weren't used very much, and the difference between comments and notes was confusing to many readers. I have left the remainder of the text of this chapter as it was before I became aware of this development, but readers should be aware that the notes function no longer exists as of 2013.)

Comments and notes in *PLOS ONE* are very much like other short, relatively informal modes of online communication, like comments on a blog. The comments are generally intended to be directed at the research article as a whole, whereas notes can be directly appended to particular passages. E-letters in *Science* are formal communications that are vetted by an editor before publication. On the surface they closely resemble traditional letters to the editor, but they are also accessible directly from the online edition of the article to which they are directed. They also may be accompanied by formal replies from the original authors of the article. Letters to the editor in *Science* are very much like the e-letters in most respects, except that they are published in the print edition of the journal as well as online.

For the textual analysis in this study, a dataset was assembled by collecting comments and notes from *PLOS ONE* and e-letters and letters to the editor from *Science* under a set of parameters described below. The goal in assembling the dataset was to have a substantial, representative selection of comments and notes from *PLOS ONE* and enough e-letters and letters to the editor in *Science* from roughly the same period of time to support a reasonable comparative analysis. New forms of online communication are a more central part of the culture of *PLOS ONE* than of *Science*,[3] so the sample would likely emphasize the comments and notes in *PLOS ONE*, and this in fact turned out to be the case.

In order to control for differences in the use of online feedback tools that may exist across disciplines, only comments, notes, e-letters, and letters to the editor attached to research articles in the field of genetics and genomics were used. All comments and notes on *PLOS ONE* articles bearing the journal's "genetics and genomics" subject tag and published between December 20, 2006 (the journal's launch date), and June 30, 2007, were collected and analyzed. This period was chosen in order to mark the beginning of the online discussion features particular to *PLOS ONE* so as to establish a baseline for possible future diachronic studies of the evolution of scientific communication online. During this approximately six-month span, 151 articles with the "genetics and genomics" subject tag were published in *PLOS ONE*, of which 48 bore at least one comment and 32 bore at least one note.

Science does not use subject tags to organize its articles, so I screened the articles by hand, selecting e-letters and letters to the editor only from those articles that in my judgment fell reasonably within the field of genetics and genomics, based on my own background in the biological sciences and in comparison with the articles bearing that tag in *PLOS ONE*. *Science* publishes not only original research but also news items and reviews, so for this study only articles categorized as "brevia," "research articles," and "reports" were used. (For simplicity, in this chapter, I refer to all of these types of articles generically as research articles.) The e-letters and letters to the editor in *Science*, which were less numerous than the comments and notes in *PLOS ONE*, were collected from articles published over a longer span of time—December 1, 2006, to December 31, 2007—in order to ensure an adequately sized sample. The sample of e-letters and letters to the editor in *Science* was still considerably smaller than that of comments and notes in *PLOS ONE*, but this reflects the greater use of online communication tools in *PLOS ONE* than in *Science*.

The dataset was then segmented into units for quantitative analysis, generally following the method of Geisler (2004). Within running text, paragraphs were used as the standard unit of segmentation because they provide a strong visual cue demarcating parts of the comment, note, e-letter, or letter. Smaller units such as subject lines, salutations, signatures, and contact information were also treated as individual units in the segmentation scheme. In this sample, another advantage of paragraphs over smaller units of segmentation such as t-units was that paragraphs were more self-contained than t-units usually were. In other words, the actions performed by the text seemed to occur largely at the level of the paragraph rather than the t-unit.

---

[3] At the time of this study, *PLOS ONE* even had a staff member in the position of "online community manager" to promote and manage communication in its online forums.

Coding Scheme

The empirical study discussed here was aimed at understanding what the texts produced in the online feedback tools do and what aspect of the research article they act upon. The coding scheme used in this study is based in part on the concept of the *speech act*, which was introduced by Austin (1962) and refined by Searle (1969, 1979). The coding scheme consists of two parts: a primary set of codes corresponding to the most common speech acts performed by the texts examined in this study and a secondary set of codes corresponding to the objects of discussion—that is, the particular aspects of the research article in question that are acted upon by the texts in the comments, notes, e-letters, and letters to the editor.

Primary Codes (Speech Acts)

The first test applied to the data is a set of codes corresponding to the most prominent speech acts performed by these texts. A summary of the primary codes used in this study can be found in Table 5.1.

The first six codes are used for segments that address the status of the research article in question as a knowledge artifact. Text segments taking a positive or negative code in this study push the claims of the research article toward either greater or lesser stability as knowledge artifacts, as in Latour's (1987) positive and negative modality of knowledge claims. Also addressed by these codes are the rhetorical tactics (Howard, 2005) used in making arguments about the epistemic status of the claims in the research article and thus corresponding to Searle's (1979) degrees of commitment in an assertive speech act. In this scheme, negotiative rhetorical tactics indicate a contingent argument that acknowledges that the matter is open to discussion or debate, whereas revelatory rhetorical tactics implicitly or explicitly close off discussion and debate and present the argument as, in effect, revealed truth. It should be noted that the apparent degree of commitment expressed in the text may not necessarily correspond exactly to the degree of commitment actually held by the speaker, since the normative conventions of scientific communication include hedging (Hyland, 1998; Penrose & Katz, 2004), which can disguise the speaker's true degree of commitment.

The other primary codes are used for segments that do not directly make claims about the epistemic status of the research article, although some may do so implicitly. These codes include suggesting extensions of the work, asking a question about the work, providing additional information, or posting a correction to the article.

Interrater reliability was determined with a second coder having domain knowledge (a PhD and postdoctoral research experience) in molecular genetics, using 101 text segments in the *PLOS ONE* comments (24.9% of the comments; 14.9% of the entire data set). The reliability was substantial (Cohen's $\kappa = 0.7439$)

Table 5.1 Primary Code Corresponding to Speech Acts

Primary code	Definition
Positive-Negotiative	Solidifies the claims of the research article in question as real, acceptable, true, or fruitful scientific knowledge and accepts that this evaluation is itself open to discussion or debate
Positive-Revelatory	Solidifies the claims of the research article in question as real, acceptable, true, or fruitful scientific knowledge and closes off debate on this matter
Positive-Evidence	Provides data or other evidence to support an argument (in other segments) that the claims of the research article in question are real, acceptable, true, or fruitful scientific knowledge
Negative-Negotiative	Denies the claims of the research article in question to be real, acceptable, true, or fruitful scientific knowledge and accepts that this evaluation is itself open to discussion and debate
Negative-Revelatory	Denies the claims of the research article in question to be real, acceptable, true, or fruitful scientific knowledge and closes off debate on this matter
Negative-Evidence	Provide data or other evidence to support an argument (in other segments) that the claims of the research article in question are not real, acceptable, true, or fruitful scientific knowledge
Extension/Suggestion/Criticism	Poses an extension of the work described in the research article in question or *helpfully* suggests a modification to that work
Question/Clarification	Asks a question about the work in the research article in question or requests clarification on an aspect of that research or the article reporting it
Information	Provides additional information that may be of interest to readers to the research article in question
Link	Provides an Internet hyperlink for further information that may be of interest to readers of the research article in question
Politeness/Convention	Serves only to fit the conventions of discourse in this context. Examples of segments that may be coded thus are signatures and salutations
Correction	Corrects some part of the research article in question, either in its claims or in supporting material such as contact information. Often used by article authors or journal staff
Other	Does not make a claim about the validity, reliability, or fruitfulness of the research reported in the article in question and does not fit any of the codes above. Neutral, descriptive titles of posts will usually fit into this category

for the data coded with the codes. When the negotiative, revelatory, and evidential portions of the first six codes were ignored, such that all positive-modality and all negative-modality claims were grouped together, interrater reliability was even greater (Cohen's $\kappa = 0.7957$). The negotiative/revelatory and evidential codes were more subjective because, as noted above, the verbal clues about negotiative and revelatory rhetorical tactics are more subtle and more difficult to interpret than those of positive or negative claim types.

Secondary Codes (Objects of Discussion)

Each text segment was then coded a second time according to the particular aspect of the research article—methods, interpretation, importance, reporting, or "other"—that is addressed by the segment in question (Table 5.2). Interrater reliability for these codes, using 88 different segments in the *PLOS ONE* comments (21.7% of the comments; 13.0% of the entire dataset), was also substantial (Cohen's $\kappa = 0.7884$).

RESULTS

In terms of general textual features, perhaps the most readily apparent difference between the tools examined here is the "formality" of the e-letters and letters to the editor compared to the comments and notes. Although this can

Table 5.2 Secondary Codes Corresponding to Objects of Discussion

Secondary code	Definition
Methods	Addresses the validity or appropriateness of the experimental, observational, or computational methods described in the research article in question
Interpretation	Addresses the validity or reasonableness of the interpretation of the data as reported in the research article in question
Importance	Addresses the significance of the research reported in the research article in question. Such claims may address such issues as the novelty, scope, explanatory power, or fruitfulness of the research or how it fits into the current conversation in the field
Reporting	Addresses the way the research is presented in the article. Such claims may address such issues as the quality of prose, the appropriateness or clarity of figures, or the choice of what data to report and what to leave out of the research article
Other	Any segment that does not fit into one of the other secondary codes above

be a subjective measure, in this case, formality is evidenced by the much greater presence of salutations, institutional affiliations, and contact information, as well as rich descriptions of the topics to be addressed (in order to provide context for the argument) and thorough explanations of points made. The following is the opening paragraph of a letter to the editor in *Science* that was included in the dataset:[4]

> In the report "A common variant on chromosome 9p21 affects the risk of myocardial infarction" (8 June, p. 1491; published online 3 May), A. Helgadottir et al. use relative risks to describe an association between myocardial infarction (MI) and a common sequence variant on a specific chromosome. They conclude that individuals in the population homozygous for this variant have an estimated 1.64-fold greater risk of suffering MI than noncarriers and a 2.02-fold risk for early onset MI cases. Although calculating relative risks and relative risk reduction is widely used to represent experimental results, great care needs to be taken when reporting, interpreting, and characterizing health risks and benefits based primarily on relative risks.[5]

The paragraph opens with a concise summary of the research article it is addressing, including the title of the article and an abbreviation of the list of authors ("A. Helgadottir et al."). This is followed by a concise statement, in the passive voice, of a problem that the authors of the letter see in the interpretation of the data presented in the article. This example is representative of the style of communication across the e-letters and letters to the editor in the dataset used in this study.

Similarly, formal communication can be found in the *PLOS ONE* notes and comments, but much of the communication in these forums does not have these characteristics and reads much more like off-the-cuff conversation. This communication is still professional but more conversational, as in the opening two paragraphs of a comment in *PLOS ONE*:

> [Subject line:] Major problem in the estimates of the rate of gene family extinctions.[6]
>
> This paper addresses an important question: what is the rate and pattern of evolution of the gene repertoire in mammals ? [sic] Indeed, whereas the

---

[4] Throughout this chapter, examples from the dataset are given in the following format. The subject line (if one is present) appears first, followed by the body text. Identifying information for the authors of the examples given is omitted, but idiosyncrasies in writing or presentation, such as typographical errors, are retained. Each paragraph or other segment of text is followed by a footnote listing the primary and secondary codes (speech act and object of discussion, respectively) for that segment.

[5] Speech act: *negative-negotiative*; object of discussion: *interpretation*.

[6] Speech act: *negative-revelatory*; object of discussion: *interpretation*.

evolutionary forces shaping the rate of sequence evolution have been well studied, little is known about the frequency of gene losses or gene gains.[7]

The problem of [this] paper is that the identification of gene losses and gene creations (or duplication) relies exclusively on the analysis of the content of Ensembl gene families. An Ensembl gene family that includes only human genes is considered as a gene family "creation" in the human branch. Conversely, a gene family that is present in chimpanzee and dog but that does not include any human gene is considered as being "extinct" in human. [*sic*][8]

The differences between this comment and the letter excerpted above are subtle but apparent. The comment directly indexes the research article rather than referring to it through a citation, and the style is professional, but several typographical errors are present.

Other examples take a more "familiar" tone, as in this comment (in its entirety) praising the article to which it is attached:

[Subject line:] Very interesting[9]

I found this article to be very interesting. Although ribosomes are ubiquitously required for protein synthesis, discerning the effects of changes in individual ribosomal proteins or rRNA nucleotides has been technically challenging, particularly in vertebrates. We have traditionally had to rely on nature providing us with rare mutants (e.g. Blackfan anemia) for such insight. The gene knockdown approach used here represents a tremendous breakthrough for the field.[10]

Still other comments adopt a similar tone in criticism, as in this comment (also in its entirety):

[Subject line:] The C. elegans ALP/Enigma gene is called alp-1[11]

This paper incorrectly identifies the C. elegans ALP/Enigma as eat-1. It is NOT eat-1. The C. elegans ALP/Enigma was published as alp-1 (see reference 50). The eat-1 gene has not been cloned and maps to a different genetic locus from alp-1. The alp-1 gene encodes the C. elegans ALP/Enigma. Please keep this in mind, the nomenclature for the C. elegans gene is completely wrong in this manuscript.[12]

---

[7] Speech act: *politeness/convention*; object of discussion: *importance*.

[8] Speech act: *negative-revelatory*; object of discussion: *interpretation*.

[9] Speech act: *positive-revelatory*; object of discussion: *importance*.

[10] Speech act: *positive-revelatory*; object of discussion: *importance*.

[11] Speech act: *negative-revelatory*; object of discussion: *reporting*.

[12] Speech act: *negative-revelatory*; object of discussion: *reporting*.

These last two examples also directly index the article in question, and their sentences are shorter and more direct. They have more of the flavor of a personal note than a published article or letter.

If the comments in *PLOS ONE* can be characterized as, by and large, somewhat shorter and less formal versions of the e-letters and letters to the editor in *Science*, the notes in *PLOS ONE* are another step removed. They frequently have the flavor of conversation in the lab, as in this one asking for clarification on the food given to *Drosophila* fruit flies used in an experiment: "Should this be molasses? Apologies if I'm wrong."[13] In this case, the note is attached directly to a passage in the methodology section of the article discussing the media in which the flies are raised, rather than linked from the header of the article as comments are. It's a brief interruption in the description of the methodology, much like a quickly raised hand in a seminar. Unlike a seminar question, however, the note becomes a permanent part of the research article, readable by others as long as the article remains online.

The differences between comments, notes, letters, and e-letters are due at least in part to the editorial policies of *Science*, which include vetting by the journal's editorial staff, and the relatively less rigid standards of *PLOS ONE*, whose comments and notes are vetted only after publication and only if a concern is raised about a comment or note's adherence to "the norms of civilized scientific discussion" and the journal's terms of use. Additionally, the *PLOS ONE* notes are attached directly to the appropriate passage in the research report, which serves to establish context, so this does not need to be done in the text of the note. With regard to antecedent genres (Jamieson, 1975), the e-letters are clearly related to traditional letters to the editor, as they share many of the same formal characteristics such as salutations and careful attention to detail and establishing of the context for the argument—and in fact, the current letters to the editor really are traditional letters that happen to be published in both the print and online editions of the journal. By contrast, the *PLOS ONE* notes and comments have the appearance of blog comments, although some bear a closer resemblance to letters. In fact, it would be possible to divide *PLOS ONE* comments into categories of "blog-like" and "letter-like," based on their level of formality and the presence of conventions such as salutations, signatures, and institutional affiliation. In general, though, they are often informal in tone and sometimes contain typographical errors and infelicities in usage, and they are typically shorter than the e-letters and letters to the editor in *Science*.

The e-letters and letters to the editor also are often accompanied by replies that are solicited by the journal and published alongside the original letters, whereas the comments and notes are published immediately, without formal vetting, and can be replied to at will. The e-letters and letters to the editor also

[13] Speech act: *correction*; object of discussion: *reporting*.

contain names and institutional affiliations and other contact information, whereas the comments and notes in *PLOS ONE* frequently do not. In fact, the comments and notes examined in this study are often pseudonymous, which may very well affect the communication that occurs using those tools. (*PLOS ONE* now requires commenters and annotators to register using their real names and geographical locations.)[14]

Quantitative Textual Analysis

As described above, the text segments in the dataset were subjected to analysis using a 2-part coding scheme analyzing the speech acts enacted by each segment and the objects of discussion that they addressed. The details of this analysis are less important than the broad trends, so I present the results here in summary.

Textual Analysis: Speech Acts

The first test applied to the dataset was an examination of the speech acts (Austin, 1962; Searle, 1969, 1979) enacted by the texts analyzed in this study. The speech acts in the *PLOS ONE* comments and notes demonstrate how different the uses of two fairly similar online communication tools can be. The predominant speech acts in the comments are those employed in the service of politeness or fulfilling the conventions of scientific writing (21.5%), extensions/criticism (13.9%), and positive-revelatory claims (12.7%). "Other" speech acts not covered in the other codes (such as subject headings in replies) make up 13.7% of the sample. In the notes, the predominant speech acts are corrections (24.9%), information (21.4%), links (10.9%) to other material such as blogs mentioning the work reported in the research article, and negative-revelatory claims (8.6%), with "other" speech acts making up 12.1% of the sample.

As noted above, the notes are generally shorter and less formal in tone than the comments. They contain much less of the conventional components of a scientific document such as institutional affiliation and contact information, and like the comments, they may or may not even be signed with the real name of the author. At the time of this study, the Public Library of Science, the publisher, required those who wished to post comments or notes to register, but they were not required to provide information that could positively identify them, although many commenters and annotators are identifiable. (*PLOS ONE* now requires all

---

[14] Authors of research articles may sometimes comment on their own articles. Authors in *PLOS ONE* often post notes on their own articles in order to update contact information, correct typographical errors, or direct the reader to supplementary material available elsewhere on the Web. In the *Science* pieces in this dataset, authors wrote only formal replies to letters and e-letters written by others, and no replies were published by parties other than the article authors.

registered users to provide their full first and last names, geographical location, and a valid email address.)

The e-letters and letters to the editor in *Science* show marked differences both with one another and with the comments and notes in *PLOS ONE*. The predominant speech acts in the e-letters are politeness/convention (36.7%), positive-negotiative claims (22.4%), and negative-negotiative claims (14.3%). "Other" speech acts not covered in the other codes made up 12.2% of the sample. In the letters to the editor, the predominant speech acts are politeness/convention (46.7%), positive-revelatory claims (10.0%), negative-revelatory claims (also 10.0%), and negative-negotiative claims (5.0%). "Other" speech acts make up 20.0% of the sample.

One interesting result here is the difference in rhetorical tactics between the e-letters and the letters to the editor, with the former exhibiting a greater tendency toward negotiative rhetorical tactics and the latter a greater tendency toward revelatory tactics. The predominance of negotiative rhetorical tactics in the e-letters reflects the hedging style that is typical of the professional scientific literature (Hyland, 1998; Penrose & Katz, 2004). There is not an obvious explanation for the difference between the letters and e-letters, but it could indicate an expectation that electronic communication will be more conversational than communication in print media. This trend, however, does not extend to the comments and notes in *PLOS ONE*.

Given the small sample size from *Science*, these results shouldn't necessarily be taken as representative of e-letters and letters to the editor in general. Still, within this particular dataset, the difference between the *PLOS ONE* tools and the *Science* tools is noticeable. The more formal nature of the e-letters and letters to the editor in *Science* relative to the comments and notes in *PLOS ONE* is accompanied by the prominence of the negotiative modality claims and the politeness/convention code. The e-letters and letters to the editor in *Science* are largely used for formal, detailed criticisms of the research articles to which they respond. The *PLOS ONE* notes and comments are less formal but also more diverse in the speech acts that are carried out in them.

Textual Analysis: Objects of Discussion

After the first coding pass for speech acts, each text segment was also coded according to the aspect of the research article that it addresses. This step also uncovered some important differences between the four feedback tools.

In the comments, the most prominent object of discussion is importance (24.1%), followed by methods (16.3%) and interpretation (15.5%). "Other" made up 34.3%. In the notes, reporting (38.5%) was easily the most prominent object of discussion, followed by interpretation (23.7%), with "other" making up 19.5%.

In the e-letters, the predominant objects of discussion were interpretation (40.8%) and importance (16.3%). "Other" objects of discussion constituted

42.9% of the sample, and no text segments (0.0%) in this relatively small sample were addressed to methods or reporting. The letters to the editor were also heavily associated with importance (23.3%) and interpretation (21.7%), with "other" objects of discussion making up 48.3% of the sample. A few segments (6.7%) in the letters to the editor were addressed to methods, and again, no segments were addressed to reporting.

A significant purpose of the comments and letters to the editor, therefore, seems to be to negotiate the status of the work in the research article (cf. discussions of peer review in Berkenkotter & Huckin, 1995; Myers, 1989), either by addressing its importance and significance or the competence or thoroughness of the work, whereas the notes tend to address matters concerning the writing of the manuscript, although, as noted, some notes do address the conclusions drawn from the data, which is also a primary purpose of the e-letters.

DISCUSSION: GENRES IN THE NETWORK

The following paragraph appears in the discussion section of an article published in *PLOS ONE* in December 2006 entitled "Regulated Polyploidy in Halophilic Archaea" (numbers in square brackets below are references listed in the article):

> It has been proposed that a selective advantage of polyploidy in prokaryotes could be a higher resistance to DNA damaging conditions, especially those that induce DNA double strand breaks. The radioresistant species *D. radiodurans* can survive X-ray dosages that lead on average to more than 150 double strand breaks per chromosome [25]. However, a study where the genome copy number of *D. radiodurans* was altered by growth in different media found no correlation between ploidy and resistance to gamma or UV radiation [26]. *H. salinarum* is also extremely resistant to X-ray irradiation. The D_{10} values (10% survival) are 10 kGy for *D. radiodurans* and 5 kGy for *H. salinarum* [27], [28]. For comparison, the D_{10} value of *E. coli* is 0.25 kGy [29]. However, *H. volcanii*, which has a similar genome copy number to *H. salinarum*, is not particularly radioresistant (D_{10} = 1 kGy, unpublished data).

The essence of the argument in this paragraph is that one might reason that having more than one set of chromosomes (a condition known as polyploidy) might confer upon an organism an evolutionary advantage by mitigating the effect of damage to a chromosome, since the organism would have another copy of the chromosome that would be unlikely to have similar damage. However, altering the number of copies of the chromosome set of a particular species of bacterium, *Deinococcus radiodurans*, was found to have no effect on its resistance to x-ray radiation. Also, two species of a primitive single-celled archaeon in the genus *Holoferax*, *H. salinarum* and *H. volcanii*, have very different levels of resistance to radiation despite their having similar numbers of copies of their genomes. Attached to the concluding sentence of this paragraph, about *H. volcanii*, is a note posted by a reader of the article:

> [Subject line:] More detail on radiation resistance of H. volcanii [15]
>
> It would be useful to provide some more information about your results on H. volcanii radiation resistance. I realizeyour [*sic*] comment is about X-rays, but in my hands, H. volcanii is pretty resistant to UV irradiation. Although my work on Haloferax was not published, some of the detail can be found in my PhD thesis which I have put on Google base here: http://www.google.com/bas.... [Note: In the original note this is a working hyperlink.] [16]
>
> I believe (but am not 100% sure) that McCready and others have also shown Haloferax to be UV resistant. Are your results specific for X-rays? Or do you also see little resistance for H. volcanii in terms of UV? [17]

The note asks for more information about the work on radiation resistance in *H. volcanii*. The writer of the note says that she or he has found this species to be "pretty resistant" to ultraviolet radiation and includes a link to the writer's PhD dissertation where some work on UV resistance in *Holoferax* was reported. The writer asks if the article author observes in *H. volcanii* high resistance to UV radiation and low resistance to X-ray radiation or if their results for UV radiation resistant are conflicting. In response, one of the authors of the article wrote a reply attached to the original note:

> [Subject line:] RE: More detail on radiation resistance of H. volcanii [18]
>
> In our hands, Haloferax volcanii is not particularly resistant to UV. The D10 for dark repair of UV-B (254 nm) is around 60-90 J/m2, which is not very different to Escherichia coli. An example of a UV-killing curve for Haloferax can be seen in Guy et al (2006) J Mol Biol 358: 46-56. [19]
>
> Much to [*sic*] the UV-resistance of haloarchaea appears to be due to efficient photolyases, as shown for Halobacterium by McCready et al. However, I do not think that these authors have tested Haloferax volcanii. [20]

This author reports that his research team found *H. volcanii* not to be very resistant to UV radiation and argues that the typically high UV resistance in

---

[15] Speech act: *extension/suggestion/constructive criticism*; object of discussion: *reporting*.

[16] Speech act: *extension/suggestion/constructive criticism*; object of discussion: *reporting*.

[17] Speech act: *question/clarification*; object of discussion: *reporting*.

[18] Speech act: *other*; object of discussion: *other* (because it is simply carried over from the original note).

[19] Speech act: *information*; object of discussion: *interpretation*.

[20] Speech act: *information*; object of discussion: *interpretation*.

similar species appears to be due to the efficiency of their DNA-repair enzymes known as photolyases. One could wonder how the discrepancy between the findings of the two research groups might be reconciled, but the discussion ends there—at least at the time of this writing.

In this example, a small aspect of the research reported in the article has been called into question, namely, the inclusion or exclusion of particular information from the article relating to radiation resistance in a certain kind of microorganism. One of the authors of the article replied by supplying the requested information and offering a possible explanation for why the results turned out the way they did. When scientific journals were found exclusively in print media, this same conversation could have occurred, but it likely would have taken place in private correspondence between the interlocutors.[21] In online journals like *PLOS ONE*, which provide open communication tools such as comments and notes, this conversation happens in the open, and every subsequent reader of this article can read it.

But this is just one example. As discussed above, the four tools for online feedback examined here—comments and notes in *PLOS ONE*, e-letters and letters to the editor in *Science*—are quite diverse, both in the variety of speech acts and objects of discussion found within each tool and in the uses of each tool compared to the others. The diversity of uses of these tools suggests that each tool could support multiple genres—taken as recurrent forms (distributions of speech acts and the objects of discussion that they address) linked to particular social actions—just as, for example, email messages come in many different types serving often very different social functions (Devitt, 2004, p. 45). An added dimension to these results is that unlike different kinds of email messages, which are found in the same medium, the affordances (Gibson, 1986; Norman, 2002) of the online feedback tools in this study are different in sometimes subtle but important ways: The comments, e-letters, and letters to the editor can be attached to the research article as a whole, but only the notes can be specifically targeted to a particular passage. Also, not only might each tool support multiple genres but it appears that any particular genre could be found in more than one tool, although some genres are more prevalent in certain tools than in others. There seems to be, then, some relationship between genres and tools, but it also seems that this correspondence does not account for all variation in the sample. Furthermore, looming in the background throughout all of this are the research articles. We need to understand how the new tools for online feedback and postpublication review interact with the research article in the milieu of the online scientific journal.

---

[21] It also seems unlikely that this conversation would have taken place in letters to the editor, because the perceived importance would not be high enough to justify the publication of a letter occupying space in a print journal.

How Online Texts Can Interact

There are three primary ways that online feedback tools could potentially interact with online research articles: (a) by altering the discursive environment in which the research article sits and thereby altering the conditions of its uptake over time, (b) by altering the text of the research article itself, and (c) by causing the research article to be written differently in the first place than it would have been for a journal without online feedback and postpublication review. In the first of these modes of interaction, the feedback text, such as a comment or e-letter, can be attached to the article, changing the immediate context of the article and creating a cluster of texts that can act in concert as a knowledge artifact. The addition of texts to the article's discursive environment can then alter the article's uptake, contributing to an evolution of the expectations, perceptions, and interpretive frameworks of readers. This differs from printed texts because when online texts are associated in this way, they are linked for every reader, whereas this is not necessarily the case for printed texts, where a single copy may be seen by only a small portion of the intended audience and where, for example, a subsequent letter to the editor has no necessary proximity to the original research article. In the second mode of interaction, the feedback text might actually amend the existing text by questioning or expanding on an argument within the article directly at the point in question. Notes in *PLOS ONE* are often used by article authors to amend their own texts and by other readers to raise questions about specific portions of the article. In the third mode of interaction, the research article may potentially be composed differently than it would be if the author did not anticipate online feedback, so this would constitute a kind of preemptive interaction. A discourse community may discover that a research article intended to act as the seed of an ongoing discussion should be presented differently than one standing alone in a print journal.

The first two modes of interaction were in fact observed in this dataset, while no clear evidence for the third was found outside of one respondent to a brief survey, an author of an article in *PLOS ONE* who indicated that the possibility that others might leave comments or notes on the article affected how she or he wrote it. (The other six respondents to this question indicated that this possibility did not affect how they wrote their articles.) The first mode of interaction, putting a text in the same online space as the article, is exemplified in the *PLOS ONE* comments and the *Science* e-letters and letters to the editor. Below is an example of such a text *PLOS ONE* comment criticizing the methodology in the article to which it is attached:

[Subject line:] Flaws in this paper[22]

The result shown in Figure 1 with FLPe is wrong. A stable selection protocol like the one used here will give nearly 100% recombination with FLPe. Indeed even wtFLP will give nearly 100% recombination in a stable experiment. The authors equate their experiments with experiments in reference 8 to confirm that FLPe gives only 5% recombination with mosaicism. However the experiments of reference 8 were transient expression experiments without selection, not stable expression experiments with selection as performed here. These two types of experiments cannot be compared. Furthermore, the authors show no evidence that codon alteration improved FLP mRNA or protein expression levels. For example, if existing FLPe constructs contained cryptic splicing signals, these can be detected by RT-PCR. Minimally, improved protein expression levels are needed to draw the conclusions presented. Rather, the conclusions are based on a fundamentally flawed experiment that has no control. The simplest explanation of the FLPe result of Figure 1 is that the expression construct is damaged. Hence there is basis to conclude that FLPo is better than FLPe. It may be, but these experiments do not permit that conclusion.[23]

In this case, the comment changes the discursive environment of the original article. A similar comment could have been made about an article in a print journal, but in that case, the commentary would not necessarily be expected to become known to any reader of the article. The comment might appear in a letter in a later issue of the journal, or it might have existed ephemerally as a spoken comment in a research group meeting where the article was brought up in the discussion. In *PLOS ONE*, this comment pushing the article's claims, in Latour's (1987) terms, toward the conditions of their origin, questioning the methods by which the claims came to be made, has become a permanent part of the article. The relationship between the research article and this negative-revelatory argument against its acceptance as canonical scientific knowledge is more than just ephemeral or intertextual (Bakhtin, 1986; Barthes, 2001; Devitt, 1991); they are yoked to each other, part of a single textual unit.

An example of the second form of interaction is exemplified by this note in *PLOS ONE* attached to a different article and posted by one of the authors of that article:

[Subject line:] Plasmids available at Addgene[24]

Please visit http://www.addgene.org/pgvec1?f=c&identifier=PUBMED .. . to find the plasmids from this article.[25]

[22] Speech act: *negative-revelatory*; object of discussion: *other*.

[23] Speech act: *negative-revelatory*; object of discussion: *methods*.

[24] Speech act: *information*; object of discussion: *methods*.

[25] Speech act: *link*; object of discussion: *methods*.

Here, the text of the article is altered by the addition of a link within it to supplemental information, in this case, information on some of the materials used in the experiments reported in the article. This example isn't nearly as dramatic as the previous one, but it still represents an alteration of the text after publication. In the print era, such a notice could be placed in a future issue of the journal, or it could be circulated among an article author's "invisible college" (Crane, 1972) of colleagues working in the same area or related fields, but the article itself would be unchanged.

So it seems that either of these texts could conceivably have existed in another forum as print or oral speech, but their relationship to the research article would have been different. The differences, from a genre-theory perspective, involve a change in the "ecological" relationships between genres.

The Genre Ecosystem of Science

Let's consider here how the particular tools examined in this study might affect what we could call the "genre ecosystem" of science. I use the term *ecosystem* here to mean something similar to the genre ecologies described by Spinuzzi (2002; Spinuzzi & Zachry, 2000) but without their commitment to the principles of cultural-historical activity theory because, as Miller (2007) has argued, such a conception can be problematic for the symbolic and social nature of genres. Rather, what I draw from the genre-ecology concept is the intrinsic relationships between texts that make the enacted genres *dynamic* and *decentralized* players within the larger genre ecosystem. These properties are readily apparent in the texts examined in this study. All texts exist in a fluctuating pool of other texts, but there is a greater diversity of relationships between online texts than between print texts. All texts are used in a particular textual environment. A scientific laboratory usually has a variety of books—textbooks, monographs, laboratory notebooks, and theses and dissertations by former lab members, to name just a few examples—as well as recent issues of one or more scientific journals (although print subscriptions for individuals are becoming less necessary when institutions purchase electronic subscriptions). These texts can be read one after the other, often drawing mental connections between them. In this sense, they exist in the same discursive environment. However, the articles in the journals are connected in a way that two textbooks, say, are not. They have a different relationship to each other. The relationships between online texts are similarly varied, but there is an added dimension to online texts in that they can be linked to each other in more complex patterns, via hyperlinking, and these relationships can be altered much more easily and with much wider effect. Any individual can rip an article out of her copy of a journal or magazine or add marginal notes to one of her books, but those changes occur only in her copies. In online media, these changes can be made universal.

Implications for the Research Article

Even as its discursive environment changes with its move online and the development of various tools for online feedback and postpublication review, the research article as a textual form does not seem to be changing drastically in response to these developments. Articles in *PLOS ONE* and *Science* typically maintain the traditional IMRAD structure common in the scientific literature, and I have seen no overt references to online communication in the articles outside of the occasional link to online supplemental information. Owen (2007) concluded from his own similar observation that the scientific article has undergone "encapsulation"—that is, that its form and content have remained steady even as it has moved into a new medium—and that utopian predictions of its drastically changing or becoming obsolete are misguided. However, the research article in *PLOS ONE* and *Science* has changed in terms of the niche that it occupies in its ecosystem of texts. It's possible, of course, to make too much of a biological metaphor when writing about inanimate things like the written word, but there are some parallels. Just as introducing a new species into a biological ecosystem alters the niches filled by the native species and thus may alter those species, so does introducing new genres into an ecosystem of texts alter the niches occupied by the existing genres and thus possibly those genres.

If print journals are sometimes complex amalgamations of various genres such as research articles (Bazerman, 1988), review articles (Myers, 1991), short communications (Blakeslee, 1994), editorials, news features, book reviews, and others, then electronic journals are even more so, with the introductions of discussion forums, annotation functions, and other features mentioned above. The textual environment in which the research article sits is changing significantly, at least in the journals that employ some form of online feedback or postpublication review. Bazerman (1988) contrasted books and journal articles in Newton's time by writing that, due to their comparatively slow publication time and limited distribution, "books tend to present self-contained universes, accounts complete in themselves with little opportunity for response, except in the muffled comments of the unsatisfied reader" (p. 130). Journals, by contrast, had shorter publication times and wider distribution, and Newton found, to his dismay, that they encouraged public criticism of his ideas:

> Just as correspondence networks had served to increase the amount and immediacy of criticism, the journal made the critical activity public, casting the natural philosopher into the regular role of public defender of his work. The role of the third-party audience became important in the resolution of disputes. (p. 135)

In some senses, electronic media represent another step in an organic evolution from book publishing to the circulation of journals, in that the publication cycle decreases further and the scope of distribution can increase. But in other senses, online media are as different from print media as the latter are from oral speech, particularly in the ways that texts can be collaboratively edited, added to, and modified. The results above show that the new online feedback tools appearing in the milieu of the research article in some online journals fosters a kind of communication that would probably have greatly troubled Newton. The research article in these spaces is even less a discrete unit of scientific argument than it had been in the print media. In online journals, the research article is the core around which a cluster of texts arises, which can significantly affect it as a knowledge artifact. It therefore constitutes a new genre that will be of continuing scholarly interest.

REFERENCES

Austin, J. L. (1962). *How to do things with words*. Cambridge, MA: Harvard University Press.

Bakhtin, M. M. (1986). The problem of speech genres. In C. Emerson & M. Holquist (Eds.), *Speech genres and other late essays* (pp. 60–102). Austin, TX: University of Texas Press.

Barthes, R. (2001). The death of the author. In V. B. Leitch, W. E. Cain, L. Finke, B. Johnson, J. McGowan, & J. J. Williams (Eds.), *The Norton anthology of theory and criticism* (pp. 1466–1470). New York, NY: Norton.

Bazerman, C. (1988). *Shaping written knowledge: The genre and activity of the experimental article in science*. Madison,: WI University of Wisconsin Press.

Bazerman, C. (1994). Systems of genres and the enactment of social intentions. In A. Freedman & P. Medway (Eds.), *Genre and the new rhetoric* (pp. 79–101). London, UK: Taylor & Francis.

Berkenkotter, C., & Huckin, T. N. (1995). *Genre knowledge in disciplinary communication: Cognition/culture/power*. Hillsdale, NJ: Lawrence Erlbaum.

Blakeslee, A. M. (1994). The rhetorical construction of novelty: Presenting claims in a letters forum. *Science, Technology, & Human Values, 19*(1), 88–100.

Crane, D. (1972). *Invisible colleges: Diffusion of knowledge in scientific communities*. Chicago, IL: University of Chicago Press.

Crawford, S. Y., Hurd, J. M., & Weller, A. C. (1996). *From print to electronic: The transformation of scientific communication*. Medford, NJ: Information Today.

Devitt, A. J. (1991). Intertextuality in tax accounting: Generic, referential, and functional. In C. Bazerman & J. Paradis (Eds.), *Textual dynamics of the professions: Historical and contemporary studies of writing in professional communities* (pp. 336–355). Madison,: WI University of Wisconsin Press.

Devitt, A. J. (2004). *Writing genres*. Carbondale,: IL Southern Illinois University Press.

Garvey, W. D., & Griffith, B. C. (1972). Communication and information processing within scientific disciplines: Empirical findings for psychology. *Information Storage and Retrieval, 8*(3), 123–126.

Geisler, C. (2004). *Analyzing streams of language: Twelve steps to the systematic coding of text, talk, and other verbal data*. New York, NY: Pearson Longman.

Gibson, J. J. (1986). *The ecological approach to visual perception*. Hillsdale, NJ: Lawrence Erlbaum.

Hahn, K. L. (2001). *Electronic ecology: A case study of electronic journals in context*. Washington, DC: Association of Research Libraries.

Howard, R. G. (2005). Sustainability and radical rhetorical closure: The case of the 1996 "Heaven's Gate" newsgroup campaign. *Journal of Communication & Religion*, *28*(1), 99–130.

Hyland, K. (1998). *Hedging in scientific research articles*. Amsterdam, The Netherlands: John Benjamins.

Jamieson, K. M. (1975). Antecedent genre as rhetorical constraint. *Quarterly Journal of Speech*, *61*(4), 406–415.

Latour, B. (1987). *Science in action: How to follow scientists and engineers through society*. Cambridge, MA: Harvard University Press.

Miller, C. R. (1984). Genre as social action. *Quarterly Journal of Speech*, *70*(2), 151–167.

Miller, C. R. (1994). Rhetorical community: The cultural basis of genre. In A. Freedman & P. Medway (Eds.), *Genre and the new rhetoric* (pp. 67–78). London, UK: Taylor & Francis.

Miller, C. R. (2007). Tracing genres through organizations [Book review]. *Technical Communication Quarterly*, *16*(4), 476–480.

Myers, G. (1989). *Writing biology: Texts in the social construction of scientific knowledge*. Madison, WI: University of Wisconsin Press.

Myers, G. (1991). Stories and styles in two molecular biology review articles. In C. Bazerman & J. Paradis (Eds.), *Textual dynamics of the professions: Historical and contemporary studies of writing in professional communities* (pp. 45–75). Madison, WI: University of Wisconsin Press.

Norman, D. A. (2002). *The design of everyday things*. New York, NY: Basic.

Orlikowski, W. J., & Yates, J. (1994). Genre repertoire: The structuring of communicative practices in organizations. *Administrative Science Quarterly*, *39*(4), 541–574.

Owen, J. S. Mackenzie. (2007). *The scientific article in the age of digitization*. Dordrecht, The Netherlands: Springer.

Penrose, A. M., & Katz, S. B. (2004). *Writing in the sciences: Exploring conventions of scientific discourse* (2nd ed.). New York, NY: Pearson Longman.

Schryer, C. F. (1993). Records as genre. *Written Communication*, *10*(2), 200–234.

Schryer, C. F. (1994). The lab vs. the clinic: Sites of competing genres. In A. Freedman & P. Medway (Eds.), *Genre and the new rhetoric* (pp. 105–124). London, UK: Taylor & Francis.

Searle, J. R. (1969). *Speech acts: An essay in the philosophy of language*. London, UK: Cambridge University Press.

Searle, J. R. (1979). *Expression and meaning: Studies in the theory of speech acts*. Cambridge, UK: Cambridge University Press.

Spinuzzi, C. (2002). *Modeling genre ecologies*. Paper presented at SIGDOC'02, Toronto, Canada.

Spinuzzi, C. (2004). *Four ways to investigate assemblages of texts: Genre sets, systems, repertoires, and ecologies*. Paper presented at SIGDOC'04, Memphis, TN.

Spinuzzi, C., & Zachry, M. (2000). Genre ecologies: An open-system approach to under-standing and constructing documentation. *ACM Journal of Computer Documentation*, *24*(3), 169–181.

Swales, J. M. (1990). *Genre analysis: English in academic and research settings*. Cambridge, UK: Cambridge University Press.

Swales, J. M. (2004). *Research genres: Explorations and applications*. Cambridge, UK: Cambridge University Press.

Yates, J., & Orlikowski, W. (2002). Genre systems: Structuring interaction through communicative norms. *Journal of Business Communication*, *39*(1), 13–35.

http://dx.doi.org/10.2190/SCIC6

CHAPTER 6

The Chemistry Liveblogging Event: The Web Refigures Peer Review

Michelle Sidler

ABSTRACT

This chapter examines the connections and tensions between Web 2.0 technologies and traditional scientific peer review. Specifically, it considers the role that the blog of British chemist Paul Docherty played in the global critique of an article accepted by the well-respected *Journal of the American Chemical Society* (*JAC*). Questioning the article's claims, Docherty and others replicated a key experiment, and Docherty liveblogged his experiment, uploading photographs and data in real time. This public, interactive, and visual refutation ultimately led to the paper's withdrawal. The Docherty case shows that digital technologies can blur the line between manuscript and published work, resulting in a disruption of the established peer review process. This controversy also demonstrates that even publications in the most prestigious journals are vulnerable to the near-instant access and scrutiny afforded by the Internet.

On August 17, 2009, Carmen Drahl began a story in *Chemical & Engineering News* (*C&EN*) with the following passage:

On July 21, the *Journal of the American Chemical Society* published new papers online. That was nothing out of the ordinary. But within 24 hours, something extraordinary happened. Chemists from around the world converged online, at an organic chemistry blog, to discuss one of those manuscripts, repeat its experiments, and examine its conclusions. The story is a particularly vivid example of how the Web is changing communication in science and should encourage more chemists to tune in to online discussions. (p. 47)

99

The incident Dahl describes is the online reaction to a peer reviewed article in the *Journal of the American Chemical Society* (*JACS*), "Reductive and Transition-Metal-Free: Oxidation of Secondary Alcohols by Sodium Hydride," by Wang, Zhang, and Wang (2009). The chemical reaction reported in the article was extraordinary—even unbelievable—to many chemists, prompting a worldwide informal peer review that demonstrated how powerful online communications have become in the scientific community. Leveraging the speed and connectivity of blogging, scientists—most notably Paul Docherty, who liveblogged the experiment in his *Totally Synthetic* blog—challenged X. Wang et al.'s findings in a flurry of discussion and reporting over a period of just a few days. This controversy demonstrates that even publications in the most prestigious journals are vulnerable to the near-instant access and scrutiny afforded by the Internet. This chapter will explore the connection between Web 2.0 technologies and the demise of X. Wang et al.'s article, tracing the manuscript progression from initial online publication on the *JACS* website to its eventual withdrawal from the journal. The Docherty case shows that digital technologies increasingly blur the line between manuscript and published work, resulting in a disruption of the established peer review and reception process that has traditionally been central to scientific discourse.

Drahl's (2009) reporting of Docherty's liveblog in *C&EN* adds another rhetorical layer to this story as well: *C&EN* is the weekly magazine of the American Chemical Society (ACS), the flagship organization for chemists and the world's largest scientific society, with more than 164,000 members and 39 journals (ACS, 2012). All ACS members have access to *C&EN*, so Drahl's article reflects ACS's recognition of the growing impact of online scientific communication, including discourse published outside the mainstream of peer reviewed journals. Such recognition is doubly significant because it comes from ACS, whose scholarly communication and publishing practices are fairly conservative compared to most chemistry societies. And, like many science journals, the process of maintaining *JACS* has been something of a black box: peer review is secretive, material production is a private enterprise, and access to the published work is reserved for those with costly subscriptions. Consequently, scientists who advocate for more open online publishing practices have encountered resistance from the ACS.

Increasingly, the Internet is loosening the tight grip of publishers like the ACS, offering scientists the opportunity to both publish new findings and respond to others' findings without the sanction of proprietary publishing entities. Docherty's liveblogging event, for example, is a salient example of what Michael Nielsen (2012) calls "networked science," the 21st-century turn from scientific discourse in its "inert, passive state" to a "unified system that brings that information alive" (p. 207). In *Reinventing Discovery: The New Era of Networked Science*, Nielsen presents a manifesto for science and society, arguing that digital tools have the potential to change the way all knowledge is constructed and alter the way science works. Networked science catalyzes the process of discovery, rhetoric, and reception in ways that print-based publishing practices cannot. Nielsen argues that knowledge production is happening in spaces outside of traditional journal publications with unprecedented speed and innovative multimodal tools. By following the trail of online discussions, rhetoric of science scholars can capture information about the reception of scientific works in near-real time, identifying the strategies scientists use to both support and refute claims—and how technological tools have become a part of scientific rhetoric. Even more significant, we have the opportunity to be virtual witnesses to—and reporters of—a potential paradigm shift in scientific discourse practices.

PEER REVIEW AND RECEPTION STUDIES

The peer review of scientific journal articles has received substantial attention from the rhetoric of science community (Berkenkotter, 1995; Berkenkotter & Huckin, 1994; Gross, 2006). Gross (2006) analyzed peer review documents from a biology journal and argues that peer review is a contentious process, producing a series of critical negotiations between authors, editors, and reviewers. Building from Gross' research, Berkenkotter and Huckin (1994) performed a qualitative study of one biologist during her submission, revision, and eventual acceptance of a journal article. They found that positive response from reviewers often depended on the referees' acceptance of knowledge claims about work that happens in scientists' laboratories. Both studies reveal a series of argumentative strategies steeped in conventional illocutionary acts that "get things done in the world, either through direct or indirect means" (Berkenkotter & Huckin, 1994) and illustrate the deep professional expectations and cultural conventions surrounding the peer review process.

Both studies also highlight the adversarial role of reviewers: at the core of peer review is the science community's trust in scholars to arbitrate quality research. Editors are also crucial in this trust relationship because they ultimately judge manuscripts to be worthy of publication, determining the endpoint of the prepublication peer review process. Gross (2006) notes that once this certification occurs and papers are sent to print, evidence of peer review exchanges is lost:

> Publication obliterates all traces of the procedure by which the knowledge it asserts is certified; as a consequence of this obliteration, publication renews the credibility peer review undermines. The candidate knowledge in published papers is now ready to be tested against broader consensuses of scientists and, more importantly, again the world. (p. 109)

Once articles are published, records of the reviewers' concerns are not accessible, and the wider scientific community is free to draw its own conclusions about the scientific research. Whereas peer review is a process of social consensus and trust, vetting among the community involves scrutiny within the world, including comparison to other data and even potentially replications of the experiments.

Gross (2006) argues that the two processes—peer review and broader scientific reception—are fairly distinct, separated by the official recognition that accompanies an article's publication. This distinction has been implicitly invoked by advocates of reception studies as well, who recommend more studies to examine the impact of scientific works after their publication. Paul, Charney, and Kendall (2001) most vehemently critique the rhetoric of science community for concentrating too much on processes like peer review that occur before or during "the moment," which is "when an article is accepted for publication by a journal and the history that leads up to that acceptance" (p. 372). They contend that to understand how scientists receive the work of others, long-term studies of published works that follow the reception of texts after the "moment" are needed. To achieve this, Paul et al. advocate a multimethodological approach, which recognizes a range of empirical and hermeneutic methods intended to explore the reactions of both individuals and the larger scientific community. Harris (2005) and Ceccarelli (2005) maintain that reception studies are already occurring in rhetoric of science scholarship, but they also call for more research that employs a variety of methods for tracking the long-term impact of scientific publications. Harris (2005) in particular notes that the field has already laid the groundwork for this research with its original focus on the "production" of scientific discourse (p. 253).

In short, scholars of scientific peer review and those who advocate reception studies of scientific discourse are two sides of the same critical coin. Scholars of peer review concentrate on the certification of scientific knowledge before and during "the moment" and advocates of reception studies call for studies of impact long after it, but both imply "the moment," a distinct time when that research is accepted and published. Using "the moment" as a focal point, both peer review scholars and advocates of reception studies share several goals: to illustrate the life cycle of scientific discourse, to discover the expectations and practices that lead to accepted research, and to understand the ways in which rhetorical strategies and generic conventions impact the perceived quality of scientific works.

Largely missing from both camps are discussions about the discourse technologies involved in the publication process and their resulting impact on peer review, long-term reception, and even the certainty of a distinct "moment" of publication. Karen Lunsford (2007) argues that digital technologies facilitate what she calls "distributed publication systems," wherein "information necessary to support a specific claim may be scattered among different resources" and that information may be released and certified at different times using a variety of digital media. Moreover, I would add that peer review and reception of scientific works create distributed review systems, involving various genres, time frames, and technologies to understand the quality and impact of scientific research. Nowhere is the distribution of scientific discourse more noticeable than in the controversy involving X. Wang et al.'s (2009) article, wherein several groups of chemists interpreted the authors' reported lab findings through the larger body of chemistry research—even citing older studies not mentioned in the original work—and then took that narrative into their own laboratories in order to re-create it. The case is one example of technologies' tendency to disrupt scientific discourse practices, calling into question both the peer review process and the division between prepublication review and long-term reception itself.

Other chapters in this volume explore the ways in which digital technologies are breaking down the time distinction between peer review and print publication. Gross (2006) describes *Retraction Watch*, a blog dedicated to exposing and discussing cases of plagiarism and fraud. Although the journalist-authors of this blog generally report on cases that occur after official publication, these papers are often retracted from publication, calling into question the prepublication peer review process itself. Gross contends that no other medium could accommodate the rhetorical parameters of *Retraction Watch*: appealing to a small but dedicated readership while at the same time both maintaining a large archive of past cases and reporting on current cases as they occur. Christian Casper's chapter in this volume reports on postpublication peer review encouraged by online journals like *PLOS One*, which allows public comments in the same space as published research. The editors argue that this process allows the scientific community to more quickly and accurately vet published research. In addition, the editors encourage publication of preprint referee comments alongside published works, hoping "to make the review process more transparent as well as stimulating informed debate about published papers" (PLOS One, 2012) Rather than "obliterating" the process of peer review, *PLOS One* opens it up to scrutiny. The editors use the space and speed afforded by the journal's online-only status to create ecologies of discourse surrounding articles that span both prepublication and postpublication review. The article itself is only one text—and one genre—among many, enacting Nielsen's (2012) culture of networked science as part of the formal editorial process.

PAUL DOCHERTY'S BLOG

In the Introduction to this volume, Jonathan Buehl describes the blog of Rosie Redfield and its impact on the Mono Lake project; Paul Docherty's *Totally Synthetic* blog is well known in the chemistry community for performing similar critiques (see Figure 6.1). Primarily moderated and authored by Paul Docherty, a medicinal chemist, *Totally Synthetic* is a blog written by and for organic chemists; its purpose is to summarize and critique published research about chemical syntheses. The blog's title, *Totally Synthetic*, is a reference to total

Figure 6.1. The homepage of *Totally Synthetic* (Docherty, 2012).
Copyright © 2009 Paul Docherty. Reproduced with permission.

synthesis, the process by which smaller compounds are combined to create complex organic compounds. From 2006 to 2012, Docherty wrote in his blog about twice a month, each time discussing a recently published article. He critiqued articles for their accuracy, effectiveness, and eloquence when reporting syntheses. His critique of individual articles often led to broader comments about the editorial decisions of the host journals. The website has other features, including an editorial page and a section for news updates. However, the journal article review pages are by far the most populated areas of the site.

In addition to his own critiques, Docherty invited comments from other chemists about the articles he reviewed. Over the course of 6 years, *Totally Synthetic* gathered a community that included about a dozen regular commenters plus hundreds who left only one or two comments. Blog entries averaged about 20 comments each, but the average was much higher during the blog's most active period in 2008 and 2009. Most entries and comments are informal, but they are written to other chemists who perform similar work, as evidenced by the nomenclature, which is generally unfamiliar to lay readers and often written in a truncated style. This dense, shorthanded discourse reinforces the commenters' *ethos*, allowing them to reference complex information in what often appears to be a rapid-fire discussion format.

The participants' *ethos* also rests in their ability to reference other scientific research or scientists as well as the major journals in which they publish. For example, Docherty's (2009a) blog post from March 30, 2009, entitled "Vincorine," is a critique of the paper, "Total Synthesis of the *Akuammiline*

Alkaloid (±)-Vincorine" by Zhang, Huang, Shen and Qin (2009), which purports to describe the first total synthesis of this compound. Docherty is not convinced of its novelty and ends his critique by stating that the published synthesis is not new:

> From here, the synthesis is fairly unremarkable (and I must say I'm surprised that it was deemed JACS worthy—though all the total syntheses seem to be going into Angewandte [*sic*] these days . . .). Nice stuff in some ways, but there's nothing very new here.

Docherty is surprised that this research, which seems to replicate previous published work, would be accepted for a prestigious journal like *JAC*. The first commenter to respond to Docherty's post, whose login name is 9-BDH, disagreed: "Actually, it is the first synthesis of this target. Vollhardt and Levy only completed the tetracyclic core, while Overman's work on this particular molecule is unpublished." This brief correspondence is rich with expert knowledge of the field and its major players. First, 9-BDH refutes Docherty's contention that this paper replicates others, showing gaps in the published research and identifying scientists who research vincorine, including those who have unpublished work, which may not be as well known. Second, and more significant to discussions about the future of scientific publishing, is Docherty's side commentary about the place of publication. He critiques *JACS* for publishing this article and then notes that another journal, *Angewandte Chemie* (the flagship journal for the German chemical society which Docherty shortens to Angewandte), has been publishing more total syntheses than *JACS*. This critique is one of many that Docherty applies to *JACS* throughout the blog. Indeed, both Docherty and several of his commenters use *Totally Synthetic* as a space to scrutinize *JACS* for what they often believe are problematic publishing standards and practices. In the process, these scientists not only hold the published works up for critique, but the major journals as well. Such discussions offer a rich opportunity for rhetoric of science scholars to understand the reception of not only research articles but the also the journals who publish them. Throughout the *Totally Synthetic* blog, comments, questions, and insights about the peer review process are evident as well, providing a written record of the ways in which scientists negotiate publishing practices and knowledge construction.

LIVEBLOGGING AND SCIENTIFIC RECEPTION

Increasing disappointment in the publishing practices of *JACS* set the stage for the X. Wang et al. (2009) controversy, catapulting Docherty and his blog into an international discussion about publishing and peer review within chemistry. On July 21, 2009, Docherty (2009b) posted a fairly routine blog entry, summarizing and complimenting an article from *JACS* entitled "Total Synthesis and Structural Revision of (±)-Tricholomalides A and B" by Wang, Min, and Danishefsky (2009). However, within hours of posting the entry, regular readers of Docherty's blog left comments about the X. Wang et al.'s (2009) paper. X. Wang et al.'s article describes the oxidation (loss of electrons) of benzylic alcohol, turning it into a ketone compound. Ketones are important compounds in organic chemistry because ketones are prevalent in humans (and other mammals) and because of their usefulness as solvents. As a result, organic chemists often look for more efficient and effective syntheses for converting common alcohols to ketones. The authors claim to have used NaH (sodium hydride) as an oxidant, which would be a breakthrough in this process because NaH is a hydride and should not combine to make ketones. As Docherty commented in an interview for *Chemistry World*, "A quick inspection of Wang's results astounded me, as he seemed to suggest that black was apparently now white" (Hadlington, 2009). Implicit in this skepticism is the conventional scientific understanding that counterintuitive, paradigm-shifting results should have received intense scrutiny throughout the peer review process. Wiley-Blackwell Publishing ran a story about this case in its newsletter that sums up the community's concerns about the peer review process:

> Here, something had gone wrong with pre-publication review—the paper had got past the reviewers and the editors at this journal, which seems quite extraordinary when the results being reported were surprising and the potential flaws so obvious to many in the chemistry community immediately on publication of the article. (Hames, 2010)

The extraordinary nature of this publication prompted many scientists to question not only the results of the experiment but also the peer review process itself. And this scrutiny began almost immediately after the ASAP publication of the article, further casting doubt on the quality of its peer review.

Figure 6.2 is a screenshot of the first comments regarding X. Wang et al.'s (2009) article that appeared below Docherty's original post. The commenters almost exclusively ignore Docherty's discussion of Wang, Min, and Danishefsky's (2009) article; instead, they link to, and then question, the X. Wang et al. piece.

The discussion begins with Liquidcarbon's comment, "WTF is going on here? —> http://pubs.acs.org/doi/abs/10.1021/ja904224y." This short entry performs two distinct tasks while exploiting several technical and cultural devices. First, Liquidcarbon employs the truncation "WTF" in all caps to get the attention of blog readers, pulling them away from the discussion of Z. Wang et al.'s (2009) text and toward the link for X. Wang et al.'s (2009) article (hence the arrow). With his use of WTF to indicate extreme concern about the article, Liquidcarbon's comment disrupts the broader conversation and power dynamic of Docherty's blog entry. Like other chemists who have written about the article, he

Figure 6.2. Comments from Docherty's blog post "Total Synthesis and Structural Revision of (±)-Tricholomalides A and B." Copyright © 2009 Paul Docherty. Reproduced with permission.

recognized immediately that the reported result "goes completely against received chemical knowledge" (Murray-Rust, 2009). Although it was not uncommon for commenters on *Totally Synthetic* to veer off the topic of the article to which they were responding, it was extraordinary for a commenter to utterly ignore the article and introduce a completely new topic in the Comments section. In Docherty's own words, the commenters "hi-jacked" his post (Docherty, 2009c).

In addition to his overt disruption of Docherty's post, Liquidcarbon's comment includes a link to the article in question. The anatomy of this link is worth describing, because it is the result of a series of what Bowker (2008) calls protocols: agreements and standards that facilitate digital archiving and memory practices (pp. 23–24). Included in the link are two pieces of information: first is the place of publication, *ACS*, as indicated by pubs.acs.org, and second is the Digital Object Identifier (DOI), encompassed by the sequence of numbers, 10.1021/ja904224y. DOIs act as stable identifiers for online artifacts such as individual journal articles. Most science blogs, including *Totally Synthetic*, use DOIs to easily locate and retrieve journal articles that are available through online databases and portals. Many times, as is the case with the X. Wang et al.'s (2009) manuscript, articles are available online well before they appear in a print volume, in a process often called As Soon as Publishable (ASAP). ASAP papers are usually available on journals' websites before they are even assigned volume, issue, and page numbers (and in some cases they even appear in draft form rather than print-ready copy). Articles can exist in this pseudo-published state for weeks or even months, so DOIs substitute for other citation information and allow easy online linking. The DOI system, a seemingly mundane identification tool, is in reality another indication that the linear scientific publishing process has become dispersed and recursive. Traditionally, the moment when an article is "published" has been constructed as a pivot point of knowledge production, the time and space when an article is officially made available to the larger scientific community. For most scientific journals, this easy distinction is no longer applicable: by publishing manuscripts as soon as they are accepted, editors have exposed the drafting process of journal articles and made them available for review and critique before they are finalized. The publication cycle is sped up, and scientific reception can occur almost instantaneously.

Referencing scientific papers through DOI linking is a commonplace occurrence in online scientific discourse, but as the X. Wang et al. (2009) case unfolded, this DOI protocol became a reminder that scientific publishing practices have accelerated scientific reception. Within a few hours after Liquidcarbon posted his comment on *Totally Synthetic*, another commenter, J., suggested that the community test X. Wang et al.'s findings: "Does anyone want to pull a few things off the shelf and see if this actually works?" Docherty agreed to replicate a crucial element, which he was able to do because the experiment involved standard chemicals found in his Arrow Therapeutics lab and took less than a couple of days to perform. Along with Docherty, at least five other scientists attempted to recreate X. Wang et al.'s experiment—each using slightly different conditions to try out different oxidation scenarios—but Docherty's attempt drew the most attention because he actually performed a liveblog, recording the events of his experiment as they unfolded. Scientists from around the world followed Docherty and others as they reported results in near-real time online.

Docherty used both textual descriptions and visual images to relay data at each stage of the experimental process, further exposing the black box inner workings of both peer review and laboratory practices. Textually, Docherty described each stage of the process in detail and included a timeline to verify the length of the experiment. Unlike formal scientific publications, which generally employ second person or even passive voice (Gross, Harmon, & Reidy, 2002), Docherty's blog reads like a first-person narrative account, including a conversational tone, personal details, informal speech, and typos:

> 10.30 – Took the dried flask out from the oven, flushed it with nitrogen and vacuum. Added (dry) THF, and cooled with ice water. Also, found the big ice scoop I've been looking for ages on the biology floor. Thieving bastards . . .

> 10.40 – Added the alcohol (626 mg, 4 mmols), left it for a couple of minutes and then stuck in the sodium hydride (60% dispersion in oil, 320 mg, 8 mmols) in one go. Cue fizzing.

Although informal, these passages authenticate Docherty as an expert in organic chemistry, displaying sophisticated knowledge of the field through dense shorthanded terminology. His expert credibility is heightened by his attention to true-reporting detail: exact measurements are recorded and detailed preparations are described. Less predictably, the playful language Docherty employs, like the phrase "Cue fizzing," permeates the liveblog (and Docherty's site as a whole). In many ways, the liveblog served as an open lab notebook along the lines described by Wickman in this volume, facilitating informal recordkeeping for Docherty, describing a protocol for others to replicate and supplying primary data for further analysis. Like open-lab notebooks, Docherty's goal is to share and compare his results with others, hastening the speed of scientific reception and destabilizing the traditional black box of closed peer review as well as the linear process of print publication. The X. Wang et al. (2009) case illustrates that the temporal space between draft manuscript and final publication of an article is increasingly nebulous, and scientists in the online community often spontaneously colonize that space, crowding the conversation while article manuscripts are still in the ASAP publication stage.

Along with social networking tools, Docherty employed several other digital media to report his results in near-real time, including mobile technologies and digital inscription devices (Latour & Woolgar, 1986). Docherty took pictures on his iPhone to upload in near-real time, affirming the authenticity of both his liveblog and the results he reports. Figure 6.3 and 6.4 are photographs of the reaction taken on Docherty's iPhone.

In addition, Docherty uploaded digital renderings of the liquid chromatography–mass (LCM) spectrometry and the nuclear magnetic resonance (NMR) spectrometry to show primary data results as they were produced, in near-real time. He accessed all of these communication devices—including the blog itself—in the space of the physical lab, allowing him to record and publish his results in near-real time. Such devices serve as Latourian "plug-ins," various applications and abilities that create a discursive assemblage of information, more diverse and distributed than traditional scientific genres (Latour, 2007, p. 207). Such plug-ins also allow Docherty to circumvent the traditional print publication process by self-publishing his replication results and his evaluation of X. Wang et al.'s (2009) article. Rather than follow the prescribed genres of postpublication peer review (such as submitting a response letter to the journal), Docherty leveraged digital, open access, and interactive discourse tools to speed up the process of postpublication peer review, create a multimedia collection of supporting information, and provide space for other comments as the experiment unfolded. Here, Docherty implicitly critiques mainstream publishing practices, offering a proof of concept for the notion that Web 2.0-enabled science is more efficient, accurate, and collaborative than the print-based journal model.

Figure 6.3. The fizzing reaction from the Docherty's liveblogged experiment.
Copyright © 2009 Paul Docherty. Reproduced with permission.

Figure 6.4. The orange color reaction resulting from the Docherty's
liveblogged experiment, which demonstrates the synthesis.
Copyright © 2009 Paul Docherty. Reproduced with permission.

PROOF OF CONCEPT FOR ONLINE
PEER REVIEW

The efforts of Docherty and other scientists quickly affirmed most skeptics' suspicions that X. Wang et al.'s (2009) results were probably caused by an oxygen contaminant in the experiment. Within weeks after the online post-publication peer review began, X. Wang et al. responded by posting supporting information on the *JACS* website that included experiment protocol descriptions and spectra printouts, but generally, the scientific community dismissed this data. Meanwhile, *JACS* editors were silent about the controversy, and the online manuscript remained conspicuously in its ASAP form without going to print. On December 23, 2009, a correction note was added to it, and then on January 20, 2010, the correction was replaced with a formal retraction statement. Sometime shortly after that, the original manuscript was pulled completely off the *JACS* site, and now only one sentence is available to anyone who searches for the article: "This manuscript has been withdrawn for scientific reasons."

In the end, the fate of this one individual manuscript is less important than the proof-of-concept it demonstrated. Many in the online science community praised the work of Docherty and others, arguing that this case establishes blog review as another element of the review process (Hames, 2010; Murray-Rust, 2009), and as of August 2012, Docherty's liveblog entry had accumulated over 128,000 views and more than 200 comments. Shortly after the liveblogging event, Chris Smith (2009) interviewed Docherty for a *Chemistry World* podcast. Smith described Docherty's work as a

> stage beyond peer review, we've now got blog level peer review, which is putting researchers like you [Docherty] onto interesting things and then getting you looking at them in a new way and finding novel things about them, even catching people out.

Docherty tacitly agreed with Smith but emphasized the importance of speed and *ethos* to the success of the review:

> I think one of the most useful things is we are able to draw some new conclusions very quickly, I think within 40 hours, the reactions were all done, the results were there, but I think very important to this was everybody knew who I was. If I had been anonymous at this point, I could have been saying anything, even if it affected my career. The fact that the blog is identified as being owned by me brings some credibility to the results.

Like Smith, Docherty argues that blogs provide a new space and time for peer review that occurs much sooner than response outlets in peer reviewed journals. However, Docherty adds that this process depends on bloggers' willingness to forego anonymity and establish their credibility through quality laboratory work and extensive online interactions. Blogs and other social networking tools are often critiqued for their accommodation of anonymity, supporting the proliferation of potentially false or misleading information (Peer Pressure, 2009; Waldrop, 2008). Ironically, the increased awareness of online anonymity calls into question traditional peer review practices, which are performed mostly through anonymous blind peer review. Like the *Totally Synthetic* community, many in the online science community openly critique blind peer review as counterproductive and inefficient (Giles, 2007; McCabe, 2012; Neylon, 2011).

One notable critic of blind peer review and champion of Docherty's blogging efforts is Jean-Claude Bradley, a chemist and blogger at Drexel University. Bradley is well known within the online science community for his advocacy of open peer review practices and open-lab notebooks (His open-lab notebook, *UsefulChem*, is considered an exemplar.) Soon after Docherty's liveblogging event, Bradley discussed the X. Wang et al. article in his chemistry class, prompting researchers in his lab, Khalid Mirza and Marshall Moritz, to attempt the replication. They posted several short YouTube clips depicting their experiment on *UsefulChem*'s OpenNotebook and logged each step of the 6-hour experiment (Mirza & Moritz, 2009), offering both a visual and textual chronology that further supported the findings of other scientists. On his own blog, Bradley summarizes the experiment and presents NMR spectra showing that none of the benzene alcohol converted to acetophenon. He concludes the blog entry by referencing other online conversations about the manuscript and making another pointed statement about the value of online scientific discourse:

> In a comment on Carbon-Based Curiosities, European Chemist points to a 1965 paper where oxidants on the surface of NaH are likely responsible for oxidative behavior (Lewis JOC). This would certainly explain why some researchers are reporting some oxidation products but with widely divergent yields. For example, Totally Synthetic reported a 15% NMR yield for the conversion of the 4-chloro derivative to the corresponding ketone while Wang isolated the product in 86% yield. (Bradley, 2009, underlined phrases were hyperlinks in the original text)

The first paragraph in this quote references a blog post in *Carbon-Based Curiosities*, another organic chemistry blog written by three graduate students (Excimer, 2009). Like *Totally Synthetic*, blog postings in *Carbon-Based Curiosities* often focus on recently published journal articles. One commenter on this blog found a journal article published in *The Journal of Organic Chemistry* (Lewis, 1965) that offers a reason for the oxidation of the benzene alcohol: surface contamination containing oxygen. Bradley uses this example to critique X. Wang et al. (2009) for not performing adequate background research. To illustrate this point, he links seamlessly through several texts in different mediated spaces, including older journal articles and the current article under discussion.

The final paragraph of Bradley's blog entry elevates his discussion to a broader commentary on scientific publishing: "As many have pointed out, this is a very good example of the way Web2.0 [*sic*] tools and community can complement traditional publishing to move science forward" (Bradley, 2009). Bradley's own blog post demonstrates this principle as well, collecting laboratory work, classroom experiences, previously published research, and online discussion in one discursive space to further elaborate on both the particulars of this case and the greater implications of online scientific discourse. Like many other scientists who leverage online tools for greater openness and collaboration in science, Docherty and Bradley are well aware that they must perform two roles: they are chemists first and foremost, but they are also advocates for a new way to understand scientific publishing practices.

Docherty, Bradley, and other advocates of networked science are also richly technologically literate, exploiting laboratory equipment and emerging digital tools to further proliferate both scientific knowledge and the cause of networked science. These scientists reflect Latour's (2007) description of the emancipated actor, one who is "*well*-attached" (p. 218, his emphasis) to a collection of mediators, including, among other things, inscription devices and plug-ins. Latour contends that mediators enable associations and lead to action: "The more attachments it has, the more it exists. And the more mediators there are the better" (p. 217). It was just such an ensemble of mediators that propelled Docherty's liveblogging event. He employed myriad attachments, including laboratory equipment, blogs, DOIs, inscription devices, and iPhone images to replicate X. Wang et al.'s (2009) experiment, report on the results, critique their manuscript, and question the efficacy of *JACS*'s peer review process. As Bradley's blog post demonstrates, advocates of networked science believe that the more scientists leverage such tools, the faster and more completely it can address problems of the natural world.

WITNESSING THE (R)EVOLUTION

The future of networked science is by no means certain, and the long-term impact of projects like *Totally Synthetic* and Bradley's lab notebook are not yet known. Even in his manifesto for networked science, Nielsen admits that many hurdles exist, not the least of which is time (2012, p. 198). Most networked science projects are initiated from the bottom up by scientists who perform this work while simultaneously negotiating the professional pressures of research, publications, and grant applications. Docherty often admitted in his blog that he simply did not have the time to post entries for the many total syntheses he reads. Like many technologically literate science bloggers, Docherty initiated a Twitter feed in August 2011 to complement his blog writing and circulate information about a greater number of research articles. Unlike his critical work on the blog, the tweets are strictly informative, with each tweet consisting only of the research article's title and author as well as a retrieval link. Soon after he started tweeting, the frequency of Docherty's blog posts declined, and it appears that he ceased blogging altogether in January 2012. Docherty continues to tweet regularly—about every other day on average, which is a much greater number of articles than he covered in the blog—but his transition was disappointing for the *Totally Synthetic* community, who noted his absence in comments on his final blog post. The cessation of blog posts also ended the extensive, rich discussion that came to constitute the *Totally Synthetic* community, which is also unfortunate for scholars of scientific communication. The *Totally Synthetic* community is now dormant, and the dynamic exchange of ideas, critiques, and celebrations that accompanied the community's reception of scientific works has ended.

Nielsen argues that new technologies and revised incentives for scientists will solve at least some of these time constraint problems, but the extent to which networked science will revolutionize discourse practices like peer review and reception is still uncertain. Digital publishing is destabilizing the traditional publication cycle and offering spaces for disruption; the open access movement offers a more transparent framework for certifying and owning knowledge. Many (but by no means all) scientists recognize the value of making this transition, but no consensus about the best way forward has been reached. Even Nielsen admits that change will come in increments before a major cultural shift can occur (2012, p. 206). In the meantime, rhetoricians of science have an opportunity to observe, analyze, champion, and inform members of the scientific community throughout this process as well. Online discourse offers new windows for rhetoricians of science to glimpse the inner workings of scientific research practices, publishing conventions, and laboratory work. Through online genres like blogs, we can witness the movement of what Paul et al. call "the microcosm of lab findings" to the "macrocosm of the discipline and its accumulated knowledge" (2001, p. 384).

REFERENCES

American Chemical Society (ACS). (2012). *Homepage*. Retrieved from http://www.acs.org

Berkenkotter, C. (1995). The power and the perils of peer review. *Rhetoric Review, 13*(2), 245–248. Retrieved from http://www.jstor.org/stable/10.2307/465828

Berkenkotter, C., & Huckin, T. (1994). *Genre knowledge in disciplinary communication: Cognition/culture/power*. London, UK: Routledge. Retrieved from http://psycnet.apa.org/psycinfo/1995-97008-000

Bowker, G. (2006). *Memory practices in the sciences*. Cambridge, MA: MIT University Press.

Bradley, J. (2009, August 5). Our attempt to reproduce an oxidation by NaH. *Useful Chemistry* [Blog post]. Retrieved from http://usefulchem.blogspot.com/2009/08/our-attempt-to-reproduce-oxidation-by.html

Ceccarelli, L. (2005). A hard look at ourselves: A reception study of rhetoric of science. *Technical Communication Quarterly, 14*(3), 257–265. doi: 10.1207/s15427625tcq 1403_3

Docherty, P. (2009a, March 30). Vincorine. *Totally Synthetic* [Blog post]. Retrieved from http://totallysynthetic.com/blog/?p=1605

Docherty, P. (2009b, July 21). Tricholomalides A & B. In *Totally Synthetic* [Blog post]. Retrieved from http://totallysynthetic.com/blog/?p=1896

Docherty, P. (2009c, July 22). NaH as an oxidant—liveblogging! *Totally Synthetic* [Blog post]. Retrieved from http://totallysynthetic.com/blog/?p=1903

Docherty, P. (2012). *Totally Synthetic* [Blog]. Retrieved from http://totallysynthetic.com/blog

Drahl, C. (2009). Communication dot com. *Chemical & Engineering News, 87*(13), 5160. doi: 10.1021/ja904224y

Excimer. (2009, July 22). NaH: Magical oxidizing pixie dust. *Carbon-based Curiosities* [Blog post]. Retrieved from http://www.coronene.com/blog/?p=842

Giles, J. (2007, January 4). Open access journal will publish first, judge later. *Nature, 445*, 9. doi: 10.1038/445009a

Gross, A. (2006). *Starring the text: The place of rhetoric in science studies*. Carbondale,: IL Southern Illinois University Press.

Gross, A., Harmon, J., & Reidy, M. (2002). *Communicating science: The scientific article from the 17th century to the present*. New York, NY: Oxford University Press.

Hadlington, S. (2009). Peer review by live blogging. *Chemistry World*. Retrieved from http://www.rsc.org/chemistryworld/News/2009/July/27070901.asp

Hames, I. (2010). Live blogging and collaborative community review. *Wiley-Blackwell Publishing News*. Retrieved August 31, 2012, from http://blogs.wiley.com/publishing news/2010/02/18/live-blogging-and-collaborative-community-review/

Harris, R. A. (2005). Reception studies in the rhetoric of science. *Technical Communication Quarterly, 14*(3), 249–255. doi: 10.1207/s15427625tcq1403_2

Latour, B. (2007). *Reassembling the social: An introduction to actor-network theory*. New York, NY: Oxford University Press.

Latour, B., & Woolgar, S. (1986). *Laboratory life: The construction of scientific facts*. Princeton, NJ: Princeton University Press.

Lewis, G. E. (1965, July). The reaction of sodium hydride with p-Nitrobenzaldehyde. *The Journal of Organic Chemistry, 30*(7), 2433–2436. doi: 0.1021/jo01018a080

Lunsford, K. J. (2007). Remediating science: A case study of socialization. *Kairos, 11*(3). Retrieved August 31, 2012, from http://kairos.technorhetoric.net/11.3/topoi/prior-et-al/lunsford/index.html

McCabe, T. (2012, June 20). Why academic papers are a terrible discussion forum. In *Less Wrong* [Blog post]. Retrieved from http://lesswrong.com/lw/d5y/why_academic_papers_are_a_terrible_discussion/

Mirza, K., & Moritz, M. (August 4, 2009). Exp243. *Usefulchem*. Retrieved from http://usefulchem.wikispaces.com/Exp243

Murray-Rust, P. (2009, July 28). Junk science? The blogosphere thinks so. *Petermr's Blog: A Scientist and the Web* [Blog post]. Retrieved from http://blogs.ch.cam.ac.uk/pmr/2009/07/28/junk/

Neylon, C. (2011, January 25). What is it with researchers and peer review? or; Why misquoting Churchill does not an argument make. *Science in the Open* [Blog post]. Retrieved from http://cameronneylon.net/blog/what-is-it-with-researchers-and-peer-review-or-why-misquoting-ch/

Nielsen, M. (2012). *Reinventing discovery: The new era of networked science.* Princeton, NJ: Princeton University Press.

Paul, D., Charney, D., & Kendall, A. (2001). Moving beyond the moment: Reception studies in the rhetoric of science. *Journal of Business and Technical Communication, 15*(3), 372–299. Retrieved from http://jbt.sagepub.com/content/15/3/372.short

Peer Pressure. (2009). *Nature Chemistry, 1*(8), 585. Retrieved from http://www.nature.com/nchem/journal/v1/n8/full/nchem.434.html

PLOS One. (2012). *PLOS One guidelines for reviewers.* Retrieved from http://www.plosone.org/static/reviewerGuidelines.action

Smith, C. (Host). (2009, September). Chemistry world podcast—September 2009 [Podcast transcript]. *Royal Society of Chemistry (RSC).* Retrieved from http://www.rsc.org/chemistryworld/podcast/Transcripts/2009/September.asp

Waldrop, M. (2008). Science 2.0. *Scientific American,* 1–8. Retrieved from http://www.nature.com/scientificamerican/journal/v298/n5/full/scientificamerican0508-68.html

Wang, X., Zhang, B., & Wang, D. Z. (2009). Reductive and transition-metal-free: Oxidation of secondary alcohols by sodium hydride. *Journal of the American Chemical Society, 132*(2), 890. doi: 10.1021/ja910615z

Wang, Z., Min, S., & Danishefsky, S. (2009). Total synthesis and structural revision of (±)-tricholomalides A and B. *Journal of the American Chemical Society, 131*(31), 10848–10849. Retrieved from http://pubs.acs.org/doi/abs/10.1021/ja9049433

Zhang, M., Huang, X., Shen, L., & Qin, Y. (2009). Total synthesis of the akuammiline alkaloid (±)-vincorine. *Journal of the American Chemical Society, 131*(16), 6013–6020. Retrieved from http://pubs.acs.org/doi/abs/10.1021/ja901219v

Note: Since the writing of this chapter, the *Totally Synthetic* website has been completely removed and subsumed into the *Organic Chemistry Portal* at http://www.organic-chemistry.org/totalsynthesis/totsyn03/majusculone-taber.shtm. Links to *Totally Synthetic* will redirect to that site. Sadly, Jean-Claude Bradley passed away in 2014. His open data is still open and accessible at *UsefulChem*: http://usefulchem.wikispaces.com/.

http://dx.doi.org/10.2190/SCIC7

CHAPTER 7

Controversies on the Web: The Case of Adult Human Neurogenesis

Jeanne Fahnestock

ABSTRACT

Controversies in science are common, and they may be resolved by further evidence, by mitigating claims, or simply by loss of interest in the absence of new data. A recent controversy over whether the adult human brain exhibits neurogenesis in the neocortex offers a case study in how the resolution of scientific controversies can be affected by the Internet. With its ability to reach and even create audiences, the Internet spread claims about brain renewal from the original research reports to news outlets, to disease advocacy sites, and to health and wellness sites, with inevitable distortions along the way. With its speed, the Internet allowed the creation of new (and sometimes fake) online journals, quickly proliferating less vetted research. With its interactivity, the Internet has amplified uninformed responses to various research reports, impeding the creation of an informed public. Because overall it obscures chronology and makes superseded materials easily available, the Internet can give disputed claims a purchase they do not have among experts and retard the resolution or even the simple fading away of a controversy.

Can the adult human brain grow new neurons and, if it could, would these new neurons repair or even enhance its powers? These questions fascinate most people because they concern human beings and the most distinctive organ in humans, the brain. Unfortunately, they can be answered in multiple ways depending on what is meant by "adult," "brain" and "neurogenesis." Over the past two decades, whether and where the brain can show new growth has been a source of controversy among brain researchers who have disagreed over the evidence for claims of neurogenesis and over their implications and medical applications. But in the popular media, expanded in online niches, the potential for growing new brain cells is asserted enthusiastically, with chatty advice on how to stimulate mental renewal and bright promises of cures for devastating brain diseases.

This chapter examines the adult human neurogenesis controversy and identifies features of its public airing on the Internet through a process that could be called *refraction*, the skewed reflection of a topic through different media and outlets. Some features of refraction also occur in print media since, whenever a subject travels through different genres to different audiences, it undergoes inevitable changes in its presentation. So a further attempt is made in this chapter to identify affordances and consequences unique to the Internet as they impact a scientific controversy. Of course whether in print or on the Web, the spread of a controversy also engages the general and still curiously neglected issue of what constitutes an acceptable version, summary, or paraphrase of an argument as it moves through other texts. But this chapter focuses on how the Web, with its extended speed, reach, and interactivity, can affect the dynamics of controversy resolution in the sciences as it refracts a subject through different sites.

DEFINITIONS OF CONTROVERSY

The sense of *controversy* used here first requires some clarification. For purposes of this study, a controversy is not synonymous with any disagreement or with the presence of conflicting views on a topic. For instance, the label *controversy* does not really fit when a new phenomenon stimulates different explanations. At that stage, researchers offer plausible, tentative theories, and there is a period of testing and discussion, as in the 1950s over the "genetic code," until eventually the less productive explanations fall away. Nor does a controversy occur when nonexperts resist a consensus among experts, as in the case of the vaccine/autism link, or when there is overwhelming agreement in a field but one credentialed expert continues to object, as in the case of Emilio Golgi's insistence on a reticular theory of brain organization (Raviola, 2006) or Peter Duesberg's continuing denial that HIV is the cause of AIDS (Corbyn, 2012).

A *controversy*, as stipulated here, requires a disagreement among participants with the stature to command a hearing in a field, and it has to be recognized *as* a controversy. It may involve two or more incompatible theories (characterizations or causal explanations), or it may involve a salient and unanswered refutation to a claim. The controversy over the nature of the Flores "hobbit" fits the first definition with its two conflicting accounts of the diminutive remains found on an Indonesian island: either those skeletons represent a distinct miniature species of humans, or they represent a population of *Homo sapiens* dwarfed by disease or malnutrition (Culotta, 2006; Kaplan, 2011). A controversy in the second sense involves a claim and its refutation, as in the case of arsenic metabolizing bacteria mentioned in the introduction to this volume, a claim refuted within 2 years of its much-touted assertion (Schiermeier, 2012). Clearly, burden of proof is an issue in the difference here. A controversy from incompatible claims, more likely to be called a debate, leaves the burden with both parties either to refute the other and/or to generate further support. But a controversy generated by a cogent refutation, which can seem more damaging to the threatened position, switches the burden back to the originators. The precise issues fueling either kind of controversy can involve the available evidence (how it was collected or what it actually signifies), or the reasoning from that evidence, or even who has the expertise to generate evidence or reason about it. Controversies should not, however, involve a free-for-all of standards. Instead, there should be agreement on what would end the controversy, even if that "what" is unattainable. The controversy over adult human neurogenesis fits the second sense of *controversy* stipulated here when it first erupted 12 years ago. It involved major figures in neuroscience on both sides, it pitted a claim against a refutation, participants shared a sense of what should count as evidence pertinent to the case, and they referred to their own disagreement as a controversy (e.g., Gage, 2005; Gould, 2007).

Scholars in ethics and social science have suggested several ways that controversies can resolve or merely end. Among the means of resolution are (a) sound argument creating a consensus, (b) adjudication or negotiation directed from a recognized institution, and (c) natural death through loss of interest (see Engelhardt & Caplan, 1987, pp. 28–35). The first method would be preferred in science: reasoning from evidence accepted by all parties yields a resolution. The second method of closure, an adjudication as in a court proceeding or a negotiated settlement as in a labor dispute, is not really available in scientific controversies. Formally, there is no court of appeal, though the closest thing to adjudicatory boards in the sciences, namely, granting agencies or peer reviewers, do deny funding and exposure to less popular views. And informally, parties in a controversy may "negotiate" by mitigating their claims, in effect giving in on some things to the other side. The third ending, a natural death through declining interest, certainly does occur in science, especially when a challenging finding receives no reinforcement from further work. Whether and how the adult neurogenesis controversy was resolved will be discussed below.

ADULT HUMAN NEUROGENESIS

There is a firm and long-established consensus that neurogenesis, the formation and growth of neurons in the brain, occurs during fetal and neonatal development in all species. From the late 19th century and the first histological mappings of the brain by Cajal and others, prevailing opinion held that the neurons formed before and just after birth constitute an unchanging, lifetime population. Brain tissue never regenerates itself the way epithelial or muscular tissue does, and a fixed number and articulation of neurons in a brain appears to be an evolutionary adaptation to make the storage of learned routines and long-term memories possible.

Challenges to this view emerged through new techniques of labeling and assaying cells in general and brain tissue in particular, most of the latter developed in work on rodent brains. In 1962, Joseph Altman tentatively offered evidence of adult neurogenesis in a *Science* article aptly titled, with a question, "Are New Neurons Formed in the Brains of Adult Mammals?"[1] Altman, then at MIT, created lesions and simultaneously injected radioactively labeled thymidine into rat brains. Since the thymidine could be incorporated into nuclear DNA, it was taken as a test for DNA synthesis and hence of cell division. Altman exposed sections of labeled brain tissue to photographic plates for two months and reported seeing labeled glia cells in the area of the lesions as well as the "labeled nuclei of some neurons" (p. 1128). Altman speculated at the time that although neurons were never observed to undergo mitosis, it was possible that "new neurons might arise from non-differentiated precursors" (p. 1127). Experiments like Altman's were repeated in the 1970s by Michael Kaplan and James Hinds, who added electron microscopy to examine the labeled tissue, thus addressing uncertainties in Altman's identification of the cells involved (Kaplan & Hinds, 1977). In the 1980s, Shirley Bayer, who had worked with Altman, demonstrated a linear increase in granule neurons in rats between 30 and 365 days old (Bayer, 1982).

This early work on rodent brains was reinforced by a series of papers in the 1980s from Fernando Nottebohm and colleagues who studied the seasonally changing volume of songbird brains. Female canaries given testosterone also showed this growth and developed the ability to sing like male canaries. Seeking the underlying brain changes, the researchers discovered through radioactive

---

[1] Altman's work is characterized in a review article by Charles Gross (2000) as "ignored or dismissed as unimportant for over two decades." According to Gross, who was a co-author on controversial papers with Elizabeth Gould, "The neglect of Altman's demonstration of adult neurogenesis is a classic case of a discovery made 'before its time'" (p. 68). He characterizes Altman as a self-taught post doc working on his own in a psychology department at MIT and then says he was denied tenure there and switched his research to more conventional issues. Some 15 years later, according to Gross, Altman was "vindicated." Gross finds another victim in Michael Kaplan, who did his research as a graduate student and post doc but eventually left academia for medical school. Kaplan used the same methods of H-thymidine labeling but added electron microscopy for a more careful identification of neurons as the cells labeled with H^3-Thymidine. The lone forerunner producing early and perversely neglected work is a common theme in the history of science. The citation histories of Altman's articles do not suggest neglect.

thymidine labeling that while the treated birds did show a proliferation of glial and endothelial cells, both the treated birds and, surprisingly, the controls showed signs of persisting neurogenesis from, the researchers inferred, "ventricular zone precursor cells" (Goldman & Nottebohm, 1983, p. 2394). The researcher most responsible for knowledge of fetal neuronal development in primates, Pasco Rakic, was prompted to investigate and to report that a similar phenomenon did not occur in the macaque brain (1985).

But later research with mice, rats, and even tree shrews did confirm neurogenesis in the hippocampus, part of the brain's limbic system associated with short-term memory and spatial orientation (LeDoux 2002, pp. 100, 113), and in the subventricular zone (SVZ), a layer of cells under the ventricles, the mid-brain cavities. Researchers in the 1990s, including a group working in Bruce McEwen's lab at Rockefeller University, took advantage of a new labeling technique with bromodeoxyuridine (BrdU) incorporated into replicating DNA and detectable with an antibody assay rather than autoradiography, and they confirmed the previously reported neurogenesis. Versions of these findings have often been repeated, and the results are now widely cited and referred to as established. Thus, if "brain" means the hippocampus or the SVZ, if "neuron" means a granule neuron or interneuron rather than the prototypical projection neuron, and if "adult" means a laboratory animal that has reached full growth, then the claim that neurogenesis occurs in the adult mammalian brain is uncontroversial and has been for over 10 years (Rakic, 2002c; Sierra, Encinas, & Maletic-Savatic, 2011).

But steps beyond this consensus came in several papers at the end of the 1990s, the "decade of the brain," establishing striking new claims about adult neurogenesis. In 1997, Fred Gage of the Salk Institute and his colleague Gerd Kemperman, following up on similar studies of stress-related changes to the brain, reported research on adult rats placed in an "enriched" environment who, unlike similar rats kept in small cages, grew new granule neurons in the hippocampus. This result circulated widely in the media, immediately yielding a moral easily applied to humans that an "enriched environment means a better brain" (Kemperman, Kuhn, & Gage, 1997). A year later, Gage and colleagues took advantage of a special population of patients with brain cancer who had been injected with bromodeoxyuridine (BrdU) to test for tumor growth. Under normal circumstances, humans cannot be given BrdU because it is itself carcinogenic. Autopsies of the brains of these patients revealed BrdU antibody staining in the same brain areas showing neurogenesis in birds and rodents (Eriksson, Perfileva, Bjork-Eriksson, Alborn, Nordborg, Peterson, & Gage, 1998). Here was the first evidence that the adult *human* brain exhibited neurogenesis.

Also in 1998 and again in 1999 came striking reports under lead author Elizabeth Gould of Princeton University. In the first paper published in *PNAS* with her mentor from Rockefeller University, Bruce McEwen, Gould reported the presence and reduction of hippocampal neurogenesis in adult marmosets, a primate species, as a result of "stress," operationally defined in this case as being placed in the cage of another monkey: "A single exposure to this stressful experience results in a significant reduction in the number of these proliferating cells" (Gould, Tanapat, McEwen, Flügge, & Fuchs, 1998, p. 3168). The next year, collaborating with Charles Gross of Princeton, Gould and colleagues claimed to find neurogenesis not only in the hippocampus and subventicular zone but also migrating from the latter source to the neocortex of adult macaques. (It is an unusual and amazing feature of perinatal neurogenesis that new neurons form deep in the brain and migrate in streams to their final destination.) Gould, Reeves, Graziano, and Gross's paper (1999), which included electron micrographs labeled as streams of migrating neurons, offered the first evidence that an adult primate could presumably incorporate new neurons into the intricate architecture of the neocortex.

Perhaps because of the high profile news coverage given the Gould papers (Blakeslee, 2000; Kolata, 1998), there was pushback the following year, primarily from two established neuroscientists: Pasko Rakic, noted above as the discoverer of the mechanics of developmental neuron generation and migration, and Richard Nowakowski, pioneer in the use of BrdU labeling on brain cells.[2] Nowakowski and his collaborator Nancy L. Hayes sent a lengthy letter, "New Neurons: Extraordinary Evidence or Extraordinary Conclusion?" to *Science*, where the original Gould and Gross article appeared. It was published in May 2000 as a "Technical Comment" and was followed by a detailed "Response" from Gould and Gross. (Both the Comment and Response are grouped as the "New Neurons Debate" and all pages are numbered 771a.) Rakic published two refutative review articles in 2002 with less challenging titles, "Neurogenesis in Adult Primate Neocortex: An Evaluation of the Evidence" in *Nature Reviews Neuroscience* (2002a) and "Adult Neurogenesis in Mammals: An Identity Crisis" in *The Journal of Neuroscience* (2002b).

Nowakowski and Hayes's (2000) first criticism involved complications in interpreting BrdU data. Nowakowski, who had introduced BrdU assays, and Hayes pointed out that its labeling is not "stoichiometric," that is, its detection does not correlate with the amount of a dose and that, furthermore, it can be taken up in cells only undergoing repair rather than replication. They also puzzled over the reported result that multiple injections of the same monkey did not yield a detectable increase in labeled cells. (Since BrdU is incorporated into replicating cells within minutes after injection, each subsequent injection should affect a new cohort of cells and animals sacrificed at different times should show differences.) Nowakowski and Hayes also noted that the Gould results required extremely fast

---

[2] Of interest are the differing disciplinary locations of the contending parties. Elizabeth Gould and Charles Gross are both in the Psychology Department at Princeton. Rakic and Nowakowski are neuroscientists in medical schools, the first in Yale's Department of Neurobiology and the second, at the time, in the New Jersey-Robert Wood Johnson School of Medicine.

neuron migration and that the three labels used to identify the BrdU cells as neurons and not glia cells or astrocytes did not in fact exclusively label neurons. The critics also wondered why there were no standard histological and imaging data of the new neurons in the neocortex.

Gould and Gross's (2000) follow-up letter accused their critics of misreading and failed logic. Since Nowakowski and Hayes (2000) numbered their criticisms, Gould and Gross numbered their responses, but they did not answer quite the points raised. They argued that the time lag between BrdU labeling in subcortical areas and then in the cortex provided evidence of the labeling of new neurons, created in one place and migrating to another, rather than the labeling of those undergoing repair. They claimed not to have seen a larger population of neurons, as their critics thought they should, because the critics misread a particular diagram. And they claimed, on the basis of new evidence not yet published, that in fact the new neurons do not survive for long, thus discounting the problem of finding them in any numbers in the neocortex. In a sense, they "negotiated" by mitigating their claim: the cells do appear, but not for long. This compromise confirmed their reported findings and at the same time preserved cortical neuronal architecture from the complications of intrusive newcomers (for the new data, see Gould, Vail, Wagers, & Gross, 2001).

Rakic's rebuttal pieces in 2002 were harsher in their criticism of BrdU as evidence of neurogenesis. He pointed out that DNA replication occurs not only in repair and mitosis, but it can also precede cell death. Hence, BrdU is a fallible label of cell proliferation. He also noted that the visual evidence provided by Gross and Gould did not include images through a sufficient number of layers in the microscopic field, so they were likely detecting glia cells associated with neurons and not BrdU labeled neurons. He discounted the electron micrographs of streaming neurons as in fact the endothelial cells of capillaries. Overall, Rakic's refutation creates a quantitative impression of significant uncertainty given the many things that might go wrong with the available evidence. Over the next few years, attempts to replicate the Gould and Gross results failed or were at best ambiguous.[3] But the later criticisms and negative evidence did not receive the popular coverage that the original sensational findings received.

Another source of evidence was recruited into the controversy in a 2006 paper by Bhardwaj, Curtis, Spalding, Buchholz, Fink, Bjork-Eriksson et al., which counted as a refutation. These researchers used the fact that ^{14}C levels in the

---

[3] The debate over neocortical neurogenesis had the effect of reinforcing consensus on hippocampal neurogenesis according to Fred Gage. A classic concession structure stepped in. In the context of discussing the resistance to his own first papers on hippocampal inducement through stress, Fred Gage wrote, "There was also a controversy about the cortex, and whether neurogenesis was going on there. By virtue of everyone looking at that very, very carefully to see whether or not it occurred in the cortex, it became clear that it certainly did occur in the hippocampus" (Gage, 2005).

atmosphere doubled during the time of above ground nuclear testing (roughly 1955–1963) after which it returned to previous levels. Children born in those years, and the neuronal population in their brains, incorporated this isotope, reflecting the ambient concentrations. DNA is stable after cell division, so the ^{14}C level in DNA serves as "a date mark for when a cell was born and can be used to retrospectively birth date cells in humans" (Bhardwaj et al., 2006, p. 12564). If neurons in the brain turned over during their lifetimes, those new cells would show later ^{14}C levels. The Bhardwaj group sampled brain tissue from people born during those years and others and concluded that "whereas nonneuronal cells turn over, neurons in the human cerebral neocortex are not generated in adulthood at detectable levels but are generated perinatally" (p. 12564). This result was aggressively promoted by the same two researchers who had weighed in against the earlier Gould papers. The issue of *PNAS* carrying the carbon brain dating paper also contained a preview piece by Nowakowski (2006) with a title ("Stable Neuron Numbers from Cradle to Grave") overstating the Bhardwaj paper, which did admit other areas of neurogenesis. That same month, Rakic published a "Perspectives" piece in *Science* (somewhat unusual in that it did not concern an article in that issue) touting the Bhardwaj results under a title showing that everyone watches too many Seinfeld reruns: "No More Cortical Neurons for You" (2006). Here, the subtitle claims that the "contentious question" of new neurons in the cortex of the adult human brain has been answered in the negative.

The researcher whose work was challenged did not remain silent. Elizabeth Gould was allowed or invited to write a Perspectives piece in *Nature Reviews Neuroscience* labeled "Opinion" (2007). In it, she deftly defended her research program. Among her skillful tactics is a reminder of consensus on neurogenesis in the hippocampus and SVZ and then of "evidence" for neurogenesis elsewhere—"neocortex, striatum, amygdala and substantia nigra"—a list that places her own findings among a cohort (p. 416). Gould does report on failures to repeat the detection of neurogenesis in the cortex, but she then raises a series of technical concerns about the refutations, not unlike those that had been aimed at her. What is obscured in her paper, thanks to the conventions of in-text citation lacking dates in scientific publishing, is that the positive findings she cites are all dated between 1999 and 2003, while the rebuttals come afterwards.

Elizabeth Gould's riposte appeared in 2007. Over the next few years, no further evidence for adult neurogenesis in the neocortex of primates, or in other mammals, appeared. Gould's Princeton Web presence and CV lists subsequent studies on the hippocampus. The web page for "Research" in "The Gould Lab" describes work focusing on the hippocampus and lists neurogenesis in the neocortex as a last item of interest and *as* controversial. In the same venues, Charles Gross, an aggressive proponent a decade ago (2000), describes his work as involving spatial orientation and, down the list, the continuing study of cortical neurogenesis with Gould. Thus, the controversy over cortical neurogenesis in 2006–2007 could fade through lack of attention, and perhaps among researchers it has.[4]

However, neurogenesis anywhere in the brain remains a high-interest issue, in part because it has been pulled into the vortex of interest in stem cell research. The source of the new neurons became the focus. Since neurons apparently do not undergo mitosis, they must proliferate from other less differentiated cells that do divide. Altman had labeled these "nondifferentiated precursors" (1962, p. 1127). In 1983, Goldman and Nottebohm did use the term "stem cells" once, but preferred the synonymous terms "neuronal precursors" or "precursor cells." In 2000, researchers reported growing neurons *in vitro* from what they called "neuronal progenitor cells" (Roy, Wang, Jiang, Kang, Benriass, Harrison-Restelli et al., 2000). In fact, for decades the cells giving rise to a particular line were called *progenitors* or *precursors*, that is, immature versions of the cells eventually derived. But by 2005, "undifferentiated progenitors" were relabeled "neural stem cells" (Watts, McConkey, Anderson, & Caldwell, 2005). When the public thinks of stem cells, they tend to think of embryonic stem cells that are pluripotent, capable of differentiating into any cell in the body. But under a precise definition, a stem cell is actually any cell capable of replicating itself and also of differentiating into other cells types, though not necessarily into any other cell type. Thus, the term has been extended to immature but already specialized cells (e.g., *neural* stem cells), a usage that still invokes associations with pluripotent stem cells and thus with high-profile and highly fundable research and novel therapies. Studying uncontroversial neurogenesis in the hippocampus and SVZ or controversial neurogenesis in the neocortex can readily be presented as stem cell research.

CONTROVERSIES ON THE INTERNET

The primary literature in the controversy over cortical neurogenesis, summarized above, can be identified and accessed on the Web, largely from PubMed or from journal websites (through a university portal or by fee). The possibility of someone not in a field accessing its disciplinary literature, and doing so with ease and speed, has been so facilitated by the Internet that the situation before could almost be described as no access. The Internet indeed, as often noted, offers its users three affordances so different from other media quantitatively as to be different qualitatively: reach (the extended population addressed through a variety of websites), speed (an accelerated rate of access), and finally,

[4] Another pair of papers illustrates the quick fate that some claims could have. In 1998 in the *Journal of Theoretical Biology*, Shankle et al. claimed that neurons doubled in number in the human cortex in children between 15 months and 6 years of age. This paper was aggressively refuted in the same journal the following year as a physical impossibility (Korr & Schmitz, 1999), but it is still sometimes cited as evidence of human cortical neurogenesis.

interactivity (the ability to respond to and not just consume sources). The question here is how these affordances influence or alter the representation and resolution of controversies like that over cortical neurogenesis.

Reach: The Proliferation of Online Niches

Part of the affordance of "reach," as defined here, is the number of interested parties and special groups who can amplify an issue online and the new audiences that can be addressed through this expansion of web niches. The list of online genres or sites that can feature discussions of adult human neurogenesis to reach selected audiences includes the following:

1. Scholarly articles not available without special access accounts (through subscriptions or libraries) or without paying a fee per article; e.g., *Nature*, *Science*, *Journal of Neuroscience*.
2. Scholarly articles in open access journals, such as the *PLOS ONE* and *Frontiers* series and others available through PubMed and other databases.
3. Foundation and institute websites, such as the Dana Foundation, the Riken Brain Institute, and the National Institute of Neurological Disorders and Stroke.
4. Scientific organization websites, such as the Society for Neuroscience, offering news, member profiles, and bibliographies.
5. Websites of specific labs and researchers.
6. Wikipedia and Scholarpedia entries.
7. Science news available on the Web; some also available in print versions (*NYT Science Times*, *Science News*) and some only online, such as esciencenews.com.
8. Disease/health issue websites, such as the Alzheimer's Reading Room.
9. Blogs such as Neuroskeptic or Neurophilosophy, some individually initiated and others sponsored by publications such as *Discover Magazine*'s Not Exactly Rocket Science.
10. Wikis from interested groups, such as the neurowiki and neurowiki2012.
11. Course websites, postings, and wikis.

Any browser prompted with "adult human neurogenesis" will produce a mixture of these sources depending on its search algorithm. While searches can be inflected by a user's geographical location and past search history, topic-based searches usually list sites based on frequency of hits. Search terms such as "new brain cells" will of course produce a different selection. But in any search, the order in which sites are retrieved can mask the date of their posting. Of the array of sites that may discuss neurogenesis, many have print analogues, but a handful are worth further attention as examples of reach because of their special online presence: *first*, the web-unique encyclopedias, *second*, the news sites that spread press releases, which feed in turn, *third*, the disease advocacy and health/wellness sites that repackage this news to groups with common medical interests. Though disease advocacy groups existed long before the Internet (e.g., cancer, heart disease, infantile paralysis), the Web has facilitated the creation of virtual discourse communities coalescing around a shared interest not only in the major health threats but also in rarer conditions and diseases. Each of these areas of reach to nonexpert audiences exhibits inevitable but problematic language changes that are worth reviewing first.

Language Complications

Potential misunderstandings, like those created by slightly altered paraphrases, always emerge in the accommodation of expert discourse to nonexpert audiences. These happen whenever arguments are passed along in a textual chain, and they can occur in print as well as on the Web. Distortions may, however, be magnified when consensus is absent. For example, the precise point at issue in a highly technical controversy is often not passed on to nonexpert audiences. These practitioner issues may be explainable, but not in the space constraints typical in news reports and not in their nondiscursive aspects. In the case of the adult cortical neurogenesis controversy, the problems with BrdU and other neuron labeling techniques are complex, as are the technical problems with imaging through a deep field microscopically. These are "matters of art," areas where the experienced may disagree. Not acknowledging these details in a news report on a controversy is a repairable problem of omission.

Problems of commission occur through other inevitable language habits such as substitution with hypernyms when carrying a notion across a text (Fahnestock 2011, pp. 63–67). The obvious and overwhelming problem in this case study is using the word "brain" instead of labels for the specific structures of the brain that are involved in neurogenesis. For most nonexpert readers, the "brain" is a single organ, and prototypically it refers to the human neocortex, the external "shell" of the brain most frequently imaged. But in the current consensus on adult neurogenesis, new cell growth appears primarily in a part of a part of a part: the subgranular zone of the dentate gyrus of the hippocampus. Yet in an article reporting on Gould's 1998 research on the hippocampus, the headline in the respected *Science Times* claimed, "Studies Find Brain Grows New Cells" (Kolata, 1998). The text does go on to limit this claim, but such stipulating is not the norm, and for readers sampling only headlines, the damage is done.

There are also problems with inclusive terms for organisms. Results from studies with rodents are typically taken to indicate conclusions about "the mammalian brain," a hypernym in relation to the mouse, monkey, or human brain. Rodents, however, are not the prototypical mammal, nor in most contexts where the term is used does "mammal" suggests a human being. Yet conclusions about the "mammalian brain" derived from studies of mice and monkeys are routinely applied to humans. In another case, promising early studies of neurogenesis in songbirds (Goldman & Nottebohm, 1983) was characterized as involving the "vertebrate brain," a hypernym with considerable extension including mammals and therefore humans. The terms used to characterize inclusion can be organized on the following "ladder" of abstractions (Hayakawa, 1978, p. 155).

> Brain
> Vertebrate brain (includes work on birds, amphibians, and all other vertebrates)
> Mammalian brain (includes work on mice and all other mammals)
> Primate brain (includes work on monkeys and other primates)
> Human brain

By default protocols of language use, all the higher terms on this list seem to include the lower, though in popular usage, "brain" at the top usually means "human brain" at the bottom. But in animal studies, the logic of inclusion built into the language can be misleading. Species often represent niche special-izations, and the species under a genus are not quite the same as the members of a set. Nottebohm's work on songbirds, for example, is referred to in the citation of his award of the Benjamin Franklin Medal in Life Science as "his dis-covery of neuronal replacement in the adult vertebrate brain" (Franklin Institute, 2006), but the specializations in bird brains to learn seasonal songs are not likely to apply to all vertebrates.

Another language problem not unique to but common in web texts is the use of words in their general rather than discipline-specific senses. For example, the term "adult" in "adult neurogenesis" is used in the research literature to refer to experiments on mice or monkeys that are adult in senses quite different again from common usage where "adult" presupposes a mature human. Aside from the problem of how "adult" is read by nonexpert readers, there can be a problem in how it is applied to other species, as Rakic pointed out in 2002:

> Results obtained in 4- to 6-week-old rats or monkeys <3 years old should not be generalized to the adult brain. Sometimes juvenile animals are clas-sified as adults. The common use of weight as an index of an animal[']s age is also not a sufficient criterion. (2002b, p. 616)

Rakic suggested defining adulthood as reaching the midpoint of the average lifespan of a species—3 years for a rat and 10 for a macaque (Rakic, 2002b, p. 617). That stipulation would invalidate most of the published research. To put this issue in perspective, human adolescents would be defined as adult in most research protocols because they have typically reached adult height and weight. But the human adolescent brain is widely acknowledged to differ in significant ways from the adult human brain (Luciana, 2010).

Wikipedia and Scholarpedia

Nonexperts looking for information are first likely to investigate an unfamiliar subject through a Wikipedia entry. When they read the Wikipedia entry on "Neurogenesis," exclusively on its occurrence in adults, they will find an incoherent and skewed pastiche that receives low ratings from WikiProject overseers in medicine and neuroscience (though these ratings are not obvious without a little digging).[5] From sentence to sentence, the language careens from a formal and disciplinary to a less specialized register, statements are made and then immediately contradicted or doubted, and the topics covered in subheaded sections lack a rationale. A history of the edits to this article reveals a continual accretion of insertions and citations, some apparently provided by the researchers themselves. Shirley Bayer, for example, made 10 edits, placing herself in an overview of research on the topic of adult neurogenesis as someone who sparked its renewal. Michael Kaplan then added his own work, and others added a section on the "Role in behavioral sensitization," citing articles actually on fibroblasts and synaptogenesis. Inevitably, it seems, there is a section on the "Effects of Marijuana," which has one citation claiming stimulation of neurogenesis and a subsequent sentence citing nullifying research. The specific issue of neocortical neurogenesis is characterized as a stalemate based on citations to research 10 or more years old:

> Further, some authors (particularly Elizabeth Gould) have suggested that adult neurogenesis may also occur in regions within the brain not generally associated with neurogenesis including the neocortex.[14][15][16] However others[17] Others [sic] have questioned the scientific evidence of these findings, arguing that the new cells may be of glial origin. (Wikipedia, 2012; footnotes 14–16 are to papers 1999–2003 and footnote 17 is to Rakic in 2002b).

[5] The Medicine WikiProject rates the entry a "C," assessing it as "substantial" but "still missing important content or contains a lot of irrelevant material. The article should have references to reliable sources, but may still have significant issues or require substantial cleanup." It is described under "Reader's Experience" as "Useful to a causal reader, but would not provide a complete picture for even a moderately detailed study" and under "Editing suggestions" as "Considerable editing is needed to close gaps in content and address cleanup issues." The WikiProject Neuroscience rates it lower as "Start," an "article that is developing but that is quite incomplete and may require further reliable sources." Furthermore, "It needs references to reliable sources and substantial improvements in content and organization."

The much-touted democratic project that is Wikipedia often produces such entries marred by a chaotic voice-address situation overall and written from no controlling perspective for no controlling purpose. In this sense, Wikipedia will never replace the genuine encyclopedia entry or textbook explanation that has a single editorial voice that constructs a consistently located reader. The Scholarpedia page on "Adult Neurogenesis" does not have the deficiencies of the Wikipedia entry. But then it has named and credentialed authors (Aimone, Jessberger, & Gage, 2011). Its register features a consistent "expert author to highly informed reader" address, indistinguishable from a review article, and its arrangement has a principle of organization, moving from established evidence on neurogenesis in the hippocampus and subventicular zone to research attempting to explain its effects. It makes no mention of neocortical neurogenesis. A comparison of the Wikipedia and Scholarpedia entries suggests that Einstein's "accommodation paradox" has not been overcome: explanations are either clear but incomplete, or complete but unclear.

News and Health Websites

Science "news," ferrying new findings to interested publics, long antedates the Internet, but its presence on the Internet is especially rich. Older print sites, both dedicated publications like *Scientific American* and more general publications like *Newsweek*, which occasionally feature science news, have a significant Web presence and offer easy access to even recent issues. In addition, there are multiple Internet-only sites offering science news, such as escience.com and sciencenewsdaily.com. The typical path to published news on such sites starts with a press release from a university, institute, or corporate research center. News websites often merely copy and paste from such sources, sometimes with slight alterations, sometimes not. For example, the following claim about a possible facilitation of neurogenesis occurred in a press release issued on the 10th of August, 2011, from the University of Virginia, home institution of the authoring researchers (see Lu, Elliott, Chen, Walsh, Klibanov, & Ravichandran, 2011): "Until now, scientists have not fully understood how this process [phagocytosis] works, which phagocytes are unique in the brain and how removal of dead neurons influences the production of new ones" (UVAToday, 2011). On the 12th of August, the website Medical News Today offered this version: "Researchers have not completely understood how this process works, which phagocytes are unique to the brain and how the removal of dead neurons influences the creation of new neurons, until now" (Rattue, 2011). This deft paraphrase (with its dramatic final adverb *until now*) represents the slight refractions that occur in news reports. For the most part they are harmless, but they can be amplified on the Internet into refractions of refractions in a funhouse of mirrors.

Disease Advocacy Sites

In addition to increasing readership overall, the notion of "reach" involves access to and even the creation of audiences with special interests. Beyond news sites, the websites extending the reach of the Internet have a more complicated set of goals tied to their intended audiences. The goals of websites devoted to particular diseases, for example, include promoting awareness of the disease, raising funds for research, and providing information and support for patients and their families. These sites will report on apparently relevant research, but it is not usually in their interest to report controversies about that research. Neurogenesis is a promising topic for sites devoted to diseases that compromise brain function since in these conditions some form of regeneration seems desirable: for example, stroke, Huntington's disease, schizophrenia, depression, Parkinson's disease, and all forms of progressive dementia as well as Alzheimer's disease. Patient advocacy sites that have featured neurogenesis research include the Multiple Sclerosis Research Centre (mrsc.com.uk) and WrongPlanet.net, "The online resource and community for Autism and Asperger's." (This site posted a typically titled article, "Myth Busted: Adults DO Grow New Brain Cells," summarizing research actually on nerve cells growing dendrites.) To take another advocacy site as typical, the Alzheimer's Reading Room, started, according to the site, by a caregiver, is now the main site (as least as far as Google is concerned) for advice through postings, archived articles, and further links. In a page posted on August 14, 2011, this site reported on the press release from the University of Virginia, discussed above. The third paragraph of the press release contained a potential medical application of the reported research on the ability of some neurons to engulf and digest dead cells. According to the UVA spin doctors, this "pivotal discovery . . . could one day help scientists devise novel therapies to promote neurogenesis in the adult brain. This could re-establish brain function in patients suffering from depression, post-traumatic stress disorder and other mental disorders in which adult neurogenesis is impaired" (UVAToday, 2011). This claim is amplified in the Alzheimer's Reading Room posting and expressed in a way that makes it relevant to the site's concerns: "These findings raise the possibility that this newly discovered process could be manipulated to rejuvenate the brain by regulating the addition of new neurons" (Alzheimer's Reading Room, 2011). Neither this statement, tweaked from the press release, nor the wording of the release itself, are warranted by the original research report, whose farthest claim of application restrains itself to "Identifying phagocytosis as an unexpected further property of neuronal cells may have a significant impact on further understanding adult neurogenesis in physiological and pathological conditions" (Lu et al., 2011, p. 1083). In an interview with his university's public relations office, the lead author did suggest medical applications, a standard gesture in such accommodated reports. There is however no consensus that impaired *neurogenesis* is a causal agent in mental disorders and certainly none to the step beyond of controlled therapeutic neurogenesis in any part of the brain. But because patient advocacy sites serve an overall claim—"things can improve"—and assume as an unstated cause for that improvement—"thanks to us"—material is invariably inflected toward a hopeful, attainable future. No one contributes to hopeless causes.

Health and Wellness Websites

Sites offering lifestyle advice could be described as bottom feeders catching the detritus floating down from science news sources. Pedaling products from supplements to online courses, many offer "scientific" ways to improve the brain. At the more respectable end are sites like The Wellness Advisor, sponsored by the Cargill Corporation—its posting "Yes, You Can Grow New Brain Cells!" was written by an MD who, among other good habits for a healthy brain, advises eating fish oil and flossing (Keenan, 2012)—and the Livestrong.com site, associated with the Lance Armstrong Foundation, which suggests that exercise stimulates a brain protein driving "the production of neurogenesis and stem cells" (Garvin, 2011). At the less respectable end, the blog "4 Mind 4 Life", created by "Drew," describes itself as "offering health tips to help you improve your physical and mental health." This blog features information on "brainwaves, brainwave entrapment experiments, and the latest brain research news" and suggests that "to help get you started with brainwave entrapment, check out my 'recommended products' section" (Drew, 2008). A further posting titled "7 Scientifically Proven Ways to Stimulate Brain Cell Growth" actually specifies that neurogenesis occurs in the hippocampus, but then generalizes the results:

> Though thousands of new brain cells are formed and produced via the hippocampus each and every day, many die quickly after birth. When we can keep them alive for this crucial period after birth, we are able to effectively boost the power of the human brain by adding new brain cells to the bank of existing cells. (Drew, 2008)

The seven ways include exercising and living in an enriched environment, advice derived from Gage's work a decade earlier with rats in larger cages, but Drew also recommends eating blueberries and wearing an "infared [*sic*] light helmet." On these "wellness" sites, an undifferentiated neurogenesis is an uncontested fact. In this way, fragments of legitimate science are annexed to dubious enthusiasms, an effect more likely to occur in the case of research with potential medical relevance.

Speed: The Eruption of Authorizing Sites

Speed remains the premier asset of the Internet. Research reports accepted in journals with print versions are now typically published online before they appear in print. Open source or online journals post articles quickly after acceptance, and indeed the rationale for "periodical" publication with its cyclic delays has disappeared. Everything is available more quickly, especially the initial reporting of "discoveries."

In the following discussion, "speed" will, however, be given a special interpretation as the speed with which an authorizing "publication" can come into being on the Web. This Internet-enabled facility is crucial because a containing "publication" suggesting institutional authority and peer review is still a necessary warrant in legitimating scientific research. A case illustrating the ease of creating online publications is the *Frontier* Journals enterprise.[6] These web publications advertise themselves as a new type of academic journal following a "4th generation publishing model." The sponsors promise an expedited review process and transparency in listing reviewers on publications. But the main feature of this open access model is its system of tiered journals, tier 1 for a specialty, tier 2 for a field, tier 3 for a domain. So under the domain of "Science" is the field journal *Frontiers in Neuroscience* and under that is the specialty journal *Frontiers in Neurogenesis*. (Researchers are also invited to create sites for "hot topics" within a specialty by collecting at least 10 submissions. These are then bundled and made available as an ebook.) The site also describes higher tier 3 publications for a domain (e.g., Science, Medicine) and tier 4 for "the ultimate distillation of the most relevant and excellent research written for public understanding," but no tier 3 or 4 publications were available on the site in mid-2012. The *Frontier* tier 1 specialty journals are created by contributors themselves, and these narrowly titled journals clearly solidify the identity of a research area. Such specialty journals are presumably maintained so long as there is a "healthy" number of submissions. The *Frontiers* journals require authors to pay for publication (as do many science journals) and 2012 fees for a regular submission were a hefty €1,600.

Once an article or review is published in a tier 1 specialty journal, the *Frontiers* system tracks its viewings and downloads to, as they put it, "democratically assess" the article's importance. The top 10% of articles measured by this method are then advanced to the next tier. Thus, a review article on adult human

---

[6] *Frontiers in Neuroscience* was in fact the first of the *Frontiers* journals. It was founded by Henry and Kamila Markram, researchers at the Ecole Polytechnique Federale de Lausanne in Switzerland. Markram, something of a media star, is known for his current high profile "Blue Brain" project, attempting to reconstruct a human brain on IBM supercomputers, a multiyear project that is also being filmed along the way.

neurogenesis originally appearing in *Frontiers in Neurogenesis* received enough hits to advance it to *Frontiers in Neuroscience*, an elastic publication without a limiting physical size. The *Frontier* site brags that access and download counting shows the social importance of research and frees it from "interests." But this automatic bibliometry is not a substitute for citation history as a sign of importance since an article may be accessed but then dismissed. And while the *Frontier* journals may have some credibility and staying power, there is little barrier to any interested party representing a research field who wants to start an online journal, thereby in effect creating that research field. In fact by 2012, "counterfeit journals" exploiting open access and the author-pay model may account for, according to one expert, 5% to 10% of all open access publishing, endangering the entire enterprise (Beall, 2012a; Butler, 2013). The creators of ersatz journals have apparently gone as far as fabricating whole issues to forge a legitimating track record (Beall, 2012b).

Irrespective of how quickly they get into circulation, once in circulation, articles invite responses. Print media allow such responses in subsequent issues (as in Nowakowski and Hayes's [2000] response to Gould and Gross [2000]). But the speed of response is facilitated by the Internet, not only in comments posted on journal sites, but also through the work of bloggers who echo "interesting" articles quickly. For example, in a July 2009 posting, the blogger known as "Neuroskeptic" summarized, just 2 days after its appearance, a much-noticed article linking antidepressants with increased hippocampal neurogenesis (Boldrini, Underwood, Hen, Rosoklija, Dwork, Mann, & Arango, 2009).

Also unique to the Web are the quick "responses to responses" in the Comment sections to postings and blogs, a space that may or may not be policed. So within hours of Neuroskeptic's summary of the article on antidepressants, the first comment, from someone who reports not being able to access the full article, draws attention to anomalies in the article's data as reported by the blogger. The original article reported counting neural progenitor cells (NPCs) in post-mortem samples from three populations: people neither depressed nor on antidepressants, those depressed and not on antidepressants, and those depressed and on antidepressants. (The total sample size was 19.) The control group's population of NPCs numbered 360, the untreated depressed people 1,119, and those on antidepressants 17,229. The implication of this study was that antidepressants were having a good effect by increasing neurogenesis, yet those labeled normal in the sample had very low neurogenesis. Furthermore, of the sample on antidepressants, 5 out of 7 committed suicide. The comment to Neuroskeptic's blog summary pointed out that it would be worth asking whether neurogenesis, if induced by antidepressants or even by the underlying disease process, was really therapeutic. Neuroskeptic responded by noting the commentator's "excellent question": "The authors don't even try to explain the finding that depressed people have more NPCs than controls. Which is the opposite of what you'd expect if you think 'depression = low neurogenesis.'"

And he concludes that the news is not good for neurogenesis theory "if some people can get by with much lower rates of neurogenesis than others." In this case, demonstrating the affordance of speed, the posted summary, and the comment and response raised a valid criticism within 3 days of the article's publication.

Interactivity: The Facility of Feedback

The third and most distinctive affordance of the Web is its interactivity. Interactivity, as in the case just cited of blogs and comments, means that readers/ responders can publicly post their perspectives, sometimes along with the original, in venues subjected to varying degrees of control. In the case of responses to the link between hippocampal neurogenesis and antidepressants, however, while the contribution discussed above did engage the substance (but perhaps never reached the original authors), all the remaining comments to the original posting wandered off point, musing on whether antidepressants work at all, on whether standards for licensing psychiatrists have declined, and on whether anyone still believes in monoamine theories of depression or schizophrenia (Neuroskeptic thinks "few serious people do"). Finally, a self-proclaimed "layman," who describes himself as having asymptomatic bipolar disorder, reports liking the idea of antidepressants as a fountain of youth but wonders if neurogenesis could just take place while people experience antidepressant-induced sleep. In short, the comments are mostly tangential, and on their evidence, the blog's refraction of this article to nonexpert audiences is of doubtful value.

Furthermore, the interactivity afforded to users is sometimes detrimental. For example, in the aftermath of the ^{14}C study and its coverage, the blog Not Exactly Rocket Science, sponsored by *Discover Magazine*, picked up on the Seinfeld allusion in the Rakic (2006) paper with the posting "No new brain cells for you—settling the neurogenesis debate" (December 7, 2006). The blogger, Ed Yong, identified as an award-winning British science writer with a considerable list of publications, introduces the issue as "one of the most hotly contested questions in neuroscience," over how the neocortex adapts throughout life and whether it does so through neurogenesis. Referring to Gould's work without naming the source, he writes, "A reported sighting of newly-made neurons in primate brains fanned the flames of debate but could not be con-firmed." He then gives a credible summary of the Bhadwaj et al. (2006) paper. Among the 13 posted comments is one that claims there are "a ton more articles" and "tons of research" on the issue showing that "cells move to whatever part of the brain needs repaired." When asked by the blogger Yong to cite references, none were forthcoming. Another posting, from someone claiming to be at the "Center for Neural Science" stated outright that "neurogenisis" [*sic*] in the neocortex merely slows during adulthood, that the study was invalidated because it took dying cancer patients (actually it did not) and it ends with the accusation that "if you are a scientist what you say is almost outrageous—remember A cornerstone of biology is that for every problem there is a good experimental system or task paradigm to exploit the answer. This was not one of them." These comments provoked a sharp response from the blogger about the elitism and arrogance in the post and the nonsense of its final point. In short, the exchange amounted to little more than name-calling.

The facility for commenting and responding in the "webverse" brings up again the potential problems with refracting specialists' discourse to the uninitiated and the soliciting of their voices in return. Such interactivity has perhaps been the most celebrated affordance of the Web, leading to visions of a democratized science with citizen-scientists contributing to research. The typical Comments sections sampled in this case raise doubts about such visions. Substantive responses do occur. But these would probably have been made in venues that would have reached the original researchers. Instead, the "net" result of the comment/response affordance seems to be a display of immediate reactions to and free associations on a topic. These are no doubt personally satisfying to the responders, but the enabling of what is essentially consumer feedback in the "marketplace of ideas" is something less than citizen participation in science.

Another interactive affordance created by the Internet comes from a special population. These are the postings or wikis generated by students, and they have a special role in the case of scientific controversies. Two contributions are representative. The first is a paper posted by a student in a course called Great Controversies in Neurobiology, offered at Brown University in 2008, a themed course no doubt reflecting the "teach the debate" principle of course design that has caught hold in academics. The student was evidently assigned Elizabeth Gould's 1999 article for analysis and critique. In 2010, this student posted a detailed summary for anyone to access. His conclusions about the paper's methods and reasoning were largely positive, giving the paper currency 11 years after publication and in spite of contrary evidence (Brown University, 2008). While this assignment is an excellent one for developing a student's ability to understand and paraphrase an extended disciplinary argument, its status as a public document is surely problematic. A second and more impressive student-generated performance is the course wiki produced by an Advanced Neuroscience class at Lafayette College in 2010. This entire course was devoted to the then-current Neurogenesis Debate, and the wiki produced has separate pages, a video interview with a professor, and clarifications of research methods using BrdU and confocal microscopy. The Lafayette students produced a professional, image-rich site on the topic of neurogenesis, with attention to its controversial aspects. But overall, such course postings, though furthering laudable academic goals, can keep controversial topics current.

WEB REFRACTION:
PROLONGING CONTROVERSIES

Complaints and concerns are often expressed about the Web's impermanence. Servers crash or cease to be maintained; links fail. But so long as links and servers remain accessible, the parties to a controversy do not go away, even when the consensus goes against them. Of course parties in controversies conducted in print also remain available, if documents survive. But they do not have the atemporal currency that comes from being listed among browser links. Nor are old papers in bound volumes always sitting on open shelves in public libraries.[7] So by simply prolonging access, the Internet can defeat closure on a controversial issue. Articles subsequently refuted or reviews of a field replaced by more recent ones remain in a suspended state of currency by virtue of their appearance in browsers, typically out of chronological order and apparently dated "now" in every download.

The specific controversy examined here, over the location and extent of neurogenesis in the adult mammalian neocortex, had a unique history on the Web. Though its initial spread from the research literature to science news sources was predictable, its further refraction to disease advocacy or health and wellness sites was due to its potential crossover with high-interest health issues, not a feature of a controversy like that over the Flores "hobbit." Once in circulation on these sites, the claims grew larger and less precise, due in part to inevitable patterns of language use but also to the pressures on these sites to meet their audience's expectations, whether for hopeful medical news or self-improvement advice. Once "out of the bottle," the diffused message that the "brain" has overall regenerative powers is difficult to recall.

Whether this case should lead to a positive or negative overall assessment of the Internet as a medium for scientific controversies depends on initial assumptions. Prolonging a controversy and keeping a refuted view in circulation are not necessarily unfortunate consequences. No one believes that research on neural progenitor cells should cease, and access to the entire body of research on the subject is important. Furthermore, the medical exigence for this line of inquiry is undeniable. However, once outside the primary literature, as the subject refracts through Wikipedia, blog entries and comments, course postings and websites with narrower agendas, the content becomes unreliable. The Internet carries an enormous undertow of gunk, and its chaotic refractions can confuse the state of knowledge in a field. Given the further dangers of ersatz open access

---

[7] The problem of apparent currency is illustrated by a PDF on "The Life and Death of a Neuron," posted by the National Institute for Neurological Disorders and Stroke (NINDS; 2002), which makes promising references to adult neurogenesis and Gould's work. It was written 10 years ago but a still-available early version shows that versions updated to 2012 do not change the wording referring to the promise of a generalized adult neurogenesis.

journals and of voting on the importance of research by accessing rather than citing it, the assessment turns negative. But then again, a positive or negative assessment is moot for a medium that is beyond any single agent's control.

REFERENCES

Aimone, J. B., Jessberger, S., & Gage, F. H. (2011, October). Adult neurogenesis. *Scholarpedia*. Retrieved from http://www.scholarpedia.org/article/Adult_neurogenesis

Altman, J. (1962, March 30). Are new neurons formed in the brains of adult mammals? *Science, 135*, 1127–1128.

Alzheimer's Reading Room. (2011). *Researchers help explain how the adult brain cleans out dead brain cells and produces new ones.* Retrieved from http://www.alzheimers readingroom.com/2011/08/researchers-help-explain-how-adult.html

Bayer, S. (1982, May 21). Neurons in the rat dentate gyrus granular layer substantially increase during juvenile and adult life. *Science, 216*, 890–892.

Beall, J. (2012a, September 13). Predatory publishers are corrupting open access. *Nature, 489*, 179.

Beall, J. (2012b, October 18). New journal publishes seven issues of bogus articles to appear successful. *Scholarly Open Access* [Blog]. Retrieved from http://scholarlyoa.com/2012/10/18/bogus-articles/

Bhardwaj, R. D., Curtis, M. A., Spalding, K. L., Buchholz, B. A., Fink, D., Björk-Eriksson, T., et al. (2006, August 15). Neocortical neurogenesis in humans is restricted to development. *Proceedings of the National Academy of Sciences, 103*(33), 12564–12568.

Blakeslee, S. (2000, January 4). A decade of discovery yields a shock about the brain. *New York Times* [Science Times]. Retrieved from http://www.nytimes.com/2000/01/04/science/a-decade-of-discovery-yields-a-shock-about-the-brain.html?pagewanted=all&src=pm

Boldrini, M., Underwood, M. D., Hen, R., Rosoklija, G. B., Dwork, A. J., Mann, J. J., & Arango (2009, 15 July). Antidepressants increase neural progenitor cells in the human hippocampus. *Neuropsychopharmacology, 34*, 2376–2389.

Brown University. (2008). Neurogenesis in the neocortex of adult primates. *Great Controversies in Neurobiology* [Course wiki]. Retrieved from https://wiki.brown.edu/confluence/display/BN0193S04/Neurogenesis+in+the+Neocortex+of+Adult+Primates

Butler, D. (2013, March 28). Investigating journals: The dark side of publishing. *Nature, 495*, 433–435.

Corbyn, Z. (2012, January 5). Paper denying HIV-AIDS link secures publication. *Nature.* doi: 10.1038/nature.2012.9737. Retrieved from http://www.nature.com/news/paper-denying-hiv-aids-link-secures-publication-1.9737

Culotta, E. (2006, August 25). Skeptics seek to slay the "hobbit," calling Flores skeleton a modern human. *Science, 313*, 1028–1029.

Drew. (2008). 7 scientifically proven ways to stimulate brain cell growth/neurogenesis. *4 Mind 4 Life* [Blog]. Retrieved from http://4mind4life.com/blog/2008/08/18/7-scientifically-proven-ways-to-stimulate-brain-cell-growth-neur/

Engelhardt, H. T., Jr., & Caplan, H. L. (Eds.). (1987). *Scientific controversies: Case studies in the resolution and closure of disputes in science and technology.* Cambridge, UK: Cambridge University Press.

Eriksson, P. S., Perfilieva, E., Björk-Eriksson, T., Alborn, A., Nordborg, C., Peterson, D. A., et al. (1998, November). Neurogenesis in the adult hippocampus. *Nature Medicine, 4*(11), 1313–1317.

Fahnestock, J. (2011). *Rhetorical style: The uses of language in persuasion.* New York, NY: Oxford University Press.

Franklin Institute. (2006). *Fernando Nottebohm, Ph.D.* Retrieved from http://www.fi.edu/winners/2006/nottebohm_fernando.faw?winner_id=4385

Gage, F. H. (2005, November). Salk's Fred H. Gage on neurogenesis in the adult brain. *Science Watch, 16*, 6.

Garvin, S. (2011, March 28). How does exercise help the brain? *Livestrong.com.* Retrieved from http://www.livestrong.com/article/410524-how-does-exercise-help-the-brain/

Goldman, S. A., & Nottebohm, F. (1983, April). Neuronal production, migration, and differentiation in a vocal control nucleus of the adult female canary brain. *Proceedings of the National Academy of Sciences, 80*, 2390–2394.

Gould, E. (n.d.). The Gould Lab. *Princeton University.* Retrieved from http://www.princeton.edu/~goulde/research.html

Gould, E. (2007, June). How widespread is adult neurogenesis in mammals? [Perspectives/Opinion]. *Nature Reviews Neuroscience, 8*, 481–488.

Gould, E., & Gross, C. G. (2000, May 5). Response [following Nowakowski & Hayes, New neurons: Extraordinary evidence or extraordinary conclusion]. *Science, 288*, 771a.

Gould, E., Reeves, A. J., Graziano, M. S. A., & Gross, C. G. (1999, October 15). Neurogenesis in the neocortex of adult primates. *Science, 286*, 548–552.

Gould, E., Tanapat, P., McEwen, B., Flügge, G., & Fuchs, E. (1998, March). Proliferation of granule cell precursors in the dentate gyrus of adult monkeys is diminished by stress. *Proceedings of the National Academy of Sciences, 95,* 3168–3171.

Gould, E., Vail, N., Wagers, M., & Gross, C. G. (2001, September 11). Adult-generated hippocampal and neocortical neurons in macaques have a transient existence. *Proceedings of the National Academy of Sciences, 98*, 10910–10917.

Gross, C. G. (2000, October). Neurogenesis in the adult brain: Death of a dogma [Perspectives/ opinion]. *Nature Reviews Neuroscience, 1*, 67–73.

Hayakawa, S. I. (1978). *Language in thought and action* (4th ed.). New York, NY: Harcourt Brace Jovanovich.

Kaplan, M. (2011, August 8). "Hobbit" just a deformed human? *Nature.* doi: 10.1038/news.2011.466. Retrieved from http://www.nature.com/news/2011/110808/full/news.2011.466.html

Kaplan, M. S., & Hinds, J. W. (1977, September 9). Neurogenesis in the adult rat: Electron microscopic analysis of light autoradiographs. *Science, 197*, 1092–1094.

Keenan, J. (2012). Yes, you can grow new brain cells! Here's how to protect and nurture them. *The Wellness Advisor.* Retrieved from http://www.thewellnessadvisor.com/2012/01/yes-you-can-grow-new-brain-cells-heres-how-to-protect-and-nurtur/

Kempermann, G. H., Kuhn, G., & Gage, F. H. (1997, April 3). More hippocampal neurons in adult mice living in an enriched environment. *Nature, 386*, 493–495.

Kolata, G. (1998, March 17). Studies find brain grows new cells. *New York Times* [Science Times]. Retrieved from http://www.nytimes.com/1998/03/17/science/studies-find-brain-grows-new-cells.html?pagewanted=all&src=pm

Korr, H., & Schmitz, C. (1999). Facts and fictions regarding post-natal neurogenesis in the developing human cerebral cortex. *Journal of Theoretical Biology, 200,* 291–297.

Lafayette College. (2010). Neurogenesis. *Neuroscience 401* [Advanced neuroscience wiki]. Retrieved from http://sites.lafayette.edu/neur401-sp10/

LeDoux, J. (2002). *The synaptic self: How our brains become who we are.* New York, NY: Penguin.

Lu, Z., Elliott, M. R., Chen, Y., Walsh, J. T., Klibanov, A. L., Ravichandran, K. S., & Kipnis (2011, September). Phagocytic activity of neuronal progenitors regulates adult neurogenesis. *Nature Cell Biology, 13*(9), 1076–1083.

Luciana, M. (2010, February). Adolescent brain development: Current themes and future directions. *Brain and Cognition, 72*(1), 1–5.

National Institute of Neurological Disorders and Stroke. (2002). *The life and death of a neuron.* Retrieved from http://www.ninds.nih.gov/disorders/brain_basics/ninds_neuron.htm

Neuroskeptic. (2009, July 17). *Antidepressants and neurogenesis in humans* [Blog]. Retrieved from http://neuroskeptic.blogspot.com/2009/07/antidepressants-and-neurogenesis-in.html

Nowakowski, R. S. (2006, August 15). Stable neuron numbers from cradle to grave. *Proceedings of the National Academy of Sciences, 103*(33), 12219–12220.

Nowakowski, R. S., & Hayes, N. L. (2000, May 5). New neurons: Extraordinary evidence or extraordinary conclusion. *Science, 288,* 771a.

Rakic, P. (1985, March 1). Limits of neurogenesis in primates. *Science, 227,* 1054–1056.

Rakic, P. (2002a, January). Neurogenesis in adult primate neocortex: An evaluation of the evidence. *Nature Reviews Neuroscience, 3,* 65–71.

Rakic, P. (2002b, February). Adult neurogenesis in mammals: An identity crisis. *The Journal of Neuroscience, 22*(3), 614–618.

Rakic, P. (2002c). Neurogenesis in adult primates. In M. A. Hofman, G. J. Boer, A. J. G. D. Holtmaat, E. J. W. Van Someren, J. Verhaagen, & D. F. Swaab (Eds.), *Progress in brain research* (Vol. 138; pp. 3–14). Amsterdam, The Netherlands: Elsevier Science.

Rakic, P. (2006, August 18). No more cortical neurons for you. *Science, 313,* 928–929.

Rattue, G. (2011, August 12). Ridding brain of dead cells and creating new ones, How it's done discovered. *Medical News Today.* Retrieved from http://www.medicalnews today.com/articles/232685.php

Raviola, E. (2006, November 16). A complex mind. Review of Paolo Mazzarello, *Il nobel dimenticato: La vita e la scienza di Camillo Golgi. Nature, 444,* 273.

Roy, N. S., Wang, S., Jiang, L., Kang, J., Benriass, A., Harrison-Restelli, C., et al. (2000, March). *In vitro* neurogenesis by progenitor cells isolated from the adult human hippocampus. *Nature Medicine, 6*(3), 271–277.

Schiermeier, Q. (2012, July 9). Arsenic-loving bacterium needs phosphorus after all. *Nature.* doi: 10.1038/nature.2012.10971. Retrieved from http://www.nature.com/news/arsenic-loving-bacterium-needs-phosphorus-after-all-1.10971

Shankle, W. R., Landing, B. H., Rafil, M. S., Schiano, A., Chen, J. M., & Hara, J. (1998). Evidence for a postnatal doubling of neuron numbers in the developing human cerebral cortex between 15 months and 6 years. *Journal of Theoretical Biology, 191*, 115–140.

Sierra, A., Encinas, J. M., & Maletic-Savatic, M. (2011, April 4). Adult human neurogenesis: From microscopy to magnetic resonance imaging. *Frontiers in Neuroscience, 5*(47). Retrieved from http://www.ncbi.nlm.nih.gov/pmc/articles/PMC3075882/

UVAToday. (2011, August 10). *U.Va. research helps explain how the adult brain cleans out dead cells and produces new ones.* Retrieved from http://news.virginia.edu/content/uva-research-helps-explain-how-adult-brain-cleans-out-dead-cells

Watts, C., McConkey, H., Anderson, L., & Caldwell, M. (2005, September). Anatomical perspectives on adult neural stem cells. *Journal of Anatomy, 207*(3), 197–208.

Wikipedia. (2012). *Neurogenesis.* Retrieved from http://en.wikipedia.org/wiki/Neurogenesis

Yong, E. (2006, December 7). No new brain cells for you—Settling the neurogenesis debate. *Not Exactly Rocket Science* [Blog]. Retrieved from http://notexactlyrocketscience.wordpress.com/2006/12/07/no-new-brain-cells-for-you-settling-the-neurogenesis-debate/

http://dx.doi.org/10.2190/SCIC8

CHAPTER 8

Radiolab and Parasites: Podcasting Horror and Wonder to Foster Interest in Science

Sarah Wardlaw

ABSTRACT

Podcasts—digital media content you can download from the Internet—offer a novel means to communicate science. Radiolab, a one-hour radio broadcast from WYNC and NPR that is available online, employs creative narrative to communicate science to a general public. Episodes organize around a theme and loosely address scientific questions with an interdisciplinary approach. Thus far, the majority of rhetorical analyses regarding science popularizations have been limited to textual works. This chapter will evaluate the strategies used to popularize science in text versus podcast by comparing the popular science book *Parasite Rex* (Zimmer, 2000) to Radiolab's episode *Parasites* (2009b). I find that both sources employ strategies articulated by Fahnestock (1986) and Myers (1990), including wonder appeal and narratives of nature. However, Radiolab's audio production privileges emotional appeals to horror and wonder over scientific content to make the case for parasites and invoke curiosity. Listener feedback left on Radiolab's blog supports the success of emotional appeals to generate interest in science. These findings complicate foundational works in the rhetoric of science by challenging the idea that science popularizations primarily exist to relay factual scientific information to its audience.

In his 2008 commencement speech at the California Institute of Technology, Robert Krulwich, science reporter, urges pending graduates to discuss science with nonscientists. Krulwich makes the case that "scientists need to tell stories about science because science stories have to compete with other stories about how the universe works and how the universe came to be." Krulwich claims that scientific narratives can tell stories about nature that, while still true and complicated, can awe, excite, and draw people in. Krulwich's call for compelling scientific narratives is reflected in the program he co-hosts, Radiolab.

Radiolab, a one-hour radio broadcast from WNYC and NPR, embraces a narrative structure meant to invoke curiosity and inspire a general audience. Producers describe Radiolab as a show "where sound illuminates ideas, and the boundaries blur between science, philosophy, and human experience" (Radiolab, 2013). While each episode is organized around a theme that explores scientific and philosophical questions, this content is not bounded by any single discipline at a given time. Radiolab's hosts, Jad Abumrad and Robert Krulwich, engage a given theme with scientists, doctors, science writers, and journalists, and also members of the public who present unique perspectives or experiences. Episodes, in addition to 5- to 30-minute shorts, are available online at their website for download via podcast and are played on local radio stations all over the country.

Radiolab provides an interesting opportunity to evaluate scientific narratives in the digital age. Radiolab revitalizes an old media format, radio, via a new technology, podcasting, to foster interest in science. While work in the rhetoric of science, including foundational publications by Fahnestock (1986) and Myers (1990), has addressed strategies to popularize science, these analyses are restricted to textual works. Myers (2003) addressed the problems in establishing boundaries for what constitutes popularization and assumptions regarding the purpose of science popularization. He also notes that few analyses consider modes of communication beyond words. My examination of an episode of Radiolab and its reception will use the rhetorical framework provided by Fahnestock and Myers to consider how audio communication and digital distribution affect the popularization of science as distinct from textual works.

I will first compare a segment entitled "In Defense of Cheats" from Radiolab's *Parasites* (2009b) episode to Carl Zimmer's popular science book *Parasite Rex* (2000). The Radiolab segment is directly inspired by Zimmer's book, and even has had Zimmer on as a guest, thus this comparison will provide a means to access the unique features of audio communication. To address the listeners' response to the episode, I will examine comments left at Radiolab's website. I find that Radiolab's primary purpose is invoking a feeling over conveying accurate scientific information by appealing to its listeners' emotions. Radiolab's audio environment reinforces stories that emotionally resonate. While Radiolab still uses strategies discussed by Fahenstock (1986) and Myers (1990), such as wonder appeal and a narrative of nature, its emotional appeals complicate their analyses of textual scientific popularization by challenging the idea that the sole purpose of a scientific popularization is to impart knowledge.

Since Radiolab is a radio broadcast and podcast, its discussion first requires a meditation on what distinguishes radio from podcast and how the features of each might benefit science communication. Berry (2006) discusses the innovation of podcasting as possibly revolutionizing radio. While both podcasts and radio broadcasts consist of audio content, are freely available, are commonly listened to in solitude, and travel with us, commercial radio has become predictable and familiar in its attempt for mass appeal and advertisement sales. Podcasting presents the opportunity to explore and create new kinds of content that will appeal to niche audiences. Since the technology to produce and subscribe to podcasts is free, anyone can create and distribute a podcast. Berry notes that even large corporate broadcasters, such as BBC and NPR, have embraced podcasters to reach new and younger audiences. Though podcasts have been a growing cultural trend since 2004, they have not usurped the role of traditional radio broadcast. Edison Research's 2012 national phone survey shows that 45% of people are familiar with the term "podcast," compared to 22% in 2006, and that 29% of people have listened to an audio podcast, compared to 11% in 2006. However, Arbitron's March 2012 RADAR 112 National Radio Listening Report shows that radio listening remains strong, with 93% of the population listening to radio at least once a week. While podcasts have not replaced traditional radio broadcasts, they have reinvigorated the medium and given listeners even more ways to connect to audio content.

Audio content, regardless of distribution, poses its own advantages to communication. Reports indicate that the structural features of sound can foster increased engagement with the material at hand. Potter and Choi (2006) find that when radio messages are more complex, containing more voice changes, production effects, sound effects, and music onsets, their subjects report more arousal, attention, and can recall more features of the message. Rodero (2010) finds that when sound effects and sound "shots," environmental information connoting distance, are added to a radio story, subjects pay more attention to the story and experience more mental imagery. These reports demonstrate that listening to audio content is an active process and that the listener becomes more mentally engaged with increasingly complex auditory information. These features of sound would certainly benefit science communication by holding an audience's attention and making the content more memorable.

How listeners consume scientific information may prove just as important as the information itself. Due to wireless technology, podcasts can now be accessed remotely on mobile devices and listened to at any time. Listeners are freed from the constraints of scheduled programming and can listen on their terms. As a result, podcasts are often consumed when people are involved in other activities, like exercising or commuting. MacDougall (2011) entertains the idea that listening to content while mobile changes how we interact with the material. MacDougall postulates that listening to podcasts while out in the world and wearing headphones creates a highly personalized auditory zone where visual perception serves as a backdrop. This visual perception can integrate auditory information in complicated ways, serving not just as a reminder of what a listener heard, but also informing how ideas get applied to their world. Listening to scientific narratives while mobile might invite listeners to become more curious about their surrounding environment and perpetuate the act of questioning and investigation.

Podcasts also harbor the potential for making science more approachable to the public. Picardi and Regina (2008) have discussed that the specialization of podcasts is well suited for science communication. Podcasts can tailor information to different audiences, thus listeners can find scientific material that suits their varied interests. Furthermore, since podcasts are simple to produce and distribute, there are several instances of researchers, concerned for the public's awareness of science, embracing digital media as a means to discuss and critique research projects within their fields. Picardi and Regina specifically call out This Week in Science, The Naked Scientists, and Scientificast as examples of scientists reaching out to the public via podcast. More than scientists talking at people, podcasts can play a crucial role in providing the space for open communication about science. Picardi and Regina posit that rather than passively passing information along, podcasts create interactive dialogues by encouraging participation from listeners online in the form of forum posts or blog comments. Radiolab is able to utilize all of these novel aspects of podcasting while keeping a traditional radio format.

Radiolab attempts to make radio relevant in the digital age. Radiolab possesses the resources of a traditional radio broadcast station and also benefits from the innovation of podcasting. With WYNC and NPR's resources, Radiolab is able to employ a full staff to extensively research and edit their episodes, which are then broadcast nationally. These highly produced episodes reach a larger audience with the added contribution from digital distribution. In 2011, Rob Walker reported in the *New York Times* that about a million people listen to Radiolab on air while another 1.8 million listeners download the podcast. With its solid listener base, Radiolab is free to experiment with scientific popularization by returning to a traditional form of radio, storytelling. These stories take place in a rich audio environment in order to hold the listeners' attention, while Radiolab's online presence fosters interaction with its listeners.

Radiolab's *Parasites* episode, released on September 7, 2009, initially invokes a visceral disgust for parasites only to later instill wonder and admiration for their complexity. The tension between disgust and wonder for parasites is articulated as a debate between Carl Zimmer, a popular science writer, and Radiolab's hosts. Zimmer attempts to convince Abumrad and Krulwich that parasites are impressive creatures worthy of appreciation by telling stories about them. When comparing Radiolab's *Parasites* (2009b) to Carl Zimmer's book *Parasite Rex* (2000), I find that both utilize the strategies articulated by Fahenstock (1986) and Myers (1990) in making scientific content accessible to a general audience. However, this comparison also reveals that Radiolab consistently deemphasizes a rational engagement with the episode's content and instead relies on inciting an emotional response to foster interest in science.

In "Accommodating Science," Fahnestock (1986) observes that accommodations of science reports for a general audience employ an epideictic discourse that judges whether science deserves praise or blame. Both *Parasites* (2009b) and *Parasite Rex* (2000) judge whether parasites deserve our interest, though "In Defense of Cheats" (2009a) is more explicit in framing the segment as a trial. However, to sell parasites, they first acknowledge how parasites are commonly perceived.

In *Parasites* (2009b), Jad Abumrad introduces the topic of parasites by exploring a typical visceral reaction to the idea. He introduces Robert Krulwich to the scene in *Alien*, where an alien larva suddenly bursts out of a man. Listeners hear Krulwich exclaim in horror as the scene progresses. In defining this horror, Abumrad speculates, "It's not that the little creature is disgusting . . . it's that it was there all along." Abumrad describes parasites as "little creatures that live inside us" that are "wiggling around and doing more or less what that alien was doing and I can't even see them in you." Part of what scares us about parasites is their otherness, like an alien, co-inhabiting our bodies and escaping our notice.

By contrast, in *Parasite Rex* (2000), Zimmer rationally approaches the common prejudices against parasites by explaining their historical origins, comparing the Victorian notion of parasites as weak degenerates to the more modern notion of parasites as a horrific evil. Zimmer first cites Ray Lankester, a nineteenth-century zoologist who argued that parasites, by depending on others to live, are devolved; they drop out of the tree of life in order to simplify. Zimmer then explores how modern science fiction has cultured a horror of parasites by reflecting on the significance of the fear of parasites depicted in science fiction:

> But all these works do have something in common: they play on a universal, deep-seated fear of parasites. This horror is new, and for that reason it's interesting. There was a time when parasites were treated with contempt, when they stood for the undesirable, weak elements of society that got in the way of its progress. Now the parasites have gone from weak to strong, and now fear has replaced contempt. (p. 116)

Zimmer articulates that science fiction focuses on the control parasites exercise over their host to inspire "not just a fear of being killed; it's a fear of being controlled from within by something other than our own mind, being used for something else's end" (Zimmer, 2000, p. 116). We see parasites as evil because of the calculating manipulation they exert over their hosts. Our fear of being controlled in such a fashion cements parasites as evil others.

Both Radiolab's *Parasites* (2009b) and *Parasite Rex* (2000) recognize that we might have a cultural aversion to parasites. Radiolab explores this aversion by actually experiencing the horror with us, while Zimmer instead explains the horror in *Parasite Rex*. Radiolab continues to abandon reason "In Defense of Cheats" (2009a) when characterizing the debate.

In the segment, Zimmer serves as a "lawyer" and "defender" for parasites to argue that parasites are not degenerate. Radiolab frames this trial as "Parasites: Are they evil or are they awesome?" which actually involves the interaction of two different arguments: parasites as degenerate and worthy of contempt and parasites as evil and worthy of fear. While in *Parasite Rex*, Zimmer (2000) distinguishes the Victorian idea of parasites as degenerates from the modern notion of parasites as evil, Radiolab does not make the distinction clear and melds the two into a debate that makes no sense. Framing parasites' worth as a debate serves to foment drama and captures the listener's attention. The precise issue being debated is less important than the fact that there is a controversy to witness. Historical distinctions between arguments that parasites are degenerates or evil are not necessary to the development of that emotional response, so the two arguments can be merged without loss of audience interest.

Fahnestock (1986) distinguishes two kinds of appeals used in praising science: a "wonder appeal" and an "application appeal." Both *Parasites* (2009b) and *Parasite Rex* (2000) make the case for parasites by appealing to wonder and telling stories about parasites to bring creatures that are generally invisible, unappreciated, and misunderstood into focus. Their narratives are consistent with Myers' (1990) observation that science popularizations tend to focus on narratives of nature, where "the plant or animal, not the scientific activity, is the subject." Zimmer tells similar stories in "In Defense of Cheats" (2009a) and *Parasite Rex* to make the case for parasites, ultimately anthropomorphizing parasites. However, the audio production in the Radiolab segment privileges emotional tone over scientific fact.

When Zimmer describes the parasitic wasp in *Parasites* (2009b), he illuminates the skill involved in parasites' survival strategies. The parasitic wasp demonstrates calculated use of a host by first hijacking the nervous system and then using its body as a food reserve for its young. The Radiolab segment dwells on the host's experience, thus continuing to inspire horror and disgust for parasites. Our pity for the cockroach host is pitted against admiration of the parasitic wasp. Lulu Miller, a Radiolab producer, helps tell the story with Zimmer. Her contribution invokes sympathy for the cockroach, introducing the cockroach character by telling listeners, "for those of you that never thought you'd feel sorry for a cockroach, keep listening." When the cockroach has lost its fight with the parasitic wasp and "lost its will," Miller provides the cockroach's voice, providing the thought "I'm awake, but can't move." In effect, the parasitic wasp turns the cockroach into its "puppet," recalling the science fiction horror of being controlled from within. Radiolab emphasizes this puppet imagery by playing circus-like music after the cockroach is attacked. As a puppet with no will of its own, the cockroach has no choice but to be led and kept as food. It is kept alive long enough for the larvae to grow to adulthood and leave their host. Abumrad reacts to this anecdote as "the purest description in nature of evil that I can imagine" and empathizes with the cockroach's experience in its plight.

In contrast, Zimmer offers admiration in the segment for the skill required in the parasitic wasp's hijack. Zimmer emphasizes the precision required for the parasitic wasp to "insert its stinger into one specific part of the cockroach's brain and inject a precise little cocktail of drugs that then turns the cockroach into its slave." He makes the comparison to human skill with his comment, "I know that the wasp didn't get a PhD in neurobiology." Miller agrees the parasite's attack is "a kind of brain surgery." The metaphor of the parasite's attack as a complex experimental procedure or surgery praises the wasp's survival strategy and invites the comparison to a human expert. Zimmer's observation of the wasp's technical skill acknowledges the extensive training a human would require to master such a precise manipulation and yet the parasitic wasp requires no training. Zimmer states, "There's a complexity there that you can't deny."

In *Parasite Rex* (2000), Zimmer solely focuses on the parasitic wasp's complexity rather than belaboring a comparison to evil. He uses the parasitic wasp story as evidence that parasites are not degenerates but clever survivors. While Zimmer does call their strategy "vicious and unneighborly" (p. 48), he spends more time illustrating the parasitic wasp's complexity rather than identifying with its hosts. When describing the wasp's infection of a caterpillar, he keeps the focus on the wasp. He describes, "The wasps keep their host alive for as long as they need to develop, sparing the vital organs. After a few days or weeks, the wasp larvae emerge from the caterpillar" (p. 48). This explanation illuminates the cleverness of the wasp in precisely utilizing the caterpillar to benefit the developing larvae instead of invoking sympathy for the caterpillar host. His descriptions also introduce technical language such as the "ovipositor" (p. 48) when explaining how the parasitic wasp injects its eggs.

For the Radiolab segment, Zimmer must make an appeal beyond complexity to build the case for why parasites should be appreciated. Anthropomorphizing parasites allows Zimmer to instill wonder by appealing to their skill but also casts parasites as evil by bringing their actions into the human realm and inspiring horror. Zimmer must empathize with parasites to balance the horror they inspire. While Zimmer tells the same story of blood flukes in *Parasites* (2009b) and *Parasite Rex* (2000), his book continues to focus on the complexity of the parasite, while the Radiolab segment romanticizes blood flukes, serving as contrast to the horrific first impression of parasites.

Romanticizing blood flukes is an impressive feat, since they are parasites that target humans. *Parasites'* (2009b) story focuses on blood flukes' journey to find and stay with a mate and deemphasizes the host's experience. Once blood flukes find each other in a human, they physically attach and stay together. Zimmer describes their mating as "monogamous and loyal . . . animals to reinforce your family values" in the segment. This arrangement extends beyond a single reproduction event, as the blood flukes will stay attached for decades.

As bizarre as the blood fluke's arrangement is, Radiolab utilizes sound and music to pacify its listeners at the thought of blood fluke companionship in the human circulatory system. The story begins with a gentle overlay of water moving and it ends with calm music. The last thing Zimmer says before the music begins is "It's heaven. I mean, you're going to spend the rest of your life together." Perhaps because of the description of "heaven," the music almost feels ethereal and awe inspiring, signaling to the listener that blood fluke companionship is a phenomenon worthy of wonder. We are sympathetic for the creatures that have struggled to find their mate and relieved at the calm when their search ends. The blood flukes narrative makes an emotional appeal, bringing the hosts to actually feel sympathy for the parasites. The segment romanticizes blood flukes to such a degree that they are referred back to later in the episode as "pretty nice" and "good."

In *Parasite Rex* (2000), Zimmer gives much more detail about blood flukes, including their scientific name, how they sense their environment, and how they enter and survive in their human hosts. These details emphasize the struggle blood flukes face and illuminate the differences between blood flukes and the listener rather than romanticizing them. In entering the skin, the blood fluke loses its tail. Once it makes its way to the capillaries, it must "use a pair of suckers to inch forward" as the capillaries are "barely wider than the blood fluke itself" (p. 25). Even after the blood fluke gets past the capillaries, it is faced with the challenge of "a torrent of blood so powerful it carries the fluke away" (p. 25) and then must endure the "perpetual menace and attack" from the human immune system (p. 56). The blood fluke's journey in Radiolab (2009b), in contrast, sounds like a leisurely water park attraction. Once the blood flukes find each other in the human circulatory system, Zimmer's discussion of their companionship is more grotesque than romanticized. He comments, "They may be the most monogamous couples in the animal kingdom," as he mentions in Radiolab, but then continues to elaborate that "a male will clasp onto its female even after she has died" (Zimmer, 2000, p. 25). Zimmer builds a case for blood flukes by emphasizing their bizarre biology that is so fascinatingly complicated, yet distinct from us. If Radiolab had emphasized the blood fluke's struggle to enter the human host, it would distract from our sympathetic identification with it. The blood fluke faces challenges foreign to the listeners and poses solutions even more alien. As a result of focusing on the struggle of finding a mate rather than the struggle of entering the host, Radiolab keeps the focus of the blood flukes on their monogamy, not their lives as parasites.

While music and sound contribute to the emotional states integral to the parasites' stories, the informal dialogue structure reinforces the story by holding the listener's attention and signaling that the material is interesting. In *Parasite*

Rex (2000), Zimmer mostly speaks in his own voice, but can quote others to provide information or reinforce a point. In contrast, Radiolab provides a parasite's narrative with many voices. "In Defense of Cheats" (2009a) is produced such that Carl Zimmer's telling is interwoven with producer Lulu Miller's version. They do not directly speak or respond to each other, but the segment is produced such that they finish each other's sentences. In *Parasites* (2009b), Zimmer and Miller set up the entry of the blood fluke into the human host thusly:

> ZIMMER: Blood flukes are related to flatworms, tapeworms, so their eggs start out in the water. Fresh water in Africa, Asia, parts of South America . . .

> MILLER: And in the first part of their life they go into a snail and they come back out into the water.

> ZIMMER: And they're swimming around and they start looking for a human.

> KRULWICH: So imagine a foot going into the shallow end of the pond. I see toes, I see bottom of feet, I see ankle.

> ZIMMER: Well, if you're a blood fluke, you don't see anything. You don't have any eyes.

> KRULWICH: Oh, sorry.

> MILLER: But eventually you find a foot, secrete a little enzyme . . .

> ZIMMER: Basically turn a little bit of skin into butter.

> ABUMRAD: Ah.

> ZIMMER: And you slip into the vein and now you're going to swim my circulatory system. You're going to ride along in the blood. And now it's time to find a mate.

Both Zimmer and Miller are important as speakers since they convey the information about blood flukes. Having two speakers, one an expert and the other a member of the Radiolab production team, suggests the accessibility of the material. Even though Miller is not an expert, she fully understands and is engaged in the blood fluke narrative. Alternating the speaker of the story gives the sense of telling and retelling. Not only are the stories repeated by multiple voices, but the different perspectives vary the stories such that the listener's attention is constantly shifting. Retelling also suggests that this story is interesting enough to be worth repeating.

Abumrad and Krulrich, as the audience to the story of blood flukes, provide voices that directly interact with the speaker and the content of the narratives. They interject to react, clarify, and question. Their ready interruption of the stories offered by Zimmer and Miller creates the impression of a casual conversation. Their interest in the topic is apparent in their dynamic exchanges. Abumrad and Krulwich are excited, inviting the listener's interest and excitement. Even a comment as simple as Abumrad's noncommittal "Ah" is an important contribution to the dialogue, ensuring that the audience is following, understanding, and responding to the story. Unlike Lulu Miller, they do speak to Zimmer and often influence the shape of the story told. In the cited exchange from the blood fluke narrative, Krulwich interjects with what he envisions as the blood fluke's perspective. While Zimmer politely corrects the scientific fact that blood flukes have no eyes, Krulwich shapes how Zimmer and even Miller refer back to the blood fluke. Miller repeats that "you find a foot" and Zimmer repeats that "you slip into the vein," so the blood fluke's perspective becomes the listener's perspective.

The blood fluke narrative moves Radiolab's cohosts from an initial negative preconception of parasites to an idealized and romantic image of parasites. In this process, parasites are metaphorically granted an emotional life of committed pair-bonding. The debate concludes that parasites are both evil and awesome, often inspiring awe because of the horrifying measures they will go to in order to ensure their survival. Abumrad and Krulwich, as nonexperts with a common emotional aversion to parasites, represent how a general audience might react to these narratives. Using a narrative of nature and appealing to values held by the listeners allows Zimmer to instill an appreciation for parasites in both *Parasite Rex* (2000) and *Parasites* (2009b). Myers (1990) explores why the public understands narratives of nature over narratives of science by considering that the perspective of nature "minimizes expertise and emphasizes the unmediated encounter" while also bringing scientific knowledge to the "realm of common sense." Radiolab makes a case for parasites not through scientific evidence but by appealing to the stories parasites can tell. The stories bring parasites to the "realm of common sense" through anthropomorphism so that, in feeling for the parasites, the listener can appreciate them. The audio production in this story reinforces the emotional tone of both horror and awe. To evaluate whether listeners actually end up appreciating parasites by the end of the episode, we can turn to their online feedback.

As digital media delivered online, Radiolab episodes present opportunities for producers to interact with listeners, for listeners to interact with content, and for listeners to interact with each other. On Radiolab's website, listeners can immediately access any episode or short for free, peruse the blog, and post comments. In evaluating how well Radiolab persuades its listeners to appreciate parasites using emotional appeals, I turned to the comments left on the episode at Radiolab's website.

At the time of analysis, there were 148 comments: 136 on the page for the entire episode and 12 comments specifically on the page for the "In Defense of

Cheats" segment. Most often, listeners post to express approval (32 comments), offer more information related to the episode (18 comments), or ask about the music (11 comments). Some listeners use the website to post new thoughts inspired by the episode (10 comments). There are four instances of producers directly responding to listener comments, though this was shortly after the episode was released. If there is interaction among comments, most often it is a listener responding to another listener (11 comments). Seven of these listener-to-listener comments pertain to a debate over the meaning of theory, as the colloquial and not scientific meaning of theory was used on the episode. Four listeners mention discussing the episode with other people. One listener comments that she "was fascinated" and had been "telling everyone about the intelligent, brain surgeon wasp and the loving worm all week."

Not all listeners felt positively about the episode, as there were a handful of comments expressing disappointment (5 comments). One particular review does not take well to Radiolab's production techniques, commenting, "good facts-presentation techniques very annoying—too cute . . . the presentation methods have become more important than scientific information." While there were three comments critiquing the production, six actually praised the level of production. One comment goes as far to say that the production helped them follow the material, commenting, "I liked how the producers were able to add sound effects to the talking . . . that helped me pay attention."

Two classes were assigned to listen to the podcast and leave comments on the website. These 27 responses prove helpful since the instructors prompted their students to write more than whether they enjoyed the episode or not. A total of 17 of the comments were from a class of unknown age and location during October of 2009. These students were asked to provide a summary of the episode, describe what they learned, and explain how they reacted. Of the student comments, 10 were from students in a class from Madrid, Spain (which one student suggests are in their teens) during September of 2012. They were asked to list five facts that they learned from the podcast, what surprised them about the episode, and what they would like to learn more about.

The comments from Madrid mostly reiterate talking points from the episode. When listing facts, these students are most likely to pull phrasing directly from the episode compared to the students asked to provide a general summary. Two students used Zimmer's phrasing of "turn a little bit of skin into butter" word for word to describe how the blood fluke enters its human host. Three students were especially intrigued by the account of the parasitic wasp and interested in learning more about the science behind how it is able to neurologically control the cockroach. Very few of the Madrid comments remark on an emotional reaction to the episode beyond surprise in the information about parasites. One student is particularly sympathetic for the host cockroach, remarking, "I felt really sad that the cockroach, after being stung, cannot even lead a normal life until the wasp eggs that were laid in it grow and develop and then it dies."

Perhaps because of the nature of their prompts, the class assigned to listen in October 2009 discusses what they thought about the episode rather than simply relaying facts they learned. When providing a summary, most students described a "debate" or "argument" (16 comments) to determine the value of parasites. Surprisingly, only one student frames this decision as the choice between "evil or awesome," reporting the dichotomy in quotations as if to create distance from the strange dichotomy. Instead, more than half of the students report the deliberation as concerning parasites as "good or bad" or having "positive or negative effects." When forced to explain what was going on in the episode, students choose a rational dichotomy rather than Radiolab's irrational one.

An overwhelming amount of students (12 of the 17) comment that they found the podcast to be surprisingly interesting. They frame this surprise by noting that they expected an hour-long episode on parasites to be "extremely boring" or "the most disgusting and appalling thing I had ever listened to." Many of the students express their complicated feelings of both awe and disgust in reaction to parasites. Regarding blood flukes, one student cites that she was both "amazed and scared." Another student notes that he was "intrigued and disgusted by this podcast." Yet another student states, "I thought it was creepy, but I was intrigued as well."

Some students note the value in the information they learned, as one student notes, "I don't think many people realize what parasites are capable of doing, even what parasites are. After listening to this podcast I think people should be more educated on parasites and their ability." Another student also comments, "It gave great information about parasites which would be hard to find in many other places." However, most students stress how they felt after listening. These student reactions are paralleled by some of the other unprompted comments. Nine of the unprompted comments also express disgust or fear, including "the idea of these things being anywhere and possibly everywhere is creepy and exciting at the same time."

Radiolab's emphasis of both the horror and wonder that parasites inspire seems to be successful in capturing most listeners' interest, though there are some exceptions. Many comments reiterate feeling disgust and fear yet also surprise and interest in learning about parasites. Many listeners also seem to take notice of Radiolab's production efforts, especially when it comes to music. Radiolab's level of audio production does appear to make the content memorable, as the listeners asked to recall facts from the episode repeated phrases word for word. The online comments also show that some listeners are taking advantage of the online platform to interact with others by sharing information and asking questions, though a given listener is more likely to comment whether or not they liked the episode than interact with another listener via comments.

Robert Krulwich's call to tell compelling stories about science to captivate an audience is answered in Radiolab. Radiolab is not just concerned with educating the public about science; it also uses emotional appeals to excite its listeners and

generate interest in science. Existing rhetorical analyses of scientific popularizations provide a useful framework but are limited to information discussed in
print. While Radiolab does employ strategies similar to textual popularizations,
such as appealing to the wonder of science and telling narratives of nature,
communication via podcast allows novel appeals to emotion, utilizing audio
production to reinforce its emotional content and digital distribution to reach
a greater audience.

The *Parasites* (2009b) episode is certainly an extreme case in how emotions
inform narrative content since Radiolab must tackle what most people already
feel about parasites, yet its other episodes consistently prioritize inciting curiosity
and excitement while telling stories related to science. Many science popularizations, such as *Parasite Rex* (2000), focus on getting its audience excited about
the scientific content at hand by making information accessible, understandable,
and relatable. When comparing *Parasites* to *Parasite Rex*, I find that Radiolab
often distances itself from scientific accuracy for the sake of its emotional
message. Perhaps because of its format as podcast, which encourages innovation, Radiolab has the freedom to explore a less typical means of connecting
with science: deemphasizing scientific content. Radiolab's approach challenges
previous assumptions that the sole purpose of a science popularization is to relay
factual information. Radiolab instead connects to its audience on a very fundamental level by telling a compelling story that emotionally grabs its listeners.

Using the comments on Radiolab's website as a limited sample to understand
the reception of *Parasites* (2000), I find that Radiolab's emotional approach is
mostly supported by its listeners. While some listeners utilize these comments
to interact with each other and producers, the majority of comments generally
pertain to the episode itself. In the report "Podologues: Conversations Created by
Science Podcasts," Birch and Weitkamp (2010) directly assess the assumption
that podcasts inherently foster interactive, online dialogues by tracking online
communication about science podcasts for 6 weeks and following the listening
habits of a recruited group. Regarding WNYC's Radiolab, Birch and Weitkamp
find that users usually only posted a single comment on Radiolab's blog and
that these comments were mostly in response to the podcast itself and rarely
interacted with other comments. Their finding is consistent with what I found
with regard to the *Parasites* comments.

When Birch and Weitkamp (2010) interviewed their recruited group, they
found that interviewees generally listened to podcasts while they were doing
something else and rarely contributed to online blogs and forums, even though
they were aware of their existence. Interviewees did comment that they valued
the new information they learned from science podcasts and were likely to share
with friends and family. Birch and Weitkamp's findings challenge the idea that
because podcasts are available online it follows that listeners will interact within
an online community. Their interviews suggest that perhaps because of how
podcasts are being consumed, as people go about their lives performing other

activities, listeners are connecting to podcasts in a way that encourages them to talk to people who are in their world versus online.

My reception study has no means of accessing the listeners that are more inclined to share the episode with people they know rather than online, though there are a few online comments that mention sharing what they learned with co-workers, friends, and family. Given my findings that Radiolab fosters an emotional connection to stories about science, I would next question how listening to podcasts (everywhere and any time) affects how listeners relate to and interact with scientific content.

REFERENCES

Arbitron. (2012). *Radio's audience remains steady over the past year.* Retrieved from http://arbitron.mediaroom.com/index.php?s=43&item=808

Berry, R. (2006). Will the iPod kill the radio star? Profiling podcasting as radio. *Convergence, 12*(2), 143–162. doi: 10.1177/1354856506066522

Birch, H., & Weitkamp, E. (2010). Podologues: Conversations created by science podcasts. *New Media & Society.* doi: 10.1177/1461444809356333

Edison Research. (2012). *The podcast consumer 2012.* Retrieved from http://www.edisonresearch.com/home/archives/2012/05/the-podcast-consumer-2012.php

Fahnestock, J. (1986). Accommodating science: The rhetorical life of scientific facts. *Written Communication, 3*(3), 275–296.

Krulwich, R. (2008, June). *Commencement speech.* California Institute of Technology. Pasadena, CA. Retrieved from http://www.radiolab.org/blogs/radiolab-blog/2008/jul/29/tell-me-astory/

MacDougall, R. (2011). Podcasting and political life. *American Behavioral Scientist, 55*(6) 714–732. doi: 10.1177/0002764211406083

Myers, G. (1990). *Writing biology: Texts in the social construction of scientific knowledge science and literature series.* Madison, WI: University of Wisconsin Press.

Myers, G. (2003). Discourse studies of science popularization: Questioning the boundaries. *Discourse Studies, 5,* 265–279. doi: 10.1177/1461445603005002006

Picardi, I., & Regina, S. (2008). Science via podcast. *Journal of Science Communication, 7*(2).

Potter, R., & Choi, J. (2006). The effects of auditory structural complexity on attitudes, attention, arousal and memory. *Media Psychology, 8,* 395–419.

Radiolab. (2009a, September 7). *In defense of cheats.* Retrieved from http://www.radiolab.org/2009/sep/07/in-defense-of-cheats/

Radiolab. (2009b, September 7). *Parasites.* Retrieved from http://www.radiolab.org/2009/sep/07/

Radiolab. (2013). *About.* Retrieved from http://www.radiolab.org/about/

Rodero, E. (2010). See it on a radio story: Sound effects and shots to evoked imagery and attention on audio fiction. *Communication Research, 39*(4), 458–479. doi: 10.1177/0093650210386947

Walker, R. (2011). *On "Radiolab," the sound of science.* Retrieved from http://www.nytimes.com/2011/04/10/magazine/mag-10Radiolab-t.html?pagewanted=all

Zimmer, C. (2000). *Parasite rex.* New York, NY: Free Press.

http://dx.doi.org/10.2190/SCIC9

CHAPTER 9

Online Visualizations of Natural Disasters and Hazards: The Rhetorical Dynamics of Charting Risk

Charles Kostelnick and John Kostelnick

ABSTRACT

Scientific organizations, government agencies, and private companies are increasingly visualizing data about earth sciences (geography, geology, meteorology) on the Internet in the form of charts, graphs, and thematic maps. These displays visualize natural disasters and hazards—from hurricanes and earthquakes to fires, floods, and asteroids—in several temporal modes (past, present, and future) and often include interactive features that enable users to participate in their design and to assess risk to life and property. The displays have both forensic and deliberative elements, providing the evidence for arguments and the impetus for decision-making. Because natural disasters have huge potential consequences for users, kairos and emotional appeals also play key roles in the rhetorical process. Also, the certainty of predicting these events can be problematic, complicating their visualization and raising ethical issues for designers and users.

INTRODUCTION

In the past few decades, data about earth sciences—including geography, geology, hydrology, climatology, and meteorology—and associated natural disasters have increasingly been visualized on the Internet, making data available to the public in the form of interactive maps, charts, lists, and animations. In most cases, users can organize and articulate the data according to their needs and interests, enabling them both to see the big picture—across their state, nation, or planet—and to

157

localize the visualization in their own neighborhoods. In doing so, the public can visualize natural phenomena that continue to shape the planet—and the ways that we inhabit it—by posing risks that range from minor nuisances (sleet that lengthens a morning commute) to devastating hurricanes, tornados, and earthquakes that may seriously jeopardize life and property.

The contemporary world poses a wide array of risks, many of them produced by human activity such as the consumption of processed foods, defects in vehicles or equipment, or the consequences of polluting the environment through chemicals, fossil fuels, or mining. *Natural* phenomena, however, also continue to pose major risks around the globe, where population growth increases our vulnerability and multiplies the risk. For example, over half of the world's seven billion people now live in urban areas, many of them in coastal cities, subjecting these people to risk for hazards such as hurricanes, coastal flooding, or tsunamis. Until recently, human vulnerability to natural disasters was extreme, given the lack of science and technology to predict, plan, mitigate, and prepare for them. With the advent of the Internet and digital tools for visualizing natural disasters—those that have occurred and those that *might* occur—users can learn about and prepare for events like earthquakes, hurricanes, floods, volcanic eruptions, tsunamis, and even asteroid impacts, among others.

In this chapter, we explore how a variety of websites feature online visualizations to communicate with large, amorphous audiences by deploying several data display genres and rhetorical strategies. Although the rhetoric of data displays, both contemporary and historical, has been analyzed extensively (Barton & Barton, 1993b; Brasseur, 2003; Kimball, 2006), interactive displays as a new form of digital rhetoric have received relatively little attention (Kostelnick, 2008; Mirel, 1998). Visualizing science has been examined historically (Gross, 1996), as has communicating risk, particularly in static maps (Monmonier, 1997), but critiques of hazard visualizations delivered over the Internet have only begun to emerge (e.g., Liu & Palen, 2010; Monmonier, 2008). Moreover, scholarship has yet to focus on the visual rhetoric of online, interactive displays of hazard and risk data that are now widely available to the public.

RHETORICAL OVERVIEW OF THREE TEMPORAL MODES

Visualizing risk online entails assessments of data across both narrow and wide swaths of time, ranging from the far distant past to the distant future:

- *Past*—looking at historical data to understand hazard events that have already occurred, ranging from last week to millennia ago.
- *Present*—considering current conditions through real-time data that track the progress of an ongoing event.
- *Future*—extrapolating from past and present data to project risk scenarios of what might yet happen in a given location.

In the remainder of this chapter, we use these three temporal modes—past, present, and future—to organize our visual, scientific, and rhetorical analysis of earth science visualizations. The usability aspects of these three temporal modes are very similar in terms of perception (color, scale, animation), interpreting conventional genres (like thematic maps), and customizing the displays to match the user's needs. For example, visualizing information interactively enables users to adapt the data to their own situations, to move between what Tufte (1990) calls the "macro" level and the "micro" level, which allow users to see both big patterns and the smaller, more localized variations within that larger picture (pp. 37–51). However, other rhetorical aspects of the three temporal modes—such as evidence, arguments, timing, emotional appeals, and ethos—differ considerably across modes and situations.

Visualizations of the *past*, for example, largely entail what classical rhetoricians called "judicial" or "forensic" rhetoric (Aristotle, 2007, pp. 47–48) because they are designed to supply evidence about what happened, such as the location of known earthquakes 6.0 or greater on the Richter scale in North America over the past century. These visualizations of the past may be generated from data collected by scientific instruments, such as a seismometer, and presented in a form for users to grasp the spatial and temporal patterns of the disaster. From a user's perspective, these visualizations are typically well grounded in factual information (i.e., what happened, where, and when) and therefore engender a high level of credibility. Emotionally, users' interactions with the data remain distant and subdued because the data are highly sanitized visually and because the user can vicariously (and safely) experience the devastation of the disaster without facing any immediate consequences.

Visualizations of the *present* depict current natural disaster conditions on the ground through real-time or frequently updated data. Rhetorically, these visualizations must project *kairos*, or good timing, because the users' interactions with the data require urgency as well as accuracy, often at a very local level. Focusing on the here and now, these visualizations inform users of the current situation, enabling them to locate specific places they should avoid or where to exercise caution, such as visualizations depicting severe weather warnings and watches. These visualizations are crucial instruments for emergency managers and government agencies to warn civilians in times of crisis and to provide safety information. Users will likely be highly engaged both perceptually and emotionally: perceptually, because they must make accurate judgments, often in the context of their own communities; and emotionally, because, depending on their situation, they may feel threatened and anxious about the immediate consequences to themselves, empathy for people they know, or perhaps intense relief for having dodged a disaster.

Finally, visualizations of projected future risk foster what classical rhetoricians called "deliberative" rhetoric (Aristotle, 2007, pp. 47–48): by warning users about what might happen in the *future*, they induce users to consider actions they might take—personal steps as well as public policies and procedures—to address that risk. Predictive visualizations evoke pathos appeals by engendering varying degrees of fear and anxiety, and in doing so pose ethical issues for the data designers, who must walk the fine line between fostering compulsory vigilance and inducing wasteful prevention. Users are encouraged to assess the visualized data and scenarios to assess the likelihood that a future disaster will strike. That assessment entails consideration of geographic and temporal factors—the probability or likelihood that a hazard event will strike a given location over a specified time period (e.g., hurricanes in Miami, Florida, in early fall 2015)—as well as the consequences the hazard poses to populations, infrastructure, property, and nature itself.

Although the audiences for these groups of visualizations are rarely specified by the websites in which they appear, we can make some solid inferences about users.[1] Visualizations of the present, due to their timely dissemination of ongoing events, have broad appeal to virtually anyone in the public who wishes to stay out of harm's way during an impending disaster. Such visualizations may also appeal to more specialized audiences, such as emergency management officials who rely on real-time information from multiple sources as they coordinate disaster responses from command centers. Visualizations of the past may, in addition to a public audience, have specific pedagogical applications for teaching students about earth science processes or the catastrophic consequences of natural disasters. In addition to appealing to private citizens, visualizations of the future may attract forward-thinking urban planners, developers, local government officials, and policymakers for planning purposes prior to significant building or infrastructure projects. Certainly, visualizations of all three types are used for specialized communication between scientists within and across disciplines, such as drought visualizations that serve as a means of communication between meteorologists and agronomists.

Most visualizations of natural disasters, however, attract large public audiences: teachers, students, farmers, ranchers, developers, outdoor enthusiasts, amateur scientists, and other private individuals. Because visualizations sponsored by government agencies often serve as the "front page" for massive expenditures in sophisticated data collection endeavors, websites for these agencies gladly promote their data displays to as many curious taxpayers as possible in order to justify the investment. Regardless of the specific visualization, users may or may not have the required level of subject (domain) expertise to interpret a display fully and conventionally, a potential drawback of the easy-to-access nature of the Internet, particularly for the large public audiences we will focus on primarily.

---

[1] See Liu and Palen (2010) for a review and analysis of several design choices, including consideration of user issues, made by developers of crisis maps on the Internet.

VISUALIZATIONS OF PAST DISASTERS: (OVER)SIMPLIFYING EVENTS THROUGH INTERACTIVITY

We are inherently interested in the natural world around us: to understand it, to protect it from degradation, and sometimes to protect ourselves when it threatens us. Interactive visualizations enable a wide array of users to understand the earth, and its many scientific disciplines, by providing access to large sets of existing data about climate, geography, and geology. Visualizations of past natural events can be primarily categorized as forensic (or judicial) rhetoric designed to supply a credible record of what occurred so that arguments can be constructed (or inferred) from the visualization. The displays emphasize rational and accessible techniques that often enable users to manipulate and focus the evidence through interactivity. Although most visualizations of past disasters operate largely on the macrolevel, many embody interactive features that allow users to sort and filter vast historical datasets according to the users' needs and interests. That flexibility to select and manipulate the data greatly heightens its forensic value and its ethos, generating arguments that are multi-faceted and discoverable.

For example, Figure 9.1 shows a treemap by the Hive Group (2012), which visualizes the earthquakes of the world since 1901. Users can select the variables on the treemap according to the magnitude of the earthquakes, the loss of life, the nations in which they occurred, and specific years. By defining the variables, users can decide which aspects of the database they want to foreground. Here, the data are filtered to show all earthquakes since 1901 above 7.0 on the Richter scale and resulting in more than 50 deaths, sorted by country. Chile (top left) and Indonesia (immediately beneath) dominate the treemap, with each country displaying events of great magnitude. To their right, Japan (top), Peru (middle), and Ecuador (bottom) have also experienced major disasters, while deadly earthquakes in the United States and Europe (lower right) have occurred relatively rarely. Color indicates the deadliness of the earthquakes, with the darker shading in many of the small rectangles, where population is dense, showing high values. This display argues that the most severe events occur in a small geographic area, but high-density population areas make humans more vulnerable, even if the quake's magnitude is less severe. The forensic elasticity of this treemap can generate many different visual arguments, depending on which combination of variables users choose to visualize.

More narrowly focused visualizations of natural disasters can be found at the website of the National Weather Service's National Hurricane Center (2011), which provides temporal animations that thread together each storm's historical track, wind speeds, and associated warnings and watches along coastal areas. Users can control the speed of the retrospective animation and stop it frame by frame to see how a given storm developed and the threats it posed along its route. Although the fast-moving parts of animations can sometimes pose perceptual

Figure 9.1. Treemap visualizing earthquake size and deadliness by country since 1901 (Hive Group, 2012). Retrieved from http://www.hivegroup.com/gallery/earthquakes/. Treemap interface created by The Hive Group (www.hivegroup.com) © 2014 The Hive Group, Inc. Used with permission.

challenges (Fisher, 2010), and evaluations of the effectiveness of animated maps in particular have yielded mixed results (see Johnson & Nelson, 1998; Kostelnick, Land, & Juola, 2007; Patton & Cammack, 1996; Slocum, Blok, Jiang, Koussolakou, Montello, Fuhrmann, & Hedley, 2001), user controls of the animation, like in the hurricane display, can greatly enhance interpretation. Figure 9.2, for example, shows one frame of an animation documenting the trek of Hurricane Irene as it traveled through the Caribbean and up the U.S. coast in August 2011, threatening virtually every coastal area. In its entirety, the animation creates a macrolevel historical narrative of the disaster as it unfolded over 10 days, while at the same time it enables users to control that narrative by studying microlevel snapshots along the way.

A longer narrative appears in Figure 9.3, an animation by the U.S. Geological Survey/National Drought Mitigation Center (2012) showing the 2012 drought conditions across the United States in 2-week intervals. Users can run the entire

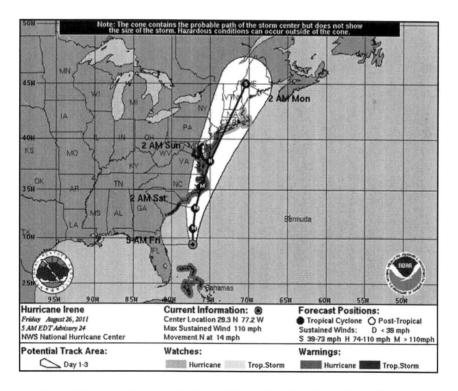

Figure 9.2. Animated visualization of the path of Hurricane Irene (National Weather Service/National Hurricane Center, 2011). Retrieved from http://www.nhc.noaa.gov/archive/2011/graphics/al09/loop_3W.shtml. Figure courtesy of NOAA (National Oceanic and Atmospheric Administration).

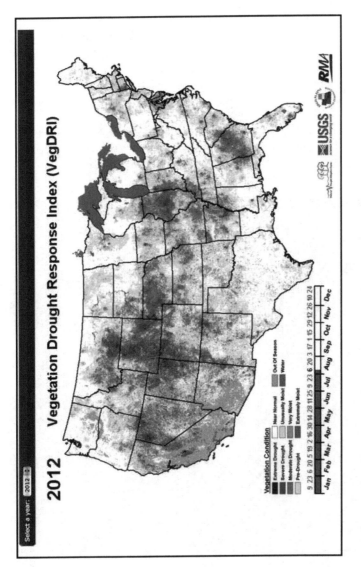

Figure 9.3. Frame from an animation displaying the drought (U.S. Geological Survey/National Drought Mitigation Center, 2012). Retrieved from http://vegdri.unl.edu/TimeSeries.aspx. The Vegetation Drought Response Index (VegDRI) is produced by the National Drought Mitigation Center at the University of Nebraska-Lincoln, in collaboration with the US Geological Survey's Center for Earth Resources Observation and Science, and the High Plains Regional Climate Center at the University of Nebraska-Lincoln.

animation to see the macrolevel patterns as they unfolded over the year they select, from 1989 to the present. Users can also view drought conditions at any 2-week interval, offering them microlevel flexibility at the temporal level. The image in Figure 9.3 shows the situation in late July and early August 2012, when several areas of the country were experiencing drought (or predrought) conditions (e.g., Wyoming, Illinois, Georgia). The conventional color spectrum runs from dark red/brown (extreme drought) to dark green (extreme moisture), with white representing normal conditions. As we'll see in other examples, this conventional color coding is deployed to show natural disasters in many different forms.

A longer-term narrative is visualized in Figure 9.4, an animation by NASA (2011) to show forest and other wildfires that have occurred globally over the past decade, with each fire represented by a red dot (here mostly in southern Malaysia, Indonesia, and northern Australia), which is displayed on a vegetation backdrop derived from satellite imagery. Users can view a macrolevel animation of the entire globe or zoom in (at the relative microlevel) to a single continent. The animation focuses not on specific disasters but rather on the broader geographic distribution of the collective whole, enabling users to detect large-scale temporal and geographic patterns in the data unavailable at closer range.

As Figures 9.1–9.4 show, natural disaster visualizations employ a wide range of temporal scales to depict the passage of time, ranging from hours and days to years, decades, or even centuries. For visualizations of an isolated event such as the path of a hurricane, the temporal scale of the visualization is often quite short and precise, influenced by the longevity of the specific natural disaster narrated from start to finish. In this case, the temporal scale may cover the period of a few weeks, spanning a typical life cycle from when a tropical storm emerges, strengthens as a hurricane, and weakens and disappears. Other visualizations that display historical trends in natural disaster events, on the other hand, require a much more extended and coarse temporal scale, such as a map-based visualization of earthquakes in a region over the past century. Here, the visualization illustrates geographic trends over time for similar natural disaster occurrences so that users can grasp these patterns and contemplate their meaning for future events.[2]

Subdued Pathos Appeals

When we see visualizations that depict the animated storm paths of hurricanes or the legions of tornadoes spawned throughout the country each spring, we can comprehend the macrolevel physical and logistical effects of such events with remarkable clarity. Over the past decade, these displays have enabled most users

---

[2] Temporal scales measure the time between disasters as well as the time that a disaster occurs. An earthquake chart might show many years between events, but the earthquakes themselves may have lasted just seconds. Several hurricanes may hit the same place several times in a season, with a short duration between each one.

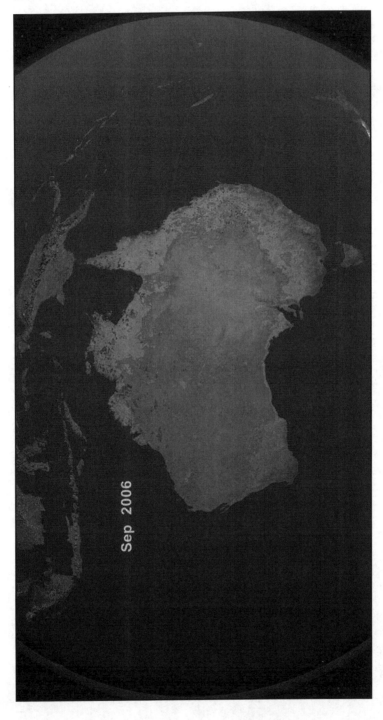

Figure 9.4. Frame from an animation displaying active fires (red) in Australia, Malaysia, Indonesia, and Oceania in September 2006 (NASA 2011). Retrieved from http://www.nasa.gov/mission_pages/fires/main/modis-10-overview.html. Figure courtesy of NASA Goddard Scientific Visualization Studio.

to lurk comfortably from afar, unaware of the death and destruction these events cause, unless abstractly invoked, as in the earthquake treemap (Figure 9.1). In these ways, historical visualizations narrating stories about the loss of life and property sanitize the data by excluding the gruesome effects on the ground, which are merely implied. As we watch the inexorable track of an Irene or a Katrina, we see the graphical macrolevel abstractions of the storm data rather than its microlevel effects at ground level. The focus is entirely on nature and its physical movements and patterns rather than on the human damage that they incur.

Historical visualizations, then, display forensic evidence dispassionately and objectively, curbing the emotions of the audience. These displays often afford user access to microlevel details, visualizing the magnitude of the earthquake precisely where it struck, the height of the flooding river, or the wind speed of the passing hurricane. Because users experience the terror of the event through the subdued lens of physical distance and abstract graphical forms, these visualizations fail to "humanize" the data, as Dragga and Voss put it (2001, p. 269). Focused on the natural phenomena themselves, the displays eschew explicit pathos appeals and remain almost entirely within the realm of logos: of highly usable, rational, and abstract representations of natural events.

Visualizing Current Disasters in Real Time: The Kairos of Exigency

In tracking current natural disasters, the Internet disseminates visualizations based on timely data that can be updated seamlessly and frequently as conditions change—daily, hourly, even minute by minute. Timely data constantly feed these visualizations so users can assess the current situation and adapt their daily activities as needed. In this way, *kairos* (or good timing) drives the rhetoric of visualizations that represent current conditions, as users focus their attention on images that matter *in the moment*. In generating such a wide array of timely, real-time displays that demand our immediate (and sometimes unrelenting) attention, the Internet has become a kairotic machine—technology that rivets audiences to natural exigencies.[3]

Perhaps the most popular of these types of visualizations are interactive, animated weather maps available from local and national news media as well as government agencies such as the National Weather Service. Such visualizations include maps layered with current data on variables such as temperature, cloud cover, precipitation, or wind conditions, often updated several times an hour. In many cases, data sources for natural disaster visualizations feed directly from

[3] Of course, users are riveted by moment-to-moment variations in other real-time Internet visualizations, such as stock market indexes, gas prices, commodities trading, and the movement of cars and airplanes, all of which create their own sets of exigencies.

scientific sensors or instruments from the natural environment, with little or no direct human mediation. One particularly appealing and effective example of such a real-time visualization is the animated wind map of the United States (Figure 9.5), designed by Viégas and Wattenberg (2012). Current prevalent wind patterns (direction and speed) are represented by the smooth-flowing vectors, updated on an hourly basis, that users can enlarge to examine microlevel conditions. In this particular map, strong southerly winds gust through the Chicago area, light westerly winds fan the Northern Great Plains, and the Mid-Atlantic enjoys relative calm.

Other real-time data maps visualize far more serious conditions. The real-time maps of stream gauge levels by the National Oceanic and Atmospheric Administration (NOAA) and the National Weather Service (2012c) enable users in the United States to assess local conditions and take necessary precautions. Figure 9.6 shows the locations of near (yellow) or minor (orange) flooding on the map of Florida in mid-July 2012 after Tropical Storm Debby had passed along

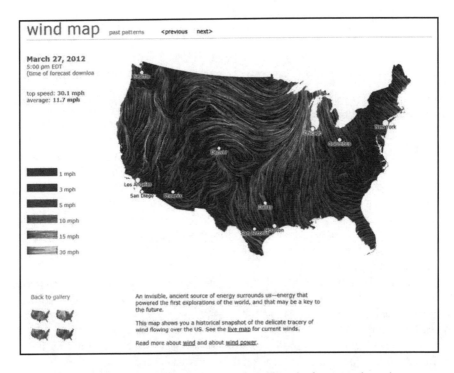

Figure 9.5. Animated wind map, updated hourly, for an early spring day in the continental U.S. (Viégas & Wattenberg, 2012). Retrieved from http://hint.fm/wind/gallery/mar-27.js.html. Reprinted with permission of Fernanda Viégas and Martin Wattenberg.

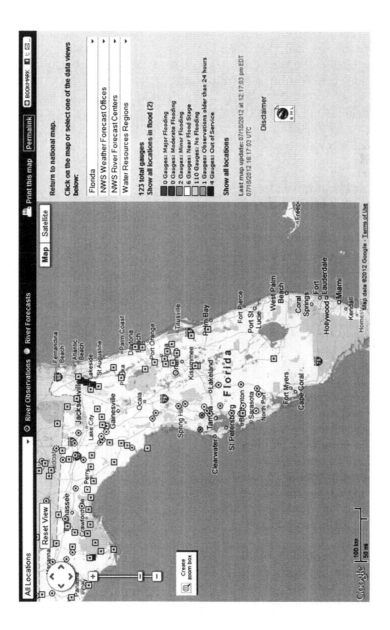

Figure 9.6. National Weather Service visualization of stream gauge readings for Florida, indicating locations of near (yellow) or minor (orange) flooding (NOAA 2012c). Retrieved from http://water.weather.gov/ahps/region.php?state=fl. Image provided courtesy of NOAA/National Weather Service.

the Gulf Coast a few weeks earlier. At this point, a recently soggy Florida had drained quite well, and for most Floridians the kairos of the display probably plummeted. Not so for users of Figure 9.7, in which the U.S. Geological Survey/ Earthquake Hazards Program (2013) shows the epicenters for recent earthquakes around the world, reminding inhabitants of coastal areas that seismic activity continues unabated, an uncomfortable reality around the Pacific "Ring of Fire." The size of the circle represents the earthquake's magnitude and the color the time of the event (red = within the past hour; orange = within the past day; yellow = within the past week). Users can access microlevel data by zooming in and by scrolling over earthquakes 2.5 or greater on the Richter scale, events often followed by numerous aftershocks.

Accessing Macro/Micro Data:
Visualizing My Own Backyard

Unlike risk in other aspects of life—health, finance, consumer products—risk from natural disasters is typically correlated with place, with a specific geographical location. Focus on place at the microlevel is particularly important for visualizations that depict ongoing natural disasters *as they occur*, as users assess the immediate danger for their own locations. However, the precision and accuracy of the geographical location may hinge on various sources of uncertainty inherent to the natural disaster, such as challenges related to pinpointing exactly where a tornado touched down in the immediate aftermath of the storm, or the precise size and location of an earthquake. Like Figure 9.7, Figure 9.8, by the California Institute of Technology Southern California Earthquake Data Center (2013), displays real-time data about earthquakes, but at a much finer microlevel—here focusing on California and Nevada, with even tiny 1.0 tremors visualized. Progressively larger squares represent the magnitude of each quake, and again color reveals time (red = last hour; blue = last day; yellow = last week). To see how close a quake has come to their own backyards, users can zoom into the map to locate a quake's precise location within a kilometer.

That microlevel precision can also be experienced through the National Weather Service website, which enables users to visualize local conditions through conventional radar as well as through rain and river gauges around the United States. At any given moment, a hydrogram chart (Figure 9.9) shows the water level at a local river or stream—here for Squaw Creek in Ames, Iowa, at Lincolnway, a key city street (NOAA/National Weather Service, 2012b). Users can then zoom in to their local situations to see the levels of rivers and streams in their areas on a display that plots time and depth at a given measuring station, allowing users to localize their views of the water conditions. The hydrogram in Figure 9.9 fosters kairos by displaying the creek's extremely low water level in summer 2012, when users were confronted with severe drought

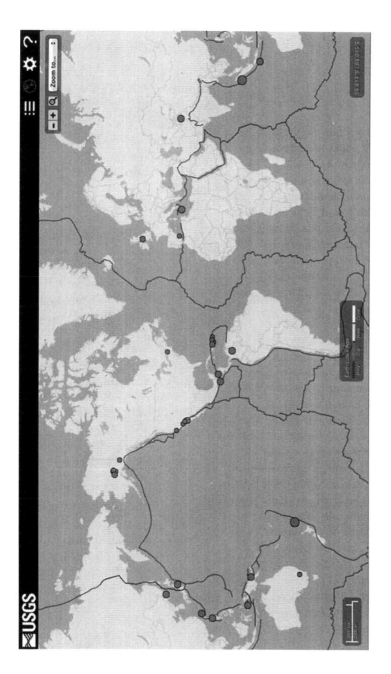

Figure 9.7. Visualization displaying locations of earthquakes 2.5 or greater on the Richter scale over seven days (U.S. Geological Survey/Earthquake Hazards Program, 2013). Retrieved from http://earthquake.usgs.gov/earthquakes/map/. Courtesy: U.S. Geological Survey Earthquake Hazards Program.

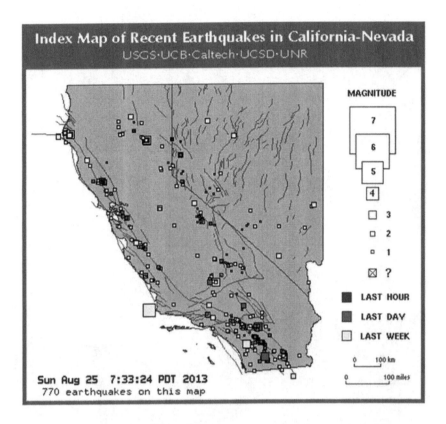

Figure 9.8. Visualization displaying locations of earthquakes in California and Nevada over seven days in real-time (California Institute of Technology, 2013). Retrieved from http://www.data.scec.org/recenteqs/. Reprinted with permission of SCEDC (2013): Southern California Earthquake Data Center. Caltech.Dataset.doi:10.7909/C3WD3xH1

conditions that stifled crops, dried up gardens and lawns, and caused unbearable heat. The low water levels visualized on the hydrogram quantified the severity of the conditions, heightening anxiety and uncertainty.

Social Media and the Citizen-Scientist: Cooperative Interaction in the Displays

Given the time-sensitive nature of some earth science visualizations, the public is invited to pitch in and assist with the disseminated data. Indeed "participation" and "creative collaboration" have been identified by James Zappen (2005, p. 321)

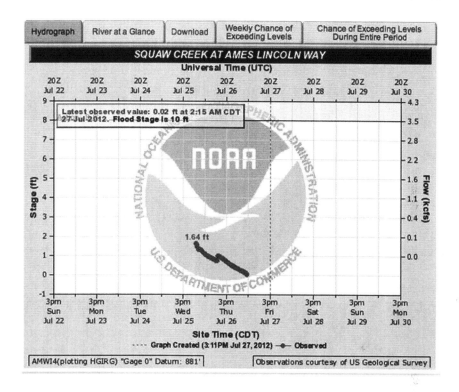

Figure 9.9. Water level on Squaw Creek in Ames, IA, at Lincolnway
(NOAA/National Weather Service, 2012b). Retrieved from
http://water.weather.gov/ahps2/hydrograph.php?wfo=dmx&gage=amwi4.
Image provided courtesy of NOAA/National Weather Service.

as key elements of digital rhetoric, and interactive displays of natural disasters often invite users to become actively engaged in shaping and communicating information. Because government (or government-funded) agencies maintain many of the websites about earth science data, accountability to the public plays a role in their design, dissemination, and evolution. Unlike static displays that appear off-line, online visualizations often allow users to provide feedback to the designers or to engage in blog conversations about the data. Through crowd-sourcing and citizen-science activities, some websites encourage users to submit actual data (or provide frequent, regular updates) utilized in constructing the visualizations. In these ways, users can contribute data, participate in the design process, and interact with other users. Goodchild (2007) has coined the term "Volunteered Geographic Information" (VGI) to describe the rapidly increasing trend of user-contributed information for map-based visualizations. In particular, social media and other forms of public participation have emerged as key components of web-based map visualizations for crises, given their conduciveness to support rapid emergency response (Liu & Palen, 2010).

Examples of natural disaster visualizations incorporating VGI are the real-time interactive disaster response maps published by the Environmental Systems Research Institute (ESRI). Figure 9.10, for example, shows one such ESRI map (2012) that focuses on wildfires in the western United States in summer 2012. Here, users can track the status of ongoing wildfire locations and wildfire potential in the continental United States, as well as ancillary map layers for current precipitation and wind patterns. In addition to having the option to explore the geographical extent of the wildfire perimeters by navigating the map at different scales and customizing it with overlays such as satellite imagery, users can also access information fetched from social media sources on the map, such as Twitter feeds, YouTube videos, and Flickr images. The social media information, added to the map as hyperlinked pushpins at the location where the information was captured or submitted, then becomes available to other users, providing a

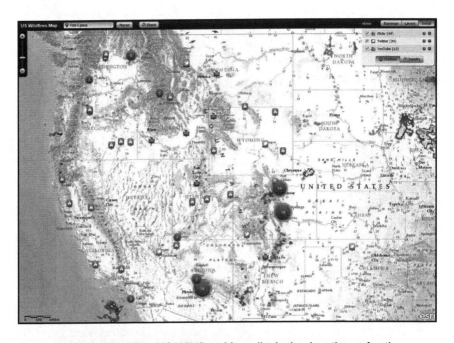

Figure 9.10. ESRI's US Wildfires Map, displaying locations of active wildfires in the American West, July 2012 (Environmental Systems Research Institute, 2012). Retrieved from http://tmappsevents.esri..com/Website/index.html. Used by permission. Copyright © 2012 Esri, NOAA, USGS, GeoMac. All rights reserved.

more personalized visualization where individuals can share their observations and experiences and tell their own stories about a given wildfire.

The National Weather Service utilizes social media in a related manner, allowing users to log comments via email and Facebook as well as to read Twitter posts by the Director. Upon request, the National Weather Service also provides email alerts or text messages via mobile phones to users when hazardous conditions arise. These interactive features commonly appear on websites of U.S. agencies. For example, the website of the U.S. Geological Survey's Earthquake Hazards Program (2013) enables users to report any earthquake activity they have experienced. The website also features a "Did You Feel It?" map on which they invite users' comments: users can report on their experiences with a specific earthquake, or they can even report tremors that do not appear already on the map. In these ways, users participate in constructing, altering, and commenting on the digital visualizations.

VISUALIZATIONS OF FUTURE DISASTERS: THE RHETORIC OF UNCERTAINTY

Visualizations of future probabilities are highly deliberative in that they warn users about what *might* happen in the future and prod them to consider what actions they might take to address the risk, however short or long term. Of course, visualizations showing past or present data often have a bearing on future events, given that users can extrapolate future patterns from the display and in this way infer what lies ahead. However, many visualizations focus specifically on the future—to *predict*, as explicitly as possible and with varying degrees of certainty, impending natural disasters. If the prediction has immediate conse- quences—say, in the next week or year, or even the lifetime of the user—the kairos (timing) of the prediction and its associated warnings and commands evoke pathos appeals for the stakeholders by engendering emotions ranging from concern and anxiety to fear or panic. However, if the prediction visualized is more long term, distant, and cosmic, it can evoke a more subdued pathos or even arouse feelings of the sublime. Because predictive visualizations affect users' decisions about how to respond to natural threats—where to live, precautions to take—these displays also raise ethical issues about their degrees of certainty or uncertainty. According to Monmonier (1997), persuasion is a primary purpose of risk maps due to their social construction, and the inevitable sources of uncertainty that abound in future projections may be manipulated by the designer and not readily conveyed to the map user.

These predicted events have varying levels of immediacy and consequences for the public, ranging from an imminent event to one not likely to occur for decades or even centuries or millennia, from an event that's merely a minor nuisance (a rainstorm) to one with long-range and perhaps catastrophic results sometime in the future (an asteroid impact). In short, these visualizations have varying levels of kairos. We might plot these variables as a scatter plot (Figure 9.11), with immediacy on the X-axis, here spanning a mere 140 years, and consequences on the Y-axis, on a scale from 1 to 100, with 1 being a minor inconvenience to 100 being total devastation.

So for example, a flood warning would be a very short-term and imminent event that might have serious consequences, depending on the location of the Internet user. Blizzards, ice storms, and other weather events would have a similar profile. An asteroid approaching Earth, on the other hand, might be a longer-term event (occurring decades or centuries in the future) and have huge consequences for some or all Internet users across the planet. The measurement of consequences, then, can be quite variable, ranging from no effect on some users to catastrophic consequences for others. If the users reside in the path of the lava flow of a predicted volcanic eruption, the risk to those users is infinitely higher than for someone living on another continent. On the other hand, over time, the plume of the volcano could affect virtually everyone on the planet in one way or another. Moreover, with the distant prospect of a galaxy collision or the solar system encountering a black hole, every living thing would be threatened in such a rare and (we hope) unlikely event.

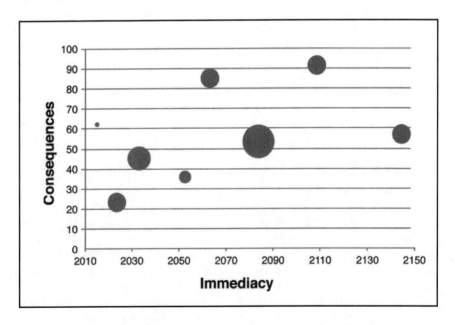

Figure 9.11. Plot showing potential consequences of predicted natural disasters. Circle size indicates relative impact on human lives.

So the number of users for which each datapoint on the scatter plot has consequences has to be qualified in some way. We do that here by enlarging the point to reflect the potential consequences to many users (the whole planet) and shrinking it to reflect the consequences to only a few (people experiencing a local flood), though by doing so, we do not wish to diminish the devastating impact of the event on those few who actually experience it.

Hedging the Future:
Certainty and Uncertainty of Predicting

Risk level for natural disasters varies with the type and by location: For example, we can envision hurricane or tropical storm risk along the coast near Miami, Florida, to be high not only due to the elevated likelihood of such storms forming there late each summer and early each fall, but also due to the potentially devastating consequences on the large populations living in the paths of these storms. A hurricane bearing down on the U.S. East Coast presents a real and imminent threat, yet one that can be tracked and allows adequate time for preparation in advance of the destruction. Earthquakes and droughts, on the other hand, are much more elusive to predict, the result of inference and extrapolation from data. And predictions of asteroid impacts are often informed guesses, based on tracking data from a limited number of previous sightings, with the probability fluctuating as new data accumulate, which can heighten or diminish the odds—and with them, public concern.

What risk pictures do data visualizations paint, and how accurate is it or can it possibly be? The water level predictions for Squaw Creek visualized in the line graph in Figure 9.12 seem to have a high level of accuracy, showing the probability of water rising to a given level over the next 3 months. Figure 9.12 by NOAA/National Weather Service (2012a) shows the overall likelihood of water levels, and an accompanying bar graph shows the likelihood in weekly intervals. The line graph emphatically predicts that Squaw Creek will not likely rise very much in the near future, with the probability of it reaching flood stage virtually nil. Reading the line graph (and accompanying bar chart), however, can be challenging for laypersons unfamiliar with this kind of statistical modeling, unlike flood or water specialists who use these charts regularly and can compare them with previous displays. Users who live in the area and understand these charts, however, can have a high degree of confidence in these predictions because they span a fairly narrow time zone in the immediate future and are based on a wide range of percentages, which allows some wiggle room and hedging.

On a much longer-term and consequential scale, the U.S. Geological Survey's Geologic Hazards Science Center (2012) offers Internet users the option to create "probability" maps that show the likelihood of an earthquake in a given location. By entering a zip code or latitude/longitude coordinates, the magnitude of a

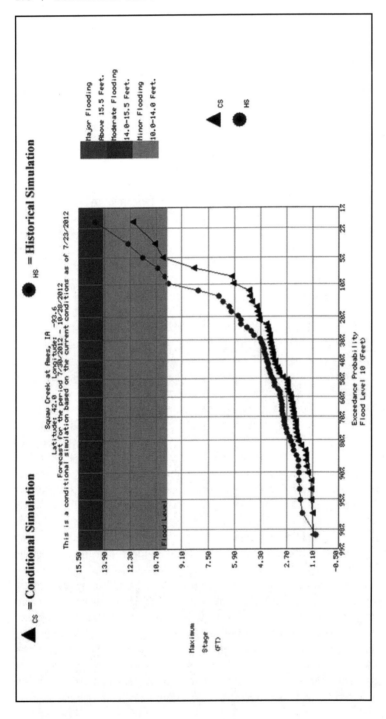

Figure 9.12. Prediction of water level in Squaw Creek in late summer and early fall 2012 (NOAA/National Weather Service 2012a). Retrieved from http://water.weather.gov/ahps2/period.php?wfo=dmx&gage=amwi4. Image provided courtesy of NOAA/National Weather Service.

possible quake, and a time span (1 year, 100,000 years), users can generate a map that shows the percentage probability of an event occurring in the surrounding area. In Ames, Iowa, for example, the chances of a severe quake (e.g., magnitude 6.0) occurring in the next millennium are very slim, not surprising because that part of the Midwest experiences very little seismic activity. However, not surprisingly, the same parameters yield a very different story for Los Angeles, where the probability is virtually certain at 100%. By entering a specific location (latitude/longitude or zip code), a time horizon (1 year to 10,000 years), and a magnitude on the Richter scale (5.0 and up), users can generate a color-coded map that indicates the level of risk for those variables (the darker the shading, the higher the risk). In this way, users can customize the prediction at the microlevel to see what's likely to happen in their own neighborhoods. Obviously, though, kairos diminishes with each zero added to the time scale: users may experience considerable anxiety with a 10- or 20-year time frame, but they may be unfazed (or even amused) by events predicted over a span of 10,000 years, however likely. Still, even though their persuasive power diminishes with time, the earthquake hazards maps are compelling and therapeutic, and their short-term predictions may be able to provoke action.

The predictive variations based on place can be instructive (and sometimes surprising). Figure 9.13 shows probability of an earthquake striking the Los Angeles area over the next 100 years. The dark shading indicates an extremely high risk in these places, 100%, which we might expect. A similar map generated by the website for Normal, Illinois, is entirely white, indicating that an earthquake 6.0 or greater in the next 100 years is extremely improbable, even though central Illinois lies in the realm of the potent New Madrid fault. These predictions, of course, are fairly easy for users to anticipate, given the geological histories of these two very different places. However, even the 100-year prediction map for a place like New York City, which is rarely associated with earthquakes, shows a slightly higher risk than Normal, Illinois, and also shows a slightly higher risk than Philadelphia (which appears on the New York City map because of its close proximity), realizations that can either be reassuring or unsettling. Even so, given the temporal span and the low probability of an earthquake, this map will hardly induce insomnia in the Bronx.

The exact level of risk can elude scientists, especially with long-range weather forecasts that predict temperature and precipitation. In North America, those forecasts are often driven by Pacific Ocean events known as La Niña and El Niño, which represent a cooling or warming of the ocean waters and which profoundly influence weather patterns and have serious consequences for agriculture, commodity prices, and land use generally. The effects of La Niña and El Niño are measured by the Southern Oscillation Index (SOI), which typically registers a positive value for La Niña events and a negative value for El Niño events, both of which can cause flooding or drought in certain areas. In general, the more distant the prediction, the less risky the assessment. Figure 9.14 by the National

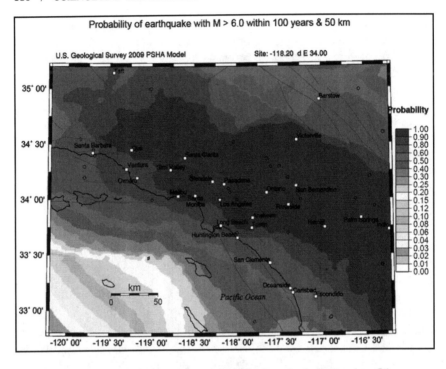

Figure 9.13. An earthquake probability map for Los Angeles, CA, generated from the U.S. Geological Survey's interactive website (U.S. Geological Survey/ Geologic Hazards Science Center, 2012). Retrieved from http://geohazards.usgs.gov/eqprob/2009/index.php. Courtesy: U.S. Geological Survey Geologic Hazards Science Center.

Weather Service's National Centers for Environmental Prediction (2012) shows the prediction for precipitation for 3 months into the future. The dark values represent a prediction of above-average dryness, and the darker the value the more severe the dryness predicted. The lighter values represent a prediction of above-average wetness, with the remainder of the country equally divided among higher, lower, or normal precipitation. Another map from the same website with exactly the same variables extends the predictions to 12 months into the future. Unlike the certainty expressed in the heavily colored 3-month map, the 12-month version contains large unshaded areas that have equal chances of higher, lower, or normal precipitation and consequently has less predictive value for users.

The level of certainty visualized in the display varies depending on the nature of the risk and the time horizon, though users may have to infer these varying levels of certainty because the visualizations do not always readily confess them. Only by inference do we suspect, for example, that the certainty in Figure 9.14 wanes in its longer-term version. The U.S Geological Survey's earthquake maps

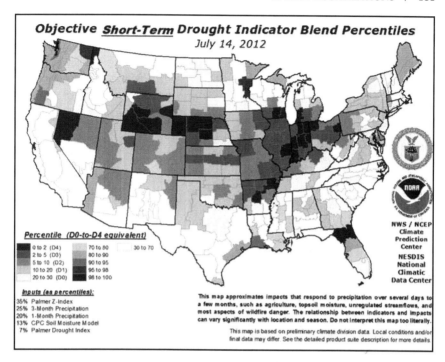

Figure 9.14. Short-term drought predictions for the U.S.
for July 2012 (National Weather Service/National Centers
for Environmental Prediction, 2012). Retrieved from
http://www.cpc.ncep.noaa.gov/products/predictions/tools/edb/sbfinal.gif.
Figure courtesy of the NOAA National Centers for Environmental Prediction.

use the same graphical display for a 10,000-year prediction that they do for a 10-year prediction, which results in greater certainty with time but which can also erase the differences among locations, which *over a long period of time* may share the same levels of risk. For vulnerable places like Los Angeles, for instance, a long time horizon colors the map evenly, homogenizing it visually and sacrificing the gradations of shorter-term maps, whose apparent precision conceals the lower level of certainty. From the user's perspective, however, the certainty of a 10,000-year map may have little bearing on the present, so as deliberative rhetoric, it may provide less impetus than the short-term map for users to ponder future plans or policies.

Assessments of risk and the certainty of predictions change as new data become available, in the process heightening or weakening the deliberative function of the displays that visualize them. For example, asteroids striking Earth pose a remote, but potentially devastating, aspect of risk that NASA's Near Earth Object Program website (2012) constantly monitors, cataloguing asteroids according to their size, orbit, and potential risk, measured on both the Palermo scale and the Torino scale. The Palermo scale measures risk mathematically according to several physical variables, while the Torino scale records gradations of risk on a 10-point color-coded scale, ranging from a 0 (white—no real risk) to a 10 (red—great potential for a major impact). Asteroids with "close approaches" to earth are measured in LDs, or lunar distances (the distance between the moon and the Earth), and the predictions of their possible impact constantly change, based on new data and observations.[4] NASA's Near Earth Object Program website (2012) visualizes dozens of asteroids and their predicted values in a detailed, interactive table that enables microlevel searching and analysis about the size of each asteroid, its time horizon, and its probability of Earth impact, including both the Torino and Palermo scales. Users can click on the probability rating to see a more detailed analysis and explanation as well as visualize the path of each asteroid in an animated solar system diagram. Although the chances of a given asteroid impacting the Earth are exponentially small, NASA does not visualize the actual risks graphically—perhaps because the possible trajectories are too complex, uncertain, and changeable and because lay audiences may too easily misinterpret such visualizations and find them potentially alarming. So as the risk profile of each asteroid evolves, so does its deliberative status, ranging from obscure and inconsequential to planetarily existential.

In most visualizations of risk, the level of certainty remains ambiguous and undisclosed, probably to reassure users and not to undermine the ethos of the visualization. Figure 9.15 by NOAA (2012), however, visualizes the level of certainty explicitly. Here, the flooding effects of sea level rise from climate change are mapped along the Gulf and Florida coasts, and users can control key prediction features (water depth, from 1 to 6 feet; frequency of flooding), and they can also visualize the *level of confidence* in these predictions. Blue areas indicate a high level of confidence and light orange high uncertainty. Figure 9.15 shows a close-up of the south Florida coast: the dark blue indicates that severe flooding would certainly occur in the Keys and the southern Everglades, with a low level of confidence in its severity in the Miami area. Given that this map is intended for "coastal managers and scientists," the uncertainty scale may bolster the ethos and value of the visualization for these users, who expect precision and full disclosure. On the other hand, private individuals with little

---

[4] This assessment of risk, obviously, is entirely Earth-centric, whereby all of the measurements and risk analyses are conducted relative to impacts with the Earth, as other planetary impacts will have no immediate consequences to lay users, even though they might fixate users who are scientists.

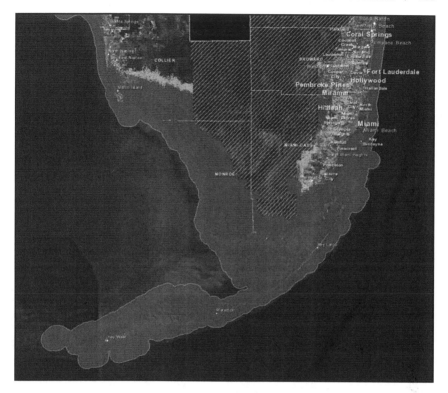

Figure 9.15. Predictions of sea level rise for south Florida (NOAA, 2012).
Source: NOAA Coastal Services Center (Digital Coast),
http://csc.noaa.gov/digitalcoast/tools/slrviewer
Used by permission. Copyright © 2016 Esri and its
data providers. All rights reserved.

scientific knowledge or experience with such data might find the different confidence levels disconcerting and confusing.

Predictions and the Rhetoric of Fear and Equanimity

Internet users who can master the interactive displays of looming natural disasters and glean precise information will feel a sense of control, masters of their data universe and empowered to respond, if necessary. Still, visualizations of natural disasters are inherently worrisome, engendering anxiety, distress, and fear. Computer models showing many divergent paths of a hurricane in a spaghetti diagram of crisscrossing paths running hither and yon may intrigue scientists in the audience, who value complexity and predictive detail; at the same time, however, that diagram will increase the angst of public users over a wider geographical area than a simpler diagram plotting the storm's most likely path. The more data-rich the visualization, the more likely it might engender anxiety and confusion—and turn empowerment into provocation.

How risk data are visualized can heighten or diminish that anxiety. Risk maps for natural disasters typically show the most dangerous areas in bright red or purple—colors in Western cultures that are associated with passion and emotion—and lesser areas of danger in lighter, cooler colors. On the earthquake prediction maps, darker colors represent greater chances of earthquakes and the lighter colors lesser chances. Clearly, these design conventions are intended to emphasize and focus users on the key risk data. So depending on the user's location, these visualizations may instantaneously engender a sense of foreboding or relief.

Variations of some of these color conventions appear on the map in Figure 9.16 (U.S. Department of Interior, 2004), which creates a vivid and alarming microlevel look at a future natural event—a volcanic eruption. Created by the U.S. Geological Survey (Hoblitt, Walder, Driedger, Scott, Pringle, & Vallance, 1998), the static map in Figure 9.16 visualizes prospective flow of lava and lahars (mudflows) that will occur with the next major eruption of Mt. Rainier in Washington State, with the range of the devastation depending on the magnitude of the eruption. Gray on the map indicates the area affected by lava in the immediate vicinity of Mt. Rainier, where population is very sparse, and shades of orange and yellow represent areas likely affected by lahars, where population is denser and which extends all the way to Tacoma. The level of certainty about the timing of major lahars—about every 500 to 1,000 years, with the last one occurring perhaps 500 years ago—is ambiguous enough to reduce immediate anxiety but specific enough to give pause to developers, homeowners, and others in their path. And given the eruptions at nearby Mount St. Helens in recent decades, the kairos and persuasiveness of this map remains strong if not urgent among area users.

So visualizations of potential natural disasters evoke a rhetoric of fear and anxiety for those users or for their friends and relatives who live in harm's way. The visualizations may deploy much of the same graphical coding that appears in historical versions, but users' interpretations are situated very differently because the visualization is oriented toward what *might* happen in the future—in the next few hours, days, or years. And that short-term imminence and a level of uncertainty foster emotional responses from users who are stakeholders, though they may not know exactly how to interpret the uncertainty (e.g., sometime in the next 500 years), which may not even be acknowledged on the display to protect its ethos. The visualizations can also engender a state of equanimity for those users who lurk from afar, have no stake in the probable event, and experience it only vicariously through the display.

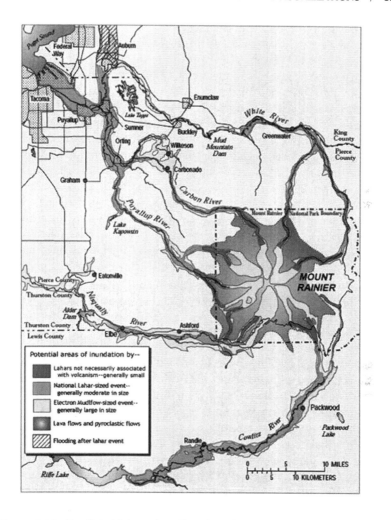

Figure 9.16. Predicted lahars (mudflows) and lava flows for Mount Rainier
in Washington State (U.S. Department of the Interior, 2004, Figure 3;
source for map is Plate 1 from Hoblitt, Walder, Driedger, Scott, Pringle, &
Vallance, 1998). Retrieved from http://nationalatlas.gov/articles/geology/a_volca
nicrisk.html. Courtesy of U.S. Geological Survey.

The Cosmic Rhetoric of the Sublime

Although visualizations predicting future events have only recently been available, natural disasters have occurred for thousands of years, with the assumption that they would repeat themselves. Visualizations enable us to see how,
where, and when those re-occurrences might take place. Contemporary science,

however, has discovered additional threats with more far-reaching consequences, creating new avenues of uncertainty and anxiety. Only in the past half century, for example, has the impact of asteroids been increasingly known—and along with that knowledge, the daunting certainty of future such events, leaving us to wonder not *if* but *when* another might occur—and what we might do in the meantime to avert these looming catastrophes.

On an even broader scale, images from the Hubble telescope are visualizing the stunning and beautiful violence of the evolving universe and fostering speculation about how similar events might shape our own destiny. That speculation is mostly reduced to mathematical calculations (a three in a million chance of such and such happening in the next billion years), happily abstracting the data into forms that most of us can't possibly comprehend, spatially or temporally. So from the standpoint of visualization, such terrifying prospects are visualized vicariously at the macrolevel with amazing clarity and brilliance, but they remain visually and existentially (and perhaps hopelessly) ambiguous at the microlevel. The ambiguity and incomprehensible size of such phenomena, along with the relative safety of their distance in space and time, are engendering—perceptually and emotionally—the sublime of Edmund Burke (2008) on a cosmic scale.

The Ethical Fine Line of Visualizing Predictions

The ethical responsibility to persuade users, by warning them and provoking them to action to a sufficient degree, always accompanies risk assessment, particularly when potential disasters are visualized. In predicting future risk, government agencies bear some responsibility for influencing the material conditions of their constituents—for example, land and home values, regulations for constructing buildings, zoning policies, as well as where people are willing to live and work and what kind of life they envision for themselves, say, near an active seismic fault. By visualizing these assessments and predictions, the Internet can profoundly affect users' decision-making in the present, long before an actual event occurs. Given the physical risks that users may foresee to themselves and their property, the visualizations may prompt them to protect themselves by taking certain actions—for example, boarding up windows for hurricanes, retrofitting buildings for earthquakes, purchasing flood insurance, or moving somewhere else. All data design has an ethical component (Kienzler, 1997), especially visualizations of risk, which can have such far-reaching consequences.

The Internet's position of authority, then, entails an ethical fine line between, on the one hand, adequately alerting users so they can protect themselves, and on the other hand, hyping up risk and causing users to overreact and squander precious resources on needless remedies. So the designers of online visualizations have the ethical responsibility to balance user safety with overly dire predictions that might create panic and distrust and cause the unnecessary expense of preventative measures.

That responsibility, however, can sometimes be confounded by entrenched visual and social conventions. To give a simple example, emergency weather outlets on the Internet typically visualize warnings by counties, which come in all shapes and sizes. However, weather phenomena rarely follow the exact contours of (largely artificial) county borders: while a tornado, hailstorm, or high winds may seriously threaten the southeast corner of a given county, users living in the northwest corner *see* exactly the same alert on their screens. By homogenizing place, the convention of visualizing by county extends the warning evenly across a whole area, though only a fraction of it may be affected. As we mentioned earlier, color conventions prevail in risk visualizations, with warm, intense colors indicating potential problems and cooler, lighter ones low risk, and in the process over- or understating risk visually. Also, what a visualization shows and does not show (Barton & Barton, 1993a, pp. 53-68) may strongly influence a user's perception of risk. A map showing tornado patterns across the central United States may intimidate a New Yorker wanting to relocate in Kansas City by isolating this one phenomenon in what otherwise may be (in terms of natural disasters) a very uneventful place. To remedy this, Barton and Barton (1993a) would advocate a more complex, nuanced, and complete picture—here perhaps by supplying links to visualizations of other natural disaster risks so that users have a broader context within which to interpret the data and make well-informed decisions.

CONCLUSION

As a form of scientific rhetoric that spans several earth science disciplines, visualizations of natural disasters—past, present, future—embody an array of rhetorical elements. These displays embody forensic rhetoric by articulating data about past natural events in logical frameworks within which users can manipulate data to highlight variables and reveal patterns. As a new form of digital rhetoric, most data visualizations invite user participation to customize displays according to their needs and preferences as well as to provide data and feedback. In displays of present and often real-time data, kairos dominates, as users experience data *in the moment*, focusing on the immediate events unfolding and how to interpret and react to them. In visualizations that predict future natural events within a range of probability, deliberative rhetoric dominates, as users assess and debate plans and policies in response to the risk. Credibility and ethics pervade all three temporal modes, particularly predictive visualizations that have decision-making consequences for stakeholders. All three temporal modes foster emotional responses, ranging from relief, anxiety, or fear to those of terror, empathy, and the sublime. Understandably, disasters stir the emotions, which visualizations can further intensify through color, animations, and ambiguity.

We have now experienced the first wave of visualizations about natural disasters, which have largely been designed to help the public sort through, understand, and respond to complex datasets. The variety of forms these displays embody—graphs, maps, lists, animations, color, interactivity, blogs—have engaged users on steep learning curves in many different rhetorical situations, ranging from learning and discovery, to responding to immediate crises, to making long-range plans. This first wave of visualizations has established a rhetorical and perceptual foundation that scientists, designers, and Internet users can build on. Ahead lie countless more Internet visualizations that ever-more numerous, engaged, and sophisticated users will learn how to interpret, critique, and act on.

REFERENCES

Aristotle. (2007). *On rhetoric: A theory of civic discourse* (G. A. Kennedy, Trans., 2nd ed.). New York, NY: Oxford University Press.

Barton, B. F., & Barton, M. S. (1993a). Ideology and the map: Toward a postmodern visual design practice. In N. R. Blyler & C. Thralls (Eds.), *Professional communication: The social perspective* (pp. 49–78). Newbury Park, CA: Sage.

Barton, B. F., & Barton, M. S. (1993b). Modes of power in technical and professional visuals. *Journal of Business and Technical Communication, 7*, 138–162.

Brasseur, L. E. (2003). *Visualizing technical information: A cultural critique.* Amityville, NY: Baywood.

Burke, E. (2008). *A philosophical enquiry into the origin of our ideas of the sublime and beautiful.* A Phillips (Ed.). Oxford, UK: Oxford University Press. (Original work published 1757)

California Institute of Technology Southern California Earthquake Data Center/ U.S. Geological Survey. (2013, August). Index map of recent earthquakes in California-Nevada [Map]. *Caltech.Dataset.* doi: 10.7909/C3WD3xH1. Retrieved from http://www.data.scec.org/recenteqs/

Dragga, S., & Voss, D. (2001). Cruel pies: The inhumanity of technical illustrations. *Technical Communication, 48*, 265–274.

Environmental Systems Research Institute (ESRI). (2012, July). *U.S. wildfires map* [Interactive map]. Retrieved from http://tmappsevents.esri.com/Website/wildfire/index.html

Fisher, D. (2010). Animation for visualization: Opportunities and drawbacks. In J. Steele & N. Iliinsky (Eds.), *Beautiful visualization: Looking at data through the eyes of experts* (pp. 329–352). Sebastopol, CA: O'Reilly Media.

Goodchild, M. F. (2007). Citizens as sensors: The world of volunteered geography. *GeoJournal, 69*, 211–221.

Gross, A. G. (1996). *The rhetoric of science* (2nd ed.). Cambridge, MA: Harvard University Press.

Hive Group. (2012, July). *Most powerful and deadliest earthquakes since 1900* [Interactive chart]. Retrieved from http://www.hivegroup.com/gallery/earthquakes/

Hoblitt, R. P., Walder, J. S., Driedger, C. L., Scott, K. M., Pringle, P. T., & Vallance, J. W. (1998). Volcanic hazards from Mount Rainier, Washington. *U.S. Geological Survey Open-File Report 98-428.* Washington, DC: U.S. Department of the Interior, U.S. Geological Survey.

Johnson, H., & Nelson, E. S. (1998). Using flow maps to visualize time-series data: Comparing the effectiveness of a paper map series, a computer series, and animation. *Cartographic Perspectives, 30,* 47–64.

Kienzler, D. (1997). Visual ethics. *Journal of Business Communication, 34,* 171–187.

Kimball, M. A. (2006). London through rose-colored graphics: Visual rhetoric and information graphic design in Charles Booth's maps of London poverty. *Journal of Technical Writing and Communication, 36,* 353–381.

Kostelnick, C. (2008). The visual rhetoric of data displays: The conundrum of clarity. *IEEE Transactions on Professional Communication, 51,* 116–130.

Kostelnick, J. C., Land, J. D., & Juola, J. F. (2007). Judgments of size change trends in static and animated graduated circle displays. *Cartographic Perspectives, 57,* 41–55.

Liu, S. B., & Palen, L. (2010). The new cartographers: Crisis map mashups and the emergence of neographic practices. *Cartography and Geographic Information Science, 37,* 69–90.

Mirel, B. (1998). Visualizations for data exploration and analysis: A critical review of usability research. *Technical Communication, 45,* 491–509.

Monmonier, M. (1997). *Cartographies of danger: Mapping hazards in America.* Chicago, IL: University of Chicago Press.

Monmonier, M. (2008). Web cartography and the dissemination of cartographic information about coastal inundation and sea level rise. In M. P. Peterson (Ed.), *International perspectives on maps and the Internet* (pp. 49–71). Berlin, Germany: Springer.

NASA. (2011, July). *Fire and smoke* [Animated map]. Retrieved from http://www.nasa.gov/mission_pages/fires/main/modis-10-overview.html

NASA/Near Earth Object Program. (2012). *Sentry risk table.* Retrieved from http://neo.jpl.nasa.gov/risk/

National Oceanic and Atmospheric Administration (NOAA). (2012, August). *Sea level rise and coastal flooding impacts* [Interactive map]. Retrieved from http://www.csc.noaa.gov/slr/viewer/#

National Oceanic and Atmospheric Administration (NOAA)/National Weather Service. (2012a, July). *Advanced hydrologic prediction service: Chance of exceeding levels during entire period* [Graph]. Retrieved from http://water.weather.gov/ahps2/period.php?wfo=dmx&gage=amwi4

National Oceanic and Atmospheric Administration (NOAA)/National Weather Service. (2012b, July). *Advanced hydrologic prediction service: Hydrograph* [Graph]. Retrieved from http://water.weather.gov/ahps2/hydrograph.php?wfo=dmx&gage=amwi4

National Oceanic and Atmospheric Administration (NOAA)/National Weather Service. (2012c, July 18). *River observations* [Interactive map]. Retrieved from http://water.weather.gov/ahps/region.php?state=fl

National Oceanic and Atmospheric Administration (NOAA)/National Weather Service/National Centers for Environmental Prediction. (2012, July 14). *Objective long-term drought indicator blend percentiles* [Map]. Retrieved from http://www.cpc.ncep.noaa.gov/products/predictions/tools/edb/sbfinal.gif

National Oceanic and Atmospheric Administration (NOAA)/National Weather Service/National Hurricane Center. (2011, August 26). *Irene graphics archive* [Animated map]. Retrieved from http://www.nhc.noaa.gov/archive/2011/graphics/al09/loop_3W.shtml

Patton, D. K., & Cammack, R. G. (1996). An examination of the effects of task type and map complexity on sequenced and static choropleth maps. In C. H. Wood & C. P. Keller (Eds.), *Cartographic design: Theoretical and practical perspectives* (pp. 237–252). Chichester, UK: Wiley & Sons.

Slocum, T. A., Blok, C., Jiang, B., Koussolakou, A., Montello, D. R., Fuhrmann, S., & Hedley, N. R. (2001). Cognitive and usability issues in geovisualization. *Cartography and Geographic Information Science, 28*, 61–75.

Tufte, E. R. (1990). *Envisioning information.* Cheshire, CT: Graphics Press.

U.S. Department of the Interior/nationalatlas.gov. (2004, May). *Mount Rainier: Learning to live with volcanic risk* [Map]. Retrieved from http://nationalatlas.gov/articles/geology/a_volcanicrisk.html

U.S. Geological Survey/Earthquake Hazards Program. (2013, August). *Latest earthquakes* [Interactive map]. Retrieved from http://earthquake.usgs.gov/earthquakes/map/

U.S. Geological Survey/Geologic Hazards Science Center. (2012, July). *2009 Earthquake probability mapping* [Map]. Retrieved from http://geohazards.usgs.gov/eqprob/2009/index.php

U.S. Geological Survey/National Drought Mitigation Center. (2012). *Vegetation drought response index: VegDRI animated series* [Animated map]. Retrieved from http://vegdri.unl.edu/TimeSeries.aspx

Viégas, F., & Wattenberg, M. (2012, March 27). *Wind map* [Animated map]. Retrieved from http://hint.fm/wind/gallery/mar-27.js.html

Zappen, J. P. (2005). Digital rhetoric: Toward an integrated theory. *Technical Communication Quarterly, 14*, 319–325.

http://dx.doi.org/10.2190/SCIC10

CHAPTER 10

Meltdowns in the Media: Visualization of Radiation Risk from The Printed Page to the Internet

James Wynn

ABSTRACT

This chapter considers whether and in what ways the Internet might be influencing risk communication about nuclear accidents. It compares the visual and verbal features of radiation maps in pre-Internet print reports of the accidents at Three Mile Island and Chernobyl with the features of online maps of the Fukushima Daiichi disaster—maps created by both mainstream media outlets and citizen activists. This investigation suggests (a) that visual representations of radiation risk vary in response to the material, sociopolitical, and/or technical conditions in which the risk communication is made; (b) that the choices of risk visualization can be driven as much by rhetorical, or persuasive goals, as communicative ones; and (c) that the Internet has fundamentally transformed visual risk communication of radiation risk.

In *Risk Society* (1992), Ulrich Beck argues that the central social concern in 20th-century Western nations is the rise of risk brought about by their regimes of scientific progress and technicization. This intuition seems to be reaffirmed almost daily as events like the Deep Water Horizon disaster in the Gulf of Mexico and the meltdown of reactors at Fukushima, Japan attract media attention and generate public debate and discourse about the risks of modern techno-industrial society. Rhetorical scholars of science and technology have been quick to pick up on and investigate the growing importance of risk and its consequences for argument and communication. Carolyn Miller, for instance, has written articles on a variety of risk topics, including how organizational communication influences risk (Herndl, Fennell, & Miller, 1991), how failures of risk communication impede public deliberation (Katz & Miller, 1996), and how the mathematization of risk elides ethical engagement between governing institutions and citizens (Miller, 2003). Other rhetoric and communication scholars have written on a range of risk topics, including nuclear accidents (Farrell & Goodnight, 1998), mine safety (Sauer, 2003), and bioweapons (Keränen, 2011).

Despite the significant attention to written and spoken risk discourse, virtually no consideration has been paid to visual representations and their role in characterizing risk.[1] It is also notable that rhetorical scholars have yet to explore how the introduction of the Internet might be transforming risk communication and argument. This omission seems unusual given the attention that the relationship between the Internet, political communication, and argument has garnered (Davisson, 2011; Gil de Zuñiga, Puig-I-Abril, & Rojas, 2009; Warnick, 2007). This chapter engages with these research gaps by exploring maps visualizing the radiation risk from nuclear plant accidents at Three Mile Island, Chernobyl, and Fukushima in both print and online media. In particular, it will pursue these questions: What are the strategies for visually representing radiation risk? To what extent and in what ways do visualization strategies change across accidents and media types? And what possible consequences do these changes have for the consumers and producers of risk communication?

To assess the strategies in print media for representing radiation risk and their change over time, this chapter will analyze the visual/verbal features of radiation maps in pre-Internet print stories in the *New York Times* and *Washington Post* on Three Mile Island and Chernobyl. These visualizations will be compared with online maps of the radiation risk from Fukushima created by the *New York Times* and the citizen group Safecast to gain insight into whether and in what ways the Internet might be influencing risk communication about radiation and what the consequences of this transformation might be. This investigation suggests (a) that visual representations of radiation risk vary in response to the material, sociopolitical, and/or technical conditions in which the risk communication is made; (b) that the choices of risk visualization can be driven as much by rhetorical, or persuasive goals, as communicative ones; and (c) that the Internet has fundamentally transformed visual risk communication of radiation risk.

---

[1] Lee Brasseur's work on Florence Nightingale's development of rose diagrams to show the risks of poor sanitation in military hospitals takes a step in this direction. Its goal, however, is not a self-conscious discussion of risk visualization. See Brasseur (2005). Beverly Sauer in *The Rhetoric of Risk* (2003) also talks about the role of visual mediums such as gesture and FATALGRAMS in mine safety education and discourse. This discussion, however, is limited to private specialized risk communication rather than public representation of risk. See Sauer (pp. 166–175, 232–244).

METHOD

Describing and comparing visual representations of risk across nuclear accidents requires analytical categories for visual assessment and methods that allow similarities and variations to be accounted for. To maintain comparability and a manageable sample size, the corpus of print visuals for this investigation has been limited to the *New York Times* and the *Washington Post*, while the online visual corpus has been limited to the websites NYTimes.com and Safecast.org. These corpora offer access to important slices of mainstream print and online visual representations of the three nuclear accidents. In conducting this investigation, every issue for each of the print publications was searched for risk visuals for a 1-month period following each nuclear accident. Once located, all of the visuals in the sample were assessed using a standard format. Basic background information about the visual was recorded, including the date, the source, the author, and location in the news publication. Then, a detailed qualitative evaluation of the visual was made, which included four categories of assessment: the format of the visual presentation, the information provided about radiation risk, the relationship between the visual and the text of the news story (or stories) with which it was associated, and the context in which it occurred. In the assessment of the online risk visuals on NYTimes.com and Safecast.org, these strategies of analysis were also applied with the exception of the analysis of the relationship between the text and the story. The map on NYTimes.com was linked as a resource to a number of stories rather than attached to a single one, making it difficult to identify any specific connection between the reporting and the interactive visual. Safecast.org was not a news site and therefore had no news text to analyze. However, maps and blogs posted on the website between March of 2011 and 2012 were examined.

In assessing the format of the visual presentation in all of the sources, the range of strategies for representing risk were identified and inventoried. These included features like maps and map insets, visualizations of population centers, visualizations of radiation and its magnitude, and the incorporation of words and numbers in visuals. Once the visual formats were identified, they were assessed for the type of information about risk they communicated. This assessment was made on the basis of a basic set of questions considered vital by media experts on risk reporting: What is the risk? What is its magnitude? What is its location and geographic extent? Who is affected by it? What are the consequences for those who are affected? Who/what is responsible for it? (Kitzinger, 2009; Ropeik, 2011). In cases where risk visuals were complements of news stories or blogs, the relationships between the visual risk representations and textual content were also examined. The relationship between words and visuals and the kinds of epistemological and rhetorical contributions each makes to discourse and argument has been the subject of research by a number of rhetoric and communication studies scholars (Gross, 2009; Hagan, 2007; Kress

& van Leeuwen, 2006). This study focuses specifically on the extent to which the basic questions about risk were supplied by the text of a news story, its associated visual, or both. Then, conclusions will be drawn about the role of visual and textual elements or their collaboration in communication about risk. Finally, this assessment considers the context in which the risk visualizations occur. As Birdsell and Groarke (2007) point out, visual representations need to be interpreted in a manner that fits the context in which they are situated (p. 104). Because the contextual factors influencing risk visualization of nuclear accidents are myriad and not all relevant, this investigation will focus specifically on assessing the influence of existing visual conventions on choices of risk representation, the immediate historical-political context in which the risk visuals emerge, and the technological-material factors that might affect them.

THREE MILE ISLAND

Understanding how the representation of radiation risk has changed over time requires a consideration of what the characteristics of risk visualization were at its inception. This section examines that moment by looking at visual representations of the very first widely reported nuclear accident, Three Mile Island. This examination suggests that the conventions for visually representing radiation risk were borrowed from the iconography of civil defense discourse and that borrowing this iconography had some unintended consequences for risk representation.

At 4 a.m. on Wednesday, March 28, 1979, the main cooling pump of reactor number two at the Three Mile Island nuclear plant shut down, and the auxiliary pump could not be brought on line to cool the reactor core. The plant's engineers shut the reactor down; however, pressure built in its core as the reactor's uranium rods continued to fission without being cooled. Steam building in the reactor core was released to maintain pressure; however, a stuck-open valve allowed cooling water to flow out of the reactor as well. A cascade of events followed, including the melting of more than half of the reactor core, the buildup of a hydrogen gas bubble in the reactor, and the release of radioactive water, vapor, and particulates into the area surrounding the plant. As the crisis at the plant grew, the news media descended on southeastern Pennsylvania to cover the event. The coverage of Three Mile Island represents a watershed moment in radiation risk communication because it is the first time that news reporters and designers were tasked with representing radioactive risk from a nuclear power plant accident. Though there were two other accidents reported on in the 1960s,[2] these did not

---

[2] In 1961 there was an accident at a government test reactor SL-1 in Idaho where three people were killed. *Time* magazine and the *New York Times* ran stories on it in January of the same year. See Finney (1961) and "Runaway" (1961). The second accident was a partial meltdown in the core of the Fermi nuclear plant outside Detroit in October of 1966, which was reported a month later in the *New York Times* in November of the same year. See Gamson and Modiglioni (1989, p. 14).

generate the media attention or risk visuals that the Three Mile Island accident did (Gamson & Modiglioni, 1989, p. 14). Because of their first-of-their-kind status, the verbal/visual risk representations in the media coverage of Three Mile Island offer a starting point from which to assess the developments of the conventions for visualizing radiation risk from nuclear accidents.

Though the visualizations created to describe the accident at Three Mile Island were the first of their kind, it is important to note that the accident did not immediately or directly spawn new conventions for representing radiation risk. That a conventional representation was not immediately created is evidenced by the initial variety of strategies for risk visualization used in the first two days of reporting (March 29 and 30, 1979). During this period, the *New York Times* and the *Washington Post* both carried maps of the area at risk from the accident. However, only the *Washington Post* offered a visualization of radiation, which used a shaded square to identify the supposed area affected by radioactive emissions (O'Toole, Peterson, Richards, Cohn, Lantz, Baer et al., 1979). It wasn't until March 31 that newspapers introduced maps that included a bull's-eye overlay—a set of concentric rings radiating out from a central point. This design strategy quickly became a conventional standard for representing radiation risk for a nuclear accident. After March 31, this visual element appears on every radiation map in the sample. Figure 10.1 (printed in *The Patriot-News* of Harrisburg, PA) is just one example of the bull's-eye map.

Some rhetorical scholars have argued that visual strategies seldom exist in a vacuum. Instead, conventions, or existing strategies for representation, often drive information design (Kostelnick & Hasset, 2003, p. 7). In the case of the bull's-eye overlay, its adoption as a convention for describing nuclear accidents seems to have been driven by earlier civil defense evacuation and risk assessment maps, which use the bull's-eye strategy to represent the area of risk created by a hypothetical atomic bomb attack and its consequent fallout. Visualizations of this kind appear as early as 1952 in the *Greater Boston Civil Defense Manual* and continue to be part of the format of local[3] as well as national[4] civil defense pamphlets and booklets distributed to the public into the 1960s. Though by the 1970s, civil defense against nuclear attack was no longer a priority of the government[5] and the circulation of these documents ebbed, their use in a decade of public education had likely given them an iconic status.

Their iconicity was also reinforced by their use in the media during the same period to describe the threat of a potential nuclear strike. In 1955, for example, the concern over the consequences of nuclear warfare reached a new fever pitch with the release of estimates of the area of destruction created by the

---

[3] See Office of Civil Defense, St. Louis (1955).

[4] See U.S. Department of Defense, *Fallout Protection* (1961, p. 13).

[5] See Krugler (2006, p. 184).

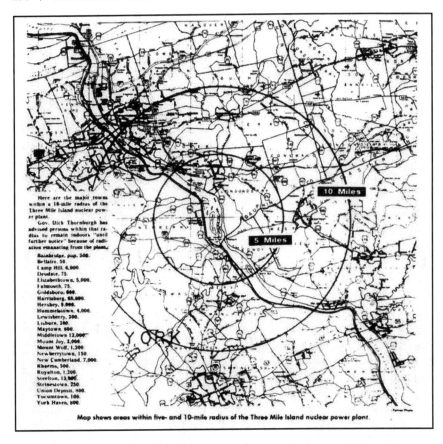

The following towns are listed on the map:

Here are the major towns within a 10-mile radius of the Three Mile Island nuclear power plant.

Gov. Dick Thornburgh has advised persons within that radius to remain indoors "until further notice" because of radiation emanating from the plant.

Bainbridge, pop. 500.
Bellaire, 50.
Camp Hill, 6,000.
Dresdale, 75.
Elizabethtown, 5,000.
Falmouth, 75.
Goldsboro, 600.
Harrisburg, 68,000.
Hershey, 9,000.
Hummelstown, 4,000.
Lewisberry, 300.
Lisburn, 800.
Maytown, 800.
Middletown 12,000.
Mount Joy, 3,000.
Mount Wolf, 1,200.
Newberrytown, 150.
New Cumberland, 7,000.
Rheems, 500.
Royalton, 1,200.
Steelton, 12,000.
Strinestown, 250.
Union Deposit, 800.
Yocumtown, 100.
York Haven, 800.

10 Miles

5 Miles

YORK

Map shows areas within five- and 10-mile radius of the Three Mile Island nuclear power plant.

Figure 10.1. An example of the bull's-eye overlay often used to represent the Three Mile Island Accident. This map appeared in *The Patriot-News*, a Harrisburg, PA newspaper. Note. © March 31, 1979 The Patriot-News. All rights reserved. Preprinted and/or used with permission.

hydrogen bomb in the 1954 Bikini Atoll tests. These tests revealed that the hydrogen bomb was more powerful than anticipated and the spread of fallout greater than expected. In the first few months after the test in 1955, stories such as "U.S. H-bomb Test Put Lethal Zone at 7,000 sq. Miles: Area Nearly the Size of Jersey Covered by Atom Fallout . . . Civilian Peril Stressed" and "City Evacuation Plan: 3 Governors and Mayor Weigh Plans to Meet H-Bomb Attack" were front page news in the *New York Times* (W. Blair, 1955; Porter, 1955). In the same period, the Associated Press (1955) produced a map, "Radiation Effects," with a bull's-eye overlay to describe the "range of possible death if an H-bomb should hit squarely on Cincinnati." In the visual, a bull's-eye overlay with three concentric circles marks off three zones of radiation risk from fallout in the aftermath of a nuclear attack. In the inner 140-mile radius circle, all persons downwind from the bomb blast could expect to receive a fatal dose of radiation. In the two rings marked off between 160 and 190 miles, 5 to 10 persons out of 100 exposed to radiation might be expected to die. Because of the iconicity the bull's-eye overlay in civil defense materials and the media, and its connection with the risks of radiation, it is not surprising that it would be co-opted for representing the radiation risk from the nuclear accident at Three Mile Island.

Though the bull's-eye overlay was uniquely suited for representing the risks associated with a hypothetical nuclear strike, there were some consequences for choosing this method to represent a real radiological disaster. In civil defense materials, for example, the bull's-eye graphic was useful because it could simultaneously represent a number of different dimensions of the risk situation, including the actual risk, the area affected by the risk, and/or the area where risk intervention had to take place. This polysemic representation of risk was useful in civil defense documents that were dedicated to educating the populous about the risks of a nuclear strike as well as informing them who would be affected and what they should do in the case of an attack. Under real emergency conditions where simple and direct communications are essential, however, this polysemy could be detrimental because it encouraged multiple ways of interpreting a risk communiqué. In addition to being polysemous, the bull's-eye overlay was also a visual strategy for generalizing risk. The concentric circles that were the hallmark of the visualization represented the possible zones of risk rather than specific details about actual risk location and intensity. In the hypothetical nuclear attack scenario described in civil defense materials, this representational strategy was required since no event had taken place. In fact, imaging the broadest range of potential risk was useful for citizens and local governments who needed to plan for a range of disaster scenarios. While the general quality of the bull's-eye overlay's concentric rings works well in a civil defense manual, in cases with real risks with specific locations, it can offer a false sense of either safety or risk because it does not account for the actual dynamics of radiation spread which typically follow an asymmetrical path.

An assessment of the first bull's-eye overlay maps in the *New York Times* and *Washington Post* on March 31 illustrates the problem of visual polysemy (Cook, 1979; Lyons, 1979). The visual polysemy of these maps seems to be associated with the prior conventional use of the bull's-eye overlay to represent different aspects of the risk situation and the presence of textual cues in news reporting that supported different readings of the visual. In both the *Washington Post* and the *New York Times*, the maps were juxtaposed with content discussing radiation levels at the plant and content about Pennsylvania Governor Richard Thornburgh's evacuation plans. In the *New York Times*, for example, the first fallout map is placed between the headline "U.S. Aides See a Risk of Meltdown at Pennsylvania Nuclear Plant; More Radioactive Gas Is Released" and its caption, which describes Governor Thornburgh's advisement of evacuation. The juxtaposition of the map with text describing these two different subjects raises questions about which of the topics the map is representing: the area of radioactive fallout or the area of evacuation ahead of the foreseeable threat from radioactive fallout. This ambiguity is further encouraged by the fact that neither the *Times'* nor the *Post's* maps are labeled to indicate whether the area within the bull's-eye represents the area of evacuation or the area affected by radiation released from the plant. The *Post's* map is titled generically, "Area Surrounding Three Mile Island Nuclear Plant," while the *Times'* map is not labeled at all. Though there is no direct reader response evidence that the polysemy of the maps created confusion or panic, the Carter administration's *Kemeny Report*, which examined the role of the media in the accident, suggests that it might have. The creators of the report noted that "A few newspapers . . . did present a more frightening and misleading impression of the accident. This impression was created through headlines and graphics, and in the selection of material to print" (President's Commission, 1979, p. 58).

In addition to facilitating polysemy, the bull's-eye visual also fosters vagueness about the location and magnitude of radiation risk. It suggests, for example, that people living in the area circumscribed by a ring of the bull's-eye would be exposed to the same amount of radioactive material, though in reality, radioactive gases and particles escaping a nuclear plant follow the path of the prevailing winds, distributing the risk of radioactivity asymmetrically across geographic areas (ApSimon & Wilson, 1986, p. 43). Further, the concentric circle design encourages the interpretation that people living in different rings are exposed to geometrically higher or lower doses of radiation than those in the rings further away from or closer to the center of the bull's-eye. Under actual conditions, however, exposure rates are never geometrical. They tend to be extremely high in areas close to the accident and fall off precipitously as distance increases (Von Hippel & Cochran, 1986, p. 18). This misconception might be easily cleared up by including radiation measurements in the visual; however, neither the *Post's* nor the *Times'* maps included these. In fact, only one mainstream media source[6] provided quantitative values for radiation in their visualizations of the Three Mile Island accident.

The obvious communicative drawbacks of the bull's-eye overlay raises questions about why the mainstream media would have adopted this strategy for representing risk or at least not tried to supplement it with numerical data and textual information. More accurate ways of representing radiation risk existed long before the accident at Three Mile Island. As early as 1957, for example, the Atomic Energy Commission (AEC) was employing basic isopleth illustrations— nested lines with assigned values—to describe the direction and concentration

[6] See Matthews, Agrest, Borger, Lord, Marbach, & Cook (1979).

of radionuclide releases from hypothetical nuclear plant accidents. Figure 10.2, for example, shows the hypothesized diffusion of radioactive material under daytime conditions from a ground-level cloud pushed by a 5-meters-per-second wind (AEC, 1957, p. 61). The figure looks like a bull's-eye overlay whose rings have been pinched together and stretched to make concentric conjoined ovals. Though geometrically this isopleth design and the bull's-eye overlay appear similar, their slight differences have important implications for the kinds of information they convey. The pinch and stretch of the isopleth allows it to represent more precisely the general physical shape of the radioactive cloud emitted from the plant, whereas the perfect circles in the bull's-eye overlay are visually ambivalent about the direction of the spread of radiation. Further, isopleth illustrations were not limited strictly to internal government publications, meaning that here they were familiar representations in the broad public discourse about radiation risk. For example, many of the popular civil defense educational materials such as the U.S. Office of Civil Defense's film *Radiological Defense* (1961) and the Defense Department's handbook on nuclear attack *Fallout Protection* (1961) used isopleths to describe the complex shape of the fallout.

The existence of more sophisticated ways of visualizing radiation and their presence in popular representations of radioactive fallout deepens the mystery of why the press did not rely on these kinds of visualizations to describe the accident at Three Mile Island. The absence of these types of representations in the daily newspapers likely had more to do with the unavailability of data in the immediate aftermath of the accident than with the media's negligence. One

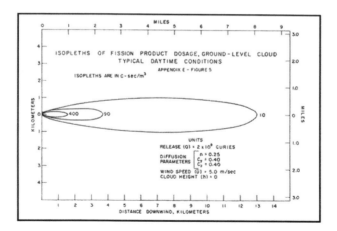

Figure 10.2. Isopleth graphic of radiation fallout from a hypothetical nuclear accident. From *Theoretical Possibilities and Consequences of Major Nuclear Accidents in Large Nuclear Power Plants* (WASH-740), by the U.S. Atomic Energy Commission, 1957, p. 61.

of the criticisms of the utilities and the Nuclear Regulatory Commission following the accident at Three Mile Island was that they failed to gather sufficient data about radiation levels near the plant and also withheld information about these levels from the public. The scarcity of data is evidenced in news reports on the day following the release of the first bull's-eye maps. On April 1, Walter Pincus of the *Washington Post* reported,

> The Nuclear Regulatory Commission yesterday began to "blanket the countryside" with devices to monitor and record accumulated radiation.
> Until yesterday, monitoring outside the plant site had consisted primarily of spot checks that determined radiation levels at a specific time and place.
> Without knowing accumulative dosages, no determination can be made on the levels of exposure of persons in the vicinity of the power plant. (Pincus, 1979, p. A1)

Without accurate comprehensive measures of the radiation levels by a distributed sensor network, there was no way for the media to know the magnitude and direction of the releases of radiation from the plant in a more precise manner. As a consequence, the bull's-eye overlay with its capacity for generalization offered the best method to describe the risk of radiation emanating from the plant.

An examination of the available visual conventions and a contextualization of data for representing radiation risk at Three Mile Island suggests that the mainstream media, though incomplete and inaccurate in their representations of risk, nonetheless seemed to have made a reasonable decision when they adopted the bull's-eye overlay. Though they might have done more to address the polysemy generated by the visual strategy, its familiarity and capacity to communicate generally about risk in a moment of ambiguity made it an appropriate and useful visual strategy for describing the accident. As we will see, however, the institutional embrace of the bull's-eye overlay in the long term, despite its shortcomings, becomes a source for critiquing institutional risk visualizations by grassroots groups like Safecast.

CHERNOBYL

With the accident at Chernobyl, there is some change in the strategy for visualization used in the mainstream media's reporting on radiation risk.[7] However, the bull's-eye overlay continues to play a prominent role in risk reporting. Like the accident at Three Mile Island, very little is known or reported about radiation risk in the early days of the accident, encouraging the media to return to the bull's-eye overlay as the primary method of risk visualization.

---

[7] The mainstream media introduces a radiation cloud visualization, which uses stippling, or black dots, to show represent the location and density of the fallout cloud.

Despite this continuity of visual representation between the two accidents, the use of the bull's-eye overlay in the Chernobyl accident incorporates a novel feature, which, when considered in the sociopolitical context of the accident, suggests that the bull's-eye overlay could be used to persuade as well as inform.

The accident at Chernobyl occurred on April 26, 1986, at 1:23 a.m. (Moscow Standard Time) during a test of the electrical backup systems in reactor four. The test was conducted under suboptimal conditions, which resulted in a spike of radioactivity and heat that blew apart the reactor core. Subsequent explosions and the extreme heat created by radioactive material in a state of uncontrolled fission set fire to exposed graphite rods, sending black radioactive smoke billowing from the plant. The nearby town of Pripyat was evacuated the next day, but there were no reports of the event in the mainstream Russian media until the evening of April 28 (Luke, 1987). The first stories in the American media appeared on April 29, three days following the accident. On the same day, the first visualizations of radiation risk appeared (Gwertzman, 1986).

Communication scholars writing at the time of the accident suggest that the Western media, particularly in the United States, endeavored to make the disaster into a morality tale by contrasting U.S. and Soviet cultures (Dorman & Hirsch, 1986, p. 56). One of the moral narratives that dominated the American media was that Russia was trying to cover up the seriousness of the accident, particularly the death toll (Dorman & Hirsch, 1986, p. 54; Luke, 1987, p. 361). The support of the *New York Times* and the *Washington Post* of this narrative is clear in the early coverage of the accident. Though it is not unreasonable for casualties to be the main focus in early reporting, the degree of unsubstantiated speculation about the number of casualties in the *Times* and *Post* suggests that the papers were developing a cover-up narrative in which the Soviets were being vilified for attempting to grossly underestimate the number of victims claimed by the accident. In the front-page story "Soviet Reporting, Atom Plant 'Disaster,' Seeks Help Abroad to Fight Reactor Fire; 2 Deaths Admitted" on April 30, 1986, for example, Serge Schmemann of the *New York Times* reports that the Soviet government "said that two people had been killed in the accident [at Chernobyl]" (p. A1). He then challenges the credibility of the Russian casualty count with skeptical statements by Reagan Administration officials. He writes, "Some Western officials questioned whether the death toll could be as low as two. In Washington, Kenneth L. Alderman, director of the Arms Control and Disarmament Agency, called the Soviet assertion 'frankly preposterous'" (Schmemann, 1986, p. A1). Though suspicion of Russian official numbers was not unwarranted given years of Cold War mistrust, the elevation of emphatic speculative comments by Western officials as counterbalance to these numbers suggests a prejudice toward the perspective that the Russian government was being deceptive and the Reagan Administration was telling the truth. The only way to move the debate beyond prejudice was to corroborate it with reliable evidence.

The *New York Times* does offer corroboration, however, it seems only to provide further evidence of their prejudice toward a massive Russian cover up. The supporting evidence appears in a text box immediately following Schmemann's (1986) story. The box is titled "U.P.I. [United Press International] Says Toll May Pass 2,000" and contains a story from an anonymous author who reports that an "unidentified Kiev resident" said that "'Eighty people died immediately and some 2,000 people died on the way to hospitals'" (UPI, 1986, p. A10). The article quotes the foreign editor at UPI as stating that "this source has never proved to be unreliable" but concedes that "it could find no Soviet official to confirm the report" (UPI, 1986, p. A10). Because there is no independent confirmation of the death toll, the story's validity rests on the Western reader's judgment of which scenario is more credible: an anonymous source vouched for by a prominent Western journalist is lying, or Soviet officials are being deceptive about casualties in an effort to obscure the scope of the accident. By creating this choice, the *New York Times* seems to be staking the credibility of its evidence on the reader's prejudice toward the latter interpretation and in so doing reinforcing as a sustaining narrative of the accident the Soviet deception about the death toll. The *Washington Post* advanced the same narrative in its April 30 edition using Kenneth L. Alderman's statement about the preposterousness of the official Russian casualty count and the UPI figure of 2,000 deaths to back up this assertion (Bohlen, 1986, p. A1).

If the casualty count of UPI's anonymous source had been accurate or the Soviet's number a substantial undercount of the death toll, the United States and the Western media would have certainly scored a major moral victory with their cover-up narrative. As it turns out, however, not only could the UPI numbers not be substantiated, but the official Soviet numbers were accepted as legitimate. By May 3, Harold Denton, an official of the Nuclear Regulatory Commission, was quoted by the *Washington Post* as saying, "It is 'entirely possible' that Soviet officials gave accurate casualty figures" (Peterson, 1986, p. A16). A month later, UPI officially retracted its story of the casualty count.

The controversy over the casualty count and the Western media's failed attempt to support its narrative of a massive Soviet cover up provides a contextual framework for understanding how slight changes in conventional radiation risk visualizations might be used to defend or advance an ideological agenda. Whereas bull's-eye visualizations of the Three Mile Island accident include basic information about the accident's location and distance from different geographic points and population centers, the Chernobyl bull's-eye map also incorporates details about the size of the population affected by the accident. Though this addition seems to be an innocent informational enhancement; in the context of the debate over casualties it also takes on the rhetorical, argumentative function of defending the ideological perspectives of the *New York Times* and *Washington Post*. The addition of information about population sizes to risk visuals seems to be a response by these papers to the problem created by their claims about the high number of casualties related to the accident and their subsequent inability to find credible evidence to corroborate them. It seems more than coincidental that the only maps that included details about the population in the area around the accident appeared in these publications on May 1 and 2, the period between the *Post* and *Times* reporting on high casualty estimates and the growing acceptance by U.S. officials that Soviet casualty numbers were legitimate. The addition of visual representations of population information to bull's-eye overlay maps is used to make the case that the casualty numbers have to be higher than the Soviet government is claiming, given the size of the population around the plant.

The first bull's-eye overlay map in the sample with population data appeared in the *New York Times* on May 1 in conjunction with the story "197 Hospitalized, Kremlin Says; Calls for West's Help Broken Off." The story revisits the discussion of casualties initiated in the previous day's reporting, though in a more subdued, the-jury-is-still-out tone. In the opening paragraphs, Philip Taubman describes the Soviet denials of the high casualty count reported by the *Times*. He uses the phrase "Western reports" to emphasize that it was not only the *New York Times* who reported these numbers: "Moscow denied Western reports that there had been thousands of casualties. It said 197 people had been hospitalized as a result of the accident, 49 of whom were discharged after examination" (Taubman, 1986, p. A1). Following the description of the Russian response, Taubman restates the commitment of Western media sources, including the *New York Times*, to the cover-up narrative, though the tone of the claim is more subdued than in the previous day's reporting. He writes, "Western assessments of the magnitude of the accident and the health dangers posed by it continued to be considerably graver than Moscow's" (p. A1).

The visual that accompanied the story was titled "The People Nearest the Damaged Reactor" and shows a map of the area, including the countries of Ukraine, Byelorussia, the Soviet Union, Moldavia, Lithuania, and Poland (The people near, 1986, p. A10). My Figure 10.3a is not the actual map from the *New York Times*, but it presents similar features and demonstrates similar rhetorical strategies. The locations of a number of population centers are marked on the map. In the middle of the map, there is a bull's-eye overlay centered on Chernobyl and Pripyat, with concentric rings marking the distance in 50-mile increments radiating out to 250 miles. All of these features also appeared in maps of the Three Mile Island accident. A notable difference, however, is in the way that the population centers are represented. In addition to being marked for location, the size of each population center is indicated using both larger and smaller dots, ringed circles, and shaded polyhedrons. A key for decoding the visualization strategies by connecting it with population size is located in the bottom right-hand corner of the map. Given that the map describes the population size around the accident in the context of a dispute over casualties and cover ups and is even juxtaposed with reporting on the dispute, it seems

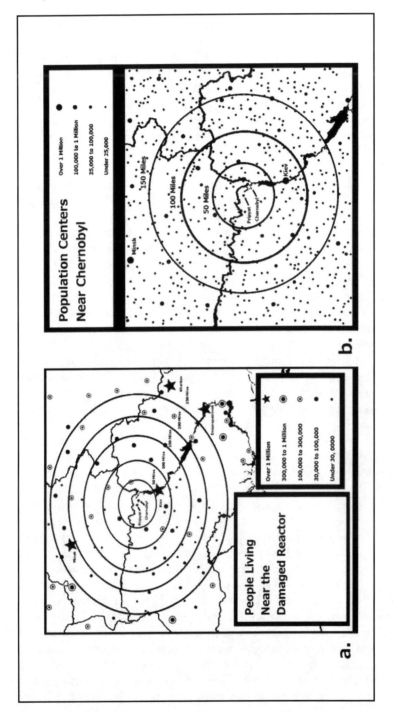

Figure 10.3. A comparison of two strategies for representing the radiation risk to the populations centers surrounding the Chernobyl site. Both maps include a bull's-eye overlay; however, a) emphasizes the size of population centers while b) emphasizes the number of population centers.

reasonable to suggest that the map is implicated in this debate. The question is how? With the Soviet backlash over high casualty counts as well as the growing insecurity in the West about the reliability of these claims, the *Times* map offers a visual defense of its argument that the risks posed by the accident are considerably graver than what Russian officials are letting on. The visual argument of the map is that there is a substantial population near the accident; therefore, the Soviet's claim that only two people were killed seems unreasonable.

One of the critiques leveled against visuals as argument is that visuals are too ambiguous to reliably make arguments by themselves. Rhetorical and critical scholars have defended the argumentative function of visuals by making the case that the problem of ambiguity is often solved by the appearance of visuals in a particular context or their juxtaposition with written or spoken discourse (Barthes, 1977, p. 156; J. A. Blair, 2004, p. 47). Though this is certainly case, I would argue the ambiguity of visuals is itself a rhetorical strength because it offers arguers a subtle and deniable method for making claims. In the case of the *New York Times*, for example, a subtle and deniable argument is required because the paper must walk a fine line between defending its narrative about the Soviet cover up and risking the further loss of credibility for doing so too forcefully under uncertain conditions of evidence. With the UPI casualty count under suspicion and no other reliable information to support its claim, the paper falls back on the probabilistic argument that the Soviet estimates have to be wrong; that is, given the size of the population near the accident the likelihood of only two people being killed seems improbable. Because this argument is speculative, making it in print might invite the charge that the paper was desperately grasping at straws to defend its casualty cover-up narrative. By using a visual to make the argument, however, the paper can avoid having its defense publicly critiqued because it would be difficult for critics in the Eastern or Western media to cite these visual arguments and too involved to explain simply in a critique.

The drawback to this strategy, however, is that the reader might miss their defensive argument. In hopes of drawing some attention to the map and the argument it is making, the *Times* offers readers a few verbal cues to help them make the connection. The map's title, "The People Near the Damaged Reactor," indicates that the focus of the map is people and their proximity to the reactor. This frames the viewer's visual experience by promoting the idea that the population centers represented in the bull's-eye are near the damaged reactor and therefore at risk from radiation. The number of people at risk is also alluded to briefly in the text of the article in a discussion about the contamination of the water supply. Taubman writes,

> There have been constant unconfirmed rumors reaching Moscow that Kiev's water supply might have been contaminated by the accident. . . . The plant is on the Pripyat River, which feeds into . . . a 50 mile-long reservoir that supplies water to Kiev, a city of 2.5 million people. (Taubman, 1986, p. A10)

The inclusion of Kiev, the Pripyat River, and the Kiev Reservoir on the map as well as in the story create a link between the text and the visual. This link might also invite the reader to connect the risks, the number of people in harm's way, and the claims about the extent of the casualties, which are also part of the conversation in the text.

The strategic use of population density visualizations to defend arguments of a Soviet cover up of casualties was not limited to the *New York Times*. On May 2, the day following the publication of the map in the *Times*, the *Washington Post* relied on a similar strategy to defend the same position. The *Post* presented a map entitled "Density of Population around Chernobyl" in conjunction with the story "Soviet Lid on News of Chernobyl Reflects Cost, Security, Image Concerns." This article, like the article in the *Times*, discusses the Russian report on injuries, noting that the Russian's claimed that "'Only' 197 were hospitalized after the accident" (Lee, 1986, p. A26). In a similar fashion, the article also informs the reader of the Soviet critiques of Western reports explaining that *Tass*, the official Soviet news agency, "charged 'bourgeois mass media' with 'whipping up the scale' of the disaster" (Lee, 1986, p. A26). The visual that appears directly below the article on the page, like the visual in the *New York Times*, supports the position that the casualties have to be higher than the Soviets are letting on. Like the *Times* map, the title of the *Post* map "Density of Population around Chernobyl" frames the visual for the reader by highlighting the number of people near the accident. Also like the *Times* map, the *Post* map includes graphic representation of the population size.

Unlike the *Times* map, however, the *Post* map marks every population center, big or small, within a 150 mile radius of Chernobyl (Cook, 1986, A26). Though the claim that the strategy is meant to support is the same—that the risk and casualties have to be higher given the number of persons living around the plant— the technique of argument here is different. As Figure 10.3a demonstrates generically, The *New York Times* visual relied on the size of the population centers near the accident to make its point. To comprehend these essential features of argument, the reader must visually jump between the cities on the map and the information about population density in a "Population Key." In the *Post* map (which was similar to Figure 10.3b), the visualization focuses on the number of population centers rather than their magnitude. Though the map also includes a population key, there is no need for the reader to look at it. Instead, a quick glance at the bull's-eye overlay region on the map densely packed with dots is sufficient to form an impression of the population density around the plant. This strategy of visualization, therefore, makes an accumulation argument in which the number of population centers at risk in the accident reinforces the visualizer's perspective.

Though the introduction of population size to bull's-eye overlays is a subtle change in risk representation, its introduction to the *Washington Post* and the *New York Times* maps during a period of debate over Russian casualty assessments seems more than a coincidence or an unconscious communicative act. Instead, it can be reasonably considered a rhetorical strategy on the part of the papers to subtly defend their ideological narrative about Russian attempts to cover up the deadly consequences of the Chernobyl nuclear accident. Their use of risk visualizations toward this end illuminates the value of the semantic ambiguity of visuals for making subtle and deniable claims about risk.

FUKUSHIMA

Whereas the previous sections have examined how visual conventions and the ideologies of risk visualizers have influenced representation, this final section will explore how new technologies, in particular the Internet, have changed it. A comparison between old and new print visualizations in the *New York Times* suggests that the affordances of the Internet have begun to change print representations of risk and that the movement from print to online media has greatly expanded the content of risk visualization. Perhaps more significantly, however, the Internet has allowed grassroots groups outside of the mainstream media to create and broadcast their own radiation risk visualizations. A comparison between the risk representations of Safecast and the online visualizations in the *New York Times* reveals that visual strategies of grassroots organizations diverge from and even challenge conventional practices of risk visualization in the mainstream media and that these divergences and challenges can be directly linked to the different goals and audiences of the two.

Perhaps the most significant change in risk representation in the mainstream media occasioned by the advent of Internet has been the use of rich multi-layered formats known as "mashups." Mashups are aggregates of discrete nodes of information that are thematically coherent but separated from each other in cyberspace. These nodes are conceptually bound together by an anchor, a text or visual that a user would encounter first while browsing, which provides a hub for accessing off-screen nodes. By clicking links embedded in the anchor, off-screen nodes appear overlaid on the text or visual or in a separate window. These features offer solutions to the problem of information density by allowing individual layers of information to be peeled off and sequestered in cyberspace. At the same time, links in the mashup connect the informational nodes to the anchor and each other, promoting conceptual connections and facilitating ease of access.

The influence of online mashups on print visualizations of radiation risk is illustrated in the graphic associated with the *New York Times* story "Data Show Radiation Spread; Frantic Repairs Go On," which appeared on March 18, 2011 (Cox, Ericson, & Tse, 2011a). The graphic is divided into two visual sections. One is dominated by a giant map of Japan with a bull's-eye overlay. The map commands the most attention, suggesting that this element is the print equivalent of the anchor in an online mashup. The other section is subdivided into four columns of information, including the distance from the risk event, the magnitude of radiation risk, the possible effects of radiation, and the population of the risk area. The content in this section emulates the format of online mashups by presenting individual nodes of information in visually separate spaces and connecting these nodes to the visual anchor using lines and brackets. Like the radiation visuals of Three Mile Island and Chernobyl, the visual anchor of the Fukushima accident includes the source of the risk, its geographical extent, and the populations affected by the risk. However, unlike previous print visualizations, the nodes in the second section include additional risk information like magnitude and risk effects.

This brief visual assessment of a sample of risk representation in the *New York Times* suggests that the style and content of the print media had been influenced by the online media mashup. The move in older print formats to emulate newer online ones seems to run counter to the process of remediation outline by Bolter and Grusin (1999, p. 45). Instead of recycling or repurposing old media, what seems to be happening here is a kind of retrocycling or retropurposing, where traditional media is being "modernized" or updated by adding stylistic elements from new media. But why is this happening? Though modernization may be one reason for retropurposing, a more pragmatic reason might be the requirements of producing news simultaneously in both print and online formats. Because they are working in two formats, it makes sense from a production standpoint to create visuals that can function in both rather than producing different visuals for each. In fact, the visualization previously discussed appeared in both the print and online versions of the *New York Times* in virtually the same format (Cox et al., 2011a; Cox, Ericson, & Tse, 2011b). Considering the requirements of news production, it seems that this visual representation of risk is a hybrid style emulating the format of a media mashup but adapting it to the limits of the printed page.

In addition to producing hybrid print/online visualizations, the *New York Times* also developed an interactive online map representing the radiation risk from Fukushima. The interactive map was included as part of a suite of interactive maps generally titled "Map of the Damage from the Japanese Earthquake." By selecting "radiation levels" on the infographic's navigation bar, the user can bring up a map of the area within a 50 km radius of the accident. Within this radius, the map includes 44 dots, ranging in color from white to dark purple, which indicate increasingly higher levels of radiation. When the user's cursor moves over a dot, a text box appears on the page that includes the radiation level measured in microsieverts per hour (μSv/h), the date of the measurement, the number of measures taken, a graph of the change in measurement over time (between March 17 and April 10, 2011), and a comparative contextualization of the measurement (Bloch, Cox, Marsh, McLean, Tse, Park et al., 2011). By providing an interactive map that included specific information about radiation levels near the accident, the *New York Times* allowed their online readership in both the United States and Asia to explore the risks of radiation from the accident in more detail than they had previously been able to thanks to the affordances of the Internet and the availability of information about radiation risk. This level and type of detail, though far richer than print representations from previous accidents, were qualitatively and quantitatively limited when compared to the visualizations created by Safecast. This disparity, I will argue, is a consequence of differences between the goals, audiences, and information-gathering practices of the producers of mainstream media and those of the citizen-science endeavor.

The organization Safecast and its website have emerged from a complex interplay of individual and collective needs and public and expert exigencies. Safecast began as RDTN.org, an online radiation mapping site conceived by Portland, Oregon designer Marcelino Alvarez and developed with the help of his colleagues at Uncorked Studios. In the days following Japan's earthquake and nuclear accident, Alvarez became frustrated with the limited information in the American media about the crisis. In his personal blog at Uncorked Studios on March 21, 2011, he explains,

> I wanted to gather all the information that the talking heads did not have time to talk about. I wanted to create a site so simple and easy to use that it would allow anyone the ability to check and see if all things were clear. (Alvarez, 2011, para. 3)

In addition to personal motives, Alvarez was also driven by a sense of democratic idealism that his website could provide information for and by the people about radiation risk, "We thought there was something noble to the notion of having people purchase their own detection devices and post data" (Alvarez, 2011, para. 5). Energized by these frustrations and convictions, he and his co-workers developed and launched the website RDTN.org on March 19, 2011, a little more than a week after the accident at Fukushima.

Alvarez's development of an online visual representation of radiation levels attracted attention early on from well-connected individuals in the computer technology and information design communities. This group, who might best be described as publicizers and networkers, included three figures who would become central to the advertisement of the site and its eventual transformation to a Japan-based alternative radiation monitoring network. They included Sean Bonner, an online entrepreneur, journalist, and activist in Los Angeles; Joi Ito, venture capitalist, high-tech entrepreneur, activist, and soon-to-be head of MIT Media lab; and Pieter Franken, an information technology manager in the Tokyo banking sector and visiting researcher at Keio University in Tokyo. On the day before the launch of the RDTN website, Alvarez and his team in Oregon were put in touch with Ito and his associates. Collectively they agreed to collaborate on developing and publicizing the site.

As RDTN began to develop and get attention in the media for its efforts to visualize risk, a parallel citizen-science endeavor for radiation measuring was starting to take shape across the Pacific in Japan. This endeavor was set in motion by American expatriate Christopher Wang, known as Akiba, who was a member of Tokyo Hackerspace, a club dedicated to modifying existing technologies to extend their utility or create new devices (Tokyo Hackerspace, n.d.). On March 15, 2011, the Tuesday following the earthquake, Akiba and his tech-savvy hacker compatriots met at Tokyo Hackerspace to decide how they could use their technical skills to respond to the crisis created by the earthquake, tsunami, and nuclear accident. They decided to build solar lanterns and to develop a Geiger counter network to collect radiation readings in Tokyo and then expand the network out into the rest of Japan. Because of his experience building custom electronic devices,[8] Akiba assumed the task of hacking or fabricating Geiger counters for the group's sensor network. On April 2, Pieter Franken, who was an electronics enthusiast, participated in one of Tokyo Hackerspace's solar lantern builds. At the event, he introduced himself to Akiba and the two discussed the group's plans to establish a radiation sensor network.

By the end of March and beginning of April, the original confederation of RDTN and Ito, Bonner, and Franken expanded to include Akiba and a few other members of Tokyo Hackerspace. The participants in this newly expanded confederation recognized that their fundamental problem was the lack of Geiger counters. To respond to this need, RDTN and Tokyo Hackerspace jointly broadcast a pledge drive for donations using the Internet fundraising site Kickstarter (Aaron, 2011). They also realized that with the expansion of the group, it was important to work more closely to coordinate their efforts. In response to this exigence, representatives from each part of the collective agreed to meet for face-to-face discussions about the enterprise at the New Context Conference in Tokyo on April 15, 2011. During the conference, they decided to "focus on collecting data and concluded that a new brand was needed to describe both the work we were doing now and in the future. . . . We were to be called Safecast" (Safecast, 2011a).

By the time the citizen-science collective officially changed its name to Safecast on April 24, 2011, the transformation of its mission from strictly visualization to data gathering and visualization had already begun. Their most significant innovation was the development of the bGeigi, a bento-box-sized radiation measuring device, which could be strapped to the side of a car and driven around to take and download continuous radiation measurements. Because of its mobility and automaticity, the device provided a simple and reasonably inexpensive method for collecting measurements across a large area, certainly a

---

[8] Akiba is the owner of Freaklabs, which designs and manufactures custom-built wireless sensor devices. See his website freaklabs.org for more details.

boon for a small grassroots organization aspiring to provide a comprehensive survey of radiation levels. As a consequence of Safecast's extra-institutional status and its unique mission to both gather and visualize radiation risk online, its representations of risk offer a unique opportunity to examine the way in which changes in the audience for and source of risk representations impact visualization (S. Bonner, personal communication, July 31, 2012).

Like the *New York Times*, Safecast was able to harness the affordances of the Internet in their Safecast map to create a risk visual that was more information-dense and visually sophisticated than its print predecessors. However, unlike the *Times*, Safecast pushes these affordances far beyond the risk visualizations created by the mainstream media. It even uses them to critique conventional risk visualization practices.

The use of color by Safecast offers one example of how the group's visual strategies go beyond those used by the mainstream media. Though Safecast, like the *Times*, employs color to describe variations in radiation levels, the role of color in Safecast's visual goes beyond representing risk at a fixed point. Instead, it is used to indicate risk at different geographical scopes. On the Safecast map, radiation levels are visualized using a grid of colored squares (Figure 10.4a). Cooler colors (green or blue) represent levels of radiation either commensurate with or barely elevated above levels of radiation previous to the accident, and hotter colors (red or yellow) are used to indicate radiation levels that are substantially higher.[9] When the user places their cursor over a colored square on the grid of the map, a textbox pops up, which includes the precise level of radiation measured in counts per minute (CPM) and microsieverts per hour (μSv/h), the GPS coordinates of the measurement, and the date on which it was taken. In addition to providing specific information about radiation levels and measurements, the map allows users to zoom in and out so that they can examine these metrics at different levels of granularity. As the user zooms out a few levels, the individual measurements are replaced with a grid of larger colored squares whose colors and radiation levels are determined by averaging all of the squares at the subordinate level that the larger square encompasses (Figure 10.4b). By zooming out even further, the user can examine the distribution of radiation risk around the whole region and, at the highest resolution, the whole country. This strategy for representation allows users, for example, to identify a hotspot 20 miles northwest of Tokyo at the regional level, which at a higher resolution can be pinpointed to a stretch of highway 2km west of Daiichi Hospital between the cities of Ota and Isesaki (Safecast, 2011b).

---

[9] Safecast has changed their color coding for risk over time. Initially, they used a conventional green-to red-risk scale. However, their most recent visualization breaks with this conventional color scheme by using a blue to light yellow risk scale.

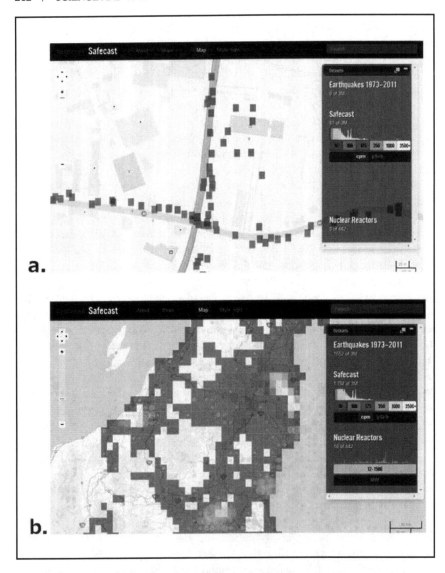

Figure 10.4. Radiation visualizations on the Safecast Map (Safecast, 2011b).
Images retrieved from Safecast.org. Used under the terms of a Creative
Commons Attribution 4.0 International Public License:
http://creativecommons.org/licenses/by/4.0/deed.en_US.

While Safecast mobilizes color in a more sophisticated fashion than the *Times* to represent the radiation risk at different geographical scopes, perhaps more impressive is the number of radiation measurements it displays and the amount of auxiliary detail it offers for contextualizing risk. Though the *Times* interactive map far outstrips its print predecessors by including radiation measures for 44 separate locations in the proximity of the accident, it seems a paltry account of risk when compared to Safecast's map, which in its very first iteration included over 100 radiation measurements and now, thanks to the bGeigi and the efforts of Safecast volunteers, boasts over 3 million individual measurements taken from the very northern to the very southern tip of the main island of Japan (Safecast, 2011b). In addition to visualizing a greater number of measurements, Safecast also includes in its risk representations more contextual details so that the reader can orient themselves with respect to the risk.

In the *Times* interactive map, dots on the map marked the places where radiation levels were taken so that a user in Japan could get a general sense of what the risk levels were at various locations and distances from the nuclear plant. However, no names for the locations are given when the user clicks on a dot and the areas in which the dots appear are devoid of most navigational features such as roadways, mountains, or rivers. Though the map does contain a few major cities as locational markers, only a very general sense of the location of the measurement sites can be extrapolated from these (Bloch et al., 2011). In contradistinction, the Safecast map provides the reader with a very fine level of detail. Not only are roads, mountains, and rivers and other navigational features marked, but each of the individual readings is tagged with a GPS coordinate that would allow any user with a GPS-capable device to locate the exact spot where the measurement was taken. In addition, because Safecast's map includes so many measurements and the capability to identify readings at scales of hundreds of meters, users of its maps living in the areas measured would be able to find the reading nearest their location with great precision.

In addition to providing a more comprehensive account of radiation levels than the *Times* online map, the Safecast map also supplies a more accurate picture of radiation distribution that avoids the weaknesses of the conventional bull's-eye overlay used by the mainstream media but incorporates its strengths. Like the bull's-eye overlay, the Safecast grid map, at the very broadest level of visualization, allows the user to have a sense of the average levels of radiation in areas around the plant. In fact, the map even incorporates a very basic bull's-eye overlay design that outlines the 20km evacuation zone around Fukushima and, in earlier iterations, also included the 50km ring marking the evacuation zone suggested by the U.S. Embassy. Because the visualization in the Safecast map is built up dynamically by continually averaging radiation values from more local measurements, it can represent, unlike the bull's-eye overlay, the asymmetry of the distribution of radiation risk from a nuclear accident. Interestingly, in talking with the media about their efforts, members of Safecast reveal a keen awareness of the value in their visual technique for overcoming the limitations of the bull's-eye overlay. In an interview in fall 2011 with PBS News Hour correspondent Miles O'Brien, Safecast's Sean Bonner illustrates this awareness in the following exchange:

> **Miles O'Brien:** Sean Bonner is one of the founders of Safecast, an all-volunteer organization that has plotted the most detailed maps of radiation contamination in Japan. . . . Radiation doesn't fit that nice neat little disk they want to paint on the map right?

> **Sean Bonner:** Yes. Radiation isn't looking at a compass radiating outward.

> **Miles O'Brien:** Yes. That's right. It's a very arbitrary thing.

> **Sean Bonner:** Yes. There is wind and topography and this crazy stuff that ends up playing into it. (O'Brien, 2011)

Here, O'Brien and Bonner take aim at the bull's-eye overlay's inability to capture the nuances of radiation movement. O'Brien, for example, critiques the overlay's inherent prejudice toward an orderly symmetrical advance of radiation with the comment/question, "Radiation doesn't fit that nice neat little disk they want to paint on the map right?" In addition, the two team up to emphasize the asymmetrical nature of the risk. O'Brien begins the critique with the statement that "It's [radiation is] a very arbitrary thing," and Bonner elaborates by talking about the variety of factors that play into its distribution: "There is wind and topography and this crazy stuff that ends up playing into it." With the grid map design, Safecast is able not only to illuminate the complexity of the distribution of radiation risk but also critique conventional styles of risk representation that have been used by the media.

The technical affordances of the Internet allow Safecast and the *New York Times* to create visualizations of radiation risk that far exceed the informational and visual capacities of their print predecessors; however, the differences between the Safecast map and the *New York Times* online map cannot be explained by changes in technological circumstances. In order to account for the divergences in visualization here we must consider the differences in the goals and audiences of the mainstream media and grassroots groups. The goal of news reporting is to get the basic facts about the accident out in an accessible and concise fashion. The *New York Times* interactive visual goes beyond the basic facts by providing some precise levels of radiation data; however, it is not surprising that the creators of the map stopped far short of providing a comprehensive set of datapoints. Although the print and online versions of the *Times* circulate in Japan and other parts of Asia, its primary audience is the American news-reading public. For the majority of this audience, providing a few datapoints in the area around the plant would be sufficient to satisfy most of their demands for information about the radiation levels. Further, geographically contextualizing these datapoints with a few navigational features would be sufficient for American readers to get the gist of the location of the radiation while at the same time avoiding information overload on the map. For Safecast, however, comprehensiveness and detail rather than sufficiency and concision are the primary design parameters. These goals are clearly spelled out in their website blog, where they write,

> Our hope in launching this site is that clear reliable data can provide *focus* on the critical relief efforts needed in Japan. . . . We have been working day and night to find and integrate new data sources that can help provide reliable data. (Ewald, 2011)

As stated, the goal of Safecast's citizen-science endeavor was to get reliable data and make it useful for victims of the Fukushima accident. Given these goals, it's not surprising that their map is far more comprehensive and includes navigational details such as roads, mountains, and rivers. Therefore, the different goals of the mainstream media and grassroots organizations seem to be as much if not more central than technological changes are in accounting for the choices made when visualizing risk.

CONCLUSION

By following the development of radiation risk visualization over time, it is possible to see how changes in informational, sociopolitical, and/or technological contexts can have important consequences for risk communication and argument. An examination of risk representation at its conception reveals that visualizers of the Three Mile Island accident relied on the existing conventions from civil defense manuals for visualizing radiation risk. Though these conventional representations were suitable models for visualization, they had significant consequences for how media consumers understood the risks of radiation from Three Mile Island and subsequent accidents. With the advent of Chernobyl, the bull's-eye strategy for visualizing risk was preserved but enhanced with population information to make it a tool for ideological argument. This analysis reveals how the *New York Times* and *Washington Post* used bull's-eye visuals with population data to discretely argue that the Soviets were covering up the number of casualties from the accident. Finally, with the accident at Fukushima, we witness a more dramatic change in risk visualization facilitated in part by the affordances of the Internet and in part with the emergence of grassroots risk visualizations. An investigation of the online group Safecast suggested that thanks to the affordances of the Internet, radiation maps could be created that juxtaposed massive amounts of information to provide comprehensive and detailed representations of risk. It also revealed, however, that even though this technology was widely available, its accessibility alone could not account for the unique character of Safecast's risk visualization strategy. A comparison between the Safecast map and the *New York Times* online interactive map suggests that differences in the goals and audiences of institutional and noninstitutional risk visualizers play a critical role in shaping visual choices of risk communication.

As attention to risk and the use of visuals to communicate about it increases, the efforts of scholars in rhetoric, communication, information design, and professional and technical writing to understand the practical and ethical consequences of these practices need to keep pace. Though important gains have been made in the last two decades to develop rhetorical perspectives on visual artifacts like murals, photographs, architecture, and video games, it's surprising that risk representation that plays a vital role in communications between governments and citizens, employers and workers, caregivers and patients, businesses and consumers has been ignored. This chapter has endeavored to make an initial contribution toward a deeper understanding of risk visualization by exploring the strengths and limitations of risk representation strategies, the variety of roles they can play in risk communication, and the myriad factors that might influences the choices of risk visualizers.

REFERENCES

Aaron, J. (2011, March 30). Japan's crowdsourced radiation maps [Blog post]. *New Scientist*. Retrieved from http://www.newscientist.com/blogs/onepercent/2011/03/crowdsourced-radiation-maps.html

Alvarez, M. (2011, March 21). *72 hours from concept to launch: RDTN.org* [Blog post]. Retrieved from http://uncorkedstudios.com/words/page/3

ApSimon, H., & Wilson, J. (1986). Tracking the cloud from Chernobyl. *New Scientist, 111*, 42–45.

Associated Press. (1955, March 4). *Radiation effects* [Fallout map]. Retrieved from http://www.apimages.com

Atomic Energy Commission. (1957). *Theoretical possibilities and consequences of major nuclear accidents in large nuclear power plants* (WASH-740). Washington, DC: U.S. Government Printing Office.

Barthes, R. (1977). Rhetoric of the image. In C. Handa (Ed.), *Visual rhetoric in a digital world* (pp. 152–163). Boston, MA: Bedford.

Beck, U. (1992). *Risk society: Towards a new modernity*. Thousand Oaks, CA: Sage.

Birdsell, D., & Groarke, L. (2007). Outlines of a theory of visual argument. *Argumentation and Advocacy, 43*, 103–113.

Blair, J. A. (2004). The rhetoric of visual arguments. In C. Hill & M. Helmers (Eds.), *Defining visual rhetorics* (pp. 344–363). Mahwah, NJ: Lawrence Erlbaum.

Blair, W. (1955, February 16). U.S. H-bomb test put lethal zone at 7,000 sq. miles. *New York Times*.

Bloch, M., Cox, A., Marsh, B., McLean, A., Tse, T. M., Park, H., et al. (2011). *Map of the damage from the Japanese earthquake* [Radiation map]. Retrieved from http://www.nytimes.com/packages/flash/newsgraphics/2011/0311-japan-earthquake-map/

Bohlen, C. (1986, April 30). U.S. experts see situation as more serious than admitted. *Washington Post*, pp. A1, A18.

Bolter, D., & Grusin, R. (1999). *Remediation: Understanding new media*. Cambridge, MA: MIT Press.

Brasseur, L. (2005). Florence Nightingale's visual rhetoric in the rose diagrams. *Technical Communication Quarterly*, *14*(2), 161–182.

Cook, D. (1979, March 31). Area surrounding Three Mile Island nuclear plant [Radiation map]. *Washington Post*, p. A8.

Cook, D. (1986, May 2). Density of the population around Chernobyl [Radiation map]. *Washington Post*, p. A26.

Cox, A., Ericson, M., & Tse, A. (2011a, March 18). The evacuation zones around the Fukushima plant [Map]. *New York Times*, p. A11.

Cox, A., Ericson, M., & Tse, A. (2011b, March 25). The evacuation zones around the Fukushima plant [Map]. *New York Times*. Retrieved from http://www.nytimes.com/packages/flash/newsgraphics/2011/0311-japan-earthquake-map/

Davisson, A. (2011). Beyond the borders of red and blue states: Google maps as a site of rhetorical invention in the 2008 presidential election. *Rhetoric and Public Affairs*, *14*(1), 101–124.

Dorman, W., & Hirsch, D. (1986). The U.S. media's slant. *Bulletin of the Atomic Scientist*, *43*(1), 54–56.

Ewald, D. (2011, March 23). *Open dialogue* [Blog]. Retrieved from http://blog.safecast.org/2011/03/open-dialogue/

Farrell, T., & Goodnight, T. (1998). Accidental rhetoric: The root metaphors of Three Mile Island. In C. Waddell (Ed.), *Landmark essays on rhetoric and the environment* (pp. 75–105). Mahwah, NJ: Lawrence Erlbaum.

Finney, J. (1961, January 5). Atom aides scan effect of blast. *New York Times*, p. 19.

Gamson, W., & Modigliani, A. (1989). Media discourse and public opinion on nuclear power: A constructionist approach. *The American Journal of Sociology*, *95*(1), 1–37.

Gil de Zuñiga, H., Puig-I-Abril, E., & Rojas, H. (2009). Weblogs, traditional sources online and political participation: An assessment of how the Internet is changing the political environment. *New Media and Society*, *11*(4), 553–574. Retrieved from http://dx.doi.org/10.1177/1461444809102960

Gross, A. (2009). Toward a theory of verbal-visual interaction: The example of Lavoisier. *Rhetoric Society Quarterly*, *39*(2), 147–169.

Gwertzman, B. (1986, April 29). Plume of radioactive material spread from accident at Pripyat [Radiation map]. *New York Times*, p. A1.

Hagan, S. (2007). Visual/verbal collaboration in print: Complementary differences, necessary ties and an untapped rhetorical opportunity. *Written Communication*, *24*(1), 49–83.

Herndl, C., Fennell, B., & Miller, C. (1991). Understanding failures in organizational discourse: The accident at Three Mile Island and the shuttle *Challenger* disaster. In

C. Bazerman & J. Paradis (Eds.), *Textual dynamics of the professions* (pp. 279–305). Madison, WI: University of Wisconsin Press.

Katz, S., & Miller, C. (1996). The low-level radioactive waste siting controversy in North Carolina: Toward a rhetorical model of risk communication. In C. Herndl & S. Brown (Eds.), *Green culture* (pp. 111–140). Madison, WI: University of Wisconsin Press.

Keränen, L. (2011). Concocting viral apocalypse: Catastrophic risk and the production of bio(in)security. *Western Journal of Communication, 75*(5), 451–472.

Kitzinger, J. (2009). Risk and regulation advisory council. *Department for Business Innovation and Skills.* Retrieved from http://bis.ecgroup.net/Publications/AboutUs/RiskandRegulationAdvisoryCouncil.aspx

Kostelnick, C., & Hassett, M. (2003). *Shaping information: The rhetoric of visual conventions.* Carbondale, IL: University of Illinois Press.

Kress, G., & van Leeuwen, T. (2006). *The semiotic landscape: Language and visual communication. Reading images: The grammar of visual design* (2nd ed.). London, UK: Routledge.

Krugler, D. (2006). *This is only a test: How Washington D.C. prepared for nuclear war.* New York, NY: Palgrave Macmillan.

Lee, G. (1986, May 2). Soviet lid on news of Chernobyl reflects cost, security, image concerns. *Washington Post*, p. A26.

Luke, T. (1987). Chernobyl: The packaging of transnational ecological disaster. *Critical Studies in Mass Communication, 4*, 351–375.

Lyons, R. (1979, March 31). Children evacuated. *New York Times*, p. A1.

Mathews, T., Agrest, S., Borger, G., Lord, M., Marbach, W. D., & Cook, W. J. (1979, April 9). Nuclear accident. *Newsweek*, pp. 24–33.

Miller, C. (2003). The presumption of expertise: The role of ethos in risk analysis. *Configurations, 11*(2), 163–202.

O'Brien, M. (2011, November 10). Safecast draws on power of the crowd to map Japan's radiation. *PBS News Hour.* Retrieved from http://www.pbs.org/newshour/bb/science/july-dec11/japanradiation_11-10.html

Office of Civil Defense, St. Louis. (1955). *Escape from H-bomb: St. Louis county and city* [Fallout map]. Retrieved from http://www.historyhappenshere.org/archives/4193/

O'Toole, T., Peterson, B., Richards, B., Cohn, V., Lentz, P., Baer, J., et al. (1979, March 29). Radiation spreads 10 miles from a-plant mishap site. *Washington Post*, pp. A1, A7.

Peterson, C. (1986, May 3). Plume believed deadly for miles. *Washington Post*, pp. A1, A16.

Pincus, W. (1979, April 1). Radiation monitors installed to check exposure. *Washington Post*, pp. A1, A6.

Porter, R. (1955, March 12). City evacuation plan: 3 governors and mayor weigh plans to meet H-bomb attack. *New York Times*, p. 1.

President's Commission on the Accident at Three Mile Island. (1979). *Report of the President's commission on the accident at Three Mile Island.* Washington, DC: U.S. Government Printing Office.

Ropeik, D. (2011, June 27). Risk reporting 101. *Columbia Journalism Review.* Retrieved from http://www.cjr.org/the_observatory/risk_reporting_101.php?page=all

Runaway Reactor. (1961, January 13). *Time*, pp. 18–19.

Safecast. (2011a). *History.* Retrieved from http://blog.safecast.org/history/

Safecast. (2011b, August). *Maps.* Retrieved from http://blog.safecast.org/maps/

Sauer, B. (2003). *Rhetoric of risk: Technical documentation in hazardous environments.* Mahwah, NJ: Lawrence Erlbaum.

Schmemann, S. (1986, April 30). Soviet reporting, atom plant "disaster," seeks help abroad to fight reactor fire; 2 deaths admitted. *New York Times*, p. A1.

Taubman, P. (1986, May 1). 197 hospitalized, Kremlin says; call's for West's help broken off. *New York Times*, p. A1, A10.

The people nearest the damaged reactor. (1986, May 1). [Radiation map]. *New York Times*, p. A10.

Tokyo Hackerspace. (n.d.) *What is Tokyo hackerspace?* Retrieved from http://tokyo hackerspace.org/en/what-is-tokyo-hackerspace

UPI says toll may pass 2,000. (1986, April 30). *New York Times*, p. A10.

U.S. Department of Defense. (1961). *Fallout protection: What to know and do about a nuclear attack.* Washington, DC: U.S. Government Printing Office. Retrieved from http://ia700300.us.archive.org/7/items/falloutprotectio00unitrich/falloutprotectio00 unitrich.pdf

U.S. Office of Civil Defense. (1961). *Radiological defense* [Motion picture]. Retrieved from http://archive.org/details/Radiolog1961

Von Hippel, F., & Cochran, T. (1986). Estimating long-term health effects. *Bulletin of the Atomic Scientist*, *43*(1), 18–24.

Warnick, B. (2007). *Rhetoric online: Persuasion and politics on the World Wide Web.* New York, NY: Peter Lang.

http://dx.doi.org/10.2190/SCIC11

CHAPTER 11

Intersections: Scientific and Parascientific Communication on the Internet

Ashley R. Kelly and Carolyn R. Miller

ABSTRACT

We examine the purported "erosion," suggested by Trench (2008), of boundaries between expert and non-expert spheres of discourse in science communication online. Taking online communications in response to the Fukushima Daiichi disaster as our case, we suggest that there are genres, or protogenres, of science communication emerging online that do seem to blur the boundaries between expert and non-expert spheres of discourse. These genres, we suggest, might be described as "parascientific genres," a notion from Kaplan and Radin (2011) we take up and adapt to help explore the genres we are seeing emerge online. Parascientific genres are those that function alongside traditional genres of science communication in that they borrow scientific authority and knowledge structures from the realm of science but operate without the gatekeeping and traditional reporting forms of internal science communication.

INTRODUCTION

Some decades ago, John Ziman (1968) characterized science as "public knowledge," constituted in an important way by its communication system. The "public" that Ziman referred to was not voting citizens or the mass media audience but rather the "free, intellectual consensus" of other scientists (p. 145), and much of the subsequent research on scientific communication has been devoted to characterizing expert interchange within the scientific community as it

221

sets itself apart from the "lay," "non-expert," or general public. Increasingly, however, communication with that wider public has been of interest, a development due in part to the reversals of public deference to expertise of the late 1960s and to governmental concern for acceptance of public projects and public funding of research (Cooke, 1991; Gaskins, 1992). This newer focus has given rise to several subspecialties (such as risk communication) and scholarly forums (such as *Public Understanding of Science*). One recent example is the 2012 National Academy of Science Sackler Colloquium on "The Science of Science Communication," which had as one of its main goals "To improve understanding of relations between the scientific community and the public" (National Academy of Sciences, n.d.).

This distinction between expert and non-expert communities or spheres of discourse and the boundaries between them has been central to recent views of science. Such views have been built on Thomas Kuhn's (1970) picture of disciplinary knowledge as generated and judged by a "special kind of community" (p. 167); on Toulmin's (1958) notion of "argument fields" involving "field-dependent" premises; and the sociological concept of "boundary work" necessary to distinguish one discipline from another and science from not-science (Gieryn, 1999; Taylor, 1991). The result has been that studies of scientific communication have become formulated along these same lines, with distinct lines of research devoted to, on the one hand, internal or expert communication (Ceccarelli, 2001; Gross, Harmon, & Reidy, 2002; Harris, 1991) and, on the other, to external or public communication (for example, Brossard, 2009; Bucchi, 2008; Condit, Lynch, & Winderman, 2012; Stocking & Holstein, 2009), with both presuming the distinctiveness of the two spheres of discourse. Farrell and Goodnight's (1981) classic discussion of the rhetoric playing out during the Three Mile Island nuclear disaster is built on a Toulmin-like distinction between the social or public sphere and the technical sphere and the incompatible structures of reasoning and value sustaining their differences.

In his 2008 review of the effects of the Internet on science communication, Trench (2008) reprises this distinction between internal and external communication (as does the organization of the present volume of essays). But Trench goes on to make a further point: that the Internet is "turning scientific communication inside out" (p. 185). The Internet has not simply transformed expert and public communication of science but has also transformed their relationship, "eroding" the boundaries between the scientific community and the public (p. 186). Trench's observation challenges the adequacy of our traditional view of scientific communication, the autonomous status of scientific communities, and the nature and stability of the boundaries between expert and public communities. Our aim here is to explore these challenges.

The Internet has changed even in the few years since Trench (2008) wrote, and so have the possibilities for communication within and about science, within and through those supposedly eroding boundaries. It would be impossible (or at least would require a much larger project than this can be) to document and inventory all those possibilities. The proliferation of Internet technologies and platforms continues apace. Rather than focusing on specific platforms or technologies in an attempt to update Trench's observations, we look to a particular event as an initiating exigence from which we might trace how emerging affordances of the Internet are put to work, for what reasons, and to what effect. We look specifically at some of the ways the online communication figured in responses to the disaster at the Fukushima Daiichi nuclear power plant, following the March 2011 earthquake and tsunami that crippled the site. We choose this event, sometimes known as 3/11, for three reasons. First, as an unprecedented combination of events—the earthquake, tsunami, and breach of the operating nuclear power plant—the disaster was beyond immediate comprehension, scientific or public; there were, therefore, both immediate and longer-term efforts to gather information, to understand and track what was happening. Second, the event galvanized an enormous amount of Internet activity, both within Japan, because other modes of communication (cell phones and landlines) did not function (Jung, 2012), and worldwide, as the traditional media have become incapable of controlling information flow (Friedman, 2011). And third, it exemplifies the kind of event that may become increasingly common in a highly interconnected and technologically mediated world, an event unpredictable in its particulars, global in its potential consequences (Beck, 1992), and complex in its tight coupling of natural forces and human artifacts: as Perrow (2011) has noted, "despite the best attempts to forestall them," accidents are inevitable "in the complex, tightly coupled systems of modern society, resulting in the kind of unpredictable, cascading disaster seen at the Fukushima Daiichi Nuclear Power Station" (p. 44).

In order to explore how the Internet mediated science-related communication about Fukushima Daiichi, we will be looking for evidence of rhetorical genres in the uses of selected Internet platforms. Using genre as a probe in this way will provide a complex perspective on the ways these platforms are shaping communication. Genres represent relatively stable agreements about what kinds of "utterances" (Bakhtin, 1986), or communicative actions (Miller, 1984), are being undertaken and what they mean, but the agreements and the meanings are relative to a community of actors. Thus, by implicit agreement, established genres internal to the scientific community, such as the research report, the referee's report, the call for proposals, make a certain kind of claim, invoke certain communally held premises, rely on certain forms of authorization, take a certain form, exploit certain media affordances, and invite certain kinds of responses. In short, each is taken as a typified meaningful action that is recurrent and predictable to a certain extent. The same is true for genres that carry scientific information within public communities: news reports, popular science magazines, science textbooks, patient package inserts for prescription drugs, museum displays, information about blood and organ donation, public service advertising for eating disorder awareness or other mental health issues. And the agreements are relative to the communities in which these genres circulate as typified meaningful utterances (Medway, 2002; Miller, 1992; Swales, 1990); as Berkenkotter and Huckin put it, "genre conventions signal a discourse community's norms, epistemology, ideology, and social ontology" (1993, p. 475). Thus, in order to explore the ways in which the boundaries between scientific communities and public communities are eroding (or perhaps being otherwise disrupted), we can look at the constitution and circulation of genres, these recurrent patterns of communication, as they develop in relation to various Internet platforms.

We will suggest that some of these genres may be characterized as "parascientific," to adopt a notion from Kaplan and Radin (2011). They use the term specifically with reference to the trade journal *Chemical & Engineering News*, which exists "alongside" peer reviewed scientific journals and addresses audiences both within and outside the scientific community, aiming to influence ("deliberately intervene in") scientific practice, particularly through its access to elite audiences in the media and policy arenas (p. 460). The need for such a characterization of an old medium like a trade journal suggests that the binary division of science communication into internal and external has been an oversimplification all along.[1] We will use the term in a more general way than Kaplan and Radin do: to refer to a variety of genres that do not fit clearly into the more traditional internal/external binary.

Our argument will begin with a brief review of the events at Fukushima Daiichi in March 2011 and then examine the ways in which various communities of users and communities of concern deployed several established Internet platforms to address the exigence of this event as they constructed it. We will briefly examine three sites that might be characterized as social media, which afford the creation and exchange of user-created content. First, we look at the very popular microblogging site, Twitter.com, used by about 15% of online adults (Smith & Brenner, 2012). Second, we examine the ways that science bloggers took up the issue, using the relatively well-established conventions of blogging for purposes arising out of this singular event. Third, we look at the social encyclopedia, Wikipedia, which the Pew Research Center reports as a source of information for 42% of all Americans who are online (Zickuhr & Rainie, 2011). We then turn to a somewhat different community that made different uses of the capacities of the Internet, creating its own technology platform: a group calling itself Safecast and often characterized as "citizen science,"[2] though we will find that the situation is somewhat more complicated. In

---

[1] See also Miller's discussion of "contact zones" between expert and public forums (2005).

[2] See, for example, *Scientific American*'s online database of citizen science projects, which includes Safecast.

each case, we will ask what *exigence* is being constructed, assumed, and shared by those using the platform. As exigence represents the social knowledge at the core of situation, and recurrent exigence is the core of genre (Bitzer, 1968; Miller, 1984), identifying the recurrent exigences in the uses of the Internet allows us to determine whether online activity surrounding the accident at the Fukushima Daiichi power plant can be described in terms of genres and whether those genres are well established or newly emerging. Looking across a spectrum of Internet use, then, we can focus on the ways that perceptions and responses are turned into typified motives for those engaging in rhetorical action.

EVENTS AT FUKUSHIMA DAIICHI

Fukushima became a globally recognizable signifier for the 2011 Tōhoku earthquake and subsequent tsunami that ravaged the coast of Japan, causing numerous failures at the Tokyo Electric Power Company's (TEPCO) Fukushima Daiichi Nuclear Power station. Crippling the plant, the 9.0 magnitude earthquake occurred Friday, March 11, 2011, at 5:46 UTC, with its epicenter near Sendai, which triggered the automatic shutdown of several reactors at the site, a mechanism designed to safely cool reactors to prevent meltdown in the event of power loss (U.S. Geological Survey, 2011). While reactors were automatically shut down, a 14-meter high tsunami overtook the protective seawall, resulting in further damage to the plant and creating new problems by interrupting the automatic cool down. As the site flooded, backup generators designed to ensure that the reactors are safely cooled failed, and approximately 6 hours later an evacuation order was issued for the surrounding area. After a cascade of additional failures, the site became increasingly worrisome to experts and the community alike, and almost a month after the accident, the International Nuclear Event Scale rating for the site was raised to Level 7, the site now standing atop the nuclear event scale with one notorious companion, Chernobyl. More than 2 years later, accidents are still occurring, such as the discharge of radioactive water, and the condition as well as future of the site remains unclear. With such an unprecedented nuclear disaster—Chernobyl, while being more deadly and dangerously scattering radioactive material when it exploded, was a less complex accident in that only one reactor was damaged, whereas the Fukushima site has several damaged reactors—the response to the accident has been equally unprecedented. Despite the enormous amount of scientific expertise focused on the event, there was considerable debate about radiation levels and safety for those living near the site, later questions about safe levels for those near the exclusion zone, and uncertainty about how the food chain might be affected, with the possibility of radiation effects extending across Japan. The cascading uncertainty was exacerbated by the unwillingness of Japanese authorities to release information and the minimal amount of information that the authorities did have.

EXIGENCE I: NEED FOR INFORMATION

With the situation at Fukushima Daiichi worsening, and reports leaking through the mainstream media, speculation began. Many citizens would turn to social media sites in an attempt to find more information about what was happening and how dangerous it was. Those on the ground in Japan turned to social media as an outlet to share what they were seeing and experiencing. In both cases, the traditional channels of information flow from experts to journalists to the public were disrupted. We look to Twitter, which saw dramatically increased usage following the earthquake, as an example of a social media platform put to use to create public knowledge about complex, unfolding events. Our examination of the other two media platforms, blogging and Wikipedia, will also focus on their informational uses in the immediate aftermath of the tsunami.

Twitter

In *The Philosophy of Literary Form*, Burke (1941) profitably elucidates the process of joining a conversational space, such as a discipline or community of practice, through the metaphor of an unending conversation. Burke's metaphor asks the reader to imagine arriving late at a parlor, with conversations long preceding their arrival. Because the conversation has already started, and there is no time for pause, the reader must listen for some time to determine the nature of the conversation and subsequently join (pp. 110–111). Burke's metaphor is helpful for understanding social media landscapes, particularly for our purposes. First, sites like Twitter.com often see patrons come and go without much fuss, no formal system of check in or check out. The fluid, informal nature of the conversational space is made evident by the fluctuating discursive spaces within which conversations dwell. Second, as one is free to come and go from the conversational space, the antecedent threads of the conversation isolate and push back against those who come late and wish to join. Similarly, while social media sites can be relatively open conversational spaces, conventions begin to emerge as a user base is established and users learn to utilize the system for their communicative ends. Discovering the conventions of the place allows for fuller engagement within the conversational space. For example, on Twitter, the use of hashtags and @replies and the understanding of supplementary functionality such as TwitPic and TweetDoc allow a richer conversational experience. Finally, as one would not walk into the parlor and address a lamp with the full force of their argument, one would not join Twitter and broadcast to a following of none. To fully engage in conversations in some platform, one must first identify the opponents and allies and then engage them. A response is not guaranteed, but voices also go unheard in parlors, and some voices are never allowed into the parlor.

With its continuous, even relentless, flow of brief messages, Twitter provides real-time information about current events, from news stories, to conference discussions, to crisis events like 3/11 (Acar & Muraki, 2011; Binder, 2012; Sakaki, Okazaki, & Matsuo, 2010; Thomson, Ito, Suda, Lin, Liu, Hayasaka et al., 2012). A survey of Japanese college students about the social-media platforms they used on the day of the earthquake found differences from previously documented patterns: although Facebook was more heavily used that day, Twitter usage was higher when compared to usage rates before the earthquake (Jung, 2012). In this study, Twitter use was associated with a goal of understanding or getting information, whereas Facebook was associated with a goal of interpersonal connection; that is, checking on the safety of friends and family. The surge of Twitter use that has been documented during the early stages of 3/11 (even before the nuclear plant accident), with Twitter reporting a 500% increase of tweets originating in Japan alone (Chowdhury, 2011), is thus consistent with an identification of the need for information as a central exigence.

Two previous analyses of Twitter data relevant to the 3/11 events are useful here: one from tweets originating in Japan and the other from tweets originating in the United States. Doan, Vo, and Collier (2011) provide an analysis of tweets originating within Tokyo during the period of March 9, 2011, to May 31, 2011. They collected over 1.5 million tweets to determine some of the social attitudes during this period, and the corpus data provide insights about the use of Twitter as the earthquake and tsunami hit, analyzing Japanese- and English-language tweets separately for keywords concerning the earthquake and tsunami, keywords concerning radiation, and keywords concerning anxiety. In this corpus, the first tweet arrives, in Japanese, 1 minute and 25 seconds after the earthquake began (p. 61). Shortly after messages about the earthquake, those about the tsunami followed, with a retweeted message from someone on the coast who wrote that they could see the tsunami coming (p. 62). Finally, within 9 minutes, there are worries about nuclear plants, and Doan et al. provide the following examples posted within hours of the earthquake: "Is the nuclear power plant okay?," "In detail RT @u_tips: Fukushima Dai-ni power plant is on alert," and "The Fukushima plant is in a really bad situation. . . . I hope that the government won't deceive the public" (p. 63).[3] Though the range of their study demonstrates that discussion about the accident at Fukushima Daiichi, and possibly other sites such as Fukushima Dai-ni, had a significant volume for the first month, they provide two excellent examples of the kinds of messages delivered through Twitter early

---

[3] All examples, including translations, are from Doan et al. (2011), though we have reversed the order, putting English first because the collection to which this chapter is contributed is an English-language anthology. Another consideration these examples forward concerns writing systems. Kenji Ito (2011) notes that the Japanese character system allows for more to be communicated in any given number of characters of Japanese than in a comparable number of English characters. In the first example above, there are 32 English characters to the 8 in Japanese; in the second, 63 to 33; and, in the third, 101 to 32. Given Twitter's strict 140-character limit, the difference in writing systems should be of considerable interest.

on where, on March 13, a user writes, "People are asked to close window, door; not to use AC; use mask & not to drink tap water #Fukushimasradiation" and another "210 becquerel iodine (normal 100 becquerel) discovered in Tokyo tap water. Infants are urged to avoid drinking it #Fukushimasradiation" (p. 64). These examples suggest something of the variety of exigences being addressed, from the need for information (news), to a responsibility to warn or instruct others, and the impulse to express and share anxiety.[4] These may not represent distinct genres, but they can be considered something like proto-genres (or perhaps what Bakhtin [1986] might call "primary genres"), as they are more like conversational speech acts than like fully typified discursive genres.

The categories that Doan et al. (2011) offer also provide some substantiation for Binder's (2012) assessment of the function of tweets within the first few days of the crisis at Fukushima. Binder examined a sample of English-language tweets originating within the United States within the 2 weeks immediately following the tsunami (March 11–25). He looked for keywords related to risk and classified the tweets as either "informative" (descriptive information) or "interpretive" (attributions of cause or significance). He found that neither the number of tweets per day nor the proportion of "interpretive" tweets changed over this period but that mentions of risk were most likely in informative tweets near the beginning of this period. While the informative/interpretive distinction is not quite the same as the news/warning/anxiety distinction seen in Doan et al., the informational function fits the "news" data, and the warnings and anxiety expressions are similar to interpretive tweets concerning risk. Once again, as the proportions of the different categories of tweets changed over time, we can understand these as protogenres invoked by the changing construction of exigence as the events unfolded and associated needs changed. Nevertheless, these genres or protogenres are ones associated with or available within the genre ecology of the media platform in each case.

Science Blogs

A Google Blogs search for "Fukushima" shows a dramatic, though unsurprising, increase in bloggers' attention to the events in Japan, increasing from some 3,160 results for the month of February to 45,200 results in March, and 54,300 in April. "Blogs take many forms," Miller and Shepherd write in their 2004 account of blogs and genre, and indeed blogs address many exigences and thus have become many genres (Formal Features section, para. 1). Blogs, in many forms, took note of the events in Japan, but we are particularly interested in the responses of bloggers who were attempting to redress technical and scientific misinformation about the accident at the Fukushima plant. The blogging form

---

[4] These functions are similar to three of the classical stases: existence (news), translation or policy (warnings), and quality or value (sharing states of mind).

known as science blogging is an increasingly favored method of pushing scientific stories to nonspecialist audiences, and many popular science publications have sections devoted to the science blog, including *Scientific American, National Geographic,* and *Wired.* Is there a distinctive genre here? What is the purposeful action that such blogs accomplish? Bora Zivkovic, former Blogs Editor at *Scientific American,* writes that, "much of what science bloggers do—and do very well—is critique the science coverage by the mass media" (2012). Such critique indeed motivated much science blogging about 3/11 and was extended to address both traditional mainstream media and various online discussions as questions about the accident at Fukushima arose. *Scientific American* provided coverage of the events unfolding in Japan, making connections to other social tools: for example on March 14, 2011, the editors posted a short note, reading,

> Conditions are changing rapidly at the Fukushima power plant, where at least two of its six nuclear reactors have partially melted down. The editors of *Scientific American* are following the developments, and part of the effort involves following various *Twitter* users. Here are a few we are following:
> International Atomic Energy Agency (@iaeaorg)
> Geoff Brumfiel, one of our colleagues at Nature (@gbrumfiel)
> The Japan Times (@japantimes)
> U.S. Geological Survey (@USGS)
> American Red Cross (@RedCross). (Scientific American, 2011)

An application allowing Twitter feeds to be displayed, showing real-time messages, is embedded in the blog post and several websites are linked. More posts were soon to follow, many exhibiting either the impulse to clarify or an admission about how difficult clarity was to achieve. "The extent of the damage at Japan's Fukushima nuclear facility is still unknown," writes Rita King on March 12 in *Scientific American*'s guest blog, and then asks whether the analogies comparing the unfolding event to a "Chernobyl-like" disaster are accurate (King, 2011). In a lengthy account of the unfolding event, Chris Rowan's March 14 article concludes with tips for keeping updated. He cites geologists who are blogging and tweeting, should one "want to go beyond the media coverage" (Rowan, 2011). What if you "really want to understand what's going on at the nuclear reactors at Fukushima?" Rowan, a geologist himself, cites geologist-blogger Evelyn Mervine's interview with her nuclear engineer father, Callan Bentley's blog that provides "early, in-depth and comprehensive coverage of the geological story," and a blog post that lists more bloggers and blog sites (Rowan, 2011). *Scientific American*'s March 11 blog post came from Zivkovic (2011), who shared Cyranoski's blog article, posted by Brian Owens to *Nature News Blog.* "Some phone lines are dead, but my Internet is working. I'm writing minutes after the earthquake, stuck on a train that screeched to a halt and then bounced on the tracks," Cyranoski writes (2011). At 12:37 GMT on March 11, Mark Peplow submitted a post titled "Update 1: Japan declares nuclear emergency," saying that "Nuclear Engineering International reports that Onagawa, Fukushima Daiichi, Fukushima Daini and Tokai nuclear power stations have all automatically shut down" and that "*Nature's* Tokyo correspondent, Cyranoski, Japanese media are reporting that the emergency core cooling system (ECCS) at the Fukushima #1 plant is not working due to a loss of electrical power" (Peplow, 2011). Days after the event, the confusion was evidenced in several posts. "The television and various news sources are clogged with radiation numbers and experts trying to explain them," writes Geoffery Brumfiel, concerned whether the use of micro- and millisieverts by different sources might confuse "the public" (Brumfiel, 2011). By March 24, things were only the more confusing: "There is now so much disparate data from many sources, in different units, and on various aspects of radiation, that there still seems much confusion about what it all means," writes Declan Butler (2011).

A group of graduate students in MIT's Nuclear Science and Engineering program began a blog, the first post dated March 13, 2011, with the "intent of providing unbiased, accurate information on the disaster . . . borne out of frustration among the students at the misinformation and hysteria that characterized initial reactions to the disaster" (Pierpoint, 2011, p. 56). The purpose of the blog was also to vet what was believed to be questionable sources or accounts of the events unfolding in Japan (Pierpoint, 2011, p. 56). The MIT blog describes itself as "maintained by the students of the Department of Nuclear Science and Engineering at MIT with the support of the NSE faculty" with the goal of providing "non-sensationalized, factual information about the situation in a manner that the general public can understand" (mitnse.com). The blog addresses key topics, including "What are Spent Fuel Pools?," "What is Decay Heat?," "Introduction to Radiation Health Effects and Radiation Status at Fukushima," "On Worst Case Scenarios," and "Impact of Plutonium on Human Health"; and the site within which the blog is embedded also features an FAQ with common questions that are posed to the bloggers (mitnse.com). This effort is similar to much public risk communication, with the assumption by the scientific community of public ignorance and miscomprehension and thus of their own responsibility to explain. What this "deficit model" of risk communication (Bucchi, 2008) leaves out is the very evident confusion on the part of scientists evidenced just above.

All of this blogging activity demonstrates a substantial conversational space where rhetorical work on behalf of science is being done. This rhetorical work taken on by scientists, though in some cases functioning as boundary work to maintain the "integrity" of scientific knowledge, often aims deliberately to bridge the boundary—even to violate it—thus contributing to what Trench (2008) called its "erosion." None of these efforts, or the perceived exigences to which they respond, are necessarily new; what is new is the use of blogging to address them. As a platform, blogging does not require peer review or the editorial gatekeeping and distribution infrastructures of institutionalized science or trade journalism. Whether there is one genre of science blogging or many, this brief account cannot determine, but it seems clear that one of its distinctive features is exactly its ability to work on, around, and through the putative boundary between science and the public. There are science blogs that look more like scientific reports, which certainly feature different characteristics than crisis reporting might, but that does not detract from the argument that the way scientists are communicating is changing, and good evidence for this is the genre (or genres) of science blogging. Indeed, we might consider this genre to be very much in line with Kaplan and Radin's (2011) notion of "para-scientific" genres, in that science blogging borrows scientific authority and knowledge structures from the realm of science but operates without the gatekeeping and traditional reporting forms of internal science communication. In other words, it borrows some features from the internal discourse of science without the whole complex of features upon which the epistemic authority of science depends. However, these genres, unlike popular science genres, forego the rhetorical accommodations outlined by Fahnestock (1986), such as appealing to "wonder." Rather, the parascientific genres are concerned with the collection, arrangement, or application of scientific knowledge in contexts formally external to but somehow involved with the scientific community.

Wikipedia

On March 12, at 15:50 UTC, a Wikipedia page titled "Fukushima Daiichi Nuclear Disaster" was created by user Kslotte; this page linked to a section on "2011 earthquake events" of the article on "Fukushima I Nuclear Power Plant" (Wikipedia, 2012a). It included a standardized disclaimer at the beginning:

> This section documents the Fukushima I nuclear incident, a current nuclear event. Information regarding it may change rapidly as it progresses. Although this section is updated frequently, it may not reflect the most current information about this nuclear event for all areas.

There was no further activity that day, but by the end of the next day, March 13, there had been 396 edits, and the entry had grown from 1,737 to 2,871 words, with 75 source citations and 5 external links. By the end of the month, nearly 4,000 edits had been made, there were nearly 13,000 words, with 383 source citations, 9 external links, 9 photos, 2 tables, 4 diagrams, and 2 maps. On May 22, the earthquake section was moved from the page on the power plant to the page on the disaster and became a separate article, with a link in the first sentence to "Fukushima I Nuclear Power Plant."[5] By the end of May, there had been nearly 5,000 edits, and the article had nearly 14,500 words, 478 references, 16 external links, 13 photos, 2 tables, 7 diagrams, and 2 maps. Editing still continues as we write, though at a much slower pace than in the early days, and the article now has just over 22,000 words, 448 citations, 25 external links, 8 photos, 10 diagrams, 5 maps, and 1 table.[6]

Who did all this work? Of the 1,516 "editors" who contributed, 12 made more than 100 edits each, with 281 the most by any one person; all but one of these top 12 began contributing in the first 5 days (by March 17), but only 3 were still contributing in 2012. None of these most-frequent editors self-identifies as a scientist on Wikipedia's associated User Page, and only two mention interests specifically relevant to the Fukushima accident: Johnfos, with 109 edits, focuses on energy, renewable energy, and the antinuclear movement, and Shinkolobwe, with 122 edits, a native speaker of French, is interested in chemistry and geology; for 4 of these top 12 contributors, no user information is available at all. The user who started the page on the accident, Kslotte, made 26 contributions between March 12 and March 18 but then ceases to be involved; his user page indicates that he is Finnish, owns an information technology company, and "seldom contribute[s] with content," focusing mainly on organizing, copyediting, and ensuring adherence to Wikipedia policies. Another frequent contributor in the first days of the event, Marie Poise, with 57 edits between March 13 and 19 and none subsequently, provides no biographical information. Many of these contributors describe themselves as experienced but not expert Wikipedians, with an interest in implementing the rules and policies and in offering information that is correct and useful. The "About" page of Wikipedia indicates that "Wikipedia is written largely by amateurs . . . [and] is not subject to any peer review." The advantage claimed is that amateurs have more free time and can thus make "rapid changes in response to current events," as clearly was the case here (Wikipedia, 2012b, para. 31).

It is a bit difficult to track readership because the data before May 22 are for the entire page about the power plant, not just the section on the earthquake and ensuing events at the plant and beyond, which became the separate article. Nevertheless, because "Fukushima I Power Plant" shows virtually no readers until March 11, a dramatic spike on March 12 to over 300,000, and a readership for the month of over a million and a half (an average of over 72,000 readers

---

[5] There was a fair amount of talk among the editors about whether this article should be headed "accident" or a "disaster," based on comparison with similar events and the way that the event was commonly referred to by the press.

[6] These data are as of August 10–12, 2012.

per day after March 11), it seems reasonable to assume that this interest repre-sents a search for information pertaining to the earthquake and nuclear disaster. In April, the readership is one-tenth that, with an average of 7,700 per day. In May, the average readership drops to 976 per day on that page, but for the new page, "Fukushima Daiichi Nuclear Disaster," the rate averaged 2,418 per day after May 22, with readership in the next five months varying between about 2,500 and 6,500 per day. The average readership per day for the page on the power plant itself decreased steadily from 543 in June to 277 in October, suggesting that sustained reader interest was indeed in the disaster and not the plant itself. User ratings of the page (as of mid-August 2012), on a scale of 5, are "trustworthy" 4.2, "objective" 4.3, "complete" 4.8, and "well-written" 4.6 (with the number of ratings ranging from 234 to 253), indicating substan-tial reader confidence in the information provided, although it has not been designated as a "featured" or "good" article, designations that would add editorial authority to the high user ratings.[7]

We can learn a great deal about the ways that Wikipedia functions for users from the "Talk" pages associated with the edits as the article is built out over time. What was it that the editors thought they were doing and why? How did they evaluate and improve the article over time? The answers to these questions will tell us something about how they understood the exigence they thought they were facing and thus the ways they shaped their actions to fit the genre of the Wikipedia article. In addition to the rich data available on the talk pages, an extensive system of self-governance and policies have developed since Wikipedia's founding in 2001, including a set of official aims and ideals, and criteria for excellence, all of which inform the reasoning of the editors as they do their work.[8] In scanning through the talk pages, we see the contributors enjoining each other to add information, to evaluate sources, to have patience as an unfolding event gets reported, to explain in ordinary language, to avoid sensationalizing. As an exploratory study, we examined the 57 editorial discus-sions in Archive 1, which covers March 11–13, 2011, coding them for references to these Wikipedia policies (Wikipedia, 2011a). The policy most frequently invoked (36 times) was "verifiability," meaning that "Other people have to be able to check that you didn't just make things up. This means that all quotations and any material challenged or likely to be challenged must be attributed to a reliable, published source using an inline citation" (Wikipedia, 2012d). The next most frequently invoked criterion (18 times) was that of comprehensiveness, meaning that the article "neglects no major facts or details and places the subject

---

[7] Page ratings were added to Wikipedia sometime after July 2011, well after the initial response to Fukushima, and ratings of earlier versions have apparently not been archived (Fung, 2011).

[8] For example, see the Content Criteria article on Wikipedia, as well as articles listing the Core Content Policies, the Five Pillars, Featured Article Criteria, and "The perfect article."

in context"; followed by "no original research" (11 times), "neutral point of view" (9 times), and "well written" (8 times) (Wikipedia, 2007).

The most obvious invocation of genre in this archive (7 times) was reference to the fact that Wikipedia is an "encyclopedia," a mandate that contributors took seriously by pointing out that it is "not a news source," that editors should "stop using PRESENT TENSE," that "Wikipedia must not be sensationalistic," and "it's not wikipedia's job to keep on top of things: this site is supposed to be an encyclopedia, which is appropriate for getting to the bottom of things."[9] Indeed, the criteria of verifiability, comprehensiveness, no original research, and neutral point of view are all part of the understanding of Wikipedia's specific genre identity as an encyclopedia. The most serious tension in the early hours of Wikipedia's treatment of the unfolding events at Fukushima Daiichi was between the archival function of the encyclopedia, with the need to provide stable and authoritative information, and the chaos of the unfolding event for which only partial and imperfectly reported and comprehended information was available. The multiple editors working together functioned as checks on each other to provide the most authoritative and most comprehensible version they could manage at each moment. Wikipedia thus distinguishes itself from journalism; it also distinguishes itself from science as not subject to expert peer review and not presenting original research.[10] The prior understandings of the capabilities and responsibilities of the encyclopedia genre informed the ongoing reflective construction of the exigence by the Wikipedia editors who labored over the articles about Fukushima as the events unfolded—and thus informed and reinforced the genre of the Wikipedia article.

EXIGENCE II: NEED FOR DATA

To this point, we have examined the ways that established Internet platforms were used to engage in a variety of rhetorical actions as the events of 3/11 unfolded. In each case, we see evidence of lack of information, lack of comprehension, uncertainty, and confusion. In each case, we find that the 3/11 events at Fukushima elicited uses of these established platforms in familiar ways, drawing on typifications of social needs and audience roles that would be already available to both rhetors and audiences, making perhaps minor adaptations to the flow of events in March 2011, to perform familiar social actions addressing a

---

[9] See also the policy page, where the understanding of Wikipedia as an encyclopedia is developed contrastively (Wikipedia, 2012c).

[10] For a time in 2006, Wikipedia experimented with the use of formal "scientific peer review" for articles on scientific topics but in 2007 reverted to internal review by editors upon request because of a lack of use of the "scientific" process and in the interests of efficiency. See Wikipedia (2011b) and the associated "talk" page.

general and widely understood exigence. We see how available typifications underwrote the attempts to deal with this series of unprecedented events. We turn now to a different sort of effort that marshalled the capacities of the Internet in new ways to address a somewhat longer-term exigence related to the lack not only of information about what had happened but of detailed data that could be used to assess the future, that is, to understand risk.

Originating as the combination of RDTN.org[11] and the efforts of Sean Bonner, Joi Ito, and Pieter Franken, the group that would become known as Safecast began with frustrations regarding the lack of information about specific radiation levels and exposure risks to those at various locations in Japan. Bonner, Ito, and Franken began an email exchange after the accident, asking after friends and family in the impacted region, which soon turned to attempts to secure Geiger counters for said family and friends, but the scope grew, as did their network of connections (Safecast, n.d., History). Ito, Director of the MIT Media Lab, described Safecast's initial creation as a response to several problems, including a lack of information released to the public, the lack of existing information, and the lack of tools to obtain that information (J. Ito, 2011). RDTN founder Marcelino Alvarez expresses similar motivations, saying the project was motivated to aggregate and validate data,[12] following the confusion resulting from 3/11, but the project would evolve into an effort to collect the data as well. A Kickstarter appeal for funds[13] was launched on April 7, 2011, with the following project description:

> Safecast.org (formerly RDTN.org) is a website whose purpose is to provide an aggregate feed of nuclear radiation data from governmental, non-governmental and citizen-scientist sources. That data will be made available to everyone, including scientists and nuclear experts who can provide context for lay people. In the weeks following launch, it has become evident that there is a need for additional radiation reporting from the ground in Japan. This Kickstarter project will help us purchase up to 600 Geiger Counter devices that will be deployed to Japan (Alvarez, 2011a, para. 1).

The appeal went on to indicate that a map of radiation detection in Japan showed "many holes where no data is being captured whatsoever. Some of those are very close to Fukushima while others are well outside of Tokyo. The initial set of [detection] devices will be utilized in areas where coverage is sparse" (Alvarez,

---

[11] RDTN.org was founded within 72 hours of the accident. Another group, Bonner, Ito, and Franken, were also beginning to coordinate. These two groups were connected and then merged their efforts, rebranding as "Safecast" (from "safe" and "broadcast").

[12] For an account of RDTN's founding, see Alvarez's (2011b) "72 Hours from Concept to Launch: RDTN.org" blog post.

[13] Kickstarter is a social platform that allows users to pitch a project and attempt to secure crowd-sourced funding through the Kickstarter community.

2011a, para. 4). The idea was to distribute the devices "to people on the ground who have been trained in how to use them. It could be a teacher, a university student, or a citizen-scientist looking to contribute to the project" (Alvarez, 2011a, para. 14).

Safecast designed a response to the need for data, moving from delivering information, to collecting and contextualizing information, and even building tools for the collection of data. As of July 2012, Safecast reported having a team of 100 volunteers, mostly located in Tokyo, with 135 sensors in varied form deployed and more than 3,500,000 data-points collected (Safecast, n.d., About). We might characterize the response to this second exigence as data collection to help alleviate the lack of information about radiation levels and exposures that could endanger those in the area. Safecasters themselves say, "After the 3/11 earthquake and resulting nuclear situation . . . it became clear that people wanted more data than what was available" (Safecast, n.d., About, para. 1).

Data is central to the story of Safecast. Safecast employed many genres of coordination, organization, and sharing, based in technology platforms such as email, Skype, and the website, and such to collect and aggregate data. However, we suggest that the data, and more specifically, the rhetorical construction of data within and by databases also merit consideration in terms of genre.[14] This is a particularly interesting topic to pose with the rise of "Big Data."[15] But how might we begin to describe the rhetorical nature of data (bases or structures)? The creation and organization of a database are not determined processes: there must be an organizer, and the organization and standards to which data are held are the product not merely of technological affordance and constraint, but of consensus among a community of users and of anticipations of the functions the data will be serving. If the database can be seen as rhetorical, then we might pose questions about its generic function and form. Are there genres of databases? Are databases components of other genres?[16]

---

[14] Since James Wynn treats the rhetorical nature of the maps generated by Safecast in this collection, we will restrict our discussion to the data collection and sharing efforts of Safecast.

[15] "Big Data" is a term with increasing currency, as evidenced by the NSF solicitation for "Core Techniques and Technologies for Advancing Big Data Science and Engineering (BIGDATA). An account of NSF interest in big data more generally can be found in press release 12-060: http://www.nsf.gov/news/news_summ.jsp?cntn_id=123607.

[16] Manovich (2000, 2007) and Brooke (2009) treat this question somewhat differently, suggesting that the purposes to which databases are put vary with users and can be reflected in their queries. Following Manovich, Brooke suggests that the database is like Saussurean "langue," which in itself "does not actually mean anything; it is only when it takes the form of utterance, when it is put into practice, that meaning is generated. The same thing is true of databases" (Brooke, 2009, p. 101). When a user queries a database, it responds with an "utterance," and each database is capable of multiple utterances, increasing with the complexity of the database itself and the sophistication of the query routines and user goals.

For example, in asking "what constitutes a 'scientific' database?" Pfaltz (2007) argues that it is the effort to construct scientific knowledge, maintaining that the "actual hallmark of a scientific database is the ease with which the underlying hypotheses, scientific assertions, rules or implications (call them what you may) can be obtained from the observed data" (p. 9). Pfaltz further suggests that what distinguishes them from business databases is the need for scientific databases to accommodate spatial and/or temporal data and to allow for unforeseen data attributes and new hypotheses to be accommodated. Constructing a scientific database requires not only technical decisions, but also rhetorical decisions, just as formulating hypotheses, constructing lab experiments, justifying methods, and various other work in the laboratory are (also) rhetorical work. Scientific databases are rhetorical in that they are constructed to respond to particular exigences, constrained by the very nature of the scientific enterprise. They are rhetorical both from the perspective of the creator(s) and from the perspective of the user(s). As a genre,[17] the scientific database is a recognition of recurrent characteristic needs and functions and of conventional (and emerging) ways of engaging those needs and functions. Safecast's efforts are built on this set of recognitions.

Using a sensor network of both stationary and mobile radiation-detection devices throughout Japan, Safecast collects data through a crowd-sourcing approach. As the data are collected, they are added to the database and thereby organized, and then published on the Safecast website through a Creative Commons Universal license. The quality of the data collected has been considered by the group, who not only quickly acquainted themselves with the literature on radiation, but also participated in experimental work to ensure its quality. For example, Safecaster Joe Moross, in an interview with *IEEE Spectrum*, describes determining whether or not vehicle motion interferes with readings by testing their "theory" and finding that there did not appear to be evidence for concern (Cherry, 2011). If we take the data to be accurate, since it results from considered methods and collection protocols, we can then turn to questions of the database design itself. The data collected includes time stamps, latitude, longitude, altitude, and radiation events in counts per minute, among other information. Though it is certainly notable that the Safecast data correlate to "real-world" events, a characteristic of the scientific database for Pfaltz (2007), what is important is that decisions about what data would be collected, what units of measure would be used, and what kind of structural relations the data would have were all determined by Safecasters themselves. That is, they are

---

[17] A somewhat different case has been made by Folsom, following Manovich (2001), arguing that the database "is becoming a new genre, the genre of the twenty-first century" (Folsom, 2007, p. 1576). Both contrast database with narrative, seeing these as mutually exclusive forms of storage, structure, and access, but these general forms are not genres in the rhetorical sense.

not collecting data to be compiled into a structure determined by scientific experts (they are not acting as field technicians); rather, they are making their own decisions about what to include and exclude and how to organize it. The data are then accessible through Safecast's website, where anyone can download the CSV (comma-separated value) file in a relational database. While sites like Yahoo! Japan and the Scanning the Earth project[18] have used the data, the data are also being shared in less conventional ways, with strategic placement of stickers showing radiation readings (microsieverts per hour) at that location and the date the reading was recorded.[19] At least some Japanese residents are apparently using the data to make judgments about evacuation and personal safety, and some local governments in the Fukushima prefecture are making Safecast data available to residents (Kageyama, 2012).

We should clarify the roles of the participants, both the organizers and the data collectors. The Safecasters were none of them trained scientists, though many have technical backgrounds, and many key members in the development of the group have some connections to the hacker/do-it-yourself (DIY) culture: the connection to the DIY community through the Tokyo Hackerspace was essential to the development of the sensor network Safecast uses.[20] In addition to off-the-shelf Geiger counters (Inspector Alter and the CRM-100), Safecast and the Tokyo Hackerspace helped to build mobile monitoring devices. These devices, called a bGeigie (for the bento-box form and Geiger counter), include a standard Geiger counter and an in-house electronic recording system to track and save the readings and the GPS coordinates (Safecast, n.d., Devices). The electronics are bundled into a water resistant box and mounted to an automobile to take readings. These devices have been distributed to volunteers on the ground in Japan. The volunteers might be characterized as citizen-scientists, except for the fact that the usual model of the citizen-scientist assumes that an ordinary untrained person is working with direction from scientists who have designed a research project, established the data protocols, will do the data analysis, and will publish in a peer reviewed forum with the aim of making a sanctioned scientific claim (Cohn, 2008). In the case of Safecast, these marks of institutionalized science are absent: the data-collection devices and protocols were designed by largely self-taught Safecasters with the goal of producing

---

[18] Scanning the Earth consortium is a research project affiliated with Safecast and uses their data. Safecast co-founder Pieter Franken is a Senior Visiting Researcher at the university housing the project, Keio Research Institute at the Shonan Fujisawa Campus.

[19] Safecast provides examples on its blog: http://blog.safecast.org/2012/03/information-disbursement/.

[20] Definitions of hacker vary and have negative connotations in colloquial use, but we mean hacker in terms of a recognized level of technical interest and capability in technical systems (hardware or software). Hackerspaces, as defined by hackerspaces.org, are "community-operated physical places, where people can meet and work on their projects."

information for the public that institutionalized science had not provided. We believe it's fair then to call Safecast's work "parascientific," genuinely "alongside" the work of science and quite deliberately positioned on the increasingly questionable boundary between the expert and the public spheres.

Given that databases are rhetorical, and given that Safecast's database is a parascientific construction, we would argue that it functions here as a possible new genre, the parascientific database. Similar efforts of citizen monitoring have the capacity to produce similar databases, such as the Bucket Brigade's work with air pollution monitoring.[21] Safecast itself has branched out with Safecast Air, in development, which will monitor air quality. This particular effort is being led by Ariel Levi Simons, a high school science teacher in Los Angeles, suggesting significant opportunities for student participation and learning (Bonner, 2012). A new Geiger counter was developed by a Safecaster[22] and will be produced by International Medcom, manufacturer of radiation detection instruments. While many of the strategies of Safecast, such as crowd-sourced funding, community-based monitoring of radiation levels, and open access publishing of data, are being used in different ways within institutional science, they are hardly routine and thus probably not solidly generic in that environment yet. And one major difference between institutionalized science and an enterprise like Safecast is the expertise or professionalization of participants, and the concomitant cluster of motivations, interests, and ambitions they bring to the project. Are they "scientists" by virtue of their careful information-gathering and dissemination? To what extent do they ally themselves with science or draw upon scientific practices? In what ways do they define themselves and their project as distinctly "outside" science? We can learn something about this from the rhetorical work that Safecast members have done to define themselves as a group. We may find that the erosion of boundaries between science and the public and the emergence of new genres of parascientific discourse entail new roles for participants, such as the role of the "citizen-scientist" and "citizen-monitor," or perhaps even the "parascientist." We believe that Safecast illustrates some of the ways that new technologies, new roles, and new genres are changing the relationship between science and the public sphere.

FINAL REMARKS

The examples we have examined here tell us some important things about genre emergence and change, processes that are central to understanding

---

[21] See, for more information, https://gcm.rdsecure.org//section.php?id=9.

[22] Read about the development process of the Safecast Geiger counter, designed by Andrew "bunnie" Huang, here: "Safecast Geiger Counter Reference Design" http://www.bunnie studios.com/blog/?p=2218.

science in the age of the Internet. With the social media tools we outlined under Exigence I, we see that platform development provides new affordances to users for social, collaborative, and communicative ends. While we might trace antecedent genres or technologies to find similar rhetorical work being accomplished—perhaps Twitter has some lineage to the telegraph that would be insightful about how news information travels within communities and globally—there are notable changes with online social media. Primarily, we are talking about scales of attention and time. Under Exigence II, we provided an account of Safecast, which responded to the lack of data about radiation levels in Japan after 3/11. Here we depart from our study of what might be strictly characterized as "social media" and look to the way in which the group used the affordances offered by the Internet to connect rapidly with others and begin to coordinate a massive data-collection program. Certainly Safecast employed a variety of social media tools in this effort, but we focus on their development of a database to move beyond the comfortable space of social media, already staked out by rhetoricians and media theorists, and begin to look at the database as a site of rhetorical work. We speculate about the kinds of rhetorical work that construct the database and, indeed, the rhetorical work the database is doing. Whether we focus on characterizing the various genres that might be found on Twitter, science blogs, or elsewhere on the Internet, or use other rhetorical perspectives to understand events like Fukushima, it is evident that the landscape of scientific communication has undergone and continues to undergo massive changes.

Approaching this chapter, we asked whether boundaries between scientific and public spheres could fairly be characterized as "eroding" (Trench, 2008). If so, might we see genres emerging in response to these erosions? We also considered whether we might see new exigences crystallized with the aid of new media platforms (Miller & Shepherd, 2009). In the three cases of social media, it seems that new genres did not emerge specifically for Fukushima, unprecedented though it might have seemed as an exigence. The recognized uses of available technologies were appropriate and adequate for most information needs, both those of people directly affected by conditions in Japan and those around the world seeking to understand what was happening. In each case, however, we observe that these uses either assumed or contributed to the erosion of the boundary between the scientific and the public sphere and thus often between the roles of expert and public: Twitter users bypass experts and officials to disseminate immediate observations, and Wikipedia works to make scientifically authorized information useful to nonscientists; science blogs work from the other side of the boundary, enabling scientists to adopt the role of public educator or public advocate or even particularly knowledgeable citizen.

The Safecast example is different in that there was no Internet community or platform readily available to meet the recognized need for monitoring data and no immediate capacity in the expert sphere to do so. The DIY ethos and Internet savvy of those who spearheaded the effort enabled them to construct what they needed—including the detection devices, the data-collection network, and the community of action—and to adopt the genre of the scientific database to their specific purposes. Again, they bypassed, or simply ignored, the expert/public boundary and have subsequently worked with both non-expert citizens and with expert advisors as the project has developed since the events of 3/11. We can call this work "parascience" insofar as it works alongside science and outside the formal authorizing and gatekeeping institutions of science. But is there another sense in which this work is science? Or an intimation of the future of science? If the erosion of boundaries—between spheres, between roles, and between genres— continues, then the parascientific may become the new model for science.

Farrell and Goodnight's (1981) study of Three Mile Island expressed par- ticular concern about the apparent impoverishment of the public sphere and its domination by technical reason, which grounds the expert sphere. The erosion of this boundary they saw as a threat, a "usurpation" (p. 273) of the role of an empowered public to deliberate its own fate. Technical reason fails, they say, "to offer communication practices capable of mastering the problems of our age" (p. 271). Yet it could equally be argued that social reason, which grounds the public sphere, is inadequate to the problems of our age, as the worldwide stalemate over political measures to address global warming illustrates. Perhaps as Ceccarelli (2011) has recently argued, rhetoricians should not be satisfied only with critique of scientific orthodoxy, but must account for the manufac- turing of controversy and turn their critique on the public sphere as well in order to understand the intersection of the two. With the cases here, with these para- scientific genres, we can begin to examine the complex relationships of science and its publics, not only the publics that support science but also the publics that science supports. Whether the Internet's capacities to erode boundaries will lead to new ways of doing science or to a reconfiguration of these spheres of reasoning, it seems clear that institutionalized science will continue to be challenged by these new capacities and the new genres they enable.

REFERENCES

Acar, A., & Muraki, Y. (2011). Twitter for crisis communication: Lessons learned from Japan's tsunami disaster. *International Journal of Web Based Communities*, 392–402. Interscience Publishers.

Alvarez, M. (2011a). RDTN.org: Radiation detection hardware network in Japan. *Kickstarter.com*. Retrieved from http://www.kickstarter.com/projects/1038658656/ rdtnorg-radiation-detection-hardware-network-in-ja

Alvarez, M. (2011b). 72 hours from concept to launch. *RDTN.org*. Retrieved from http://uncorkedstudios.com/2011/03/21/72-hours-from-concept-to-launch-rdtn-org/

Bakhtin, M. M. (1986). The problem of speech genres (V. W. McGee, Trans.). In C. Emerson & M. Holquist (Eds.), *Speech genres and other late essays* (pp. 60–102). Austin, TX: University of Texas Press.

Beck, U. (1992). *Risk society: Towards a new modernity.* London, UK: Sage.

Berkenkotter, C., & Huckin, T. N. (1993). Rethinking genre from a sociocognitive perspective. *Written Communication, 10*(4), 475–509.

Binder, A. R. (2012). Figuring out #Fukushima: An initial look at functions and content of US Twitter commentary about nuclear risk. *Environmental Communication: A Journal of Nature and Culture, 6*(2), 268–277.

Bitzer, L. F. (1968). The rhetorical situation. *Philosophy & Rhetoric, 1*(1), 1–14.

Bonner, S. (2012). Monitoring air quality [Blog]. *Safecast.* Retrieved from http://blog.safecast.org/2012/04/monitoring-air-quality/

Brooke, C. (2009). *Lingua fracta: Toward a rhetoric of new media.* Cresskill, NJ: Hampton.

Brossard, D. (2009). Media, scientific journals, and science communication: Examining the construction of scientific controversies. *Public Understanding of Science, 18*(3), 258–274.

Brumfiel, G. (2011, March 16). Confusing radiation numbers swirl around Fukushima [Blog]. *nature.com.* Retrieved from http://blogs.nature.com/news/2011/03/confusing_radiation_numbers_sw.html

Bucchi, M. (2008). Of deficits, deviations and dialogues: Theories of public communication of science. In M. Bucchi & B. Trench (Eds.), *Handbook of public communication of science and technology* (pp. 57–76). New York, NY: Routledge.

Burke, K. (1941). *The philosophy of literary form.* Berkeley, CA: University of California Press.

Butler, D. (2011, March 24). Fukushima nuclear data proliferation [Blog]. *nature.com.* Retrieved from http://blogs.nature.com/news/2011/03/fukushima_nuclear_data_prolife.html

Ceccarelli, L. (2001). Rhetorical criticism and the rhetoric of science. *Western Journal of Communication, 65*(3), 314–329.

Ceccarelli, L. (2011). Manufactured scientific controversy. *Rhetoric & Public Affairs, 14*(2), 195–228.

Cherry, S. (2011, November 17). Crowdsourcing radiation monitoring. *IEEE Spectrum.* Retrieved from http://spectrum.ieee.org/podcast/geek-life/hands-on/crowdsourcing-radiation-monitoring

Chowdhury, A. (2011, June 29). Global pulse [Blog]. *Twitter.* Retrieved from http://blog.twitter.com/2011/06/global-pulse.html

Cohn, J. P. (2008). Citizen science: Can volunteers do real research? *BioScience, 53*(8), 192–197.

Condit, C. M., Lynch, J., & Winderman, E. (2012). Recent rhetorical studies in public understanding of science: Multiple purposes and strengths. *Public Understanding of Science, 21*(4), 386–400.

Cooke, R. M. (1991). *Experts in uncertainty: Opinion and subjective probability in science.* New York, NY: Oxford University Press.

Cyranoski, D. (2011, March 11). Japan earthquake: Report from Tokyo [Blog]. *nature.com.* Retrieved from http://blogs.nature.com/news/2011/03/post_74.html

Doan, S., Vo, B.-K. H., & Collier, N. (2011, March). An analysis of Twitter messages in the 2011 Tohoku earthquake. *eHealth 2011 conference,* pp. 58–66.

Fahnestock, J. (1986). Accommodating science: The rhetorical life of scientific facts. *Written Communication, 3*(3), 275–296.

Farrell, T. B., & Goodnight, G. T. (1981). Accidental rhetoric: The root metaphors of Three Mile Island. *Communication Monographs, 48*, 271–300.

Folsom, E. (2007). Database as genre: The epic transformation of archives. *Publications of the Modern Language Association, 122*(5), 1571–1579.

Friedman, S. M. (2011). Three Mile Island, Chernobyl, and Fukushima: An analysis of traditional and new media coverage of nuclear accidents and radiation. *Bulletin of the Atomic Scientists, 67*(5), 55–65.

Fung, H. (2011, July 15). "Rate this page" is coming to the English Wikipedia. *Wikimedia Foundation.* Retrieved from https://blog.wikimedia.org/2011/07/15/%E2%80%9Crate-this-page%E2%80%9D-is-coming-to-the-english-wikipedia/

Gaskins, R. (1992). *Burdens of proof in modern discourse.* New Haven, CT: Yale University Press.

Gieryn, T. F. (1999). *Cultural boundaries of science: Credibility on the line.* Chicago, IL: University of Chicago Press.

Gross, A. G., Harmon, J. E., & Reidy, M. (2002). *Communicating science: The scientific article from the 17th century to the present.* New York, NY: Oxford University Press.

Harris, R. A. (1991). Rhetoric of science. *College English, 53*(3), 282–307.

Ito, J. (2011, September 4). Safecast presentation. *Ars Electronica.* Linz, Austria.

Ito, K. (2011, November 2). *Twittering a nuclear disaster: Circulation of technoscientific knowledge and politics of expertise in emergency.* Paper presented at the 4S annual meeting, Cleveland, OH.

Jung, J-Y. (2012). Social media use and goals after the great East Japan earthquake. *First Monday, 17*(8). Retrieved from http://www.uic.edu/htbin/cgiwrap/bin/ojs/index.php/fm/article/view/4071/3285

Kageyama, Y. (2012, July 9). American praised for getting Japan radiation data. *Yahoo! Finance.* Retrieved from http://finance.yahoo.com/news/american-praised-getting-japan-radiation-data-074518244—finance.html

Kaplan, S., & Radin, J. (2011). Bounding an emerging technology: Para-scientific media and the Drexler-Smalley debate about nanotechnology. *Social Studies of Science, 41*(4), 457–485.

King, R. (2011, March 12). Failure of imagination can be deadly: Fukushima is a warning [Blog]. *Scientific Americans.* Retrieved from http://blogs.scientificamerican.com/guest-blog/2011/03/12/failure-of-imagination-can-be-deadly-fukushima-is-a-warning/

Kuhn, T. (1970). *The structure of scientific revolutions.* Chicago, IL: University of Chicago Press. (Original work published 1962)

Manovich, L. (2000). Database as a genre of new media. *AI & Society, 14*(2), 176–183.

Manovich, L. (2001). *The language of new media.* Cambridge, MA: MIT Press.

Medway, P. (2002). Fuzzy genres and community identities: The case of architecture students' sketchbooks. In R. Coe, L. Lingard, & T. Teslenko (Eds.), *The rhetoric and ideology of genre: Strategies for stability and change* (pp. 123–153). Cresskill, NJ: Hampton.

Miller, C. R. (1984). Genre as social action. *Quarterly Journal of Speech, 70*, 151–167.

Miller, C. R. (1992). Kairos in the rhetoric of science. In S. P. Witte, N. Nakadate, & R. D. Cherry (Eds.), *A rhetoric of doing: Essays on written discourse in honor of James L. Kinneavy* (pp. 310–327). Carbondale, IL: Southern Illinois University Press.

Miller, C. R. (2005). Risk, controversy, and rhetoric: Response to Goodnight. *Argumentation and Advocacy, 42*(1), 34–37.

Miller, C. R., & Shepherd, D. (2004). Blogging as social action: A genre analysis of the weblog. *Into the Blogosphere.* Retrieved from http://blog.lib.umn.edu/blogosphere/blogging_as_social_action.html

Miller, C. R., & Shepherd, D. (2009). Questions for genre theory from the blogosphere. In J. Giltrow & D. Stein (Eds.), *Genres in the Internet: Issues in the theory of genre* (pp. 263–290). Amsterdam, The Netherlands: John Benjamins.

National Academy of Sciences. (n.d.). *The science of science communication.* Retrieved from http://www.nasonline.org/programs/sackler-colloquia/completed_colloquia/science-communication.html

Peplow, M. (2011, March 11). UPDATE 1: Japan declares nuclear emergency [Blog]. *nature.com.* Retrieved from http://blogs.nature.com/news/2011/03/japan_declares_nuclear_emergen.html

Perrow, C. (2011). Fukushima and the inevitability of accidents. *Bulletin of the Atomic Scientists, 67*(6), 44–52.

Pfaltz, J. L. (2007, July 9). *What constitutes a scientific database?* SSDBM 19th International Conference on Scientific and Statistical Database. Retrieved from http://www.ursuletz.com/~jlp/07.SSDBM.pdf

Pierpoint, L. (2011). Feeds: Informing the public in a digital era. *The Electricity Journal, 24*(6), 53–58.

Rowan, C. (2011, March 14). Japan earthquake: The explainer [Blog]. *Scientific American.* Retrieved http://blogs.scientificamerican.com/guest-blog/2011/03/14/japan-earthquake-the-explainer/

Safecast. (n.d.). *Homepage.* Retrieved from http://blog.safecast.org/

Sakaki, T., Okazaki, M., & Matsuo, Y. (2010). Earthquake shakes Twitter users: Real-time event detection by social sensors. *Proceedings of the International World Wide Web Conference,* pp. 851–860. Raleigh, NC: ACM.

Scientific American. (2011, March 14). *Japan's nuclear crisis and tsunami recovery via Twitter and other Web resources* [Blog]. Retrieved from http://blogs.scientificamerican.com/observations/2011/03/14/japans-nuclear-crisis-and-tsunami-recovery-via-twitter-and-other/

Smith, A., & Brenner, J. (2012). Twitter use 2012. *Pew Research.* Retrieved from http://www.pewInternet.org/Reports/2012/Twitter-Use-2012.aspx

Stocking, S. H., & Holstein, L. W. (2009). Manufacturing doubt: Journalists' roles and the construction of ignorance in a scientific controversy. *Public Understanding of Science, 18*(1), 23–42.

Swales, J. M. (1990). *Genre analysis: English in academic and research settings.* Cambridge, UK: Cambridge University Press.

Taylor, C. A. (1991). Defining the scientific community: A rhetorical perspective on demarcation. *Communication Monographs, 58,* 402–420.

Toulmin, S. (1958). *The uses of argument.* Cambridge, UK: Cambridge University Press.

Thomson, R., Ito, N., Suda, H., Lin, F., Liu, Y., Hayasaka, R., et al. (2012). Trusting tweets: The Fukushima disaster and information source credibility on Twitter. *Proceedings of the 9th International ISCRAM Conference,* pp. 1–10.

Trench, B. (2008). Internet: Turning science communication inside-out. In M. Bucchi & B. Trench (Eds.), *Handbook of public communication of science and technology* (pp. 185–198). New York, NY: Routledge.

U.S. Geological Survey. (2011, March 11). *Magnitude 9.0 - Near the east coast of Honshu, Japan.* Retrieved from http://earthquake.usgs.gov/earthquakes/eqinthenews/2011/usc0001xgp/

Wikipedia. (2007, April 26). *FACR.* Retrieved from http://en.wikipedia.org/w/index.php?title=Wikipedia:FACR&oldid=126251043

Wikipedia. (2011a, May 22). *Talk: Fukushima Daiichi nuclear disaster/Archive 1.* Retrieved from https://en.wikipedia.org/wiki/Talk:Fukushima_Daiichi_nuclear_disaster/Archive_1

Wikipedia. (2011b, October 26). *Scientific peer review.* Retrieved from http://en.wikipedia.org/w/index.php?title=Wikipedia:Scientific_peer_review&oldid=457477974

Wikipedia. (2012a, March 29). *Fukushima I Nuclear Power Plant.* Retrieved from http://en.wikipedia.org/w/index.php?title=Fukushima_I_Nuclear_Power_Plant&oldid=484538029

Wikipedia. (2012b, October 3). *About.* Retrieved from https://en.wikipedia.org/wiki/Wikipedia:About#Strengths.2C_weaknesses.2C_and_article_quality_in_Wikipedia

Wikipedia. (2012c, December 20). *What Wikipedia is not.* Retrieved from http://en.wikipedia.org/w/index.php?title=Wikipedia:What_Wikipedia_is_not&oldid=529003301

Wikipedia. (2012d, December 22). *Verifiability.* Retrieved from http://en.wikipedia.org/w/index.php?title=Wikipedia:Verifiability&oldid=529228726

Zickuhr, K., & Rainie, L. (2011). Wikipedia, past and present. *Pew Internet: Internet & American Life Project.* Retrieved from http://www.pewinternet.org/2011/01/13/wikipedia-past-and-present/

Ziman, J. (1968). *Public knowledge: The social dimension of science.* Cambridge, UK: Cambridge University Press.

Zivkovic, B. (2011, March 14). Nature: Earthquake dispatches from the correspondent in Japan [Blog]. *Scientific American.* Retrieved from http://blogs.scientificamerican.com/guest-blog/2011/03/11/nature-earthquake-dispatches-from-the-correspondent-in-japan-upd/

Zivkovic, B. (2012, May 15). The SA incubator, or, why promote young science writers? [Blog] *Scientific American.* Retrieved from http://blogs.scientificamerican.com/a-blog-around-the-clock/2012/05/15/the-sa-incubator-or-why-promote-young-science-writers/

http://dx.doi.org/10.2190/SCIC12

CHAPTER 12

Why People Care About Chickens and Other Lessons About Rhetoric, Public Science, and Informal Learning Environments

Stacey Pigg, William Hart-Davidson,
Jeff Grabill, and Kirsten Ellenbogen

ABSTRACT

This chapter is drawn from a larger discourse analysis project analyzing interaction in *Science Buzz*, a community blog facilitated by the Science Museum of Minnesota. After describing how our findings intersect with recent scholarly conversations about everyday science learning and participation, we focus on one *Science Buzz* blog posting entitled "The Chicken and the Egg" and its comment stream in order to discuss which discursive moves are common in an online science conversation that has continually garnered high participation over several years. Drawing on a close analysis of this case example, we argue that constructing *useful* science learning environments where participants ask and answer practical questions about matters of concern can create high levels of public science engagement. When facilitated with care, online social media spaces can act as forums that encourage links between scientific knowledge and local concerns, including the ethical, political, emotional, and experiential issues that arise with a question such as "How should one best care for chickens?"

When, where, and how do people learn science? In response to this question, the National Academy of Sciences report, "Learning Science in Informal Environments" (Bell, Lewenstein, Shouse, & Feder, 2009) stressed the importance of

247

everyday experiences, designed spaces like museums and science centers, non-school science education programs, and science media. The report built on an array of scholarship attuned to science learning as a lifelong, often self-motivated endeavor. The findings are not surprising. In all cases, we spend more of our lives learning outside of classrooms and other formal learning institutions than we do inside them (Gerber, Cavallo, & Marek, 2001). The situation is analogous when we think about when, where, and why people engage public science. Often the scholarly literature focuses on deliberation in related normative forums, yet most of us engage science issues in ways (and in places) less structured and more connected to circumstances of daily life (Barron, 2006; Falk, Storksdieck, & Dierking, 2007). Indeed, in these less structured forums, what we do would not often be considered "deliberation" at all by scholars. This is particularly true for learning and engagement online, which can be easily understood as too messy to be useful (Grabill & Pigg, 2012).

We made a number of claims in that first paragraph, and in what follows, we intend to be more precise in developing our thinking. Our chapter dwells in the informal and the digital and focuses as well on learning as important to science communication. Specifically, we argue that scientific communication in an age of social media might benefit from focusing more on creating engaging and *useful* learning environments than on transmitting scientific information. Online learning environments can tap into interests of public participants and facilitate engagement with both scientific concepts and scientific ways of thinking and making knowledge. With their ability to act as both collective memory and epistemic medium, online writing environments can involve participants in ongoing inquiry-based learning. This is a fundamentally different way of thinking about the role writing can play in mediating public encounters with science—as a tool for knowledge creation, rather than reception.

In this chapter, we provide a descriptive example of this approach to science communication through findings from a recent study of the Science Museum of Minnesota's *Science Buzz*, a popular blog that uses writing to create space for conversation about current science. Our larger study provides us with a way to characterize the nature of the discourse on *Science Buzz* and to discuss indicators of learning in this forum. However, we spend much of our chapter discussing one key blog entry entitled "The Chicken and the Egg," which has generated hundreds of public comments over several years. This thread, known as the "Chicken Thread," demonstrates a model of knowledge building driven by the interest and identities of participants who leverage experiences caring for chickens to engage science. To be more precise, the participants are most often discussing chicken *eggs* and exploring the conditions of incubation. A text analysis of this thread to isolate important terms reveals that two words in particular stand out as used far, far more often than others (by an exponent of nearly 3, in fact): "egg" and "if." When we read the threads in both systematic ways as researchers and as interested observers following the conversation, we are reminded that science is driven by quite practical questions like "If the eggs get too cold, will they still hatch?"

But is this how we think of science in policy discussions about enhancing STEM learning? Do we understand the forms of reasoning central to "doing science" to be grounded in deeply practical questions and answers? The answer, we suggest, is not nearly often enough. With science itself driven by questions of application and practical import and embedded in complex political, ethical, and linguistic webs, it is only natural that online learning and engagement environments should open conversation to practical scientific questions that matter deeply to citizens. In response, we forward this conversational dynamic of shared concern, multiple stakeholder engagement through practical questioning and answering, and persistence through writing as a model for 21st-century online science learning.

COMPLEXITIES OF PUBLIC SCIENCE CONVERSATION, ENGAGEMENT, AND LEARNING

Public understanding of science scholarship has long called for engagement efforts that place scientists and nonscientists in conversation about matters of concern (see Irwin & Michael, 2003). How these dialogues are to be structured, however, and to what ends remains a matter of debate. For example, Bickerstaff, Lorenzoni, Jones, and Pidgeon (2010) identified tensions in Royal Society National Forum dialogues facilitating public discussions between scientists and nonscientists. They argued that within the National Forum project, "choices about problem framing and purpose, roles and identities, as well as the detail of the day's structure, were predefined by the Society" (pp. 482–483). With responsibility for framing solely in the institution's hands, members of the public were given "very little capacity to either shape the trajectory of debate or, subsequently, the ways in which the outputs were (institutionally) interpreted and deployed" (p. 489).

Bickerstaff et al. (2010) suggested that argument framing, or shaping the parameters of discussion, often becomes a latent influence controlled by *someone* or *something* in public engagement discourse. When tightly controlled framing undercuts the public's capacity to participate, it recalls the perceived hierarchies between scientists and members of the public that have been the focus of public understanding of science scholarship for 20 years now. Wynne (1992), for example, argued that the social gulf between stakeholder groups led to the difficulty for scientists and nonscientists to learn from one another's expertise. As Wynne pointed out, with different "social identities" come different understandings of argument and how it functions. Discussing post-Chernobyl interactions between scientific authorities and Cumbrian sheep farmers, Wynne showed how "each side only recognized even as possible evidence, claims expressed within its cultural style" (p. 296). Thus, Wynne concluded that significant differences between scientists and nonscientists are generally "social conventions" that distribute "relative authority in ways which may be inappropriate" (p. 297). Renegotiating these hierarchies is key to productive conversations between scientists and nonscientists. Gross (1994) connected this conversation to rhetoric studies through his focus on the contextual model's "interaction between science and its publics," whereby public understanding becomes "the joint creation of scientific and local knowledge" (p. 6).

In spite of this work, assumptions like those foundational to a "deficit model" of public science knowledge have not disappeared. As Bauer, Allum, and Miller (2007) have described, survey-based measures of scientific literacy in the 1980s measured public knowledge by "quiz-like textbook items," and low scores on individual items in these inventories were often reported as "indicators of public ignorance and reasons for moral panic" (p. 81). Indeed, with the current similarly perceived crises related to high-stakes standardized test performance across educational sites and levels, science learning contends not only with scientific institutional hierarchies and tensions but also educational ones. The problem with this scenario is not only its negative positioning of publics, but also its narrow view of science, which becomes reduced to a mass collection of facts divorced from contexts of production and use.

Against this backdrop, however, recent approaches to science learning emphasize the need for developing habits of mind that lead to inquiry and ongoing interaction with science over time. These approaches reframe science learning not as passive reception of established facts but rather an active process of interacting with—not merely aligning with—scientific ways of knowing. Recognizing that science language use in general (Lemke, 1990) and scientific argumentation in particular (Bricker & Bell, 2008; Duschl & Osborne, 2002) are central to science learning, Goldman, Duschl, Ellenbogen, Williams, and Tzou (2003) focused on the role online discourse can play in creating "thinking spaces" that support peer argumentation and scaffold dialogues in which learners reason through science thinking together. According to Goldman et al., online systems for science dialogue mediate thinking space differently for at least two reasons: they restructure spatial/temporal expectations of participation, and they make insights concrete and visualized: part of a collective memory as a "written record of the dialogue" that is "available for inspection and reflection at any time" (p. 3).

We build on this scholarship as we call for increased attention to the possibilities new web-based social writing platforms offer for facilitating science learning and engagement through interactive communication. Outside of classrooms, it is hard to imagine individuals encountering the scaffolded systems Goldman and her colleagues (2003) describe. However, less structured networked writing systems like blogs and social networking sites are already an active part of many individuals' social lives (see Lenhart, Purcell, Smith, & Zickuhr, 2010). These online writing environments support characteristics of exchange that have proven successful in classroom implementations. For example, social software generally create collective memory through written archives that can be revisited and extend participation possibilities by making conversations available to individuals who would not be able to attend formal dialogues due to space/time constraints. In addition, with their logic built on a flattened participatory rather than top-down transmission model, online networked writing systems hold promise for building new forms of social community (Wellman & Guilia, 1999; Zappen, 2005). Although power dynamics clearly do not disappear online (Nakamura, 2011), social writing spaces can potentially support written interaction among individuals with different forms of expertise, an important component of both science engagement and learning.

SCIENCE BUZZ:
PUBLIC SCIENCE MEETS ONLINE PARTICIPATION

Before moving to our extended example of online science learning and engagement, we should first provide context about the particular online science forum we are discussing, as well as the methods used to systematically analyze it. *Science Buzz* is a nationally recognized blog maintained by the Science Museum of Minnesota (SMM). *Science Buzz* engages a broad audience about relevant science topics ranging from health to earth science to the latest findings from chemistry and physics. The blog postings on *Buzz* are written by a group of moderators who compose short writings intended to garner interest, promote feedback, and sustain ongoing argumentation. Broader conversations develop within the comments attached to these initial postings, and we focus primarily within these conversational comments to discuss public learning and engagement.

We take our analysis in this chapter from "Take Two: A Study of the Co-Creation of Knowledge on Museum Web 2.0 Sites," a multiyear study of the impact of Web technologies on museum learning and practice. "Take Two" explored whether and how blogs and other web-based technologies support outcomes that are important to museums and other institutions of informal learning. Supported by the Institute of Museum and Library Services (IMLS), "Take Two" brought together a multi-institutional team of investigators focused on the following questions:

- What is the nature of the community that interacts through *Science Buzz*?
- What is the nature of the online interaction?
- Do these online interactions support knowledge building for this user community?
- Do online interactions support inquiry, learning, and change within the museum; i.e., what is the impact on museum practice?

This chapter reports on the results of the discourse analysis, which focused on participant interaction on *Science Buzz* and enabled us to identify indicators of learning.

Because many Internet-based interactions are written, discourse analysis provides a systematic method for describing, characterizing, and understanding what is happening in online interactions. One of the initial tasks of the study was to build an analytical tool that could accurately describe the discourse on *Science Buzz*. Taking an approach that emphasizes rhetoric in detail (Johnstone & Eisenhart, 2008), our analytical tool focused on how participants build argument, identity, and community, as well as how they explore new ideas. Our data analysis was structured in two phases. In the first phase, we coded the *Science Buzz* sample at the T-unit level, focusing on indicators of argument, identity, community building, and the invention of new ideas.[1] In the second phase, we used a more interpretive analytic that built on the coding results of the first phase but was explicitly structured by the National Academies report "Learning Science in Informal Environments: People, Places, and Pursuits" (Bell et al., 2009).

Our results suggest that the activity and community that form *Science Buzz* are highly complex and variable. Some topics and threads attract a large number of participants with diverse levels of knowledge and perspective and who participate from locations both inside and outside the physical museum. Furthermore, argumentative strategies such as making claims are the most common discursive moves on the *Buzz* blog. These reasoning strategies are the focus of many prior discourse-based studies of concepts like "learning" in group environments. Yet our analysis of the *Buzz* blog also shows a range of strategies that we associate with constructing individual identities (more common) and group identities (less common). These discourse strategies are often ignored in studies of learning or knowledge construction, but they are clearly integral to any understanding of online spaces made available by museums to the public.

Our analysis also shows *Science Buzz* to be a learning environment. When we offer the claim that *Buzz* is an informal learning environment, we are doing so in a precise fashion: we are not claiming that there is learning per se, which is extremely difficult to measure and impossible given the context and methods of this study. Rather, we are claiming that there are *indicators* of learning in evidence in meaningful representations, patterns, and densities. In particular, our discourse analysis identified practices that are aligned with categories of informal learning identified by the National Academies as important, such as developing interest in science, engaging in scientific reasoning, and identifying with the scientific enterprise.

For example, as we look across our sample, we see considerable evidence that participants are interested in science and that they are compelled to participate in conversations about science for a number of reasons, ranging from

---

[1] We computed simple agreement for each code combination for a subsample of threads. By code combination, we mean that we expected agreement not at the level of the category "building an argument," for instance, but rather at the level of the discourse move within the category ("building an argument, claim"). Agreement was well above 90% on most codes.

entertainment to intellectual engagement to fear and anxiety. We also see indicators of scientific reasoning in each thread, including a number of argument
moves (e.g., use of evidence). In addition, there is evidence of inquiry (asking
questions and engaging in a process of answering them). We see numerous
examples of participants applying ideas, concluding with and from evidence and
thinking with others in conversation. In some threads, we also see sophisticated reasoning practices and people thinking together to work through ideas.
Finally, identity work is persistent and complex. In some threads, participants are
authorizing "expert" and/or "expert-like" identities. Sometimes these dynamics
lead those who identify most strongly with the scientific enterprise to dominate
threads and ignore questions from those less knowledgeable or comfortable
expressing expertise. However, this is not always the case. Performing identities
also allows people to draw from experience in productive ways and call for
answers to questions of concern. This is particularly important in threads where
people are motivated to discuss scientific issues because of their relationship
to problems that directly affect them.

Science Buzz is thus substantial in terms of both the amount of science
discourse it has generated and the extent to which it aligns with what we
know about how people learn about science in informal environments. As we
have suggested, the various threads on the site differ considerably in how these
key dynamics of interest, reasoning, and identification develop through
conversation. The remainder of this chapter explores the intersections of informal
learning, science communication, and web technologies in detail by paying close
attention to one exceptional blog conversation (in terms of participation) that has
been a part of *Science Buzz* for over 5 years. Within this exchange, we see high
levels of interest and argument—participants thinking together in writing—and
through discourse moves such as these, they construct an engaging learning
environment.

CARING ABOUT AND FOR CHICKENS:
THE CHICKEN AND THE EGG

Begun in the autumn of 2006, "The Chicken and the Egg" (see
http://www.sciencebuzz.org/blog/chicken-and-egg) has received 850 public
comments at the date of this draft (with more added every day). Key contributors
to the thread include a museum blogger and staff facilitator, a poultry scientist
from the University of Minnesota, and a number of public posters (some
self-identified and others remaining anonymous). Our analysis revealed that "The
Chicken and the Egg" contained high amounts of argument. Nearly half of the
T-units in the Chicken Thread (48%) were assigned to our code, "Building an
Argument." This is not surprising compared to our larger sample. Where the
Chicken Thread most stands out compared to other *Science Buzz* conversations
is in the intersection of this argumentation with discursive moves that build

community connectedness. Around 18% of T-units (17.71%) in the Chicken Thread were assigned the code, "Building Community Identity," compared to an average of 11.5% across our total sample. According to our analytical scheme, this meant that the Chicken Thread contained many discursive acts in which participants explicitly requested that others explain or respond, articulated shared experiences or roles, or connected their contributions concretely to ideas or people mentioned previously in the thread. This initial analysis helped us understand that the reasoning patterns of the Chicken Thread extended beyond a collection of disconnected claims. Participants were (and are) talking to and thinking with one another.

The co-presence of engagement and argumentation moves is a substantial finding in the context of our larger study, which did not always show evidence of blog commenters creating community or engaging one another. Our closer narrative analysis of the Chicken Thread helped us to understand how these moves functioned in this particular case (and perhaps gives clues to why these particular moves were not present in others). To draw on the language of the "Learning Science in Informal Environments" report (Bell et al., 2009), a key to the discursive patterns of the thread is high individual interest. Participants care about chickens. Perhaps even more importantly, they care *about* chickens because they care *for* chickens. As stewards, their public interest in conversing and learning more about poultry and poultry science is less driven by a sense of "wonder" than of "application" (Fahnestock, 1986, p. 279). When individuals are this deeply invested in a topic or problem, an online writing environment like *Science Buzz* has the potential to become an online learning environment, sustaining engagements that facilitate learning and communication. Within the Chicken Thread, we see this play out as forms of reasoning connected to application and action that prompt continually more nuanced accounts about science. This inquiry model is similar to the dynamics of scientific rhetoric in more official genres and discourse communities. Our stance here further supports the substantive role for rhetoric outlined by Gross (1994) as a means to reconstruct both the facts and the methods of science in ways that mesh with matters of importance to the general public. In order to further describe this dynamic, we first characterize the Chicken Thread's discourse in more detail before focusing on two short samples from the conversation that illustrate themes we have introduced.

"The Chicken and the Egg" and the Discourse of Engagement and Learning

Like all "threads" on *Science Buzz*, "The Chicken and the Egg"begins with a short blog post created by museum staff to facilitate a conversation. In this case, the initial post positions the museum staff as an interested, inquisitive member of the public who has a question relevant to science issues (lines 1–27).[2] She opens simply by describing how she has "noticed a lot of dead fledglings and raided nests lately" and along with one of them "an unhatched baby bird." This act of noticing, the writer says, led her to a question about everyday experience: "Are grocery store eggs fertilized?" (line 3) and to a set of follow-up questions: "Why do you never seem to see a grocery store egg with a baby chicken in it? And, if fertilized eggs are the norm, why would the chicken "spend the energy required to produce unfertilized eggs?" (line 5).

Her initial post proceeds to describe her next steps: after conducting an informal Web search, the staff member found relevant evidence from scientists to answer her questions. She cites the Howard Hughes Medical Institute to describe how chicken eggs form and develop and provides a simple discussion of the major differences between fertilized and nonfertilized chicken eggs (e.g., if kept at the right temperature, a fertilized egg will "differentiate to form a chick, which will hatch after 21 days," whereas a unfertilized egg will never differentiate, and thus yolk material remains). We don't see baby chickens in grocery store eggs, she continues, because eggs to be sold in large commercial operations generally come from chickens that never had contact with a rooster. Importantly, the poster claims that she not only found reputable sources to help her answer her question, but she also learned that "lots of other people had the same question" (line 8). She furthermore applies what she has learned to revise prior thinking. For example, she mentions how her reading helped her rethink an idea she had been taught as a child: that a "blood spot" means an egg is fertilized. Now she knows that blood spots are just broken blood vessels.

On the *Science Buzz* blog, the initial post is important. It serves a facilitative role that the museum staffer continues in subsequent engagement with thread participants. In this case, however, the initial post also models a process of learning science:

1. The post foregrounds the interest of the writer and her identification with science.
2. The post initiates an inquiry (if not scientific) by asking questions.
3. The post engages—it facilitates—by opening up the learning process to others rather than providing the answer to the original question.

Rather than simply reporting science facts, the poster models an inquiry process and way of thinking and wondering that is central to active learning (and by

[2] We include transcript line numbers in our detailed analysis of the blog comments in order to help readers orient to how the conversation is unfolding. these line numbers are not available on the *Buzz* blog. However, we have posted a segmented version of the thread in an online appendix as a reference for readers. At this time, that version of the thread is available at the following online location: http://tinyurl.com/cjnca49

extension, we suggest, to doing science as well). What makes the Chicken Thread remarkable is that the comments that follow enact a similar process of learning through inquiry but do so through argumentation that involves multiple participants. The blog comments are largely driven by what appear to be genuine questions from participants (mostly nonscientists) who are interested and/or invested in caring for chickens. Commenters in the Chicken Thread often direct questions to the facilitator, the scientific expert, or to a "you" with an unclear referent; however, people with a range of social positions offer answers based on different forms of reasoning and evidence. Active questioning and responding in the Chicken Thread connect individuals' interests to broader scientific conversations and create shared objects of concern that can be addressed from different points of view.

The following example represents one early question and several of the nested responses to it. In this case, a public participant writes for information about why her chicken has stopped laying eggs:

Why did my chicken stop laying eggs? (lines 35–37)

Staff answer: Hen may be resting (cites scientists online) or not receiving enough sunlight. Provides links to Virginia Cooperative Extension and www.poultryhelp.com. (lines 40–49)

Public answer: Alexis says hen might be 'clucky.' Cites methods for getting rid of cluckiness. (lines 51–64)

Public answer: Anonymous says hen might be moulting. Cites the look of chicken feathers during moult. References first answer. (lines 74–81)

Public answer: Eser says hens may be sick. No evidence. (line 84)

As these responses illustrate, both institutional representatives (museum staff) and other members of the public address the problem of chicken fertility raised by this poster. Notably, however, none of their answers simply settles the issue but rather brings new evidence and possibilities to bear on the question of concern by speaking of the general issue in a newly situated way.

Questions like this one about chicken fertility persist temporally within the thread discourse, as both staff and public posters add to the building collection of responses and information. They also recur and are revisited when new posters enter the conversation. In repeatedly addressing these questions, citations of online authorities become layered with descriptions of concrete experience. At times, a particular kind of evidence might more or less useful to answer a question. For example, as we describe later, there are moments in which the hypothetical response of a scientist is of little use in helping an interested citizen make a contextualized decision about future action. In the same way, a public poster's description of caring for chickens might be irrelevant or mismatched to a more theoretical question. What is consistent, however, is that multiple forms of response and evidence can be sustained through written engagement. Much like in the initial posting, the point of this exchange is not merely to transmit scientific concepts but to enact an inquiry cycle that does not end with one answer to one question. Science learning, instead, emerges as a sustained process of engagement by asking, answering, and then asking again. This process continually tests the limits of shared understanding by considering related cases of a similar phenomenon. Technologies matter here as well, of course, as a blogging platform (in this case) is also a participant in creating a thinking space in which ideas persist in spite of distances of time and space, dialoguing individuals who might not otherwise have access to one another.

Our description to this point has been concerned with making a narrow but hopefully meaningful argument, and so we have left out other issues of importance. For instance, the dynamic we have described is not flat. That is, hierarchies between experts and nonexperts exist. Indeed, it is notable that much of the thread follows an "ask the expert" logic wherein one member of the public poses a question and an expert in the thread answers that question, often by linking to relevant content on the Web. From the poster who asks the scientist whether it is possible to find yolk material on commercial chicken meat (line 1053) to the poster who asks for advice about whether it is possible to keep chickens in her neighborhood (line 1069), some questions do not launch broader inquiry. In other moments of the thread, scientific experts draw on markers of status in order to defend knowledge during moments of community negotiation, citing authority as a way to add weight to evidence built from formal scientific procedures. Clearly, power dynamics from outside *Science Buzz* influence production and interpretation of discourse and are part of how the blog functions as an environment. Dynamics that we associate with power/knowledge relationships are operational in *Buzz*, just as they are meaningful in any scientific communication process. However, it is not always the case that power/knowledge asymmetries lead to shutting down conversation and learning. Based on our work with *Science Buzz*, we suggest that such dynamics can also enable public learning. Discursive markers of authority, for instance, are used to model inquiry processes and ways of arguing, add nuance to conversations, or refine ways of asking or answering questions.

Importantly, in the Chicken Thread, science facilitators have the opportunity to model practices important to scientific thinking because public participants inquire in ways that are both useful and personally applicable. Having said this, we want to close with two examples that move beyond the basic inquiry dynamic that we have described so far and toward more subtle engagement practices characterized by participants testing the applicability of scientific knowledge and norms. We trace, first, how scientists and nonscientists differently support the persistent discussion of a question raised by a public poster, adding nuances and applications as commenters situate the question within varied experiences and knowledge bases. We follow this by focusing on a moment of community negotiation in which public posters engage science by questioning the "truth" of a forum facilitator's claim.

Asking Toward Action: Why Public Posters Reason About the Difference Between Fertilized and Nonfertilized Eggs

Within the Chicken Thread, one recurring question—how to tell whether an egg is fertilized—becomes a site from which to observe that public engagement in scientific reasoning (an important indicator of learning) is often driven by questions of future action,[3] even when that action is unarticulated. In the post that launches this conversation, a commenter named Tom asks, "Can you clarify the fertilized egg issue . . . if you have a rooster in the hen house, how can you tell which eggs are fertilized and which are not?" (line 197). Addressing an unclear "you" here, he follows his question by discussing why candling—a common method for looking through the shell of an egg to see its contents—would not be an appropriate method to answer his question. Candling is only useful after an egg has been kept at a proper incubation temperature for around 10 days. For Tom, who thinks it would be most economical to eat unfertilized eggs and hatch chickens from fertilized ones, incubating an unfertilized egg would render it inedible because of high incubator temperatures.

The museum staff member who wrote the blog's initial post is the first to take up Tom's question, claiming there is every reason to believe all eggs laid by a hen that has had previous contact with a rooster are fertilized. Elaborating this claim, the staff member assumes that a moral/value imperative had motivated Tom's question, which she addresses in her closing thoughts: "I don't think there's any reason you shouldn't eat a freshly-laid, fertile egg if that's why you're keeping the chickens. After all, if you eat the adults . . ." (line 208). Tom responds to this assumption by pointing out that, in fact, a different imperative had prompted his thinking: "My question is, how do you avoid the waste. I'm not worried about eating fertilized eggs" (line 217).

---

[3] Fahnestock's (1986) application of rhetorical stasis theory to public science provides useful vocabulary for accounting for misunderstandings thata can arise between public posters and science facilitators during interactive conversations. Drawing on a classical rhetorical invention method. Fahnestock describes how stasis "defines and orders the kinds of questions that can be at isssue," including questions of conjecture, definition, quality and finally of action (p. 290).

We understand this as an important moment in the Chicken Thread for illustrating how the public interest that motivates engagement in scientific reasoning often emerges from practical, contextualized problems that require action. While the National Academies report (Bell et al., 2009) lists participation in scientific reasoning and developing an interest in science as two separate strands of learning, it is clear that the two are closely connected in this case. The science facilitator misreads the particular motive for Tom's question but intuitively realizes that his form of interest and form of reasoning are linked. Tom's response to the staff member is further notable because he does not simply accept the general answer the facilitator provides; he persists by refining his question, building on the context that she helps to draw out. Following up, then, Tom continues by practicing a key discursive move of this conversation: he restates his original question, now situating it more clearly within the ethic of care for chickens that motivated it. He suggests that there "must be a more accurate way" of telling the difference between a fertilized and nonfertilized egg to avoid "destroy[ing] a potential chick that could have strengthened your chicken supply" while avoiding the waste of incubating eggs that are not fertilized.

Tom's refined question now invites a new kind of response. At this point, two anonymous posters suggest (again) that Tom candle the eggs to tell whether they are fertilized or not. These answers to the question miss the context Tom built earlier for why candling would not be an effective method for determining fertilization in his particular case. However, while their answers do not help Tom very much, they do prompt additional participation that adds to the ongoing knowledge building within the thread (in this instance, on the problem of fertilization identification). Specifically, their responses prompt a poultry scientist to enter the conversation. The scientist echoes Tom's sentiment that candling will not reveal whether an egg is fertilized until an egg has been incubated (something that wouldn't happen with an egg to be eaten). The role that the scientist plays at this particular point is to continue the conversation. She does not put the issue to rest by offering a definitive answer (something that does happen by those playing the role of "poultry scientist" at other moments in the discourse). Instead, she continues the process of knowledge accumulation that had begun through Tom's question, the museum blogger's response, and the ongoing refining and reiteration.

This practice of knowledge-building continues when a public poster who calls herself "a nonny mouse" echoes the museum staff member's original claim but adds new information, including suggestions on how to hatch chickens and when candling *would* be an appropriate method to determine whether an egg is fertilized. The echoing of this point by another poster who calls herself "I have chickens 2" still does not sufficiently answer the question for purposes of the thread. Almost immediately, a poster named Mel asks a question strikingly similar to Tom's but differently contextualized: "ok so my neighbor gave me and my friends these three eggs" but "i really want to know if the egg's he gave us are fertilized." Here again, the scientist responds by pointing out that candling will not reveal whether an egg is fertilized under all or even most conditions. The scientist doesn't stop here, though. She uses the opportunity of the open question to build additional knowledge into the conversation. Specifically, she shares a common method for candling, describing the process and linking to descriptions online. The scientist further uses this point to add nuance (via her insertion of hypotheticals) that continue to have resonance both for Tom's original question and for the much earlier question about chicken infertility: "If there are too many roosters for the number of hens, however, you can get a case where the roosters spend more time fighting with each other instead of mating with the hens." Following the scientist, another public poster inserts himself to address the museum staff member's focus on the moral discussion about eating fertilized and nonfertilized eggs. Here, this poster, who calls himself "Tim the Enchanter" says, "It's actually a vegetarian issue. Some vegetarians will eat non-fertilized eggs, but fertile eggs are off-limits. And of course, in that case, you wouldn't eat the adults either" (line 341).

We could continue tracing the intricacies of this fertilization conversation for many more pages. The conversation never exactly comes to a halt. For the sake of space, however, we will simply share a few more places in which the question recurs:

- line 707: "Is there any other way to tell if the egg has been fertilized, other than candling?";
- lines 724–725: "I do not know if the eggs are fertile. Will she continue to lay on the eggs for many weeks if they do not hatch and if so how long should I leave it before removing the eggs?";
- line 812: "we separated the hens and roosters for a brief time due to a large amount of feathers missing from hens back. Probably a week has gone by and one of the hens is sitting on her eggs, are these eggs fertile?";
- line 975: "how can you tell if a egg is fertile?"; and
- lines 1156–1157: "I have 10 bantam chicken eggs taken from the farm where I work. They are all in an incubator but how do I know if they are fertilized?"

Seeing this recurring question, we might easily ask, Why can't they settle on an answer? Why must the question be repeated? Is nobody listening or learning? What we hope our reading shows is that this iterative questioning process is a means of engagement that demonstrates participant interest, facilitates argument, and therefore helps to construct precisely the sort of environment in which learning is possible. What is notable about the recurring questions around incubation is not only the way rhetoric is used to bring evidence to claims, but also the way rhetoric becomes a medium for a broader construction of understanding. Gross (1994) gives this phenomenon a name: a forum of reconstruction. The "re" in "reconstruction" is especially important for Gross, as the forum functions to forge linkages between scientific knowledge and local knowledge, something that must be done over and over again to establish the truth value of scientific facts relative to what members of the lay public know from experience. We see this played out quite vividly in the Chicken Thread in a number of ways, as those who keep chickens raise questions and relate anecdotes about specific conditions and circumstances pertaining to fertilization.

The dynamics of the forum of reconstruction also reveal an important role for the Scientist vis-à-vis the public: that of the facilitator. This role is predicted by Gross' (1994) discussion of the way scientific truths in public forums are mediated by the identity of experts, rising and falling in credibility in proportion to the trust accorded to the expert. We would expect to see our poultry expert reiterating scientific facts, but doing so in relation to the subtleties of each new formulation of public understanding of the phenomenon in question. And that is precisely what we see. Yet the discourse practices of public posters are equally important. Tom's initial question initiates multiple points of connection from which others build, and his move to reiterate a question based on a clearer sense of this particular case or context draws new detail into the conversation. Motivated by the issue of how best to care for chickens, Tom's questions also test the boundaries of the applicability of scientific knowledge in everyday life. Questions of chicken stewardship are not strictly scientific. They are practical. They are rich with ethical, economic, and even emotional issues. As the conversation demonstrates, science tells us some things that can inform the conversation. But it will never give a single, definitive answer to such a probabilistic question as "How should I best care for chickens?" Thus, public science learning requires a complex synthesis of multiple forms of evidence and knowledge.

This communicative complexity, we suggest, would not be reached through a public engagement model that seeks simply to inform members of the public about science concepts. Nor would it likely emerge as part of dialogues in which scientists overdetermine argumentative frameworks, including questions or topics of concern. Acts of questioning launch an exchange of different forms of expertise from descriptions of how one should care for chickens, to lay knowledge about how many roosters are too many roosters, to scientists' takes on the best methods for candling. Posters revisit topics of previous interest that were raised in responses to questions (like when Tom picks back up the moral implications of eating fertilized eggs) and layers of new commentary emerge, even when thread participants ask questions that have already presumably been answered.

When Reasoning Styles Conflict: Why Public Posters Care if Refrigerated Eggs Will Hatch

Our analysis further suggests that conflicts may occur when learning facilitators assume a reasoning process aligned with "wondering" about a topic when public interlocutors are actually reasoning toward decisions or action

(Fahnestock, 1986, p. 334). This tension arises during a conversation between several thread participants in response to one poster's plea for advice after her child's beloved pet chicken, Sally, disappeared: "Tonight, I went to put the chickens in for the night and Sally was not around. We have three eggs from the last three days (they are in the ref.) and I was wondering if they would hatch? Please let me know" (line 87). This question was meaningful not only because it involved kids and pets—touchy subjects—but also because it was a recurring question: one that had been raised and addressed previously in the conversation. Just previously, a poster had asked, "Are unfertilized eggs that have been stored in a refrigerator considered dead or alive?" (line 87). The museum blogger at that time responded, first, by suggesting that unfertilized eggs are not living (line 92) and then by citing an expert website that says it is possible to hatch a chicken from a fertilized egg that has been in the refrigerator (under specific circumstances—when the refrigeration happens before incubation and not after).

While this answer is technically correct, the new way of posing the question involving Sally the pet chicken leads several public posters to express dissatisfaction with the staff member's original response. One writes, "If ref. is short for refrigerator and they've been in there for three days the chances of them hatching is 1 to 1,000 so don't even try to do anything about it" (line 114), and another takes issue with the initial poster's claim that an egg in a refrigerator could hatch. He writes,

> An egg cannot get below 40 degrees or it is no longer viable. You cannot put a fertilized egg in the refrigerator and expect it to hatch when you put it in the incubator. People need to do research before answering somebodies question. (line 119)

The conflict that arises in this short exchange recalls the dissonance between different stakeholders' forms of reasoning and interest illustrated in early studies like Wynne's (1992). The staff member is attempting to model a process of scientific practice by emphasizing the importance of supporting claims through the evidence of citation and peer review that comes from a record of previous research. However, public posters' reasoning toward action leads them to either misunderstand the facilitator's thinking process or to reject it as inappropriate to address the kinds of interests they have in science.

Naturally, the staff member defends her answer to the question by referencing her citation of evidence: "I cited my source—a reputable expert. And my answer was reviewed, after posting, by local poultry expert [name removed]. So I stand by it" (line 125). However, two public posters next jump in to continue questioning what constitutes an appropriate response in this case. "I have chickens 2" (also an active participant in the first thread sample we discussed) further supports the anonymous posters, claiming, "You really need to do some research before answering anyone's questions, they really want the truth and really want to know what to do, how to do it and all the how to's" (line 132). Following up, "I have chickens 2" elaborates this claim, notably drawing on the idea that it is "really like common sense" that eggs from the refrigerator would become too cold to hatch, strengthening his/her claim through his/her authority as someone with much experience caring for chickens (line 133). Important in both these responses are appeals to practical knowledge of common sense and the need for reflective action when caring for chickens.

The museum staff member, confronted by this continual questioning, suggests a return to analyze the context of the original question. She thus reiterates the initial context for inquiry: "The poster wanted to know if it was possible that eggs kept in the refrigerator for three days, that had never been incubated, could still hatch. And my answer was, it's possible" (line 143). In this discussion, the staff member reveals that her reasoning process was suited to the original question about what was possible, as opposed to the following question about practical action. She follows up by explaining that she never suggested that hatching eggs from a refrigerator was a "recommended practice," but instead just a possibility. Interestingly, a member of the public then steps in to defend the museum blogger's claim, providing evidence from her own experience: "We hatched our pet turkey Charlie from a group of four eggs that were in the refrigerator for about 24hrs. Only one of the eggs hatched so the chances are slim but possible!" (line 153). Finally, the scientist enters the argument at this point to echo the sentiments of the previous two posters. She explains that although refrigerating eggs is not recommended practice because "most refrigerators store feed at 45F, which is too cool for successful hatching of fertile eggs," it is true that "chicks are extremely resilient and anything is possible" (lines 164).

In this exchange, we see a dynamic common in many public science communication contexts: public challenges to scientific expertise. Such challenges can be (and are) understood in many different ways, most of them negative (e.g., uninformed, emotional, NIMBYism). But these participants do not appear to be merely "flaming," and instead offer reasonable challenges to a view of scientific reasoning motivated by generalized knowledge as opposed to practical action. As with the previous vignette, the questions and challenges are not merely scientific, and this is precisely one of the points we wish to make. Public communication of science is almost never simply about science. It is always also about policy, ethics, politics, experience, and so on. Efforts to isolate the technical or scientific issues and the risks associated with them often falter because of their narrowness. New technologies provide mechanisms by which participants can help frame conversations with representatives of scientific institutions. Furthermore, such technologies can help support conversations in which disagreement can happen productively and in ways that encourage participants to reexamine assumptions. In this vein, it is important not only for public posters to revisit prior scientific knowledge but also for science facilitators to develop an emerging sense of what is driving public interest in science and shaping the forms of reasoning that are possible. There are significant cultural issues at stake as well, and the primary way that we have characterized these cultural issues is our focus on "learning" rather than "communication" as perhaps a more productive way to think about structuring public engagement around science.

As we close our discussion, then, we ask, "How might we best use the resources of the Internet in the interest of advancing scientific knowledge among the general public?" Our investigation suggests that there is still value in creating what Gross (1994) calls "forums of reconstruction" that explicitly encourage experts and members of the lay public to make links between scientific facts and local knowledge. This can happen around issues that not only stir controversy but also coincide with routine matters about which people care deeply. Like caring for chickens. Or, to offer another example, caring for a loved one with a newly diagnosed chronic illness. The need to draw on scientific evidence to guide practice and decision-making in such situations creates tremendous motive for engagement. But the means to engage—the forum for reconstruction—may not be readily apparent or easily accessible for most people. Conceiving of online communicative spaces as environments for active learning and engagement is one possible first step toward reaching out to the significant number of individuals who have interests or concerns like those of the Chicken Thread's participants.

REFERENCES

Barron, B. (2006). Interest and self-sustained learning as catalysts of development: A learning ecologies perspective. *Human Development, 49,* 193–224.

Bauer, M. W., Allum, N., & Miller, S. (2007). What can we learn from 25 years of *PUS* survey research? Liberating and expanding the agenda. *Public Understanding of Science, 16,* 79–95.

Bell, P., Lewenstein, B., Shouse, A. W., & Feder, M. A. (Eds.). (2009). *Learning science in informal environments: People, places, and pursuits.* Committee on Learning Science in Informal Environments, National Research Council. Washington, DC: National Academies Press.

Bickerstaff, K., Lorenzoni, I., Jones, M., & Pidgeon, N. (2010). Locating scientific citizenship: The institutional contexts and cultures of public engagement. *Science, Technology, & Human Values, 35*(4), 474–500.

Bricker, L. A., & Bell, P. (2008). Conceptualizations of argumentation from science studies and the learning sciences and their implications for the practices of science education. *Science Education, 92,* 473–498.

Duschl, R., & Osborne, J. (2002). Supporting and promoting argumentation discourse in science education. *Studies in Science Education, 38,* 39–72.

Fahnestock, J. (1986). Accommodating science: The rhetorical life of scientific facts. *Written Communication, 3*(3), 275–296.

Falk, J. H., Storksdieck, M., & Dierking, L. D. (2007). Investigating public science interest and understanding: Evidence for the importance of free-choice learning. *Public Understanding of Science, 16*(4), 455–469.

Gerber, B. L., Cavallo, A. M. L., & Marek, E. A. (2001). Relationships among informal learning environments, teaching and scientific reasoning ability. *International Journal of Science Education, 23*(5), 535–549.

Goldman, S. R., Duschl, R. A., Ellenbogen, K., Williams, S. M., & Tzou, C. T. (2003). Science inquiry in a digital age: Possibilities for making thinking visible. In H. van Oostendorp (Ed.), *Cognition in a digital world* (pp. 253–284). Mahwah, NJ: Erlbaum.

Grabill, J. T., & Pigg, S. (2012). Messy rhetoric: Identity performance as rhetorical agency in online public forums. *Rhetoric Society Quarterly, 42*(2), 99–119.

Gross, A. (1994). The role of rhetoric in the public understanding of science. *Public Understanding of Science, 3*, 3–24.

Irwin, A., & Michael, M. (2003). *Science, social theory, and public knowledge.* Maidenhead, UK: Open University Press.

Johnstone, B., & Eisenhart, C. (Eds.). (2008). *Rhetoric in detail.* Philadelphia, PA: John Benjamins.

Lemke, J. L. (1990). *Talking science: Language, learning and values.* Norwood, NJ: Ablex.

Lenhart, A., Purcell, K., Smith, A., & Zickuhr, K. (2010). Social media and mobile Internet use among teens and young adults. *PEW Internet and American Life Project.* Retrieved from http://pewinternet.org/Reports/2010/Social-Media-and-Young-Adults.aspx

Nakamura, L. (2011). Race and identity in digital media. In J. Curran (Ed.), *Media and society* (5th ed., pp. 336–347). London, UK: Bloomsbury Academic.

Wellman, B., & Guilia, M. (1999). Net surfers don't ride alone: Virtual communities as communities. In B. Wellman (Ed.), *Networks in the global village: Life in contemporary communities.* Boulder, CO: Westview.

Wynne, B. (1992). Misunderstood misunderstanding: Social identities and public uptake of science. *Public Understanding of Science, 1*(3), 281–304.

Zappen, J. P. (2005). Digital rhetoric: Toward an integrated theory. *Technical Communication Quarterly, 14*(3), 319–325.

http://dx.doi.org/10.2190/SCIC13

CHAPTER 13

Afterword:
Social Changes in Science
Communication:
Rattling the Information Chain

Charles Bazerman

Scientific writing has always been changing, moved by multiple forces—some of them under the inventive control of writers and editors creating articles and journals; some evolving from the communal interactions of emerging and changing scientific communities and their ways of pursuing investigations; some responsive to larger organizational, political, and economic arrangements within which science operates; and some exploiting the opportunities afforded by changing communicative technologies. The forms and appearances of texts are the realizations of communicative actions within these larger sets of forces. What we may think of as the standard forms of scientific communication are only semistable sets of expectations that emerged gradually since the invention of journals in the 17th century. While some features arose early in this history, some only took on robust form in the 20th century, as science came to reside at the intersection of university departments and professional societies (with their structures of rewards and advancements), government and business interests and funding (based on their perceived needs for scientific and technological knowledge), knowledge-based professions that pervade contemporary society (with their reliance on systems of authority and credentials), expanding educated populations who look toward science for knowledge, and evolving technologies and systems for the production and distribution of texts (including cheap printing, commercial publishing companies, university and professional libraries, national mail systems, and international agreements).

Reinforcing dynamics have served to carry forward the 20th-century expectations even as technology has afforded new opportunities for the production, format, and distribution of communications as well as opportunities for institutional, financial, and social change. Disciplines had already coalesced long before the Internet around regional and international societies, with local instantiations in university departments. Standards for work became defined in the disciplinary societies relying for legitimacy on university affiliations and credentialing. Leading journals were established and built long reputations. Societies and corporations became dependent on the profits from the production of these journals. Health care, military, economies, and other social sectors became dependent on the production of this knowledge and looked to universities and academic disciplines. In recent decades, university status has increasingly come to depend on the production of research, measured by the production of refereed and cited articles. Faculty rewards have coordinately become increasingly dependent on productivity, measured by publication in recognized academic journals supported by practices of communal judgment, especially as universities and graduate programs expanded, creating more competition among themselves with an expanded job market and an even more rapidly increasing pool of job candidates. Competition has also increased for funding, status, recognition, and students. With increasing intensity, countries of all regions have entered the world of research and sought status.

At the communicative center of this competition were publications presenting the kinds of argument that would gain disciplinary acceptance as contributing to the advance of knowledge valued by the discipline. Such contributions would meet disciplinary standards, would be useful to relevant stakeholders, would raise the status of individuals, and would produce reliable knowledge. Contributions would also articulate with other contributions in the field, which might be sharply distinguished from work in even closely neighboring fields. If the contribution were to be considered of value to multiple fields, it had to speak to needs and standards of each of the disciplines and professions. The form and evaluation processes were intertwined, in that the expected forms of reporting results and arguing for claims embodied criteria of the field that needed to be addressed for credibility. Texts had to meet these criteria and make credible arguments not only to pass refereeing and editorial judgments but to become cited and used, establishing the basis for future work, creating track records for reputations of researchers and research programs, and establishing the basis for fundability of future research.

The focusing of the research question; the articulation with prior knowledge and other current results; the methods for production, selection, and display of evidence; the presentation and analysis of the evidentiary findings; and the valuation of the research for advancing the thinking of the field became important for most fields, through differences in the specifics of each field, led to major differences in the genre details in the publications of each. Additional genres arose to pursue specific elements of these functions in a more focused way (such as reviews of the literature, methodological articles, or theoretical pieces). Also, the coherence of reasoning of these parts was held together in a larger textual structure that either implied or made explicit the overall logic of the argument. On the surface, these elements typically add up to the IMRAD structure (that is, Introduction/review of literature; Methods; Results; Analysis; Discussion), but there are many variations across the fields. Further, as fields evolved, so did the methods, kinds of available evidence viewed as relevant, the accumulated literatures viewed as currently relevant, the theories that bound contributions together, the forms of analysis considered revealing, the stakeholders whose needs must be met (such as the changing roles and relationships of government regulatory and provider agencies, health providers, research funders, and healthcare business that had interest in medical and pharmacological research), and many other elements that might influence the contents and shape of articles.

Yet no matter what the particulars in each field at each moment of time with respect to each research inquiry, the article needed to present the various relevant elements in a coherent integrated structure that in its totality argued for findings or a claim. Disciplinary evaluation of the credibility of the contribution depended both on the adequate performance of each of the elements and the total argument facilitated in the total article structure. This would be true even though most readers may not read the article fully or in chronological order (Bazerman, 1985) because all elements would be there for reviewers evaluating the suitability for publication and for any readers who had need or motive to look more deeply into the claims.

During the last decades of the 20th century, digitization entered into this strongly reinforced though potentially mutable arrangement, changing the means and economics of the production and distribution of texts and data, the convenience of multimedia components, and the ease and pace of collaboration and other communicative interactions. Digitization also potentially could affect all the components of the surrounding social, organizational, and economic systems that surrounded, energized, and shaped the system of scientific knowledge production. This current volume, *Science and the Internet: Communicating Knowledge in a Digital Age*, takes up the question of what has changed, in what way, and to what degree, particularly with respect to the Internet.

So what is changing, at what level, with what consequences for future changes? What remains stable, what is facilitated, what is made more intense, what is disrupted, what is a more attractive alternative path? When do small changes coalesce in major reinvention? The chapters in this book provide a series of cases that look at texts, websites, and other textual realizations to see what is visible in the form of the text; but in these changes we see indications of less visible underlying social changes that in the long run may lead to bigger changes than anything now noticeable. That ability to expose small signs of bigger things to come is one of the advantages of case studies. Each of the chapters has taken up interesting cases—that is, cases where novel or previously unexamined or previously unappreciated changes seem to be occurring. This is not surprising because in case study research, the novelty of one's findings often depends on the novelty of one's cases—the researcher wants to be able to tell an interesting and engaging story, typically by making visible something the reader was previously unaware of. Further, each case can look into detail as to the specific elements emerging in the communications and the social and scientific histories that lie behind the communications examined in detail. Each case serves as something of a demonstration proof—something can happen because it has happened. The forces that have shaped situations and the motives that have driven those who are responsible for producing texts (this includes editors, publishers, societies, and authors) have coalesced at least once, and the choices made by the actors are imaginable and implementable because they have been made and done. Indeed, in this volume, every case is one of novel happenings. No study focuses on what remains the same, stabilizing tendencies, or cases of "nothing going on here." Even when the reported novelties are facilitations or intensifications of long-standing practices, the studies emphasize what is new rather than what is continuing in somewhat altered shape or by altered means.

While case studies are good at making visible interesting occurrences, they are less good at evaluating overall trends within a large and varied population, particularly at a time of hypothesized change where there are many experiments and many different choices being made. Only when the new situation has achieved new semistability can we determine which innovations have lasted robustly, responsive to which purposes, concerns, and interests. Even then there will not be uniformity, and minority experiments are likely to endure, depending on the rigidity and comprehensiveness of social evaluation, selection processes, and authority structures that come to rule within any particular epistemic social grouping. For examining broader trends, larger samples are needed, to some extent handled through statistical means. One chapter in this collection (Harmon) does carry out a broader survey, but before I discuss that chapter, it is useful to look more closely at a book cited by Harmon and three of the other authors in this collection: Owen's *The Scientific Article in the Age of Digitization* (2007). Although Owen's data ended in 2004 and may not have caught some more recent trends, he did examine an extensive, systematically designed sample of all digital journals. Owen found evidence of both change and stability, but found the weight dominantly on the side of stability. Reasonably enough, a set of cases making visible changes would be set in contrast to Owen's findings, as the authors in this volume who cite Owen tend to do. Yet what Owen finds is not so different from what these authors find. Seeing these two volumes in coordination rather than at loggerheads might help sort out the real forces of change that they both point toward.

Owen (2007) first reviews theoretical models that would predict change, including an entire chapter about how research moves from the laboratory into the communicative sphere. In this chapter on what he and others have called the information chain (following on an earlier article, Owen, 2002), he argues that digital production and distribution has great potential to reconfigure the scientific communication system. I quote at length because this is perhaps the most transformative element in Owen's analysis and because it bears on some of the more striking developments noted in the chapters in this volume:

> The traditional communication system has evolved towards a high level of closure with respect to functionality, actors and role divisions. However, it seems that digitization is opening up the system considerably. Publishers and libraries are taking over each other's functions, some functions are becoming embedded in the digitized network system, and others are being taken over to a certain extent by authors and readers or their parent institutions (e.g., in the form of "self-publishing"). In addition, various new functions have emerged (such as pre-publishing and long-term archiving) that require some form of control and actor-involvement. Ideas have been developed for a more radical effect of digitization, leading to a transformation towards an entirely systems-mediated form of communication without any involvement by institutional actors. We have seen, however, that many important functions of the information chain, and especially the certification function, do require such involvement.
>
> In fact, rather than becoming more simple . . . , scientific communication is becoming more complex. The flow of scientific information from author to reader is no longer a single, well-defined process, passing distinct stages governed by actors with strictly assigned roles. Digitization has resulted in an increase in genres, actors and communication modes, with multiple trajectories through which scientific information can flow, and multiple access points for users to acquire that information, depending on the stage in the life cycle of the publication. (Owen, 2007, p. 90)

Owen then presents the results of the study of a sample of 186 established and continuing peer reviewed, digital-only journals distributed across the sciences, social sciences, law and humanities. These journals were examined for 11 dimensions of article properties and 4 dimensions of editorial policies to see how much they differed from traditional print journals and took up special affordances of digital production and distribution. On some dimensions, he found little uptake of digital affordances. For example, in only a few journals were authors allowed to submit fully formatted articles; authors were generally required to submit flat formats, following fixed style guidelines, leaving the formatting and typography to editorial processes. In almost all cases, revision ended at a date of final publication. Similarly, there was little customization of articles for readers' needs (beyond allowing readers to create personal collections files of articles). On the other hand, some digital features were taken up in small but substantial numbers, often depending on discipline, such as presentation of data resources and use of multimedia. Some journals provided opportunities for reader comments, and 8% used a degree of open peer review, though often within hybrid models that maintained elements of traditional peer review. Finally, some digital opportunities gained wide acceptance, such as hyperlinks and navigational tools within articles and journals. Also, digital systems were widely used to facilitate traditional peer reviewing, and open access ideology was changing copyright policies, with half the journals asking only for rights of first publication, leaving ownership with the authors.

These findings lead Owen to conclude that uptake of digital affordances is selective based on choices that differ across situations and across disciplines. However, the features of digitality incorporated to this point have not disrupted the integrated structure of the total article, which had historically emerged and which seems to have migrated to the Internet in a process of "encapsulization." In Owen's words,

> So it is not the case that the digital medium has certain properties that will inevitably be conferred on any genre that uses it. Rather we shall (and do) see a wide range of different applications where each genre or practice of communication is made to adopt, at any point in time, a specific set of digital properties or "digitality." Some practices of communication may indeed be transformed (though not by new media as such, but by choices made by social actors that "construct" what is perceived as new media), others may stay very close to their traditional modes of representation. This view is supported by the existence of a certain amount of communicative heterogeneity between different scientific domains. There is no single "digital medium" in science but a whole range of different manifestations of digital properties. None of these has, as we have seen, transformed formal scientific communication insofar as it is based on the peer-reviewed research article. In evolutionary terms, scientific communication has adapted itself by process of encapsulation: through digitization of the journal as a container, the scientific article is able to remain relatively stable even within a digital environment. (Owen, 2007, p. 216)

Given the narrative I have presented of the robust forces aligning to shape the contemporary article and the role of the coherent argument for making claims based on systematically produced evidence and positioned as contributions within disciplinary literatures following disciplinary standards, the encapsulization Owen (2007) reports is not surprising, particularly in light of the importance of evaluation of the argument prior to publication and for use after publication. Individual and institutional rewards depend on these evaluations, which lead to publication in esteemed venues and citation following publication. Owen notes the importance of the certification function, which still seems to require institutional involvement. Encapsulization rests on social forces that hold it together, and in the long run, the greatest changes may come from the different ways people come together over shared and competitive information as individuals and as located within institutions and social groups—changes in the information chain. It is with respect to these changes that I find the analyses of the cases in this volume most interesting, and it is these changes that are starting to motivate changes in textual form and fray the solidity of encapsulization—though the ultimate result in the form of scientific communication is too early to tell.

As to the actual developments in the form of scientific articles, there is only one survey in this volume that attempts to directly answer Owen's (2007) survey. In this volume, Harmon choses a more up-to-date sample of ten articles from each of 15 journals from 2010 and 2011. He examines 10 long-standing elite journals that appear both in print and online and 5 recent journals that are digital open access. Unlike Owen's sample, Harmon's smaller sample comes entirely from the sciences. The dimensions he examines include authorship, abstracts, inter- and intratextuality, visualization, organizational structure and supplemental information, readers' comments, and journal contents pages. The samples, analytical categories, and ways of reporting results differ from Owen, making exact comparisons difficult; nonetheless, for the most part, Harmon's findings follow the trends noticed by Owen, only a few years further down the process. Owen had noticed some use of multimedia; Harmon notices an increasing use of visualization and greater use of color than in print and the use of links to allow readers to see expanded images, though videos are still a rarity. Owen had also noted some use of data supplements, as does Harmon. Owen notices a minority of journals offering opportunities for reader comments as does Harmon, but Harmon also noted some journals now provide download statistics as another measure of reader response. Owen noticed widespread use of internal and external links to heighten intra- and intertextual linkages, as does Harmon. Harmon, like Owen, notices large and increasing use of navigation devices within the article and for the journal. Harmon finds, on the other hand, no major change in article structure and widespread use of the PDF format, both of which substantiate Owen's view of the article as encapsulated as a fixed form.

Harmon additionally finds changes in dimensions not considered by Owen (2007): first, the use of simplified summaries and other accessibility devices to make the article's findings available for those who do not wish to or are not prepared to delve more deeply into the full abstract or the full text. Secondly, Harmon notices an accelerated trend in multiple authorship from diverse regions. While these on the surface appear to be minor changes in the actual form and structure of articles, they may be indicative of deeper changes going on in the social organization of scientific communication. But on the surface, Harmon only finds incremental differences from what Owen found a few years earlier, and neither found radical disruption of the encapsulated paper, only enhancements or intensification of earlier trends supported by the conveniences and affordances of digitization and the Internet. The main difference between the two sets of results is that Owen puts the weight of emphasis on the more stabilized parts, and Harmon puts more weight of emphasis on the changing parts.

While the formal changes seem gradual, facilitative to prior dynamics, and nondisruptive, the cases in the volume reveal in greater detail what these changes are, what led to them, how they operate in changing interactions, and what their implications and consequences may be for communications internal and external to science. Even more, as several chapters note, digital distribution and participation may be calling the internal/external distinction into question in both production and use of scientific communications. I would also like to consider the clues that a number of both the internal and external communication cases may say about the changing social relations and distribution of work of science, which may in the longer run be more disruptive of the encapsulization of the scientific article than anything that now has yet crystallized in a changed form of scientific article.

Four of the five cases examining internal communications of science involve postpublication commentary on published science and illustrate the communicative efficiency of the Internet in intensifying long-standing dynamics of evaluation and accountability after the fact of publication. Publication does not in itself bring long-term acceptance of claims or incorporation into the body of accepted knowledge. That has depended on how reliable and useful others have later found that work and whether they take it up in their own writings to carry the contributions forward into a lived and intertextually strengthened body of knowledge. Disputing counterpublications, failures of replications, contrary findings, questions about methods, ethics accusations and investigations, and retractions go back at least to the early days of the *Philosophic Transactions*. Such contesting communication have influenced the long-term evaluation, uptake, and codification prospects of claims that gain the attention of scientific peers, although the greatest mechanism of long-term evaluation was and remains inattention and lack of citation. Claims not considered important, interesting, or useful enough to be worth a lot of discussion and gather significant uptake, vanish, even though no one may contest them. In the past, when discussion has been excited, however, long-term processes of discussion and evaluation have been somewhat slow and sometimes porous. The four cases of scientific Internet commentary culture here indicate the Internet is providing potentials for speeding up and strengthening postpublication evaluation and codification. Buehl's introductory case of blog response to a purported breakthrough claim published in *Science,* Gross' study of the blogs *Retraction Watch* and *Abnormal Science*, Sidler's discussion of a liveblogging event, and Casper's analysis of various forms of refereed and nonrefereed online comments all show how critical questioning, accountability, and postpublication evaluation of articles have found new and highly effective sites for what had been long-standing elements of scientific communication.

The *Retraction Watch* and *Abnormal Science* blogs that Gross documents have intensified inspection of published articles and made it far more likely that serious accusations of fraud, plagiarism, other violations, and retractions do not get lost in the interstices of a loosely articulated communication system. The blogs rely not only on the visible and widely available publication and archiving space they offer, but on the rapidity of response, and the search tools of the Internet that allow more convenient and comprehensive tracking of the fate of retractions and disputations. These blogs tighten the accountability noose. They do not seem to change the nature of the articles themselves, however, except by helping police that publications live up to long-standing expectations. At what point and in what way this more intense house-cleaning may have transformative consequences remains to be seen.

Sidler and Buehl's cases, on their faces, similarly seem to be only speeding up and intensifying postpublication evaluation processes. Each reports a controversy that erupted in unrefereed blogs within a day or two after the appearance of a highly controversial claim within a prestigious refereed journal. While for centuries postpublication controversies could circulate informally among limited groups in seminars, on the floor of conferences, in letters, and in other *ad hoc* sites before they appeared in the refereed scientific literature, blogs have allowed widespread publication and professional debate outside the reviewed publication system. In Sidler's example, the appearance of extraordinary claims in the *Journal of the American Chemical Society* that seemed to contradict well-established findings led to immediate attempts at replication, including one that was liveblogged with data, images, and comment posted in real time—all self-published by the bloggers and commentators outside the review process. The original article was rapidly discredited by the blog discussion, and there was consternation as to how it passed prepublication review. For some, this case suggested that blind prepublication review might better be replaced with open peer review. Buehl's case concerned the blog questioning of an article appearing in the online version of *Science*. The article claimed discovery of life forms that replaced phosphorous with arsenic; within two days, blog critiques appeared and followed with such intensity that by the time the print version appeared 6 months later, it was accompanied by eight technical comments and an analysis of the controversy. It should be noted, however, that the publication of the peer reviewed technical comments had the effect of bringing the discussion back within the peer review system.

Rapid and unrefereed commentary is now also being invited on the same page as refereed articles appear in online journals. Casper compares such notes and comments in the online-only *PLoS ONE* with older forms of refereed and edited letters to the editor in *Science*, which appear in both print and online versions. The unrefereed notes and comments appear in proximity to the article in both time and textual space; they tend to be shorter, more informal, and more dialogic; they raise more questions about the production of work in contrast to the more polite and formal e-letters and letters to the editor, which are more concerned with the status of the knowledge claims of the article. As a result of the dialogic interchange in the notes and comments, authors sometimes amend their articles in subsequent notes also published in proximity to the article. These postpublication commentaries therefore lead to revision of the published article in ways similar to prepublication review. Casper also raises the possibility that authors may write articles differently, anticipating the kind of intense interaction that may occur in the new commentary environments, even as writers had previously come to write articles with an awareness of the review processes manuscripts would undergo. While it is too early to have clear evidence of such changes in manuscript, this is precisely the process I found in early print journals as certain kinds of issues became salient in the interactional space of journals that got lost in the more distant interactions of books. To forestall criticisms, authors preemptively wrote their articles to address concerns over conditions of observations, methods of producing results, and precise details of results (Bazerman, 1988). This process of finding more successful ways of creating arguments that would be persuasive in the new more intense forum was one of the key drivers of the emergence of what has now become standards of scientific publication, reinforced by later-emerging reviewing and editorial practices.

The cases examined by Buehl, Sidler, Casper, and, to some extent, Gross all point to a loosening of editorial control over the evaluative process and publication of critiques, but primarily postpublication, though we see some of the pre- and postpublication lines blurring, with corrections and revisions on the basis of postpublication commentary being made available with the original article. Whether and how such processes might influence prepublication processes and published articles is still unclear, but the effect on published critiques already is becoming evident. The kind of informality, methodological critique, and questioning of evidence Casper found in the notes and comments that appear following articles also seem to pervade the blogs examined by Buehl, Sidler, and Gross. Because all these comments are not preauthenticated by review processes, the weight of argument must fall even more on precise and focused reasoning in direct engagement with the articles being commented on. This intense discussion, sorting out the reliability and value of claims within a rapid-fire public space of contention, does seem to be a real change in the postreview evaluation process. In the print world, although sometimes controversies erupted in print over claims, the weight of postpublication evaluation depended on citation and reuse, and eventual codification in review essays, handbooks, and textbooks. While prepublication open peer review has only worked in a few fields (with one of the major difficulties being the lack of voluntary labor needed to vet the large number of not-yet-authenticated submissions), controversial claims upsetting expectations within published articles seem to draw the attention of critical audiences and foster heated discussion in more direct communicative spaces without publisher intermediaries.

A potentially even more radical disruption of the encapsulated article may be the open data archives described by Wickman. In the past, data notebooks or archives were the responsibility of individual researchers or research teams and were, in a sense, private resources for their own research—resources to be drawn on selectively for evidence in publications authored by the individual or research team. These data archives could have been shared or made public in particular situations and by intentional actions, such as if research had been questioned and other researchers wanted to confirm findings. Data archives could also have been made public to support further research, but in such cases, the data would have been organized and prepared as a special section of the publication to make them useable and interpretable by future users. Responsibility and accountability for the archives and the quality of the data would have remained with the initial research group that published the archives. The *OpenWetWare* site that Wickman examines adopts a Web 2.0 ideology and a wiki structure for the core data and protocol pages, thereby distributing responsibility for the regulation, design, contribution, and revision of datasets offered at the site. It also includes blog spaces for commentary, software tools for creating notebooks, and pages for groups and courses to post and share materials about their activities. The site also includes specific procedural information for syntheses of particular substances for those entering each problem area, to regularize procedures among researchers, to standardize produced samples for investigation, and to assure a common understanding of data. So the site goes far beyond a sharing of data to a shared development of common ways of work and methods of interpreting findings. The standardization of notebook formats also serves to standardize the reporting of data. This degree of sharing and co-production of procedures and data prior to publication may redefine what will count as the contribution of an individual author or research group and what decisions the author(s) will be accountable for and therefore need to argue for. Further, it is unclear how contribution to the communal tools and communal database will count for professional contribution and establish the value of each person or group's accomplishment. This may also change the balance between competition and cooperation, which has defined relationships among researchers, and the device for distribution of rewards and opportunities. In many ways, the developments being observed in the case of the open data notebook movement resemble some of Joseph Priestley's proposals made for scientific communication two and a half centuries ago, driven by a communitarian, democratic, millenialist philosophy, relying more on communal cooperation than individual achievement (see Bazerman, 1991). Indeed, all of the cases in the first half of this volume contain elements of Priestley's vision, which included advocacy of a less formal and less distant style; greater recognition of paths of development, false turns, and mistakes; fuller sharing of data and methods; critical inspection of machines and procedures; less focus on star achievers and greater recognition that knowledge comes from taking into account the experience of all; greater focus on sharing of reasoning and experience in more narrative publications; and less attempt to create irrefutable arguments. He argued against the hoarding and hiding of unique methodological and intellectual resources that accumulate advantage for one group over the other (as evident in his faulting of Newton for being like the one who paints the ceiling of a great cathedral and then removes the ladder so no one can re-create such a magnificent accomplishment). Priestley, just as the *OpenWetWare* site, provided means for the recruitment and training of young scientists and the collaborative development of common standards, methods, and modes of interpretation. While some of Priestley's vision had been incorporated in the intervening years (such as in expanded citation and review of literature practices that create narratives of the field's communal advance and collaborative construction of knowledge), the competitive empirical argument for claims became the basis of an encapsulated form rather than the more open-ended inquiry narrative Priestley espoused. Whether the Internet will provide robust tools and Science 2.0 philosophy will be robust enough to push science further along communitarian paths and forms of presentation will be interesting to watch.

The democratic engagement of wider publics in science and the textual means for accomplishing public engagement are most directly the themes of the latter six studies in this volume. While such cases might be viewed as a continuation (through more robust, accessible, and interactive means) of prior science popularization, social changes as well as changing affordances of the technology are producing higher levels of engagement—with possible consequences for further significant reconfiguration of communication. The case furthest on the popularization spectrum is Wardlaw's study of the NPR weekly broadcast Radiolab (with a radio listenership of about one million and an additional podcast download audience of 1.8 million weekly). Comparing a popular science book on the same topic as on one Radiolab episode, Wardlaw finds the show emphasizes the emotional potential of science stories as a form of entertainment over the transmission of scientific content. The display of emotionally exciting wonders for popular consumption goes back at least as far as Renaissance wondercabinets and continued through Barnum's 19th-century museums of spectacles. Ripley's Believe it or Not still survives in museums in tourist districts. Although Wardlaw emphasizes the emotionality as a corrective to theories of more sober science popularization, what I find most notable is the way the emotional entertainment is designed for an already educated audience, ready to be amused by playing with science; further, the segments of the show are sequenced to bring the audience into deeper engagement with the topic of the week. As Wardlaw comments, the episode "initially invokes a visceral disgust for parasites only to later instill wonder and admiration for their complexity." Further, based on the specifics of the episode Wardlaw cites, it appears the visceral elements of the show achieve their amusing over-the-top effect by an ironic and knowing stance. So the show allows the sophisticated audience to indulge in emotions they in a sense know better than as a prelude to more serious and even more engaging content appropriate to their level of education and sophistication. Play with scientific knowledge turns into scientific knowledge as the ultimate play.

Pigg, Hart-Davidson, Grabill, and Ellenbogen in their study of *Science Buzz*, an interactive science popularization blog run by a science museum, point to the way a nonscientific but educated audience engages science through practical reasoning in order to solve ordinary life problems. As the college-educated science-literate population has grown and continues to grow, we can expect more serious and more extensive public engagement in science for more and more life issues. This is a process that has been building at least since the 19th century, but which got an enormous boost in the postwar expansion of higher education and the post-Sputnik focus on science education. The extensive and in-depth resources that can be made available on the Internet, rapid communication of science news afforded by the Internet, the concern of scientists themselves to engage publics, and the Internet's opportunities for interactivity are perhaps supporting another moment of growth in public engagement of science to address practical challenges of life, consumption, and health.

Fahnestock documents the complexity of educated audiences seeking information on the Web and the multiplicity of resources by which information is now being made available to meet multiple needs. She examines the reporting of the discovery of adult neurogenesis and the attendant controversy in a range of websites from open access scholarly journals (with new supplementary and simplified summaries for the public), the official websites of scientific organizations, Wikipedia, science news sites, health forums, patients groups, and the health and wellness industry websites. She finds that the variety of resources, the speed of dissemination of findings through the tiers of representation, and interactivity support engagement and the varied uses of the many groups. But she also finds that controversies refract through varied interests and may remain active long after consensus is reached among scientists. In short, scientific debate takes on a life of its own among the many interested constituencies who recognize a stake in scientific findings.

Increasingly sophisticated citizens ready to look for science to reason about life problems also form the audiences for the kinds of interactive disaster information websites documented by Kostelnick and Kostelnick. These websites, using multi-tiered visualizations, allow users to investigate past disasters, track the impact of current disasters, and gain information about possible future ones. The interactivity allows users to study specific locations with which they have an interest, to pursue the data in great detail, and to customize the interface around their concerns. Because of the potential impact of disasters for website users and the strong empathetic emotions that might be aroused in constructing the effects on others, these websites may arouse great engagement and emotions, despite the factual documentary character of the presentation. The interactivity and navigable data depth afforded by the technology provide an interactive space for people to pursue their engagement and interests, drawing them further into scientific knowledge.

Wynn examines visual representations of extremely exigent cases of disaster information concerning nuclear power plant disasters for real-time evaluation of threat and action decisions. In comparing older print media (*New York Times* and *Washington Post*) representation of the unfolding Three Mile Island and Chernobyl disasters and aftermath with recent Internet representations of a traditional news outlet (*New York Times*) and a citizen-based website (Safecast), he finds that representations vary according to material, sociopolitical conditions, and rhetorical agendas, as one might expect. But he also finds that technology matters, with the Internet having a transformative effect. Part of that effect is in the multilayered display of information, allowing greater depth and combination of information, which can be pursued according to readers' needs and interests in both the traditional news outlet and the citizen-based website. An even greater effect of technology, however, is the communicative and collaborative power afforded to noninstitutional actors to create and distribute representations that reflect the needs and interests of citizens' groups rather than of institutional actors. This collaboration extends even to the collection of scientific data. In the wake of the Fukushima earthquake, tsunami, and nuclear power plant meltdown, the team that produced Safecast as an online radiation mapping tool collaborated with a citizen-science group wanting to provide citizen information. The initial motive of data visualization soon turned into citizen data gathering, as more local and changing data were needed in the turbulent, evolving disaster. Standardized inexpensive Geiger counters were designed and distributed, and reporting tools created. Also, to serve needs of individuals assessing personal risk, richer and deeper visualization tools were created, including contextual information, so one could locate that data by on-the-ground landmarks rather than just geographical coordinates.

In a related chapter, Kelly and Miller look further into the citizen needs for detailed, accurate, and up-to-the-minute data about the Fukushima nuclear meltdown and fallout. They examine the role and evolving content of the multiple platforms used to meet the exigence at different moments in the evolving situation, including Twitter, science blogs, Wikipedia, and Safecast. They also note how the need for data reorganized the flow and control of information from scientist-originated to citizen-originated. As they note, the citizen data-gatherers were not organized as teams working under the supervision of scientists who vetted and controlled their work, but were independent operators, motivated to contribute to the common good. Nonetheless, the distribution of standardized Geiger counters served to discipline and control the work of the citizen participants and assure the production of reliable data that could be coordinated and compared with the data reported by others. Well-designed and reliable technology appear in some focused circumstances to obviate the need for extensive training and control. This may have important consequences for citizen participation in science in the future.

Citizen participation in science around issues important to their life has been a growing movement since the early days of opposition to nuclear testing, when alliances were forged between citizen groups and scientists to make available information that would serve the needs of citizens. Further, in this early movement, citizens became involved in research by contributing baby teeth to document the increasing incidence of radiation in children's bones, though these samples were still to be collected and analyzed by trained scientists (see Bazerman, 2001). The environmental movement, which was a direct descendant of this earlier movement, continued to engage people in collecting data and in fact to become more trained as scientists to pursue policy-related inquiries. This engagement of science with citizen interests and citizen participation transformed the ethos and goals of some existing specialties and helped form others. But the reach, speed, and interactivity of the Internet has greatly expanded the potential for building citizen science and creating productive research collaborations between scientists and citizens when there is public exigence.

Cases in this volume indicate multiple social forces and dynamics are rearranging scientific communication, particularly with respect to the locus of control over postpublication evaluation of scientific; the broader cooperative production of data and forging of greater collaborative ethos among formerly competitive scientific teams; and of engaged, educated, informed citizenry asserting its needs for science, becoming a market for science, and even collaborating in the production of science for its own needs. Nevertheless, while some chapters in the volume take examples from open access academic publishing, this volume does not examine how digital production and distribution through the Internet are changing the economics of academic publishing, particularly in a time when university libraries are challenged financially by corporate acquisition and marketization of traditionally boutique academic publishing that was culturally congruent with academic culture. All this is challenging the information chain that supported the emergence of the encapsulated scientific article. How disruptive these new dynamics will be for already existing forms of scientific communication is uncertain. What does seem certain is that there is a proliferation of new communicative forms and forums to forge new relations, serve new needs, and exploit the potential of the Internet. Whether these emerging communicative channels and dynamics will rely on and reinforce the encapsulated article as a core reference point, whether they will displace it, or they will push it in new directions remains to be seen.

REFERENCES

Bazerman, C. (1985). Physicists reading physics: Schema-laden purposes and purpose-laden schema. *Written Communication*, 2(1), 3–23.

Bazerman, C. (1988). *Shaping written knowledge*. Madison, WI: University of Wisconsin Press.

Bazerman, C. (1991). How natural philosophers can cooperate: The rhetorical technology of coordinated research in Joseph Priestley's *History and Present State of Electricity*. In C. Bazerman & J. Paradis (Eds.), *Textual dynamics of the professions* (pp. 13–44). Madison, WI: University of Wisconsin Press.

Bazerman, C. (2001). Nuclear information: One rhetorical moment in the construction of the information age. *Written Communication, 18*(3), 259–295.

Owen, J. M. (2002). The new dissemination of knowledge: Digital libraries and institutional roles in scholarly publishing. *Journal of Economic Methodology, 9*(3), 275–288.

Owen, J. M. (2007). *The scientific article in the age of digitization.* Dordrecht, The Netherlands: Springer.

Editors' Biographies

Alan G. Gross is an emeritus professor at the University of Minnesota–Twin Cities. He is the author of *The Rhetoric of Science* and its extensive revision, *Starring the Text*. With his long-term collaborator Joseph Harmon, he has written *Communicating Science, The Scientific Literature, The Craft of Scientific Communi- cation*, and *Science from Sight to Insight: How Scientists Illustrate Meaning*. Oxford University Press will soon publish their latest book, *The Internet Revolution in the Sciences and Humanities*.

Jonathan Buehl is an associate professor and the director of Business and Technical Writing in the Department of English at The Ohio State University. His research interests include the rhetoric of science, visual rhetoric, research methodology, and digital media studies. He is the author of *Assembling Arguments: Multimodal Rhetoric and Scientific Discourse* (University of South Carolina Press) and essays published in *College Composition and Communication* and *Technical Communication Quarterly*.

Contributors

Charles Bazerman, professor of education at the University of California, Santa Barbara, is the author of numerous research articles and books on the history and practices of scientific writing, the social role of writing, academic genres, and textual analysis, as well as textbooks on the teaching of writing. Most recently he has published a two-volume work on the theory and rhetoric of Literate Action.

Christian F. Casper is a lecturer in technical communication in the College of Engineering at the University of Michigan in Ann Arbor, where his pedagogical interests lie in the first-year experience and communication in the fields of chemical, biomedical, and aerospace engineering. His chapter in this volume is based on his PhD dissertation, directed by Carolyn R. Miller in the Program in Communication, Rhetoric, and Digital Media at North Carolina State University.

Kirsten Ellenbogan is president and CEO of the Great Lakes Science Center in Cleveland, Ohio. She currently serves as co-principal investigator of the Center for Advancement of Informal Science Education, which collaborates with the National Science Foundation to advance the field of informal STEM education. She began her work in museums at the Detroit Science Center in 1987 and has worked as a demonstrator, hall interpreter, exhibit developer, evaluator, and researcher. Before joining the Great Lakes Science Center, she was senior director for lifelong learning at the Science Museum of Minnesota.

Jeanne Fahnestock, professor emeritus in the Department of English at the University of Maryland, is a Fellow of the Rhetoric Society of America. She is the author of *Rhetorical Style: The Uses of Language of Persuasion* (2011) and *Rhetorical Figures in Science* (1999/2002), and she coauthored *A Rhetoric of Argument* (3rd edition, 2004). Fahnestock has published essays on rhetorical theory, argument, language analysis, and the rhetoric of science. She served on the board of directors of the Rhetoric Society of America (co-organizing its conference in 2000) and on the council of the International Society for the History of Rhetoric.

Jeff Grabill is a professor of rhetoric and professional writing and chair of the Department of Writing, Rhetoric, and American Cultures at Michigan State University, and is a senior researcher with WIDE Research (Writing in Digital Environments). He is also a cofounder of Drawbridge LLC, an educational technology company. As a researcher, Grabill studies how digital writing is associated with citizenship and learning, including studies on informal learning in collaboration with museum partners. He has published two books on community literacy and articles in *College Composition and Communication, Technical Communication Quarterly, Computers and Composition, English Education*, and other journals.

Joseph E. Harmon is a coordinating science writer/editor at Argonne National Laboratory and has written extensively on scientific communication from a historical perspective. For the past two decades, he has had the good fortune of collaborating with Alan G. Gross on four books, the latest being *Science from Sight to Insight: How Scientists Illustrate Meaning* (University of Chicago Press, 2013). A manuscript for a fifth book—on how the Internet is transforming the communicative practices in the sciences and the humanities— is nearing completion.

Bill Hart-Davidson is associate dean for graduate studies in the College of Arts & Letters and a senior researcher in the Writing in Digital Environments research center at Michigan State University. He is co-editor, with Jim Ridolfo, of *Rhetoric & the Digital Humanities*, published in 2015 by The University of Chicago Press.

Ashley Rose Kelly is an assistant professor in the Department of English Language and Literature at the University of Waterloo, in Canada. Kelly's research examines how different communities engage in scientific research and how science communication genres are changing, especially in response to emerging networked technologies.

Charles Kostelnick is a professor in the English Department at Iowa State University, where he has taught business and technical communication and a graduate and an undergraduate course in visual communication in professional writing. He is coauthor of *Shaping Information: The Rhetoric of Visual Conventions* and *Designing Visual Language: Strategies for Professional Communicators*. He has also published articles on visual communication in several journals.

John Kostelnick is an associate professor of geography at Illinois State University. His research interests include geovisualization issues related to hazards/ risks and the integration of Geographic Information Science (GIScience) in the social and natural sciences. His published research has examined the role of cartographic issues for communicating hazard and risk in various contexts, including sea-level rise and humanitarian demining (landmine removal).

Carolyn R. Miller is SAS Institute Distinguished Professor of Rhetoric and Technical Communication, Emerita, at North Carolina State University, where she taught from 1973 to 2015. Her professional service includes terms as president of the Rhetoric Society of America and editor of its journal, *Rhetoric Society Quarterly*. She is a Fellow of the Rhetoric Society of America and a

Fellow of the Association of Teachers of Technical Writing. She has published on rhetoric of science, rhetorical theory, genre theory, and digital rhetoric.

Stacey Pigg is an assistant professor of scientific and technical communication at North Carolina State University, where she serves as associate director of the Professional Writing program. Her research analyzes the impact of mobile and networked writing technologies on learning, work, and engagement and has appeared in journals such as *College Composition and Communication, Rhetoric Society Quarterly, Technical Communication Quarterly*, and *Written Communication.*

Michelle Sidler is an associate professor in rhetoric and composition at Auburn University. She is coeditor of the collection *Computers in the Composition Classroom: A Critical Sourcebook*, and she has published numerous book chapters as well as articles in *Rhetoric Review, Computers and Composition*, and other journals. Sidler's research explores the intersections between rhetoric, technology, and science.

Sarah Wardlaw is a PhD candidate in neurobiology and behavior at the University of Washington; she has an active interest in science communication. She studies the interaction between circadian rhythms and memory in mice. Wardlaw developed her chapter in this volume while in the graduate seminar "The Rhetoric of Science," with the guidance of Leah Ceccarelli.

Chad Wickman, PhD, is an associate professor in the Department of English at Auburn University. His research locates rhetoric in the process of scientific inquiry and explores how open-access textual practices have begun to shape the epistemological dimensions of writing and knowledge making in the biological sciences. Chad's work on rhetoric of science has been published in range of venues, including the journals *Written Communication, Technical Communication Quarterly, Journal of Business and Technical Communication*, and *Rhetoric Review.*

James Wynn is an associate professor of English and rhetoric at Carnegie Mellon University. His interest is in the study of rhetoric, science, and mathematics. His first book, *Evolution by the Numbers* (2012), examines how mathematics was argued into the study of variation, evolution, and heredity in the late nineteenth and early twentieth centuries. In his most recent scholarship, he has focused on citizen science in the digital age and how it is reshaping the relationships between scientists, laypersons, and governments.

Index